THE RABBINIC TRADITIONS ABOUT THE PHARISEES BEFORE 70

SOUTH FLORIDA STUDIES IN THE HISTORY OF JUDAISM

Edited by
Jacob Neusner
Alan J. Avery-Peck, Bruce D. Chilton, Darrell J. Fasching,
William Scott Green, Sara Mandell, James F. Strange

Number 203

THE RABBINIC TRADITIONS ABOUT
THE PHARISEES BEFORE 70

PART II

THE HOUSES

by
Jacob Neusner

THE RABBINIC TRADITIONS ABOUT THE PHARISEES BEFORE 70

PART II

THE HOUSES

by

Jacob Neusner

Scholars Press
Atlanta, Georgia

THE RABBINIC TRADITIONS ABOUT THE PHARISEES BEFORE 70

PART II

THE HOUSES

by

Jacob Neusner

Originally published by E. J. Brill, 1971

Publication of this book was made possible by a grant from the Tisch Family Foundation, New York City. The University of South Florida acknowledges with thanks this important support for its scholarly projects.

Library of Congress Cataloging in Publication Data

Neusner, Jacob, 1932–
The rabbinic traditions about the Pharisees before 70 / by Jacob Neusner.
p. cm. — (South Florida studies in the history of Judaism ; no. 202–204)
Previously published: Leiden : Brill, 1971.
Includes bibliographical references and index.
Contents: pt. 1. The masters — pts. 2. The houses — pt. 3. Conclusions.
ISBN 0-7885-0574-2 (pt. I:cloth : alk. paper). —ISBN 0-7885-0575-0 (pt. II:cloth : alk. paper). — ISBN 0-7885-0576-9 (pt. III:cloth : alk. paper)
1. Pharisees. 2. Mishnah—Criticism, interpretation, etc. 3. Tosefta—Criticism, interpretation, etc. I. Title. II. Series.
BM175.P4N46 1998
296.8'12—dc21 99-41846
CIP

04 03 02 01 00 99 5 4 3 2 1

Printed in the United States of America
on acid-free paper

TABLE OF CONTENTS

PART TWO

THE HOUSES

PART THREE

CONCLUSIONS

LIST OF ABBREVIATIONS

Ah. = Ahilot
'Arak. = 'Arakhin
ARN = Avot deRabbi Natan
A.Z. = 'Avodah Zarah

b. = Bavli, Babylonian Talmud
b. = ben
B.B. = Bava Batra
B.M. = Bava Meṣi'a'
B.Q. = Bava Qamma
Ber. = Berakhot
Beṣ. = Beṣah
Bik. = Bikkurim

Chron. = Chronicles

Dan. = Daniel
Dem. = Demai
Deut. = Deuteronomy
Development = *Development of a Legend: Studies on the Traditions Concerning Yoḥanan ben Zakkai* (Leiden, 1970)

'Ed. = 'Eduyyot
Epstein, *Mevo'ot* = J. N. Epstein, *Mevo'ot le Sifrut HaTanna'im* (Jerusalem, 1957)
Epstein, *Mishnah* = J. N. Epstein, *Mavo le Nusaḥ HaMishnah* (Jerusalem, 1964²)
'Eruv. = 'Eruvin
Ex. = Exodus
Ez. = Ezekiel

Finkelstein, *Mavo* = *Mavo le Massekhet Avot veAvot deR. Natan* (New York, 1950)

Gen. = Genesis
Giṭ. = Giṭṭin

Ḥag. = Ḥagigah
Ḥal. = Ḥallah
Halivni, *Meqorot* = David Weiss Halivni, *Meqorot uMesorot* (Tel Aviv, 1968)
Hor. = Horayot
Hos. = Hosea
Ḥul. = Ḥullin

Is. = Isaiah

JE = Jewish Encyclopedia
Jer. = Jeremiah
Josh. = Joshua
Jud. = Judges

Kel. = Kelim
Ker. = Keritot
Kil. = Kila'im

Lev. = Leviticus

M. = Mishnah
M.Q. = Mo'ed Qaṭan
M.S. = Ma'aser Sheni
M.T. = Midrash Tanna'im
MT = Massoretic Text
Ma. = Ma'aserot
Mak. = Makkot
Maksh. = Makshirin
Mal. = Malachi
Meg. = Megillah
Meg. Ta. = Megillat Ta'anit
Mekh. = Mekhilta
Men. = Menaḥot
Mid. = Middot
Miq. = Miqva'ot

Naz. = Nazir
Ned. = Nedarim
Neg. = Nega'im
Nez. = Nezirot
Nid. = Niddah
Num. = Numbers

Oh. = Ohalot
'Orl. = 'Orlah

Par. = Parah
Pes. = Pesaḥim

Prov.	=	Proverbs
Ps.	=	Psalms
Qid.	=	Qiddushin
Qoh.	=	Qohelet
R.	=	Rabbah
R.	=	Rabbi
R.H.	=	Rosh Hashanah
Sam.	=	Samuel
Sanh.	=	Sanhedrin
Shab.	=	Shabbat
Shav.	=	Shavu'ot
Sheq.	=	Sheqalim
Shev.	=	Shevi'it
Song	=	Song of Songs
Soṭ.	=	Soṭah
Suk.	=	Sukkah
Ta.	=	Ta'anit
Tem.	=	Temurah
Ter.	=	Terumot
Ṭoh.	=	Ṭoharot
Tos.	=	Tosefta
Ṭ.Y.	=	Ṭevul Yom
'Uqṣ.	=	'Uqṣin
y.	=	Yerushalmi, Palestinian Talmud
Y.Ṭ.	=	Yom Ṭov
Yad.	=	Yadaim
Yev.	=	Yevamot
Zab.	=	Zabim
Zech.	=	Zechariah
Zer.	=	Zera'im
Zev.	=	Zevaḥim

TRANSLITERATIONS

א	=	'
ב	=	B
ג	=	G
ד	=	D
ה	=	H
ו	=	W
ז	=	Z
ח	=	Ḥ
ט	=	Ṭ
י	=	Y
כ ך	=	K
ל	=	L
מ ם	=	M
נ ן	=	N
ס	=	Ś
ע	=	'
פ ף	=	P
צ	=	Ṣ
ק	=	Q
ר	=	R
שׁ	=	Š
שׂ	=	S
ת	=	T

CHAPTER FOURTEEN

INTRODUCTION

The pericopae of the House of Shammai and the House of Hillel constitute the largest corpus of materials attributed to pre-70 masters. Nearly all elements in that corpus exhibit common form and structure and uniform style.

In the Houses' dispute-form we have a superscription which states the legal problem, followed by brief rulings attributed to the House of Shammai and the House of Hillel, in that order. The superscription sometimes is inserted in the Shammaite lemma, but this is readily discerned, and the primary pericope is easily restored. The Houses-opinions are usually stated in brief balanced phrases, sometimes opposing numbers, e.g., one/two, three/nine, more often in syzygies, e.g., liable, not liable, with the Shammaites nearly always in the stringent position.

A second form is the debate, in which the Hillelites normally come first, the Shammaites have the last word and win the argument. Here the Houses-sayings generally are developed and not compressed into a few words, balanced against one another.

The model used for the formation of the Houses-disputes seems to be the pattern of the pairs in M. Ḥag. 2:2, listing contrary opinions and systematically assigning them to the two authorities of a given generation:

X says	To lay
Y says	Not to lay

The Houses-form differs primarily in the provision of substantial protases, statements of a legal issue or problem, or superscriptions; further, the Houses' opinions are phrased usually in direct discourse or in intensive verbs:

House of Shammai	
say, unclean	('WMRYM, ṬM')
declare unclean	(MṬM'YN)
declare liable; say, liable	(MḤYYBYN; 'WMRYM, ḤYB)
declare unfit	(PWŚLYN)
declare ready to receive uncleanness	(BKY YTN; MWKŠRYN)

House of Hillel	
say, clean	(’WMRYM, TḤR)
declare clean	(MṬHRYN)
declare free of liability;	
say, free of liability	(PWṬRYN; ’WMRYM, PṬWR)
declare fit	(MKŠYRYN)
declare *not* ready to receive uncleanness	(L’ BKY YTN; ’YNN MWKŠRYN)

and the like. The Houses begin just where the pairs leave off, after Shammai and Hillel; Shammai's House comes first, just as does Shammai in the original chain. Later on, when the law came always to conform to the Hillelites' ruling, the masters apparently found it convenient to preserve the traditions as they had received them, and even to shape new materials following the ancient pattern. In doing so, they relieved the student of the need of memorizing decisions, since whatever the Hillelites said would be regarded as law. The few exceptions were easy to remember. The Hillelites thus effected their revolution within the antecedent forms, by making the old forms serve new purposes.

In Amoraic times masters observed the literary phenomena represented by the fixed order and rigid forms of the Houses disputes:

> R. Abba in the name of Samuel said, "For three years there was a dispute between the House of Shammai and the House of Hillel.
>
> "One said, 'The law is in agreement with us,' and the other said, 'The law is in agreement with us.'
>
> "Then an echo came forth and said, 'Both are the words of the living God, but the law follows the words of the House of Hillel.' "
>
> Since both are the words of the living God, what entitled the House of Hillel to have the law established in agreement with their words?
>
> Because they were kindly and modest. They studied their own rulings and those of the House of Shammai. They were even so humble as to mention the words of the House of Shammai before their own.
>
> (b. ʿEruv. 13b, trans. I. W. Slotki, pp. 85-6)

> On what account did the House of Hillel prove worthy that the law should be established according to their words?
>
> R. Judah b. R. Pazzi said, "Because they placed the words of the House of Shammai ahead of their words.
>
> "And not only so, but they also saw [the point of] the words of the House of Shammai and retracted their own opinions."
>
> (y. Suk. 2:8)

Clearly, it was regarded as preferable to come first. As we shall see, the "retractions" do not amount to much, and generally show a Hillelite bias.

As in b. ʿEruv. 13b, which alludes to the several explanations, it also was held that an echo had pronounced the decision:

> TNY: An echo went forth and said, "These and these are the words of the living God, but the law is according to the words of the House of Hillel."
>
> Where did the echo go forth?
>
> R. Bibi in the name of R. Yoḥanan said, "In Yavneh the echo went forth."
>
> (y. Yev. 6:6, y. Soṭ. 3:4, y. Qid. 8:1)

To be sure, Hillelites believed in echoes, and Shammaites did not (e.g., Tos. Nez. 1:1).

As in the Shammai-Hillel pericopae, the Houses are at parity; but the Shammaites predominate in both forms, giving the first ruling, the final argument in a debate. We shall see that the forms were used for a long time after the destruction of the Temple, though most of the pericopae were redacted probably before or at Usha, ca. 140-180 A.D. Some of the pericopae provoke comments of early Yavneans, e.g. Ṭarfon and ʿAqiba, and may therefore have been redacted by ca. 100 A.D. The problem of dating pericopae thus is complicated by the fact that the Houses-form was pseudepigraphically employed over a period of roughly a century, from ca. 70 to ca. 170, somewhat less commonly thereafter. We do not know whether the form was used before 70 as well; none of the pericopae can be verified by reference to named masters before 70, who never comment directly on materials attributed to the Houses or even on legal issues addressed by the Houses.

All we can hope to propose is a plausible date for the creation and first usage of the form itself: obviously not before the time of Shammai and Hillel—ca. 20 A.D.; and not after the time of ʿAqiba and Ṭarfon—ca. 90 A.D. Eliezer b. Hyrcanus and Joshua b. Ḥananiah also comment on Houses-pericopae, which pushes the *terminus* of the form back by about fifteen years. They sometimes are identified with, or regarded as equivalent to, the Houses of Shammai and Hillel. Perhaps the form itself came even before their time, right at the outset of Yavneh. Clearly, the Hillelites predominated at Yavneh, certainly after 100, and possibly after 70, for Yoḥanan b. Zakkai was alleged to have been Hillel's disciple. By contrast, no Yavnean was assigned to Shammai as a disciple. Eliezer is merely called a sympathizer. Since the Hillelites told stories both to account for Shammaite predominance in pre-70 Pharisaism ("sword in the school-house," "Shammaites one day outnumbered Hillelites," "mob in the Temple"), and also to explain the later predominance of the Hillelites ("heavenly echo came to Yavneh"), it stands to reason that the Shammaites predominated before 70, the Hillelites shortly afterward. This is further suggested by the one-sided, if limited, evidence that Gamaliel II and Simeon b. Gamaliel I followed Shammaite rules.

My guess, as I said, is that the Houses-forms were first worked out when the parties were nearly equal in influence, but when the Shammaites still enjoyed a measure of power, so that they could persist in taking precedence. Further necessary conditions are, first, the need to bring the parties together and determine normative law, and second, the presence of an authority of sufficient stature to impose the necessary compromises. These conditions can have been met only in one time and place, and that is, at Yavneh in the time of Yoḥanan b. Zakkai and Gamaliel II. The work of Yavneh required the conciliation of both parties to achieve the unification of Pharisaism for the purpose of assuming and exercising the new power and responsibility gained in the aftermath of the destruction. Yoḥanan b. Zakkai, leader of the Ḥillelite sector of Pharisaism, and Gamaliel II afterwards may have sought to conciliate the Shammaites in the redaction of existing legal materials. The generation of Gamaliel II, Eliezer, Joshua, Ṭarfon, and ʿAqiba is the first to refer to Houses-disputes in their present form. Yavneh's accomplishments thus would seem to include not only the formation of elements of the *Siddur* and perhaps the canonization of parts of Scripture, but also the redaction in Houses-form of parts of the Oral Torah of Pharisaism. This Oral Torah would have consisted primarily of Houses-pericopae, perhaps arranged in patterns to permit easy memorization. But it is the *form*, not the substance, of Houses-pericopae, which reached the final stage of development.

Yoḥanan b. Zakkai, supposedly an important leader before 70, and all other named Pharisaic authorities are excluded from the essentials of the Houses-forms. We hear chiefly of the Houses, seldom of authorities within them. The Houses-form indeed leaves no room at all for named authorities. *Aggadic* and other theological materials are rare, for the purpose of the redactors apparently was to incorporate only the legal traditions, and the forms were shaped for that limited purpose, scarcely serving as vessels for other sorts of traditions. All *aggadic* Houses-materials violate the basic form of both Houses-disputes and debates.

The analyses that follow systematically raise two questions. First, what was the substance of the law attributed to the Houses? I have explained the laws according to the commentaries of Ḥ. Albeck and, especially, Saul Lieberman, on the Mishnah and Tosefta respectively. Lieberman's *Tosefta Kifshuṭah* and *Tosefet Rishonim* have been followed throughout. While for form-critical reasons I have offered a few alternate explanations, in the main the exposition of pericopae depends upon Lieberman. The second question is, What words are essential to the pericope, and what are glosses, interpolations, developments, or supplements? What are the mnemonic patterns? I have attempted to restore the pericopae to what seem to me essential mnemonic elements, to specify glosses, and to note elements added or changed on account of redactional considerations. I bear sole responsibility for the answers to the second set of questions.

We shall survey the pericopae in the Tannaitic Midrashim (both Mekhilta's, Sifra, Sifré, and Midrash Tannaim) and Mishnah-Tosefta; to these I have added, at appropriate places, some of the more important *beraitot* of the Palestinian and Babylonian *gemarot*, but I have excluded nearly all Amoraic discussions of the Houses-materials. Israel Konovitz, *Beth Shammai-Beth Hillel. Collected Sayings in Halakah and Aggadah in the Talmudic and Midrashic Literature* (Jerusalem, 1965), provides an apparently complete compilation, in the original languages, of all Houses-materials, early and late, and arranges them according to theme. There is no need to duplicate that work.

CHAPTER FIFTEEN

TANNAITIC MIDRASHIM

i. Mekhilta de R. Ishmael

I.i.1.A. Another Interpretation: *From Year to Year* (Ex. 13:10)—

B. [This] tells that a man needs to examine the phylacteries once in twelve months.

"Here it says *From year to year*, and below it says *For a full year (YMYM) shall he have the right of redemption* (Lev. 25:29). Just as year (YMYM) there means fully twelve months, so here it also means fully twelve months"—the words of the House of Hillel.

C. The House of Shammai say, "He never needs to examine them."

D. Shammai the Elder said, "These are the phylacteries of my mother's father."

[Mekhilta de R. Ishmael, Pisḥa 17:209-216, ed. and trans. Lauterbach, I, p. 157 (M. ʿEd. 4:10)]

Comment: See above, I, p. 188. Another interpretation (A) (DBR ʾḤR) is the redactional formula. Then comes the exegesis attributed to the House of Hillel. We should have expected a contrary exegesis of *year*; the corresponding opinion of the Shammaites ought to have had something to do with Ex. 13:9-10 or Lev. 25:29. But it does not. This is suspicious, for the opening clause of the pericope, giving the Hillelite opinion, does correspond to the form of the Shammaite opinion given afterward: *one should—should not—examine.*

If we ignore the exegesis, we have this:

One examines the phylacteries—

Once in twelve months—the House of Hillel.
One never examines them—the House of Shammai

that is, approximately the expected form, but with the Houses in the wrong order.

The Shammaites ignore the exegesis of Lev. 25:29 because it has no pertinence to phylacteries at all, probably also because it is a gloss. The Hillelites hold one can introduce Scriptural testimonies on the basis of common words—the *heggēsh—from year to year*. The form *here it says/there it says* occurs, one recalls, in Hillel-stories, e.g. the coincidence of the Sabbath and Passover, so the exegetical device attributed to Hillel is likewise attributed to his House. But that does not tell us when the exegetical mode was accepted or came to be regarded as probative among Hillelites.

It also is curious that the Hillel-House precede the Shammai one, for the contrary order is far more common, just as in the Shammai-Hillel pericopae, above, I, pp. 303-340.

The pericope is a unity. One could not comprehend the Shammaite opinion outside of the context of the argument. Shammai the Elder is tacked on afterward, but the body of the argument presumably began with the opinions of the two Houses; to this Lev. 25:29 was added. The silence of the Shammaites on that attempted proof suggests, as I said, that they never saw it or did not accept it as probative so as to require a response. Therefore the Hillelites or their heirs are responsible for the final form of the pericope.

Pericopae which have not been doctored by Hillelites normally contain an even balance of materials. Whatever point, argument, or proof is introduced by one party is dealt with by the other. The Shammaites come first. Hillelite exegetical rules are not introduced, since the Shammaites either do not know or do not accept them.

The pericope before us has been augmented by a Hillelite or later hand, through both the introduction of Lev. 25:29, and the application to it of Hillelite exegetical principles. The inclusion of the precedent of Shammai himself (elsewhere, Hillel) is a late addition to the whole.

According to this theory, the memorized fundament of the pericope would be something like this:

Tefillin
BWDQYN/ʾYN BWDQYN

And the Houses are given the opinions supposed appropriate, though, as I said, the attributions are the reverse of what one would expect and place the Shammaites in the lenient position. Then the first lemma is glossed with *once in twelve months*, a necessary addition, further requiring the simple Shammaite negative to be intensified to *never*. The Scriptures are a secondary interpolation.

I.i.2.A. *Whether he have not put his hand unto his neighbor's goods* (Ex. 22:8).

For his private use (LṢRKW). You interpret it to mean for his private use. Perhaps it is not so, but means whether it be for his private use or not for his private use? But Scripture says, *For every matter of trespass.*

B. For (Š) the House of Shammai declare one liable for the intention (Lit.: thought of the heart) to "put his hand," since it is said, "*For* every *thought of trespass.*"

And the House of Hillel declare one liable only from the moment when he actually did *put his hand.*

C. Accordingly, it is said, *Whether he have not put his hand unto his neighbor's goods*, [it must mean] for his private use.

[Mekhilta de R. Ishmael, Neziqin 15:49-55, ed. and trans. Lauterbach, III, p. 117 (M. B.M. 3:12)]

Comment: The legal issue of part B is when liability begins. The House of Shammai hold that intention is tantamount to action, and the House of Hillel, that one is liable only for what he actually does. The setting is autonomous. No named masters appear in, or refer to, the passage.

The connection between parts A + C with part B is less clear than it seems at the outset. The Š, combining part B to part A, leads one to suppose that the second part bears some relationship to the content of the first, as an explanation or illustration. But the first part concerns disposition of the stolen goods, and the second, the point at which liability begins. What unites the two is a common Scripture, not theme. The Š, translated by Lauterbach as *for*, therefore is a clumsy redactional device, in fact misleading the reader to suppose what follows explains the foregoing, or at least pertains to it. The Š is a commonplace joining-element and normally makes good sense in Houses-pericopae. Part C is tacked on with LKK, but repeats A and leaves the Hillelites without a Scriptural exegesis to support their position.

The lemma about the House of Shammai does not cite verbatim the actual teaching of the House at the outset, (say, liable) but reports the opinion third-hand: (*for*) *the House of Shammai declare liable*. . . Then comes the exegesis supposedly shaped by the Shammaites to back up their opinion. Likewise with the House of Hillel, the language is not indirect, let alone direct discourse, but a report, followed by the irrelevant *therefore it is said* (LKK N'MR), not the antecedent *for it is said* (ŠN'MR), which ignores the Hillelites, as I said. The two opinions do correspond to one another: MḤYYBYN +/— 'YN.

It is further puzzling that the Shammaite opinion depends on the exegesis of KL: For *every* matter, *even intention*—an ʿAqiban exegetical principle! The primary elements ought to have been

Thought of the heart
House of Shammai declare liable (ḤYYB)
House of Hillel declare exempt (PṬR)

It is hardly necessary to develop the Hillelite lemma into *not liable except when he actually put his hand*—on which the Shammaites obviously agree. So the pericope looks post-ʿAqiban and is highly developed.

The pericope certainly is not a unity, but an artificial construction in which part B is interpolated between parts A and C, because of the reference to Ex. 22:8.

II. Mekhilta de R. Simeon b. Yoḥai

I.ii.1.A. *Between the two evenings* (Ex. 12:6). . . From the sixth hour and onwards

B. For (Š) the House of Shammai say, "Included in *evening* is only [the time] after the day has turned [= after the noon hour]."

(Mekhilta de R. Simeon b. Yoḥai to Ex. 12:6, ed. Epstein-Melamed, p. 12, lines 4-5)

Comment: The corresponding passage in Mekhilta deR. Ishmael, Pisḥa 5:118-120, ed. Lauterbach, I, p. 42, has the following:

> Rabbi [Judah the Patriarch] says, "Behold it says, *There thou shalt sacrifice the Passover-offering in the evening.* I might take this literally, i.e. in the evening. But Scripture goes on to say, *At the time that thou camest forth out of Egypt.* When did Israel go forth out of Egypt? After the sixth hour [= noon] of the day. . ."

Rabbi Judah the Patriarch thus presents exactly the same opinion as the Shammaites, but his choice of words and supporting exegesis are different.

How would the opinion of the Shammaites originally have taken shape? It is difficult to imagine that the brief lemma before us could have circulated outside of the context of the law and Scripture to which it pertains. But we have no Shammaite Mekhilta or other document collecting their opinions, except for the Mishnaic Houses-collections (below, pp. 324-343). The lemma in its present form has been attached to a Scripture but presumably was meant as a general rule of interpretation for all places in which *between the evenings* appears. Judah the Patriarch draws the same conclusion as do the Shammaites but does not refer to their exegetical proof in stating it.

I cannot imagine why 'Aqibans should have preserved the Shammaite view. After ca. 100, no normative teachers known to us were Shammaites. So why should either party have done more than preserve either already redacted collections of materials, or stories and sayings reflecting a poor opinion of the Shammaites? This saying is neutral and presented as authoritative, normally signs of early redaction. Yet there is no indication that the lemma at an early date was given official and final form in a collection. Perhaps Shammaite exegetical rules and sayings were in fact redacted but suppressed, and only bits and pieces in pretty much their original form survived later on.

See Epstein, *Mevo'ot*, pp. 328, 332, 336.

I.ii.2.A. *Every male* (Ex. 23:17)—to include (LRBWT) the children.

B. This is that which the House of Hillel say, "Every child who can hold his father's hand and go up from Jerusalem to the Temple Mount is liable for making an appearance (R'YH)."

[Mekhilta de R. Simeon b. Yoḥai to Ex. 23:17, ed. Epstein-Melamed, p. 218, lines 28-9 (b. Ḥag. 4a, M. Ḥag. 1:1, y. Ḥag. 1:1)]

Comment: The form is much the same as the foregoing: an exegesis followed by a lemma of one of the Houses, attached in the preceding by *for the House... say*, or, as here, *This is that which... say*—that is, redactional materials to link autonomous and pre-existing lemmas to the exegetical framework already established according to order of the Scriptural compilation. The Hillelite saying is independent, without the corresponding Shammaite ruling, just as in the foregoing, the Shammaite material stands by itself. The rule of B is a unity as it stands. It would have been comprehended quite outside the Scriptural framework and circulated in that form.

Part A is ʿAqiban, for KL—*to include* is a standard exegetical technique associated with ʿAqibans and later masters. It cannot be attributed to the House of Hillel. Part B ignores the exegesis, presumably has nothing to do with it, and supplies an interpretation of the Scripture unrelated to the parts of the Scripture itself (KL). The exegesis depends, rather, upon the *meaning*, not the form—*every* male will include children who can make the trip. Still, it is hard to see how the Hillelite exegesis differs from part A, for both depend upon the meaning of *every/all*. The only distinction is that part A takes for granted the ʿAqiban *formula*: KL—*to include*; while part B, saying the same thing in substance, ignores the exegetical formula. Part B is tacked on to part A because of the common theme and common reference to KL. Part B must come later than the Houses-dispute on the same subject and is borrowed from it. Compare Sifré Deut. 143, below, p. 35.

I.ii.3. *Six days shall you work and do all your labor* (Ex. 20:9)—

A. This is that which the House of Shammai say, "They do not soak ink, dyestuffs, and vetches, except so that ('L' KDY Š) they may be [wholly] soaked while it is still day.

B. "And they do not spread nets [for] beast[s] and birds, except so that they may be caught while it is still day.

C. "And they do not lay down the olive press beams or the winepress rollers unless they [the juices] will flow while it is still day.

D. "And they do not open a channel [to water] the gardens except so that it may be [wholly] filled while it is still day.

E. "And they do not place meat, onion, and egg on the fire, and not a broth (TBŠYL) into the oven except so that they may roast while it is still day."

F. And the House of Hillel permit in all of them.

G. But that (ʾLʾ Š)

The House of Shammai say, "*Six days will you work and do all your labor*—that all your work should be finished by the Sabbath eve."

And the House of Hillel say, "*Six days shall you work* [*and do all your labor*]—You labor all six days, and the rest of your work is done of itself on the Sabbath."

(Mekhilta de R. Simeon b. Yoḥai to Ex. 20:9, ed. Epstein-Melamed, p. 149, lines 15-21)

Comment: This is a late summary-repertoire of Shammai-rulings on a single problem summarized at the end, part G. They are presented in a different sort of collection in M. Shab. 1:4-11, Tos. Shab. 1:21; see below, p. 127. All that is not drawn from M.-Tos. Shab. is the little exegesis in part G; the Houses' lemmas are not balanced opposites, unlike the M.-Tos. version.

Note also Shammai in Midrash Tannaim, p. 123, Sifré Deut. 203, Tos. ʿEruv. 3:7, b. Shab. 19a, y. Shab. 1:4. Epstein, *Mevoʾot*, p. 278, notes that the House of Shammai was more stringent than Shammai, and the House of *Hillel* followed his view!

iii. Sifra

I.ii.4.A. [*Or anything about which he has sworn falsely; he shall restore it in full, and shall add a fifth to it, and give it to him to whom it belongs*] *on the day of his guilt offering* (Lev. 6:5 [MT 5:24]).

B. The House of Shammai say, "(YLQH BḤŚR WYTR) He suffers the disadvantages of loss or gain."

[So Jastrow, II, p. 718, s.v. LQY; he must pay according to the original value of his bailment in case of depreciation, or according to the present value of the misappropriated bailment in case of a rise in value.]

And the House of Hillel say, "According to the hour of removal [of the misappropriated bailment]."

C. Rabbi ʿAqiba says, "According to the hour of the claim."

(Sifra Vayiqra Parashah 13:13, ed. I. H. Weiss, p. 28b)

Comment: The whole passage occurs in M. B.M. 3:12: *If a man put to his own use what had been left in his his keeping*—

The House of Shammai say, "He is at a disadvantage. . ."

And the House of Hillel say, "[He must restore the deposit at the same value] according to the hour of removal."

R. ʿAqiba says, "At its value when claimed."

The passage here is introduced by a Scripture, in the Mishnah by a generalized rule of law, but the substance otherwise is identical, in the standard form alluded to above. Then follow later materials (part C), augmenting, but not changing, the original matter. Such a passage must have reached its final form before R. ʿAqiba's time and was never after altered. It appears in Sifra and Mishnah without alteration, except in editorial superscriptions, other opinions as supplements at the end, and (where needed) redactional material. The Shammaite-Hillelite dispute could have stood without the ʿAqiban subscription, and probably did. Part B is a unity, the pericope a composite. Since ʿAqiba supplies the *terminus ante quem*, the conventional legal form comes very early in the formation of the legal traditions after 70.

But while the form is standard, the Houses-lemmas are not, for they do not exhibit the normal antonymic, balanced relationship, in which word-choices correspond to one another. On the contrary, the Hillelite and ʿAqiban sayings are what we should have expected for the Houses:

KŠʿT HWṢʾH
KŠʿT TBYʿH

In the simplest oral form the difference would have been the single word at the end. The Shammaite saying then should be:

KŠʿT HGZLH

the time on which the man stole, therefore in substance the same as the Hillelite lemma, for HWṢʾH = GZLH.

But the Shammaite *meaning* is different; their view is that the man pays the highest possible restitution. If the object increased in value, he pays the higher value. If from the time it was left with him or he stole it, it decreased in value, he pays the value at the time it was left with him. Therefore the Shammaite lemma could not have been a fixed time, either:

KŠʿT HPYQDWN

or:

KŠʿT HGZLH

for neither specification of time would have conveyed the precise Shammaite opinion, that the value of the property could be according to *either* time—or even the Aqiban KŠʿT TBYʿH for that matter.

The Shammaite lemma therefore necessarily consists of a stock-phrase out of balance with the Hillelite one, for only that phrase could precisely convey the Shammaite opinion. 'Aqiba rejects both Houses' opinions, taking as the time for evaluating restitution the hour of the claim, whether higher or lower than the foregoing time. The Hillelites' position is not necessarily, but may be, more lenient. In this instance, the considerations of mnemonic transmission in carefully balanced lemmas must be weighed against the need for precise expression of the Shammaite opinion, which precludes KŠ'T. . .

Note Epstein, *Mevo'ot*, p. 77.

I.ii.5.A. *[But no sin offering shall be eaten from which any blood is brought into the tent of meeting to make atonement in the holy place; it shall be burned with fire.]*

All that is holy will be burned with fire (Lev. 6:30).

B. From here they said:

The flesh of the holy of holies which has been made unclean, whether with a primary source of uncleanness or with a secondary source of uncleanness, whether within or outside [the holy precinct]—

C. "The House of Shammai say, 'All will be burned *within* [the courtyard.]'

"And the House of Hillel say, 'All will be burned *outside* [the courtyard], except [that] which is made unclean with a secondary source of uncleanness—within,' "—the words of R. Meir.

D. R. Judah says, "The House of Shammai say, 'All is burned inside, except that which is made unclean by a primary source of uncleanness—outside.'

E. "And the House of Hillel say, 'All is burned outside, except that which is made unclean by a secondary source of uncleanness—within.' "

(Sifra Ṣav Pereq 8:6, ed. I. H. Weiss, p. 33a)

Comment: Even though one does not bring unclean objects into the Temple court, not even something made unclean under any circumstances, Scripture has included in the rule of *all that is holy will be burned within the courtyard* the burning of holy objects that have been made unclean, so Meir's Shammaites. The House of Hillel say all should be burned *outside*, for it is indeed forbidden to bring unclean things into the Temple court, except something unclean in a minor degree. The rulings of the Houses, in fact formulated by R. Meir and R. Judah [b. Ilai], the *terminus ante quem*, ignore B, which alleges that the distinctions explicitly stated by the Houses do not matter at all!

Afterward comes a second, and separate ruling on the same matter, deriving from R. Eliezer [b. Hyrcanus] and R. 'Aqiba. Eliezer holds that what is made unclean by a primary source of uncleanness, whether in or out the court, is to be burned *outside* the courtyard, and what is made unclean by a secondary source of uncleanness, whether outside or inside the court, is burned *inside*. This too ignores the allegation of B. Then, also contrary to B, ʿAqiba holds that what is made unclean outside, whether by a primary or by a secondary source of uncleanness, is to be burned *outside*; what is made unclean inside the court, whether by a primary or by a secondary source of uncleanness, is to be burned *inside*. Thus the *place* where the uncleanness has taken place is decisive for ʿAqiba; the *degree* of the source of uncleanness is determinative for Eliezer. Part B comes at the end, for it explicitly alludes to disagreements on whether the source is primary or secondary, inside or outside. The original lemmas of the House ought to be simply:

The flesh of the holy of holies which has been made unclean, all will be burned
House of Shammai say, *Inside.*
House of Hillel say, *Outside.*

No authority gives that picture. The Shammaite lemma of Meir conforms, but no part of Judah's does. But the whole may be heavily glossed. The glosses are readily discernible, for they are the *exceptions.* Judah's and Meir's exceptions for both Houses depend on whether the source of uncleanness is primary or secondary—all according to Eliezer. It therefore looks as if the Ushans have rephrased and developed Eliezer's opinion into a new Houses-dispute. Perhaps B is right: the Houses originally made no such distinctions as now are alleged by both the Yavneans and the Ushans.

The Scripture is connected by an inappropriate joining-formula, *from here they said.* The exegetical materials are not pertinent at all; part B artificially and erroneously joins parts C-D-E to the established redactional framework.

The pericope recurs in M. Sheq. 8:6. There it reflects the rule of Eliezer that one takes into account the distinction between primary and secondary sources of uncleanness. M. Sheq. 8:7 then presents the Eliezer-ʿAqiba dispute.

The same Houses-opinions are attached to a parallel dispute in M. M.S. 3:9 = Tos. M.S. 2:16, below, pp. 99-105.

I.ii.6.A. [The rite of circumcision of a] baby born circumcized does not override the Sabbath, for (Š)—

The House of Shammai say, "One must draw from him [a drop of] blood [as a sign of] the covenant."

And the House of Hillel say, "One does not need [to do so]."

B. R. Simeon b. Eleazar said, "The House of Shammai and the House of Hillel did not dispute concerning one born circumcized, that one does need to draw from him a drop of blood of the covenant, because it is a hidden foreskin (ʿRLH KBWŠH).

"Concerning what did they dispute? Concerning a proselyte who converted when already circumcized, for—

"The House of Shammai say, 'One needs to draw from him a drop of blood of the covenant.'

"And the House of Hillel say, 'One does not need [to do so].' "

[Sifra Tazriʿa Pereq 1:5, ed. Weiss, p. 58b (Ber. R. 46:13; for B: Tos. Shab. 3:18)]

Comment: The setting is whether various exceptional circumstances of the rite of circumcision override the Sabbath. The basic rule is given anonymously: If the child certainly has a foreskin, the circumcision overrides the Sabbath, but otherwise it does not. Then comes a ruling of Judah [b. Ilai] on the androgynous baby, followed by the ruling of the Houses.

The pericope of the Houses, however, is already redacted, and is attached to the foregoing general rule with the usual Š. Without the rule, the pericope is complete and follows the normal form, except that we do not know the antecedent of the House of Shammai's *him*, that is, the legal problem addressed by the Houses. Part B supplies an alternative theory on that question.

The actual ruling does not explicitly pertain to the Sabbath at all, but to whether or not one draws a drop of blood. Only if we already know that the law follows the House of Hillel and that the consequence of the Hillelite ruling about not drawing blood is that one also need not set aside Sabbath regulations on account of such a bloodless rite, do we comprehend the redactor's use of the Houses-sayings. Part A therefore is somewhat more complex than it appears on the surface. Its introductory statement could not have been shaped in its present form during the period that the law did not automatically follow the Hillelite House, that is, before 70 (when it probably followed the Shammaites) and presumably sometime thereafter. The presupposition of the redactor suggests a relatively late redaction for part A.

But the original language of the Houses has probably not been changed by the redactor of A *or* by Simeon, for, if either had made any changes at all, he would have had the Houses rule on the issue actually claimed to be under discussion—Sabbath or convert—rather than on drawing blood, a question peripheral to the issue at hand according to both. So Simeon has preserved the original formulation in his prologue, rejecting what must have been before him and substituting a new superscription. In what form would the sayings of the Houses have existed until his time? It had to have been as follows:

As to circumcizing one born circumcized:
The House of Shammai say, Need to draw blood.
The House of Hillel say, No need to draw blood.

Then the redactor of A would have augmented the introductory clause:

As to circumcizing one who was born circumcized, *it does not override the Sabbath*

That is to say, all that was added is *it does not override*. . . Nothing else need have been altered; adding the clause provided all necessary redactional material. I am impressed, therefore, with the faithful reproduction of the materials coming down from the Houses. Simeon has been just as faithful, in his way.

See Tos. Shab. 15(16):9 for the same dispute with regard to a circumcized convert.

I.ii.7. [*And when the days of her purifying are completed, whether for a son or for a daughter, she shall bring to the priest at the door of the tent of meeting a lamb a year old for a burnt offering. . . This is the law for her who bears a child, either male or female* (Lev. 12:6-7).]

A. *For a son*—to impose a liability for each son.

For a daughter—to impose a liability for each daughter.

B. And when it says, *or* for a daughter—[*or* is] to include (LHBY') [in the liability for a sacrifice] one who brings forth an abortion on the eve of the eighty-first day [after the birth of a girl], that she should be liable for a sacrifice, according to the words of the House of Hillel.

For (Š) the House of Shammai exempt [her] from the sacrifice.

[Note: After the birth of a girl, eighty days of cleanness have passed, during which the woman does not become unclean through discharge of blood. Now, on the eighty-first day, she is to sacrifice. If another birth takes place before the expiration of this period, no new offerings are required; but if on or after the eighty-first day, she *is* liable. The second birth (abortion) was on the *eve* of the eighty-first day. The night is generally considered part of the following day. But since the sacrifices are not offered until daytime on the eighty-first day, is the (new) abortion covered by these sacrifices or not?—So I. Porusch, trans., *Kerithoth*, p. 56, n. 8].

C.1. The House of Hillel said to the House of Shammai, "Do you not agree with us concerning the eve [Lit.: one who sees light] of the eighty-first day that she is unclean?"

2. The House of Shammai said to them, "Do you not agree concerning the woman who aborts on the eighty-first day that she *is* liable for a sacrifice?"

D.1. The House of Hillel said to them, "What is the difference between the eve of the eighty-first day and the eighty-first day? If it is equivalent to it as regards uncleanness, will it not be equivalent to it as regards the sacrifice?"

2. The House of Shammai said to them, "No, if you say [so] concerning the woman who aborts on the eighty-first day, when it occurs at a time fit to bring an offering, [can you maintain the same when she bears an abortion on the eve of the eighty-first day, seeing that it did *not* occur at a time fit to bring an offering—*supplied from M. Ker. 1:6*]?"

E.1. The House of Hillel said to them, "And behold, she who aborts on the eighty-first day that coincides with the Sabbath will prove the matter: the abortion took place at a time unfit to bring an offering, and yet she *is* liable to bring a [new] offering."

2. The House of Shammai said to them, "No, if you say [so] concerning the abortion on the eighty-first day that coincides with the Sabbath, which is not fit for offerings of an individual but is at least fit for communal offerings, will you say so concerning the woman who aborts on the eve of the eighty-first, for lo, the nights are not the time for an individual offering and not for a public offering."

F. "She who sees blood proves nothing, for she who aborts within the period of cleanness is clean, yet she is exempted from the offering."

G. The House of Hillel said to them, "And when it says, *or for the daughter*, [it is] to include her who aborts on the eve of the eighty-first, that she should be liable for the sacrifice."

[Sifra Tazriʿa Pereq 3:1-2, ed. I. H. Weiss, p. 59a (b. Pes. 3a)]

Comment: According to the words of. . . signifies a précis of the Hillelite opinion, but not the exact words of the Hillelites. They are not given here, but appear only in M. Ker. 1:6: *The House of Hillel declare obligated.* Sifra is a secondary development, as we shall see.

Since the passage is nearly identical to M. Ker. 1:6, at the outset we had best consider the synopsis:

Sifra Tazriʿa 3:1	*M. Ker. 1:6*
1. *Or* for the daughter—to include the one who aborts on the eve of the eighty-first, that she should be liable for the sacrifice, according to the words of the House of Hillel.	1. She who aborts on the eve of the eighty-first: The House of Shammai declare free of the liability of the sacrifice, and the House of Hillel declare obligated.
2. For (Š) the House of Shammai declare free of the liability of sacrifice	2. —

3. The House of Hillel said to the House of Shammai, Do you not agree with us concerning the [one who sees] on the eve of the eighty-first that she is unclean.	3. —
4. The House of Shammai said to them, Do you not agree concerning her who aborts on the eighty-first that she is liable for the sacrifice.	4. —
5. The House of Hillel said to them, What is the difference between the eve of the eighty-first and the day of the eighty-first? If it is equivalent to it as to uncleanness, will it not be equivalent to it as to sacrifice?	5. „ „ „
6. The House of Shammai said to them, No, if you say concerning her who aborts on the eighty-first, where it occurred at a time fit to bring an offering—	6. „ „ „ [Adds:] *will you say so concerning her who aborts on the eve of the eighty-first where it occurred at a time not fit to bring an offering?*
7. The House of Hillel said to them, Lo, the one who aborts on the day of the eighty-first which coincides with the Sabbath will prove [it], for it did not occur at a time fit to bring an offering, but she *is* liable to bring an offering.	7. „ „ „
8. The House of Shammai said to them, No, if you say [so] of her who aborts on the day of the eighty-first that coincides with the Sabbath, for even though it is not appropriate for a private sacrifice, it is appropriate for a public sacrifice, will you say so concerning her who aborts on the eve of the eighty-first, for lo, the nights are appropriate for neither private nor public sacrifice.	8. „ „ „ [M. Ker. has *night*, instead of *nights*]
9. She who sees blood does not prove it, for she who aborts during the period of cleanness (ML'T)—her blood is clean, and she is free of the sacrifice.	9. The *blood* does not prove, for she who aborts during the periods of cleanness, her bood is clean [MS Kaufmann: *Unclean*], and she is free of her sacrifice.
10. The House of Hillel said to them, When it says, *or the daughter*, it is to include her who aborts on the eve of the eighty-first that she should be liable to bring the sacrifice.	10. —

The important changes come in nos. 2, 3, 4, omitted by M. Ker.; no. 5, for which M. Ker. supplies the necessary conclusion; and no. 10, omitted by M. Ker. No. 2 of Sifra is contained in the Mishnah's opening statement. Sifra nos. 3-4 summarize the underlying criteria employed by each party, and the point is elaborated in no. 5. The Hillelites hold that since she is unclean, a new sacrifice is likewise required for the occasion of her new uncleanness. The Shammaites argue that since she is liable for the sacrifice for a new birth on the eighty-first day, there is no difference between the preceding evening and the day, and the same sacrifice covers both situations. Thus the two Houses begin by arguing from facts on which all parties agree and must then introduce distinctions in support of their respective decisions. The eve before the eighty-first represents a middle ground. Why M. Ker. should omit the formal introduction to the debate (nos. 3-4) is unclear to me. Everything else depends on it, for the effort to distinguish evening from the following day takes for granted that establishing such a distinction will be decisive. The exchange therefore ought not to have been dropped. The additional materials in M. Ker. no. 6 obviously are important, providing the reverse of the foregoing clause, therefore are essential, as noted in my translation, where I interpolated M. Ker. to complete the sentence. The changes in nos. 9-10 are striking; M. Ker. ought to have included the reply of the House of Hillel. Since the exegetical basis for their position is not given earlier in M. Ker., it is all the more striking that it is also omitted here. Sifra repeats no. 1 in no. 10.

The pericope before us contains an extended debate on a legal problem, in which the opposing principles of interpretation are attached to the name of authorities, as in the Hillel-Bené Bathyra debate on the Passover offering on the Sabbath. What is striking is the even balance between the arguments. The two parties are given a fair hearing; the Shammai-House does not serve merely as a foil for the Hillel-House's ingenuity, but stands upon firm logical foundations. The normal form of the Houses-pericopae therefore has been extended from legal opinion to logical argument.

We may account for this striking phenomenon in two ways. First, we may suppose that the two Houses constitute invented personnae, serving to dramatize a clash of legal principles ("They said to them," "Do you not agree with us that"). Everyone knew the Hillelites would win and the law would follow them, so it made no great difference to preserve good, if in the end rejected, arguments in the name of the House of Shammai. On the contrary, it was vital to supply the full repertoire of counter-arguments, for it was inevitable that they would be raised by later masters. Showing that all logical issues were raised and settled at the outset made the debate more persuasive than otherwise. Everyone would recognize that the Hillelites had won through the force of their reason and logic, not merely because of circumstances or heavenly instructions ("echo"). It improved the picture of the House of Hillel to show they had strong and worthy opponents. The whole would be from a historical viewpoint fictitious, the creation of the later masters. This perspective on matters would explain the Mishnah's omission of no. 10, so leaving things with the Shammaites having the last word, the upper hand.

Alternatively, the debate-elements of the pericope were shaped in much the same way as the legal opinions, that is, when both sides enjoyed relative parity with one another. The Shammaites therefore were able to secure the inclusion in the final pericope of a full account not only of their opinions but also of the reasons for them. We have ample evidence that such arguments were constructed at Yavneh, e.g., in ʿAqiban circles, and it is not far-fetched to suppose that the final redaction of the pericope was the product of a joint effort between the two Houses to secure an accurate picture of the differences between them about both principles and legal rulings.

The difference between these alternative explanations for the balanced picture before us is not great. We cannot suppose that "one day" the two Houses assembled and spoke these arguments in unison ("They said to them"). The narrative details represent nothing more than a fictitious dramatization of the argument. The fact that the Hillelites in the end won did not prevent both the fabrication and the preservation of the balanced legal syzygies: Law. . . House of Shammai say. . . House of Hillel say. . . So here too, the debate part of the pericope need not to be attributed to Hillelite-ʿAqiban or even later masters, but *perhaps* to early Yavnean redactors, responsible to give an account of matters acceptable to both sides.

As to the pericope itself, it is transparently composite. Part B of Sifra Tazriʿa and its equivalent, M. Ker. 1:6 no. 1, were shaped first of all as a complete unit. M. Ker. conforms to the pattern normal for disputes between the Houses. Sifra Tazriʿa elements no. 1-2 differ because of the inclusion of the Hillelite exegesis, with the Shammaite opinion ("The House of Shammai exempt. . .") tacked on. The exegesis was shaped without reference to the Shammaites, and the Shammaite opinion—without an exegetical foundation—was added before part B was finished. Once it was finished, parts C, D, E, and F were worked out. Part G merely repeats the exegesis of Part B, therefore making it possible for the Hillelites to win the argument. The arguments are as follows:

C.	The woman is *unclean* on the eve of the eighty-first	—Hillel
	The woman is *liable for an offering* on the eighty-first day	—Shammai
D.	What is difference between eve of eighty-first and the eighty-first day?	—Hillel
	On the eighty-first day she can bring an offering, but on the eve she cannot	—Shammai
E.	If eighty-first day coincides with the Sabbath, she is liable to bring offering, even though the offering cannot be made that day	—Hillel
	But on the Sabbath there are public offerings, while on the eve of the eighty-first day there are no offerings, private or public	—Shammai

Part F then breaks the pattern. Shammaites give a counter-argument, without the antecedent Hillelite argument. There should have been some Hillelite argument, based upon "she who sees blood. . ." This is refuted, but the refutation stands by itself. Part G remains quite outside of the pattern, as I said, for it allows the Hillelites to complete the argument by their (repeated) exegesis, to which the Shammaites make no reply at all.

The form of the argument before us thus in fact differs in one important way from the normal Houses-form: it has the Hillel-opinion first, followed by the Shammaites, and then persists in placing Hillelites before Shammaites throughout, until at the end the Shammaites are dropped entirely. M. Ker. 1:6, by contrast, conforms to the Shammaite/Hillelite pattern:

Law
House of Shammai declare free
House of Hillel declare obligated

In the arguments, nos, 5, 6, 7, and 8, we find the Hillelites preceding, as here, but with the final Hillelite argument dropped.

If the Sifra-version has departed from the norm in its primary element, part B, the reason is clear, namely, the redactional necessity of uniting a Houses-dispute with an exegesis attributed to Hillelites. It would have been impossible both to conform to the usual Shammaite/Hillelite order and also to permit the exegesis to stand in the normal form and sequence. So redactional considerations required reversing the order, allowing the exegesis to be marked, "the words of the House of Hillel," and requiring the Shammaite opinion to come second. The addition of the Shammaite House's opinion is joined with the usual Š, *for*, but the opinion is thereupon given in precisely the form one would expect. Indeed, we find in M. Ker. the proper language. No change there has been made in the substance of the opinion.

The order of arguments, Hillel-then-Shammai, represents the significant characteristic of the debate-form. This is to the Shammaites' advantage, for it allows them step by step to refute the Hillelite arguments. Therefore the whole form consistently represents Shammaite preponderance. This reenforces my guess that the debate-form may constitute not a theoretical argument framed long after the Shammaites had passed from the scene, but rather the form of an argument among parties of about equal strength, with the Shammaites able to secure for themselves the preponderant, advantageous position, both in the order in which legal opinions are given and in the order of the unfolding of the arguments. Once the materials were redacted, they were not changed. Judah the Patriarch faithfully copied the materials as they had come down to him, with the Shammaites' winning the argument.

The Mishnaic version has not bothered with the exegesis, for three reasons; first, because the Mishnah rarely gives the exegetical foundations for laws; second, because in the early third century it was unnecessary to underline the predominance of Hillelite opinions in the formation of law, for everyone knew law followed Hillelite traditions; third, because the exegesis is spurious, and not Hillelite but ʿAqiban, as usual in Sifra. That exegetical principle is a *ribbuʾi: or* for a daughter—*to include* one who brings forth. . . The *ribbuʾi* based on *or* (ʾW) is not on the list of Hillelite principles of exegesis, but belongs to Nahum of Gimzo-ʿAqiba. Original to the Hillelite school, therefore, is merely the opinion. Before ʿAqiban times (if the pericope does date before ca. 100,) the Shammaites came last and won the argument. This seems to me definitive evidence that the pericope at the outset did not contain part G, therefore part A is likewise tacked on by ʿAqibans. The essential words of the Hillelites were as given in M. Ker. 1:6, in form just like those of the Shammaites.

I.ii.8.A. *Her bloods* (Lev. 12:7)—teaches that many bloods are unclean in her: red, and black, and bright crocus color (QRN KRKWM), and a color like earthy water and like mixed [water and wine].

B. The House of Shammai say, "Also like a water in which fenugreek had been soaked and a color like the juice that comes out of roast flesh." [So Danby, p. 747, for KMYMY TLTN and KMYMY BSR ṢLY].

C. The House of Hillel declare clean.

(Sifra Tazriʿa Pereq 3:6, ed. Weiss, p. 59a = Sifra Meṣoraʿ Parashah 4:3, Weiss, p. 78a)

Comment: M. Nid. 2:6 has the following: *Five* bloods are unclean *in a woman*. . . *and* the House of Hillel. . . As usual, Judah the Patriarch has dropped the exegesis. The only other change is to link the Houses with *and*, a redactional alteration of no importance.

The form is standard: a rule of law, followed by a dispute of the Houses. In this instance the dispute concerns materials added by Shammaites to the earlier list. The original list, however, has excluded them, thus in conformity to the Hillelite view. How would the Houses-pericope have appeared at the outset? I doubt that it originally would have conformed to the Hillelite view and *then* duplicated the Hillelite opinion in part C. We should rather have expected the complete list in the name of one of the Houses, followed by the contrary view of the other House, presumably Shammai, then Hillel, thus for the Mishnah:

> [*Seven*] kinds of blood in a woman are *unclean*: red and black and bright crocus color and a color like earthy water and like mixed [water and wine] and a color like water in which fenugreek had been soaked and a color like the juice that comes out of roast flesh, according to the House of Shammai.
>
> The House of Hillel say, "A color like water. . . and a color like juice. . . are *clean*."

In this highly developed form, the pericope would have been complete and autonomous, requiring no further explanatory matter. In its present form, by contrast, the primary list makes it superfluous to specify the bloods which the Hillelites regard as clean. The pericope before us depends upon the Hillelite revision, for otherwise it is not comprehensible; that is, "*also* like a water. . ." makes no sense apart from the earlier specification. What has been changed from the (theoretical) autonomous version of the dispute is two elements in the Shammaite lemma: *seven* (if originally present) becomes *five*; *also* is added; and, additionally, the Shammaite opinion is moved to the middle of the list.

My guess is that the original form of the Houses-dispute is not before us, and I imagine it was the redactor who changed the materials, mainly to connect the whole to the context of a series of exegeses of Scripture. Had the setting been otherwise, it would have been possible to preserve the Houses-pericope in an autonomous framework, not dependent upon any information outside of the actual words attributed to the two Houses. The earlier pericope (I.ii.7) has already shown us an example of a still more drastic revision of a material to serve redactional needs. My hypothesis on the original form of the pericope before us requires the supposition of substantially fewer changes. For the Sifra version *many bloods* need not have been changed at all. The only change was moving the Shammaite opinion back two elements, and adding *also*.

Note Epstein, *Mevo'ot*, p. 439.

I.ii.9.A. [*When you come into the land and plant all kinds of trees for food, then you shall count their fruit as forbidden; three years it shall be forbidden to you, it must not be eaten. And in the fourth year all their fruit shall be holy, an offering of praise to the Lord* (Lev. 19:23-24).]

A. All *their fruit will be*—to include (LHBY') grape-gleanings (PRṬ) and defective clusters [the grapes growing in small, separate bunches = ʿWLLWT], according to the words of (KDBRY) the House of Hillel.

B. The House of Shammai say, "He has [the right to] the grape-gleanings and the defective clusters (YŠ LW PRṬ WYŠ LW ʿWLLWT). And the poor redeem [them] for themselves (WHʿNYYM PWDYM LʿṢMM)."

C. And the House of Hillel say, "It is all for the winepress (KWLW LGT)."

(Sifra Qedoshim Parashah 3:7, ed. I. H. Weiss, p. 90a)

Comment: M.ʿEd. 4:5b has the following:

The House of Shammai say, "The laws of grape-gleanings and of the defective cluster apply (YŠ LW PRṬ WYŠ LW 'WLLWT), and the poor redeem [the grapes] for themselves (WH'NYYM PWDYM L'ṢMN).

And the House of Hillel say, "The whole [yield goes] to the winepress (KWLW LGT)."

M. 'Ed. 4:5b (and parallels) preserves the classic form of the dispute, as we have already observed in similar instances:

The House of Shammai say...
The House of Hillel say...

Part A is duplicated in part C. It serves the purpose of the redactor, linking the law to the exegetical framework already established. Therefore the redactor has taken the Hillelite opinion and given it in the form of an exegesis—again in the style of the 'Aqiban exegetical rules (!). Then comes the original form, repeated without alteration in M. 'Ed., and parts B and C are integrally related to one another and stand independent of part A.

The key is *according to the words of* in part A, noted above as well (I.ii.7). The redactor so indicates that he has given the Hillelite opinion, but *not* in the form in which he has it. Then the original follows. My guess is that parts B and C have been interpolated from the Mishnaic version, an example of the dependence of Sifra on Mishnah. In I.ii.7, by contrast, the exact words attributed to the House of Hillel are *not* given at all, but are preserved only in M. Ker. 1:6. We cannot ignore the redactor's care in specifying *according to the words of* in both instances (I.ii.7 and 9), which means that he was aware of the attribution of other, *exact* words to the Houses; since he did not present those words, he has used language to signify what he did give: a summary in exegetical form, Scripture, exegesis, *then* attribution to Hillelites.

We may therefore specify both the primary form of the Houses-disputes and its secondary development in the exegetical compilations:

Primary: House of Shammai say...
House of Hillel say...
Secondary: Exegesis—[normally] according to the House of Hillel-'Aqiba
House of Shammai say...
House of Hillel say...
[Sometimes:] Repetition of the exegesis, according to...

This permits me to suggest that I.ii.7 is defective, while I.ii.9 shows what the form should have been. Originally Hillelite opinions were not accompanied by exegeses of Scripture. 'Aqibans invented what ought to have been the Hillelite-exegesis.

One of the effects of the 'Aqiban exegetical revolution was to strengthen the claim of the Hillelites to give the correct version of the law by providing a sound Scriptural basis for Hillelite opinions. The probable reason that the Shammaites generally were not supplied with equivalent exegeses—which, we may take for granted, could have been fabricated —was that Shammaites no longer predominated at Yavneh. No one therefore took the trouble to back up their legal opinions with the new ʿAqiban exegesis. It is unthinkable that, had their opinions prevailed, no one could have done so. It is equally unthinkable that the Hillelite opinions prevailed only because the ʿAqibans (or others) were able to prove they were "right."

The language of the pericope is analyzed below, M. Pe'ah 7:6, p. 59.

I.ii.10.A. [*On the fifteenth day of the seventh month* (ʾK BḤMŠH ʿSR YWM etc.) *when you have gathered in the produce of the land, you shall keep the feast of the Lord seven days; on the first day shall be a solemn rest, and on the eighth day shall be a solemn rest* (Lev. 23:39)].

A. The House of Shammai says, "One might think (YKWL) a man may offer the pilgrim's festive sacrifice (YḤWG ʾDM—so Jastrow for ḤGG) on the festival day.

"Scripture says, *Only*, (ʾK), [meaning] *only* on the intervening week-days [between the first and last days of the Festival] do you offer the pilgrim's festive sacrifice, but you do not offer the pilgrim's festive sacrifice (ḤWGG) on the festival day (BYWM ṬWB) [itself]."

B. The House of Hillel says, "One might think a man should offer the pilgrim's festive sacrifice on the Sabbath—Scripture says, *Only*, (ʾK), [meaning] on the festival day (YWM ṬWB) one offers his pilgrim's festive sacrifice, but you do not offer the pilgrim's festive sacrifice on the Sabbath."

(Sifra Emor Pereq 15:5, ed. I. H. Weiss, p. 102b)

Comment: The dispute superficially follows the conventional form. But it cannot derive from the Houses at all, for at issue is the interpretation of the particle ʾK; later ʿAqiban exegesis held that ʾK served to exclude the Sabbath from the days on which the *ḥagigah* might be offered. The Shammaites are represented as arguing that ʾK limited the *ḥagigah*-offering to the intervening days, excluding the opening and closing days of the festival itself.

The Houses here have been used as names for the attribution of disputes that in this form certainly could not have taken shape before the end of the first century, if then. Perhaps the Houses substitute for named authorities following ʿAqiba, for the attribution to the Houses of a dispute about the exegesis of the limiting-word ʾK is spurious.

M. Ḥag. 1:6 presents the Hillelite view:

He who made no pilgrim's festive sacrifice on the first festival day of the feast offers them throughout the course of the feast (MY ŠL' ḤG BYWM ṬWB HR'ŠHWN ŠLḤG ḤWGG 'T KL HRGL)—even on the last festival day of the feast.

This is the opposite of the Shammaite view, for the House of Shammai hold one may *not* offer on the festival day (YWM ṬWB) at all. The Hillelites' excluded day ('K) is the *Sabbath*, not the YWM ṬWB. Judah the Patriarch makes no reference to the dispute and presents the Mishnaic ruling anonymously.

If the Houses actually did debate this point of festival law, the exegetical basis for their respective rulings could not have been as represented here, nor as I said, could the form of the debate have focused upon the function of 'K. Since the Houses-pericopae generally survive with ʿAqiban accretions to the original form, there is no reason that this one should not likewise have come down both in an earlier form, if any existed, and in the ʿAqiban development.

We also observe that the singular verb *says* ('WMR) is used with the Houses, rather than the plural. I.ii.9 parts B and C use both *says* and *say*, and in M. ʿEd. 4:5b, Judah the Patriarch has consistently used *say*. Normally the collective nouns are given plural verbs.

Note Judah b. Dortai's view above, I, p. 147. He stands against the Hillelite view.

I.ii.11. [*But in the Seventh Year shall be a Sabbath of solemn rest for the land, a Sabbath to the Lord. . . What grows of itself in your harvest you shall not reap. . . it shall be a year of solemn rest for the land. The Sabbath of the land shall provide food for you* (Lev. 25-4-6)].

A. *And the Sabbath of the Land shall provide food for you*—from the Sabbath (ŠBWT) in the land you may eat, and you may not eat from that which is guarded (ŠMWR). From here (MYK'N) they said:

B. *A field which has been prepared* (ŠNṬYYBH)—

The House of Shammai say, "They do not eat its fruits in the Seventh Year."

And the House of Hillel say, "They eat."

C. The House of Shammai say, "They do not eat produce of the Seventh Year [if it is] by favor."

And the House of Hillel say, "By favor and not by favor."

D. R. Judah says, "The matters are reversed. This is one of the lenient [rulings] of the House of Shammai and the stringent [rulings] of the House of Hillel."

(Sifra Behar Pereq 1:5, ed. Weiss, p. 106a)

Comment: The passage recurs in M. Shev. 4:2b (M. ʿEd. 5:1), with the following synopsis:

Sifra	*M. Shev. 4:2b*
1. *And the Sabbath of the Land shall be for you*	1. —
2. From the Sabbath in the land you may eat, and you may not eat that which is guarded. From here they said	2. —
3. A field which has been prepared (ŚDH ŠNṬYYBH)	3. „ „ „
4. The House of Shammai say, They do not eat its fruits	4. „ „ „ *in the Seventh Year*
5. And the House of Hillel say, They eat.	5. „ „ „
6. The House of Shammai say, They do not eat the fruits of the Seventh Year by favor (BṬWBH)	6. „ „ „
7. And the House of Hillel say, By favor and not by favor	7. „ „ „ *they eat* „ „ „
8. R. Judah says, The matters are reversed (ḤYLWP HDBRYM). This is of the leniencies (QWLY) of the House of Shammai and of the stringencies (ḤWMRY) of the House of Hillel.	8. „ „ „

As usual the Mishnah drops the exegetical framework supplied in Sifra. From no. 3 onward, the passages are nearly identical. No. 7 of M. Shev. adds *they eat*, as a counterpart for the House of Shammai's *they do not eat* in no. 6, a stylistic improvement. M. Shev. supplies in no. 4 *in the Seventh Year* to clarify *when* the fruit may not be eaten. In Sifra this is clear from the exegetical framework. But in M. Shev. the antecedent law concerns the year *following* the Seventh Year, so it is necessary to specify the year in which the law under discussion in the subsequent segment of the pericope actually applies, namely *in*, not after, the Seventh Year. We may therefore reconstruct the original Houses-pericope as follows:

A field which has been prepared
House of Shammai say, They do not eat [its fruits]
House of Hillel say, They eat.

Then another item in the M. Shev. collection is attached:

House of Shammai say, [They do not eat fruits of Seventh Year] by favor
House of Hillel say, By favor and not by favor.

On the last point, R. Judah reverses matters and says the Shammaite position is that one may eat it both by favor or not by favor, and that the Hillelite position is that one may not eat by favor. This subscription is developed and spelled out in M. ʿEd. 5:1:

> R. Judah reports six opinions in which the House of Shammai follow the more lenient, and the House of Hillel the more stringent ruling. . .
> According to the House of Shammai, they may eat Seventh Year produce by favor or not by favor. And the House of Hillel say, "They do not eat it by favor."

Judah was one of several Tannaitic authorities who composed lists of leniencies and stringencies of the Houses. The editor of Sifra has introduced his tradition as a *reference* to the Houses' opinions. In M. ʿEd. 5:1, the reference is turned into a fully articulated dispute. So in Sifra Judah states *that* matters are reversed. M. ʿEd. presents the language to be attributed to the two Houses, *actually* reversing the opinions. This represents a secondary development of Judah's opinion. Once he held *that* the opinions should be reversed, they indeed *were* reversed. M. Shev. and Sifra Behar have preserved the primary version of Judah's logion, which in M. ʿEd. is articulated in language of direct discourse and attributed to the Houses.

The pericope before us is in three main parts, first, the superscription, part A, providing the exegetical basis for the ruling of one of the Houses. Then comes part B, a complete unit, with the rule of law and the opinions of the Houses given according to the conventional form. Part C is then attached to B, and part D to C. Parts B and C are joined because of a roughly common theme, namely, conditions in which Seventh Year produce may be eaten, even though the specific laws are unrelated in detail. Parts B-C certainly were shaped before the time of Judah b. Ilai, and afterward part D was added.

What is the relationship between part A, the exegesis, and the subsequent rulings of parts B-C? The field which has been *guarded* perhaps is in the category of the field which has been *prepared* (B); and the field in which one may not eat the produce *by favor* of the owner of the field *certainly* is a field which is *guarded* (C). Therefore the exegesis in the first instance seems to support, and in the second does indubitably support, the Shammaite position. The connection between A and B may be tenuous, but between A and C it is firm. Judah reverses things in both instances, so allowing the Hillelites to derive support from the Scriptural exegesis, *but* attributing to them the more stringent position. It is unlikely that the exegesis could serve both purposes of both Houses, and since it supports the Shammaite view in part C, we may assume the same of part B. The difficulty leading Judah to switch the positions of the Houses and to attribute to the Hillelites the unusual position of stringency had to do with the exegetical tradition on Lev. 25:6. He would have followed the ʿAqiban position that the Hillelites could normally support their positions through ʿAqiban (or other) exegesis, and the Shammaites could not. Since the dispute comes before the exegesis, we may take it for granted that the original dispute is as given in parts B-C, and that the exegesis (part A) provoked the revision of Judah (part D).

Professor Louis Finkelstein comments (personal letter, February 9, 1970):

"The simplest way of understanding the text is to assume that the exegesis of Lev. 25:6 as given in Sifra follows the view of the Shammaites, as transmitted by the colleagues of R. Judah, according to whom the Shammaites prohibited the use of produce which is *shamur* (guarded); and therefore forbade one to take any produce under conditions which required one to be obligated to anyone; and therefore also forbade anyone to ask permission to use such produce. I am not sure whether the first part of the Mishnah illustrated the Shammaitic exegesis, for, after all, a field could be ploughed twice in the Sabbatical year, and still not be *shamur*. The Mishnah is probably cited to show how the exegesis applied to the second case; the first being mentioned in passing.

"The Shammaitic view of the exegesis presents no difficulties. Note the facsimile ed. of Sifra, according to Vatican Ms. 66, which I published with an introduction discussing some problems in the text. In that introduction, pp. 8, 9, 13, 14, 38, 66, I cite examples of *beraitot* in Sifra which, properly understood, derive from the School of R. Eliezer. These may be multiplied many times; and on occasion Rabad indicates this fact with regard to some passages. In his *Sifré Zuṭṭa* Professor Saul Lieberman shows that the *midrash* bearing that name contains many passages deriving from R. Eliezer. In the *Assaf Jubilee Volume*, I have shown that the same is true of Sifré Deut. In that instance again, the examples I gave may be greatly multiplied. It thus appears that at least these three *midrashim* of the School of R. 'Aqiba really had their origin in traditions which R. 'Aqiba received from his teacher, R. Eliezer, and were actually Shammaitic.

"This fact sheds light on R. 'Aqiba's method. He was quite willing to let Scripture be *taught* in accordance with the view of the Shammaites, provided the Mishnah and Tosefta, which provided for the normative guidance for the people in their lives, followed the view of the House of Hillel. He thus expected to hold the Shammaites and the Hillelites together, giving the first the form, so to speak, and the latter the substance.

"The fact that Sifra frequently follows the view of the Shammaites, which did not escape the Rabad, of course did not escape modern scholars either. But they supposed that the pervasive influence of R. Eliezer was due to the fact that R. Judah, who was editor of Sifra at one stage (b. Sanhedrin 86a) frequently adopted the views of R. Eliezer, which he received through his father, R. Ilai (Tosefta Zevaḥim 2:17, p. 483; b. Menaḥot 18a). Possibly this is also how Rabad explained the various passages of *Sifra* which he identified as deriving from R. Eliezer.

"What apparently gave concern to Rabad in the passage before us is that M. Shev. 4:2 is quoted as following from the exegesis. In view of the fact that R. Judah is described as the editor of Sifra, the exegesis would naturally be expected to follow his view. Presumably, when R. Judah transmitted Shammaitic views, which his father had received from R. Eliezer, he did so because he considered them Hillelite; and held his colleagues mistaken in ascribing them to the House of Shammai. In that event, M. Shev. was an example of a controversy based on the fact that R. Judah transmitted R. Eliezer's views, which, really Shammaitic, he considered Hillelite. But in that event he surely would consider the exegesis in the passage under discussion Hillelite. Rabad tried to explain in several different ways how this could be.

"It is unlikely, however, that M. Shev. 4:2 had been formulated in R. Judah's time, with the addition of the words, 'R. Judah says the opposite.' Apparently the oldest form of Sifra cited only the view of R. Judah's colleagues, according to which the Mishnah shows that the exegesis is Shammaitic; the exegesis derived from R. Eliezer, who agreed with the Shammaites. It was taken over from him by R. ʿAqiba in his formulation of Sifra without change, but with the addition of the Mishnaic norm, to indicate that the exegesis was actually Shammaitic, and that the Hillelites disagreed.

"Probably, R. Judah imputed the more rigorous view to the Hillelites, because, as recorded in y. Shev. 4:2, 35b, R. Ṭarfon tried to eat some of the fruits of his own orchard (which was being guarded by the agents of the community for future use, see Lieberman in *Tosefta Kifshuṭah Shev.*, p. 583). However, in accordance with the view of the Shammaites, he was careful to take the produce without permission; for one may not take it with permission. Consequently he was severely beaten, and finally had to identify himself as R. Ṭarfon. The guards then understood that he was following his own teachings. *Yer.* there explains that R. Ṭarfon in this instance followed the views of the Shammaites, as recorded by the majority of the later scholars. However, apparently, R. Judah, who had grown up in R. Ṭarfon's home, assumed that R. Ṭarfon had followed the view of the Hillelites; and therefore R. Judah held that the views of the Hillelites were in this instance severer than those of the Shammaites; and that it was the Hillelites who forbade one to eat produce of a field, if so doing placed one under any obligation to anyone, or one had to seek permission from anyone to do so."

IV. Sifré

I.ii.12.A. *And they shall make for themselves* ṣiṣit (Num. 15:38).

. . .and already (KBR) did the elders of the House of Shammai and the Elders of the House of Hillel enter the upper chamber of Jonathan b. Bathyra, and they said, "There is no limit (ŠYʿWR) to [the length of] *ṣiṣit.*"

Similarly, they said, "There is no limit to the [length of the] *Lulav.*"

B. *And they shall make for themselves* ṣiṣit [sing.] (Num. 15:38). I might think [Lit.: I hear] that he should make it of a single thread by itself. Scripture says, *You shall make yourself GDYLYM* [plural] (tassels) [*on the four corners of your cloak* (Deut. 22:12)].

From how many tassels do you make [them]?

"Not less than three," the words of the House of Shammai [Friedman: Hillel].

And the House of Hillel [Friedman: Shammai] say, "Three of wool and the fourth of blue."

And the law is according to the House of Shammai.

[Sifré Num. 115, ed. Friedman, p. 34a (b. Men. 40a-41b, b. Shab. 25a, b. Bekh. 39b; compare b. Yev. 46)]

I.ii.13.A. *Tassels* (GDYLYM) *you will make for yourself* (Deut. 22:12).

Why is [this] said?

Because it is said, *And they shall make for themselves* ṣiṣit [sing.] (Num. 15:38). I might think [Lit.: I hear] he should make one strand by itself. Scripture says, *GDYLYM*.

B. [Of] how many GDYLYM are they made? Not less than three strands, according to the words of the House of Hillel.

The House of Shammai say, "From four strands of blue and four of white, of four strands of four-by-four fingers."

[Friedman: And the House of Hillel say, "Three."]

And the law follows the words of the House of Shammai.

[Sifré Deut. 234, ed. Finkelstein, p. 266; ed. Friedman, p. 117a (Part B: b. Yev. 5b)]

Comment: A further pertinent tradition is as follows:

TNY': A. How many threads does he put into [the hole of the corner for fringes]?

The House of Shammai say, "Four."

And the House of Hillel say, "Three."

B. And how far must the threads of the showfringes hang down [what is the length of the twisted thread, independent of the show-fringes]?

The House of Shammai say, "Four finger-breadths."

And the House of Hillel say, "Three finger-breadths."

C. And the three finger-breadths mentioned by the House of Hillel are each equal to one of the four finger-breadths of any man's hand.

(b. Bekh. 39b-40a)

. . . and already (KBR) did the Elders of the House of Shammai and the Elders of the House of Hillel go up to the chamber of *Yoḥanan* b. Bathyra and decide that there was no prescribed length for the *ṣiṣit* and no length for the *Lulav*.

(b. Men. 41b)

For I.ii.12.B., Friedman reverses the order, "No less than three," the words of the House of *Hillel*. And the House of Shammai say, "Three of wool and the fourth of blue. . ." This he has done to conform to the parallel in Sifré Deut. 234 (I.ii.13). The *beraita*, b. Bekh. 39b-40a, has Shammai's House say *four*, Hillel's *three*, as in Sifré Deut.

I.ii.12.A has the tradition of b. Bekh. 39b-40a in the form of a story. In normal apodictic form, it would have been as follows:

Length of Ṣiṣit—

The House of Shammai and the House of Hillel say (agree), There is no limit.

The story is supplied, I imagine, from the corpus of traditions explaining how the law was ultimately decided in favor of Hillel's House, in the (upper) chamber (of someone) at Yavneh (or elsewhere).

I.ii.12.B mixes an exegesis of Num. 15:38/Deut. 22:12 with the normal legal form:

From how many tassels do you make [them]?
The House of Shammai: Not less than three.
The House of Hillel: Three of wool and the fourth of blue.

I.ii.13 follows roughly similar form:

Exegesis: Deut. 22:12/Num. 15:38
Of how many GDYLYM are they made?
The House of Hillel: GDYL is not less than three strands.
House of Shammai: Four strands of blue and four of white of [four strands of] four by four fingers
(House of Hillel: Three.)

Unfortunately, we do not have the guidance of the Mishnah to help us sort out the several traditions. If we did, it would probably look something like this:

How many threads does he put into the fringes?
House of Shammai: Four.
House of Hillel: Three.

That is, the *beraita* of b. Bekh. 39b-40a = b. Men. 41b seems the simplest and formally the most conventional statement. Friedman and Finkelstein cannot be faulted in favoring the reading of Sifré Deut. 234.

I.ii.12.B. (Friedman) has the Hillel-House first, generally rare, but quite common in the Tannaitic compilations of legal exegeses. The reason for the reversed order here as elsewhere is that the exegesis supports the opinion that there should be three strands: GDYLM is plural; the smallest simple plural is three. The Shammaites' opinion is not contradicted, but any Tannaitic exegete reading GDYLYM would surely have understood it as the Hillelites did, meaning *three*, a convention in Tannaitic exegesis of any simple plural. But b. Yev. 5b has: GDYL = two, GDYLYM = four! The order in I.ii.13 is no different. I.ii.13 then adds a second matter, four strands of four-by-four fingers, for the Shammaites' ruling, and then Friedman's text ends with the Hillelites' contrary view, consistent with their earlier opinion, thus

Number of strands
Hillel — three
Shammai — four

Thickness of strands
Shammai — four
Hillel — three

The two lemmas appear separately and in proper order in b. Bekh. 39b-40a = b. Men. 41b, as we would expect: *How far must—hang down: House of Shammai: Four*; *House of Hillel: Three*. This tradition is contradicted by the story of b. Men. 41b. The anonymous editor of the Talmud neatly harmonizes the two traditions by suggesting that the limit given in the *beraita* is *a minimum*, but, the story says, there is no *max-*

imum limit. The *beraita* therefore preserves the tradition in what must be its essential, though not necessarily earliest, form. Both Sifré Num. and Sifré Deut. thus revise the order for redactional reasons. Sifré Num. drops the question of length entirely, because the foregoing story says there is *no* limit to the matter. Sifré Deut., which does not know the story of the unanimous agreement on length, preserves both laws. But it has had to divide the Hillelite ruling into two parts, so as to keep the Hillelites together with the supporting Scriptural exegesis; then come *both* Shammaite rulings, followed (in Friedman) by the separated Hillelite ruling on length. The *beraita* of b. Bekh. 39b shows what the whole looked like in one piece, and Sifré Deut. tells us what a redactor has done to the possibly original tradition so as to keep the Hillelites' opinion together with the exegesis supporting their view.

We therefore see that two contradictory traditions on the positions of the Houses with regard to the *length* of the fringes were preserved. One has them differ in the same way as with the number of threads, four vs. three. The other has them agree—there is no limit at all! Each party renounces its opinion. Such a compromise comes *after* a tradition in which each party did hold an opinion contrary to that of the other. Once people held the Houses agreed, they could not likely have invented a disagreement.

It looks to me as if a simple lemma has been developed into several parts, pertaining to two different questions of law:

Ṣiṣit
House of Shammai: Four
House of Hillel: Three

This then served equally well for two questions:

I. *Ṣiṣit: How many threads?*
House of Shammai: Four — [Expanded to] *three of wool and fourth of blue*
House of Hillel: Three — [Expanded to] *not less than...*

II. *Ṣiṣit: How far must they hang down?*
House of Shammai: Four — [Expanded to] *finger-breadths*
House of Hillel: Three — [Expanded to] *finger-breadths*

Then, as I said, comes the little fable about agreement on the length for the *ṣiṣit*, allowing the *four/three* formula to pertain only to the number of threads. The exegesis of *ṣiṣit*/GDYLYM supporting *three* was invented for the Hillelite position, and the whole was split up as in Sifré Deut. 234. The oral tradition could thus have consisted of *ṣiṣit*-four-three, in the setting of Houses-sayings. The Shammaites would naturally be assigned the first and more stringent rule, and the rest follows.

See Epstein, *Mevo'ot*, p. 104 re ŚDYN with regard to *Ṣiṣit*.

I.ii.14. [R. Ishmael, sitting, and R. Eleazar b. ʿAzariah, standing, were studying together. When the time of reciting the *Shemaʿ* came, each changed his position. R. Ishmael stood upright and R. Eleazar b. ʿAzariah reclined. Eleazar asked Ishmael why he did so.]

A. He replied, "You reclined according to the words of the House of Shammai, and I stood up according to the words of the House of Hillel."

B. Another matter: That the matter not be established as an obligation (ḤWBH).

C. For (Š) the House of Shammai say, "In the evening every man should recline and recite, and in the morning, stand up [Friedman adds: as it is said, *When you lie down and when you rise up* (Deut. 6:7)]."

[And the House of Hillel say, "Every man reads according to his way, as it is said, *And when you walk by the way*. If so, why is it said, *When you lie down and when you rise up*? But (ʾLʾ) when men lie down and when men rise up."]

[Sifré Deut. 34, ed. Friedman, p. 74b; ed. Finkelstein, pp. 62-3 (M. Ber. 1:3, Tos. Ber. 1:4, b. Ber. 11a, y. Ber. 1:6)]

Comment: The whole of part C, connected by Š (*for*) cites M. Ber. 1:3 (b. Ber. 10b-11a), without change. What is important in the exchange between Eleazar and Ishmael is the evidence of a *terminus ante quem*. The opinion of the Houses had to have been established in pretty much the present form before the pericope of the two later masters, for the story takes for granted the Houses-pericope and alludes to its contents and language.

In b. Ber. 11a, part B is developed into a part of the reply of Ishmael, "And, what is more, lest the disciples should see and fix the law so for future generations."

So Ishmael favored the Shammaites!

I.ii.15.A. *And there shall no leavened bread be seen with you, neither shall there be leaven seen with you* (Ex. 13:7).

This is a dispute (ḤYLWQ) between the House of Shammai and the House of Hillel.

B. For (Š) the House of Shammai say, "Leaven is of the size of an olive and leavened bread is of the size of a date."

And the House of Hillel say, "Both are of the size of the olive."

[Sifré Deut. 131, ed. Friedman, p. 101a; ed., Finkelstein, p. 188 (M. Beṣ. 1:1, M.ʿEd. 4:1, b. Yoma 79b, Tos. Yom Ṭov 1:4)]

Comment: The *beraita* occurs in b. Beṣ. 7b, with no change. The primary form of the *beraita* begins at part B, linked to the foregoing Scripture by Š (*for*). The Scripture is not expounded, merely cited, with the exegetical difference of the Houses given in standard form immediately thereafter. The difference between them is based on the Scripture's use of leaven (S'WR) and leavened bread (ḤMṢ). The Shammaites hold the two words refer to different measurements for each; the Hillelites do not agree.

See Epstein, *Mishnah*, p. 162.

I.ii.16.A. *Three times in the year every one of your males will appear before the Lord your God* (Deut. 16:16).

Your male[s]—to *exclude* the women.

Every one (KL) of your male[s]— to *include* the children.

B. From here they said:

"Who is a child? Whoever is unable to ride on his father's shoulder and to go up from Jerusalem to the Temple mount," the words of the House of Shammai, as it is said, *Your male.*

And the House of Hillel say, "Whoever is unable to hold his father's hand and to go up from Jerusalem to the Temple mount," as it is said (Ex. 23:14), three *festivals* [feet (RGLYM)].

C. *And he will not see the face of the Lord empty-handed.*

From charity-funds.

And the sages set a limit:

D. The House of Shammai say, "The *re'iyyah* [is] two silver [coins], and the rejoicing [offering—SMḤH] a silver *ma'ah* (M'H)."

And the House of Hillel say, "The *re'iyyah* [is] a silver *ma'ah*, and the rejoicing [offering—SMḤH] is two silver [coins]."

[Sifré Deut. 143, ed. Friedman, p. 102b; ed. Finkelstein, p. 196 (y. Pe'ah 1:1, y. Ḥag. 1:2, M. Ḥag. 1:2)]

Comment: In Mekh. deR. Simeon b. Yoḥai to Ex. 23:17, I.ii.2, the opinion of the Shammaites (B) is dropped, that of the Hillelites appears without the exegesis (RGLYM), and the whole is phrased affirmatively: "Every child who *can* hold. . . *is* liable for making an appearance."

The exegetical supports (A) for the Houses' opinions are obviously later, 'Aqiban glosses, and not very good ones.

The pericope of the Houses is attached to the foregoing by *from here they said*, rather than with the more common *for* (Š). The meaning is not what we would have expected. In Mekhilta deR. Simeon b. Yoḥai we were told that the child *was* liable to go up if he *could* hold his father's hand, and here we find that a "child is one who cannot hold his father's hand" (etc.), and yet—*Everyone of your males—to include the children.* I should have supposed that children by the definitions of the Houses have been excluded, not included. This highlights still further the awkwardness of the joining words, *from here they said*, which leads to the expectation that the foregoing exegesis will have some bearing on the following legal opinions.

The definitions of *child* cause the difficulty. If they were in the affirmative, then the whole would make sense. But in the negative they contradict the sense of the exegesis of Deut. 16:16: You *should* bring your child. These are children—and obviously one could *not* bring such as these, who either cannot ride on the father's shoulder or (all the more so) cannot make the trip by foot.

If the text before us is sound, then the joining-materials are impossible, or, alternatively, the definitions should be phrased affirmatively, as in Mekhilta deR. Simeon b. Yoḥai to Ex. 23:17. If that passage had occurred here, it would have produced a harmonious text: Children should be brought, and a child is one who can take his father's hand.

For part C-D, see below, p. 183. Part D is tacked on.

For a lucid account of the laws, see Epstein, *Mevo'ot*, pp. 373-4. He observes (p. 375) that Sifré equates SMḤH and ḤGYGH, "which are in principle one."

I.ii.17. [*And the first of the fleece of your sheep you shall give him* (Deut. 18:4).]

And how many sheep must he have so that he will be liable for the first of the fleece?

The House of Shammai say, "Two ewes, as it is said *In that day a man shall keep alive a young cow and two sheep* (Is. 7:21)."

And the House of Hillel say, "Five, as it is said *And five sheep already dressed* (I Sam. 25:18)."

R. ʿAqiba says, "*First fleece*—two. *Of your flock*—four. *You will give to him*—lo, five."

(Sifré Deut. 166, ed. Friedman, p. 106b; ed. Finkelstein, p. 216)

Comment: We may take it for granted that the exegeses are glosses; in the Houses-pericopae it is rare to find an exegesis integral to the lemma of the Houses' opinions. The original pericope would have looked something like this:

How many sheep—first of fleece:
House of Shammai: *Two*
House of Hillel: *Five.*

ʿAqiba's opinion provides a striking example of the ʿAqiban exegetical convention of parsing a verse and supplying numerical values to its elements. But what ʿAqiba does here openly is done for the Hillelites by anonymous glossators: they provide a later exegesis in support of the existing Hillelite ruling. Elsewhere when ʿAqibans do so, they attribute their exegesis to the Hillelites. Here, by contrast, a distinction between the opinion of the Hillel-House and the exegetical foundation for that opinion supplied by ʿAqiba is carefully preserved. But the reason for the preservation is that both Houses have already been given appropriate Scriptures. Had the pericope been presented without such exegeses, we might have found ʿAqiba's placed in the mouth of the House of Hillel. On the other hand, this would seem to me primarily a minor redactional consideration. I doubt that the Scriptures were assigned to the Houses so early as ʿAqiba's day. What ʿAqiba's exegesis certainly does provide is a *terminus ante quem* for the Houses' opinions.

I.ii.18. [*When a man takes a wife and marries her, if then she finds no favor in his eyes because he has found some indecency in her, and he writes her a bill of divorce and puts it in her hand. . .* (Deut. 24:1).] From here—

A. The House of Shammai would say, "A man should not divorce his wife unless he has found in her some indecency, as it is said, *Because he has found some matter of indecency in her.*"

And the House of Hillel say, "Even if she spoiled his soup, as it is said, *Because he has found some matter of indecency in her.*"

B. The House of Hillel said to the House of Shammai, "If *matter* is said, why is *indecency* said? And if *indecency* is said, why is *matter* said? For if *matter* were said and *indecency* were not said, I might say, 'She who goes forth on account of a *matter* will be permitted to marry, and she who goes forth on account of *indecency* will not be permitted to remarry.'

"And do not be surprised, for if she was prohibited from that which had been permitted to her [her husband], should she not be prohibited from that which had already been prohibited to her [any other man]? Scripture says *indecency*, *and she goes forth from his house*, *and she goes and marries another man.*

"And if *indecency* were said and *matter* were not said, I might say, 'On account of *indecency* she will go forth, on account of [any other] *matter*, she will not go forth.' Scripture says, *Matter*, *and she goes forth from his house.*"

C. R. ʿAqiba says, "Even if he found another prettier than she. . ."

(Sifré Deut. 269, ed. Friedman, p. 22a; ed. Finkelstein, p. 288)

Comment: The passage recurs in the following:

> The House of Shammai say, "A man should not divorce his wife unless he has found in her some indecency, as it is said, *Because he has found some matter of indecency in her.*"
> The House of Hillel say, "Even if she spoiled his soup, as it says, *Because he has found some matter of indecency in her.*"
> R. ʿAqiba says, "Even if he found another prettier than she, as it says, *If she find no favor in his eyes* (Deut. 24:1)."
>
> (M. Giṭ. 9:10)

The foregoing Mishnah is accompanied by the following *beraita:*

> It has been taught:
> The House of Hillel said to the House of Shammai, "Is it not already said *matter?*"
> The House of Shammai said to the House of Hillel, "Is it not already said *indecency?*"
> The House of Hillel said to them, "If *indecency* were said and *matter* were not said, I might say, On account of *indecency* she should go forth, but on account of [any other] *matter* she should not go forth. Therefore *matter* is said. And if *matter* were said and *indecency* were not said, I might say, On account of [any other] *matter* she may be married to another, but on account of *indecency* she may not be married to another. Therefore *indecency* is said."
> And the House of Shammai—*What do they do with this* [Aramaic]?' . .
>
> (b. Giṭ. 90a)

The Babylonian *beraita* preserves the argument of the House of Hillel, but suppresses the Shammaite exegesis. Sifré Deut. 269 part B likewise contains only the Hillelite view. We may take it for granted that the Shammaites' argument in both cases has been dropped, or no one has bothered to invent one. But its main outlines are evident in the primary pericope (part A) itself: the text specifies only adultery as a proper ground for divorce. The Hillelites' reinterpretation of the Scripture has to be spelled out to counter the obvious sense of the Scripture itself. But the failure of the tradents to supply the Shammaites with an appropriate reply seems to me probative evidence that while part A is within the Shammai-Hillel-Houses-tradition, part B derives from Hillelite circles only, and probably from the ʿAqiban tradents active in other parts of this compilation. Judah the Patriarch has excluded part B from the Mishnah because he normally leaves out exegeses. But he has kept the Houses-pericope intact, also a common phenomenon. ʿAqiba seems to me to supply a *terminus ante quem* for part A, standing well within the Hillelite tradition, and extending the ruling to a more extreme case than is given to the Hillelites.

The language of the House of Hillel, *Even if*. . . certainly indicates dependence of the Hillelite lemma on the Shammaite one, for by itself the Hillelite saying would not be comprehensible. The Shammaites' opinion is spelled out in full: *A man should not divorce—unless—as it is said.* The Hillelites responds to the *whole* of the foregoing: *Even if*. . .

This represents a different form from the one we have found common: *Statement of law—House of Shammai—House of Hillel.* In such statements, dropping the opinion of the first of the Houses would not on the face of it render that of the second incomprehensible. Both Houses relate to a single antecedent statement of the legal issue or theme. Here, by contrast, the House of Hillel gives a kind of gloss to the House of Shammai. This leads to the supposition that the Shammaite opinion was already framed in precisely the form and language selected by Shammaites—hence the inclusion of a strong exegetical foundation—and never thereafter changed. But the Hillelites did not merely gloss the foregoing. They have also supplied a complete response to the Shammaites, which does not permit the Shammaites a reply.

The pericope as a whole shows us what Hillelites were prepared to do, and not do, with completed Shammaite traditions. They obviously have not falsified or doctored the Shammaite pericope, but preserved it whole. They have commented on the substance, and then added a fictitious colloquy.

This dramatic encounter follows the form one would expect from similar materials clearly shaped in the encounter between the Houses:

The House of Hillel said to the House of Shammai . .

But it does not bother to give the Shammaite reply, in the version of Sifré Deut. 269; or the reply is given in formalized terms, in the *beraita* in b. Giṭ. 90a, merely so as to set the stage for the Hillelite argument, coming in any event. So the Hillelite tradents have followed the form, only so far as to lead to the expectation of the usual balanced version; but the whole of B is a Hillelite fabrication, interpolated into existing materials.

We must therefore distinguish between a colloquy shaped by both Houses and one invented by Hillelites, but given a form fictitiously implying both sides have had equal opportunity to make a case; there the Shammaites' case is inadequate and the Hillelites must win. The Hillelite colloquy copies the form of the compromise version, therefore is presumably later.

v. Midrash Tannaim

Three of the four pericopae of Midrash Tannaim occur in the foregoing materials:

1. Midrash Tannaim to Deut. 6:8, ed. Hoffmann, p. 27:
   The story of Eleazar b. ʿAzariah and Ishmael, without the citation of M. Ber. 1:3, above, p. 34.
2. Midrash Tannaim to Deut. 22:12, part B, ed. Hoffmann, p. 139:
   Ṣiṣit and GDYLH, above, p. 30.
3. Midrash Tannaim to Deut. 23:26, ed. Hoffmann, p. 154:
   Grounds for divorce, above, p. 37.

The only new item is as follows:

I.ii.19.A. *You shall not wear a mingled stuff* (Š'ṬNZ)... *You shall make yourself tassels* (Deut. 22:11-12).

From here they said

B. A linen cloak with woolen show-fringes (ŚDYN BṢYṢYT)—

The House of Shammai declare free [of liability].

[*Should read*: House of Hillel declare liable.]

C. The House of Hillel said to the House of Shammai, "Will a negative commandment set aside a positive one?"

The House of Shammai said to them, "We find with reference to all the commandments which are in the Torah that the positive commandment takes precedence over the negative commandment, but here, the negative commandment *will* take precedence over the positive commandment [just as it does in Scripture]."

[Midrash Tannaim to Deut. 22:12, ed. Hoffmann, pp. 138-9, part A (b. Shab. 25b)]

Comment: The pericope has a parallel in the following:

Our rabbis taught: A linen garment is exempt from *ṣiṣit*, according to the House of Shammai.

The House of Hillel declare it liable.

The law follows the House of Hillel.

(b. Men. 40a)

The subsequent argument in Midrash Tannaim follows the Hillel-Shammai form, allowing the Shammaites the last word. The exegesis supports the Shammaite position, moreover, for the Scripture first specifies the negative commandment (mingled stuff), then the positive one (tassels). So *from here they said* accurately attributes to the Shammaites the supporting exegesis. We need not regard the developed argument (part B) as substantially later than the original formulation of the dispute, for reasons given earlier (p. 21). I do not understand why the Hillelite lemma (part B) has been lost.

CHAPTER SIXTEEN

MISHNAH-TOSEFTA AND SOME *BERAITOT*

I. ZERAʿIM

II.i.1.A. The House of Shammai say, "In the evening every man should recline and recite (NṬH, QR') [the *Shemaʿ*], but in the morning he should stand up, for it is written, *And when thou liest down and when thou risest up* (Deut. 6:7)."

The House of Hillel say, "Every man recites it in his own way, for it is written, *And when thou walkest by the way*. If so, why is it said, *And when thou liest down and when thou risest up*? But ('L' Š) the time that men [usually] lie down and the time that men [usually] rise up."

B. R. Ṭarfon said, "I was coming on the way, and I reclined (NṬH) to recite (QR') [the *Shemaʿ*] in accordance with the words of the House of Shammai, and I put myself in jeopardy by reason of robbers."

They said to him, "You were worthy to be liable for your own [punishment] (KDYY HYYT LḤWB BʿṢMK) because you transgressed the words of the House of Hillel."

[M. Ber. 1:3, trans. Danby, p. 2 (b. Ber. 10b-11a, y. Shev. 4:2, Sifré Deut. 34, y. Ber. 1:3)]

Comment: The Scriptural supports look like interpolated glosses. None is required for the House of Shammai, which as usual relies on the obvious meaning of the Scripture. But the House of Hillel differ from that meaning and therefore require the explanation of how their position squares with the plain sense of the Scriptural commandment.

The story (part B) of R. Ṭarfon supplies a firm *terminus ante quem* for the foregoing materials, possibly in their present form, for the roots NṬH, QR' occur in both the legal lemma and the story. This suggests Ṭarfon or the person responsible for the story about him wished to underline knowledge of, or make reference to, the actual words of the House of Shammai.

The point of the story is that anyone who follows the view of the House of Shammai deserves to be punished and die, a sure sign that the issue was vivid, and that many did agree with the House of Shammai. We do not know who "they" are, but it hardly matters. Ṭarfon says precisely what "they" do, he through his story about supernatural punishment for following Shammai, "they" through underlining the lesson by generalizing on the consequences of transgressing the words of the House of Hillel.

The pericope is clearly a composite, but part A is not; it is a unity, with glosses. The highly developed story yields no clear signs of what constituted a mnemonic version. Each element is fully articulated and glossed, and the whole depends on its editorial context. *In accordance. . . Shammai* may be interpolated, but *They said. . . Hillel* is integral to the story, so the former probably also is essential.

II.i.2.A. If he said the Benediction over the wine before the meal, he need not say it over the wine after the meal.

If he said the Benediction over the savory before the meal, he need not say it over the savory after the meal.

B. If he said it over the bread, he need not say it over the savory.

But if he said it over the savory, he is not exempt from saying it over the bread.

C. The House of Shammai say, "Or over aught that was cooked in the pot."

[M. Ber. 6:5, trans. Danby, p. 7 (y. Ber. 6:5, b. Ber. 42b, 43b)]

Comment: The point of the Shammaite lemma is that if a man blessed the savory, he has not exempted from a blessing that which was cooked in the pot, but must bless that too. The saying is a gloss on the foregoing. Obviously, *Or over aught. . .* out of context could have meant nothing. Further, to construct a pericope in which the lemma could have stood as an independent and immediately comprehensible saying is not so simple as one might think. At the outset we should have expected something like the following:

> If he said it over the savory, he is not exempt from saying it over the bread or over aught that was cooked in the pot, the words of the House of Shammai.

Such a form demands: And the *House of Hillel say. . .* (contrarywise). y. Ber. 6:5 supplies:

> If he blessed the bread, he has exempted the savory *and what was cooked in the pot*, according to the words of the House of Hillel.
>
> The House of Shammai say, "He has not exempted what was cooked in the pot."

Now we have a Houses-dispute such as we should have expected, but with the wrong order. And the law is not the same. As it stands, the House of Shammai has supplied a gloss to an existing pericope on *blessing/not blessing*. One must ask, When was the antecedent set of laws redacted? They exhibit standard Mishnaic form. We may posit two possibilities. First, the pericope antedates the Houses or was shaped about the same time as they flourished. Second, the pericope comes after the Houses had ceased to play a role in Pharisaic-rabbinic circles, ca. 80-100. The opinion given in the name of Shammai's House has been provided by someone later than that House and separate from it.

As to the former possibility, we have no literary evidence whatever that legal materials were redacted in standard form before the work of the Houses. The form of the disputes of the Houses is not replicated. It is difficult to imagine that this pericope was shaped at the same time that the Houses-materials were being worked out, assuming that the range of forms available to the Houses-redactors was what we now imagine it to be.

As to the second possibility, the gloss in the name of the House of Shammai might belong to a Tanna associated with (or accused of associating with) that House. It represents the simplest alternative. But that is hardly decisive.

The Palestinian version, which sets the whole into conventional Houses-form, complicates matters. If it comes before the Mishnaic version, then why does the Mishnah fail to attribute an opinion to the Hillelites? Obviously, if it comes afterward, the existence of the Shammaite opinion has required invention of a Hillelite counterpart.

Whether the lemma of the House of Shammai, which now appears as a gloss on the foregoing materials, represents an opinion actually held by the House is difficult to say. If the Shammaites had held such an opinion, to assure comprehensibility it would have had to be transmitted in a quite different form. No oral fundament deriving from the House of Shammai can be readily discerned. y. Yer. 6:5 is another matter. There the Houses-lemmas come down to PṬR +/— L'.

For Simeon b. Sheṭaḥ in this matter, above, I, p. 112. Note Epstein, *Mishnah*, p. 1029.

II. i.3.A. These are the things wherein the House of Shammai and the House of Hillel differ [Lit.: which are between] in what concerns a meal (ŠBYN. . .BŚ'WDH).

The House of Shammai say, "One says the Benediction (MBRK) over the day and afterwards [over] the wine."

And the House of Hillel say, "One says the Benediction over the wine and afterwards over the day."

B. The House of Shammai say, "They wash (NṬL) the hands and then mix the cup."

And the House of Hillel say, "They mix the cup and then wash the hands."

C. The House of Shammai say, "One wipes his hands with a napkin and lays it on the table."

And the House of Hillel say, ["He lays it] on the cushion."

D. The House of Shammai say, "They clean (KBD) the house and then wash the hands."

And the House of Hillel say, "They wash the hands and then clean the house."

E(1). The House of Shammai say, "[The order of saying the Benedictions at the outgoing of the Sabbath is] lamp, and food, and spices, and *Havdalah*."

And the House of Hillel say, "Lamp, and spices, and food, and *Havdalah*."

(2). The House of Shammai say, "[The Benediction over the lamp is, 'Blessed art thou] who *did create* the *light* of fire.' "

And the House of Hillel say, " '. . . who *creates* the *lights* of fire.' "

(F. No Benediction may be said over the lamp or the spices of gentiles, or over a lamp or spices used for the dead, or over a lamp or spices used for idolatry. No Benediction may be said over a lamp until one enjoys its light.)

G(1). If a man ate and forgot to say the Benediction, the House of Shammai say, "He must return to his place and say it."

And the House of Hillel say, "He may say it in the place where he remembers."

(2). Until what time may he say the Benediction? Until the food in his bowels is digested.

H. If wine is brought after the food and there is but that one cup—

The House of Shammai say, "One says the Benediction over the wine and then over the food."

And the House of Hillel say, "One says the Benediction over the food and then over the wine."

I. They may answer "Amen" after an Israelite who says a Benediction, but not after a Samaritan until they have heard the whole Benediction.

[M. Ber. 8:1-8, trans. Danby, pp. 8-9 (y. Ber. 8:1, 2, 3, 4, 5, 8, b. Ber. 51b-53b, b. Pes. 103a, b. Suk. 56a, y. Naz. 7:1)]

Comment: In addition to the two conventional Houses-forms already isolated, namely, the standard dispute: *Rule of Law. . . House of Shammai. . . House of Hillel. . .* and the dramatic debates: *House of Hillel said to House of Shammai*, here we have the third, and, for the Mishnah, the most striking: the *collection* of Houses-disputes on a single theme. The form is pellucid:

These are the things which are between the House of Shammai and the House of Hillel with regard to the meal.

Then Rabbi has assembled his list(s), in briefest possible language, without superscriptions, exegeses, debates, or other extraneous materials. He has omitted the general theme of the dispute, e.g. parts A, B, C. We have already noted the existence of other sorts of collections of Houses-materials attributed to Tannaitic masters, centered, e.g., on numbers (the six places of Shammaitic leniency). By focussing on a legal theme, rather than on extrinsic characteristics, Rabbi has made it possible to insert the whole smoothly into the pertinent portion of his Mishnah.

Part A: After the superscription serving the whole composite pericope, the first dispute is introduced without an additional superscription setting forth the specific problem. Without it all we have in effect is *day/wine* vs. *wine/day*, with the same explanatory words in both opinions. From this we are supposed to know that the dispute concerns the order of Sanctification on Sabbaths and Festivals. The Shammaites hold one blesses the day, then the wine, because the day is the primary consideration, and the wine comes only on account of the Sanctification of the day. The Hillelites hold the contrary: the wine is the important thing, for without it one says no Sanctification at all.

Part B: The same form applies: No general principle, law, or superscription, merely *wash hands, mix cup* vs. *mix cup, wash hands.* The consideration is that if he mixes the cup first, perhaps some of the liquid will spill on the sides of the cup, and when the man touches the liquid before washing his hands, he may render the whole cup unclean, so the Shammaites. The Hillelites hold that one must not separate the washing of the hands from the start of the meal.

Part C: After the man washes his hands, where does he place the napkin? The Shammaites hold he leaves it on the table, so that he may dry his hands during the meal. He does not put it on the pillow on which he is seated, lest the pillow be unclean and therefore render the napkin unclean on account of the liquid that may be diffused in it, which may then make his hands unclean. The Hillelites hold that even if the man's hands become unclean, the [ritual] uncleanness of hands is not serious. But the napkin should not be left on the table, lest the table be unclean and make the napkin unclean, and, thence, the food also be rendered unclean. The Shammaites do not take account of the possibility that the table may be unclean, since one may not make use of the table in any event.

The Hillelite opinion is not a gloss on the foregoing, but rather has been abbreviated. In full form, it would read, *He dries his hands on the napkin and leaves it on the cushion.* The lemma is not to be compared to the Shammaite gloss of M. Ber. 6:5.

Part D: After the meal one sweeps the room to collect the food particles that may be scattered and then washes the hands before the concluding benediction, so that the food particles will not be spoiled by the dropping of the water used for the final washing. The Hillelites hold one completes the washing (and the Grace), and afterward sweeps the room. Meanwhile (a *beraita* explains) the servant will collect all the food-particles of an olive's size before the washing—in effect what the Shammaites think important at the outset. But if we ignore the *beraita*, the plain-sense is that the Hillelites do not take seriously the possibility of rendering crumbs unclean.

Part E. 1: The subject shifts to the order of blessings after the night meal at the end of the Sabbath. The Shammaites hold one blesses first the light one is (now) using, then the food one has (already) eaten, then the spices, finally says the *havdalah*. The Hillelites place the blessings of the light and the spices together, both being short (so Albeck, *Seder Zeraʿim*, p. 29), then the food, finally says the *havdalah*. This is Meir's version, Epstein, *Mevo'ot*, p. 105.

Part E. 2 has a related dispute, concerning the blessing for the light, whether it is past tense and singular, or present tense and plural. The supposed difference has to do with whether one blesses the creation of light at the creation of the world, or the continual creation of all sorts of lights every day.

Part F pertains to the foregoing, therefore is included, as a gloss on the dispute of the Houses. The order—lamp, spices—is Hillelite.

Part G introduces a still further dispute about the meal, unrelated to the foregoing. If a man forgot to say the blessing, the Shammaites send him back to the place where he ate, and the Hillelites say he may say the blessing wherever he remembers it. The opinions of the Houses are brief and matched. The concluding lemma serves, like part F, as a gloss on the foregoing problem, coming after the Houses.

Part H is enigmatic. The introductory superscription, stating the problem, is unusual for the collection-form. Without that phrase, the dispute looks to be about whether, in the Grace after Meals, one blesses the wine and then the food, or the food and then the wine. The superscription changes matters: *If wine comes to them after the meal and there is only that cup of wine.* The meaning of the phrase, therefore the conditions to which it refers, is unclear on the face of it. The Talmuds supply various explanations, a sign that something is wrong. Albeck gives the following: If the man wants, he blesses the wine and drinks it, and says Grace without a further cup. Or, if the wine comes in the middle of the meal and he blessed it, or if another cup is there which he will drink after the meal and over which he will say the blessing for wine, then he does not need to say the blessing of wine for the cup of the Grace. But if he did not drink wine during the meal and says Grace over the cup, he also has to bless the cup with the blessing of the wine. The House of Shammai think that he first says the benediction of wine over the cup and afterward says Grace, and the House of Hillel the contrary.

The disputes of the Houses normally are simple and straightforward. In the collection-form before us, the disputes are not preceded by superscriptions (e.g. Parts A-E). Parts G and F are separate items, therefore noteworthy both for the superscriptions and for the additional glosses or other materials at the end. ("*Until what time...*", "*They may answer 'Amen'...*"). If the Houses-sayings had come in the earlier list, obviously the superscription would have been left off; had it been left off, the meaning would have been clear on the face of it.

We shall now review the collection's components:

	Shammai		*Hillel*
A.	Day/wine	*Blessing*	Wine/day
B.	Hands/cup	*Uncleanness*	Cup/hands
C.	Table	*Uncleanness*	Cushion
D.	Sweep/wash	*Uncleanness*	Wash/sweep
E1.	Food, spices	*Blessing*	Spices, food
E2.	*Did* create *light*		*Does* create *lights*
G.	Forgot: Go back	*Blessing*	Forgot: In the place where he recalled he forgot
H.	Food/wine	*Blessing*	Wine/food

The subject-matter (within "matters pertaining to the meal") is therefore arranged in an orderly and logical way:

Before Sabbath-Festival Meals: A
During Meals: B, C, D
After Sabbath-Festival Meals: E
After Meals (special case, pertaining to *all* meals): G

and part H is an enigma.

It looks, therefore, as if the collection consists of five separate, anterior elements or collections: parts B-C-D, uncleanness rules for meals, a neat and simple collection of logia, consisting of a few words attributed to each House; part A; part E (both segments); part G; and part H.

Part H looks suspiciously like the reverse of part A:

	A	H
Shammai:	Day/Wine (YWM/YYN)	Wine/Food (YYN/MZWN)
Hillel:	Wine/Day (YYN/YWM)	Food/Wine (MZWN/YYN)

The superscription of part H thus brings more difficulties than we might have had in its absence.

This sort of list can be readily reduced to brief and alliterative mnemonic elements:

Part A: YWM/YYN vs. YYN/YWM
Part B: NṬL/MZG vs. MZG/NṬL
Part C: ŠLḤN vs. KŚT
Part D: KBD/NṬL vs. NṬL/KBD
Part E: NR/MZWN/BSMYM/HBDLH vs. NR/BSMYM/MZWN/HBDLH
Thus: MZWN/BSMYM vs. BSMYM/MZWN

The list therefore is constructed of transitive participles, generally given in third-person plural (B, D), though I see no principle that explains why one set should be plural, the next singular. Only part C is significantly glossed; there a simple superscription would have allowed the significant difference to be reduced to two substantives, as given above. Like parts A and H, parts B and D look suspiciously alike, and it may be that they began as a single lemma, only later on developed into two separate arguments. Parts A, B, D, and E all depend upon word-order, and I see no reason why part E should not have been preserved in fully articulated form right from the outset. In all, it would be difficult to invent a better model of a mnemonic list.

Part G(1) is another sort of mnemonic, apparently built out of the same words and mostly the same radicals:

ḤZR MQWM BRK vs. BRK MQWM ZKR

Clearly the order is 1,2,3, vs. 3,2,1. Only the first word of the Shammaite and the last word of the Hillelite lemma is different, and there the difference is in a single letter, Ḥ vs. K. On the whole, therefore, we may suppose the mnemonic has been only lightly reworked with the addition of the dative particles (L, B), the personal endings, and the relative pronoun Š demanded by the Hillelite lemma.

Even in the fully articulated form before us, we find obvious balances between the Houses' lemmas. They contain the same number of words throughout, e.g.

Part A: MBRK ʿL HYWM WʾḤR KK MBRK ʿL HYYN
MBRK ʿL HYYN WʾḤR KK MBRK ʿL HYWM

and these words preserve a fixed order and balance from one House-saying to the next, as is obvious above. So while the elements of a mnemonic version may well have consisted of those isolated above, it is by no means necessary to suppose that the whole collection is not now in mnemonic form, or that Judah the Patriarch did not intentionally arrange things in just this manner.

We shall compare this version with the Tosefta's below, p. 50. Note Epstein, *Mishnah*, pp. 43, 185, 1002, 1007.

II.ii.1. MʿSH B: R. Ishmael and R. Eleazar b. ʿAzariah [who] were dwelling (ŠRWYYN) in one place, and R. Ishmael was reclining, and R. Eleazar b. ʿAzariah standing up. The time of reciting the *Shemaʿ* came. R. Ishmael stood up and R. Eleazar b. ʿAzariah lay down.

R. Ishmael said to him, "What is this, Eleazar."

He said to him, "Ishmael, my brother. . ."

He said to him, "You lay down to carry out the words of the House of Hillel, and I stood up to carry out the words of the House of Shammai."

"Another matter, so that the disciples should not see and permanently establish the law according to your words."

[Tos. Ber. 1:4, ed. Lieberman, p. 2, lines 18-25 (y. Ber. 1:3, b. Ber. 11a; Sifré Deut. 34, y. Sanh. 11:4)]

Comment: See above, p. 41. This is the equivalent of M. Ber. 1:3, Ṭarfon-story. For our purposes, what is important is the further indication of a firm *terminus ante quem* for the Houses-pericope on the subject. Judah the Patriarch preferred the more explicit Ṭarfon-subscription: If you follow the opinion of the House of Shammai, you deserve punishment.

II.ii.2.A. [As to a] Festival of the New Year that coincides with the Sabbath:

The House of Shammai say, "One prays ten [benedictions]."

And the House of Hillel say, "One prays nine [benedictions]."

B. [As to a] Festival that coincides with the Sabbath:

The House of Shammai say, "One prays eight [benedictions] and says [that] of the Sabbath by itself and of the festival by itself, and begins with that of the Sabbath."

And the House of Hillel say, "He prays seven [benedictions], and begins with that pertaining to the Sabbath and concludes with that pertaining to the Sabbath and says the Sanctification of the Day in the middle."

[Tos. Ber. 3:13, ed. Lieberman, p. 15, lines 58-63 (b.'Eruv. 40a-b, b. Beṣ. 17a; y. Shev. 1:5)]

Comment: The pericope contains three disputes, the latter two combined into one:

New Year/Sabbath

House of Shammai:	Ten
House of Hillel:	Nine

Festival/Sabbath

House of Shammai:	Eight—Sabbath by self/Festival by self
House of Hillel:	Seven—Sabbath-Sanctification-Sabbath

On the readings and the legal issues involved, see Lieberman, *Tosefta Kifshuṭah* for *Zera'im*, pp. 39-40. The whole is, mnemonically, simply a descending decade. See below, pp. 181-182.

II.ii.3.A. [The] things which are between the House of Shammai and the House of Hillel as regards the meal:

The House of Shammai say, "One blesses the day, and afterward one blesses the wine, for the day causes the wine to come, and he has already sanctified the day, but the wine has not yet come."

And the House of Hillel say, "One blesses the wine, and afterward one blesses the day, for the wine causes the Sanctification of the day to be said.

"Another matter: The blessing of the wine is continual, and the blessing of the day is not continual."

And the law is according to the words of the House of Hillel.

B. The House of Shammai say, "They wash the hands and afterward mix the cup, lest the liquids which are on the outer surfaces of the cup may be made unclean on account of the hands, and they may go back and make the cup unclean."

The House of Hillel say, "The outer surfaces of the cup are perpetually unclean.

"Another matter: The washing of the hands is only [done] near [at the outset of] the meal."

They mix the cup and afterward wash the hands [= House of Hillel].

C. The House of Shammai say, "He dries his hand on the napkin and leaves it on the table, lest the liquids which are in the napkin may be made unclean on account of the pillow, and they may go and make the hands unclean."

The House of Hillel say, "Doubtful liquids so far as the hands are concerned are clean.

"Another matter: Washing the hands does not pertain to unconsecrated food. But he dries his hands on the napkin and leaves it on the pillow, lest the liquids which are in the pillow may be made unclean on account of the table, and they may go and render the food unclean."

D. The House of Shammai say, "They clean the house on account of the waste of food, and afterward they wash the hands."

The House of Hillel say, "If the waiter was a disciple of a sage, he gathers the scraps which contain as much as an olive's bulk.

"They wash the hands and afterward clean the house."

E. The House of Shammai say, "He holds the cup of wine in his right hand and sweet oil in his left hand.

"He blesses the wine and afterward blesses the oil."

And the House of Hillel say, "He holds the sweet oil in his right hand and the cup of wine in his left hand.

"He blesses the oil and smears (ṬḤ) it on the head of the waiter. If the waiter was a disciple of a sage, he smears it on the wall, because it is not praiseworthy that a disciple of the sage[s] should go forth perfumed."

F. R. Judah said, "The House of Shammai and the House of Hillel did not dispute concerning the blessing of the food, that it is first, and concerning the *havdalah*, that it is at the end. Concerning what did they dispute? Concerning the light and the spices, for the House of Shammai say, 'Light and afterward spices,' and the House of Hillel say, 'Spices and afterward light.' "

[Tos. Ber. 5(6):25-30, ed. Lieberman, p. 29, 1. 53-p. 31, 1.75 (b. Ber. 51b, 53b [= part E], b. ʿEruv. 13b, y. Ber. 8:1—5,7—8, y. Pes. 10:2; Pes. 114a, b. Suk. 56a)]

G. In the house of study—
The House of Shammai say, "One [person] blesses for all of them."
And the House of Hillel say, "Each one blesses for himself."

[Tos. Ber. 5:30, ed. Lieberman, p. 31, lines 80-1 (b. Ber. 53a)]

Comment: The formal differences between Mishnah and Tosefta are fairly consistent. For each element the Tosefta supplies the reason for the position taken by each House, as well as "another matter" further supporting the Hillelite argument.

The construction of the brief lemmas of M. Ber. 8:1ff. is to be credited to Judah the Patriarch. He has stressed the simplest possible formulation. The Tosefta constitutes not another version, but a highly glossed copy of the original, with many interpolations. Thus, the Hillelite part of B supplies reasons for, and only then gives the equivalent of, the Shammaites' primary lemma. In C, the Hillelites do not even have such an equivalent. In D the Hillelites' view is taken for granted, then explained. In E, the waiter-element has no Shammaite counterpart. So Tos presupposes and depends upon knowledge of the Mishnah, and looks like a commentary on it, with glosses as needed.

We shall see considerable evidence that Houses-forms were followed in entirely classical style as late as the period of the Ushan academy. The only hard evidence here is the appearance of Judah [b. Ilai]; he supplies excellent testimony that M. Ber. 8:5 (II.i.3.E) was before him in a form other than that of the Mishnah. He alleges that no dispute pertained to the blessing of food and *havdalah*, and this normally means that such a dispute was before him verbatim, and that he differed and planned to correct it. Judah the Patriarch has not reproduced Judah b. Ilai's version, but rather preserved the whole list of four items. b. Ber. 52b (b. Pes. 103a) has the following:

> Rava said, "These [the Mishnah] are the words of R. Meir, but R. Judah said, 'The House of Shammai and the House of Hillel agree that Grace comes first and *havdalah* last. They differ [only] about light and spices.' "

Judah the Patriarch has taken Meir's version and dropped Judah's, and the Mishnah must be dated to Usha. On this basis we cannot determine which version is older. See Epstein, *Mevo'ot*, p. 105-6.

Parts E and G contain new materials. Part E has a dispute in the extremely succinct form of M. Ber., readily reduced to the simple mnemonic elements suggested above. But the Hillelite saying not only is out of balance, but also introduces an element otherwise lacking in the Shammaite one, about the waiter—that is, what to do with excess oil. I do not understand how the issue was raised in the Hillelite lemma at all. It belongs in D.

Part G presents a problem which occurs in reference to b. 'Eruv., below, p. 138. The language of the Houses is identical, and what is changed is the superscription. The superscription comes after the Houses-sayings and is intended to provide a setting for their already redacted ruling. But we have no evidence as to when the superscription was added or the original sayings redacted.

III.ii.1. TNW RBNN: [If] they were sitting in the house of study, and they brought light before them—

The House of Shammai say, "Each one blesses for himself."

And the House of Hillel say, "One blesses for all of them, since it is said, *In the multitude of people is the king's glory* (Prov. 14:28)."

[The Shammaite reason is adduced: it is to avoid an interruption of study.]

TNY' NMY HKY: [Those] of the House of Rabban Gamaliel did not say 'good health' [to one who sneezed] in the study house because of the interruption of study.

(b. Ber. 53a)

Comment: The Babylonian *beraita* has not only reversed the rulings of the Houses, but also augmented the superscription. The further *beraita* in the Babylonian pericope supplies the information that Gamaliel followed the Shammaite principle of not interrupting study. The rulings are matched opposites.

The reversal of the assigned opinions is the problem, for the augmentation of the superscription is commonplace and does little to change the meaning. I doubt that the Toseftan redactor has switched the Houses around in order to show the conformity of Gamaliel to the Hillelite ruling; Gamaliel is not mentioned in the context of Tos. Ber.

to begin with. Redactional considerations therefore do not seem important, and I cannot account for the change; but see Lieberman, *Tosefta Kifshuṭah*, p. 97.

The mnemonic pattern is standard:

Shammai: KL 'ḤD W'ḤD MBRK L'ṢMW

Hillel: 'ḤD MBRK LKWLN

Thus the pattern is

KL 'ḤD vs. 'ḤD [L] KL [N]

that is, 1,2,2,1. For further examples of the same pattern, see M. Pe'ah 3:1, below, pp. 54-55.

III.ii.2.A. [Our rabbis taught: He who enters a privy removes his *tefillin* at a distance of four *amot* and enters. . .]

B. TNY' 'YDK *(Another beraita)*: "He who enters a permanent privy removes his *tefillin* at a distance of four *amot*, leaves them on the window near the public way, and enters, and when he goes out, he goes away four *amot* and puts them on"—the words of the House of Shammai.

And the House of Hillel say, "He holds them in his hand and enters."

R. ʿAqiba says, "He holds them in his garment and enters."

(b. Ber. 23a)

Comment: This is a singleton, not following conventional form. The superscription is interpolated into the Shammaite lemma, as often happens. ʿAqiba supplies the *terminus ante quem*, if the whole is not pseudepigraphic. The Hillelites are balanced against ʿAqiba—hand vs. garment. The Shammaite lemma—without the elements serving all parties—must be *leaves-window*. Part A follows the Shammaite reasoning, against both the Hillelites and ʿAqiba.

III.ii.3. TNW RBNN: [If] they brought before him oil and myrtle—

The House of Shammai say, "He blesses the oil, and afterward he blesses the myrtle."

And the House of Hillel say, "He blesses the myrtle, and afterward he blesses the oil."

R. Gamaliel said, "I shall decide [in favor of the House of Shammai.] We have the benefit of (ZKH) oil both for its odor and for its anointing; we have the benefit of myrtle for its smell but not for its anointing."

(b. Ber. 43b)

Comment: The items are brought after a meal, oil to clean the hands, and myrtle to smell.

The form is standard. What is interesting is the effort of Gamaliel, presumably Gamaliel II, to argue in favor of the Shammaite position, in the Toseftan style. He supplies a firm *terminus ante quem* for the dispute, before ca. 100.

II.i.4.A. [If] between olives trees [there were] plots sown with grain (MLBNWT HTBW'H)—

The House of Shammai say, "*Pe'ah* [must be granted] from every plot."

And the House of Hillel say, "From one for all."

B. But they agree that, if the ends of the rows [of grain] were confused (M'WRBYN), (that) he gives *Pe'ah* from one [plot] for all.

[M. Pe'ah 3:1, trans. Danby, p. 12 (y. Pe'ah 3:1)]

Comment: The problem is, When does a field become divided into two, so requiring that two *pe'ahs* be left over for the poor, each part of the field being obligated by itself? The issue before the Houses is whether each plot among the olive trees is regarded as separate, therefore liable. The House of Shammai take the affirmative, of Hillel, the negative. The Houses agree regarding the ends of the rows. The Shammaite position is strict with the farmer, therefore advantageous to the poor gleaners. The Shammaites often rule to the benefit of the poor.

The form is conventional. What is new is the additional specification of the limits of the dispute, "They agree..." We have not earlier seen such a careful limitation. Clearly, *the problem of law... House of Shammai... House of Hillel...* must come before *But they agree* (WMWDYM), language already familiar to us in the opening clause of the debate form (above, p. 16), *The House of Hillel said to the House of Shammai, You agree with us...* But here the agreement is a fact, rather than a debater's opening gambit. It is difficult to imagine that such an additional clause circulated separately—for obvious reasons. But was it imposed by one party on the other? The House of Shammai's position is what is limited by the agreement, since the House of Hillel have already made the same point for a more extreme situation, where the plots are actually separate, and hence obviously would hold the same where the plots are not separated, but the rows confused. The "agreement" furthermore repeats the Hillelite lemma verbatim.

Hence we are left to wonder whether the Shammaite position has been accurately represented in the *agreement*-clause. Does it serve as a Hillelite subscription, or is the clause integral to the pericope as a whole? If they were able to enforce their view of the law, indeed able to impose their reading of the tradition on Shammai-Hillel-materials, the Hillelites could as well have suppressed the entire dispute as have altered an element in it. Hence one might argue that, had the Hillelites the power to fabricate such a new subscription, they would have done a more complete job of it. So the *agreement*-clause, claiming less for the Hillelites than one might expect had the Hillelites fabricated it, looks genuine. This argument is strengthened by the conservatism of the tradents. Clearly, what the Hillelites said about Shammaites and those who hold to their views of law is before us. Yet they did not tamper with the balanced traditions—*Shammai/Hillel*, *House of Shammai/House of Hillel*, and *House of Hillel said to House of Shammai*—but preserved some of them as they must have been redacted while the two parties enjoyed parity, or while Shammaites were in control. The foundation-stone of our inquiry is the observation that the Hillelites did not change Shammai/Hillel pericopae once in final form, even though it would have been to Hillelite advantage to do so. They invented new stories of all sorts, e.g. the sword in the school-house, petulant Shammai, and so forth. But part of what was already redacted, as occasionally evidenced by discussions of the earliest Yavnean masters, evidently was unchanged.

The report of the agreement is apt to be genuine. The Shammaites' position here probably is accurately represented. The parties differed only in some aspects of the problem, agreed in others. In that case the observation that the Hillelites saw the reason of the opposition and accepted its position seems to apply also to the Shammaites, though it is not made explicit in terms of ḤZR/ŠNH, as in M. Yev. (below, pp. 200-202) and elsewhere.

The lemmas of the Houses are beautifully balanced:

House of Shammai say:

Pe'ah

MKL 'ḤD W'HD

House of Hillel say

M'ḤD 'L HKL

Pe'ah serves both lemmas. We are left with three words assigned to each, and these, excluding prepositions, are actually two: KL and 'ḤD. Further, the order is ascending-descending, as before:

MKL 'ḤD [W'HD]—M'ḤD ['L] HKL

That is, essentially, 1, 2, 2, 1. All that is out of balance is the superscription, and this is invariably the case. Thus even where the Houses necessarily have to be given words that are not the usual syzygies (ṬM'/ṬHR), their opinions are phrased in an obvious mnemonic pattern. The agreement uses the Hillelite order: 'ḤD/KL, appropriately so, since it is the Shammaites who accept the Hillelite opinion. Other agreement-mnemonics use the primary elements of both lemmas, but here that is manifestly impossible.

See Epstein, *Mishnah*, pp. 51-2.

II.i.5.A. The House of Shammai say, "[If produce is proclaimed] ownerless for the benefit of the poor [it is deemed] ownerless [and Tithe-free]."

And the House of Hillel say, "It is not [deemed] ownerless [and Tithe-free] until (ʿD Š) it is proclaimed ownerless also (ʾP) for the [benefit of the] rich, as in the Year of Release."

B. [If] all sheaves of a field [were] each of one *qab's* [bulk] and one was of four *qabs*, and he forgot it—

The House of Shammai say, "[It is] not [deemed a] Forgotten Sheaf."

And the House of Hillel say, "[It is deemed a] Forgotten Sheaf."

C. [If] a sheaf [lay] near the wall or the stack or the oxen or the implements, and he forgot it—

The House of Shammai say, "[It is] not [deemed a] Forgotten Sheaf."

And the House of Hillel say, "[It is deemed a] Forgotten Sheaf."

D(1). [Whether any sheaf at] the ends of rows [may or may not be deemed a Forgotten Sheaf] is proved by a sheaf lying over against it.

(2). [If the householder] laid hold of a sheaf to take it to the city and forgot it, they agree that this is not [deemed a] Forgotten Sheaf.

E. Two sheaves [together may be deemed] Forgotten Sheaves; three [together may] not [be deemed] Forgotten Sheaves. Two heaps of olives or carobs [may be deemed] Forgotten Sheaves; three may not. Two stalks of flax [may be deemed] Forgotten Sheaves; three may not. Two grapes [may count] as grape-gleanings; three may not. Two ears of corn [may count as] gleanings; three may not.

These [rulings] are according to the words of the House of Hillel.

And of them all the House of Shammai say, "[Where there are] three [they belong] to the poor; [where there are] four [they belong] to the householder."

[M. Pe'ah 6:1, 2, 3, 5, trans. Danby, pp. 16-17 (y. Pe'ah 1:5, 7:1 = M. 6:1; y. Pe'ah 6:1, 2, 3, 4; b. B.M. 30b, y. Ket. 8:1, b. Sanh. 88a)]

Comment: See also M. ʿEd. 4:2-4. Parts A, B, and C constitute a *compilation*, not a collection, of Houses-disputes on the laws of the Forgotten Sheaf.

Part A concerns property declared ownerless only for the poor. Is it liable to tithes? The House of Shammai say it is not, the House of Hillel that it is. In this ruling, as above, the Hillelite position is more stringent, since it diminishes the return to the poor, who have either to compete with the rich or to pay tithes. This is made explicit in y. Ket. 8:1: "The House of Shammai say, 'Ownerless to the poor is lenient for the poor and stringent for the householder.' "

The form is extremely terse:

House of Shammai: [Ownerless] to the poor (only)
[ownerless]
House of Hillel: *Also* to the rich.

Like the Year of Release is a gloss. The whole formula requires three words—or merely *to the poor*—for the Shammaites, as given, and could suffice with two for the Hillelites. The explanatory words, *It can only be deemed ownerless if it is proclaimed ownerless* fill out the sentence, but are not absolutely necessary for comprehending the position of the Hillelites. They represent a redactional supplement.

Part B follows the more complete, articulated form:

Problem of law, then the Houses.

The Houses' opinions are equally terse: *Not Forgotten Sheaf/Forgotten Sheaf*. Clearly, to understand these words, a fuller statement of the issue to which they pertain is required. The issue is, How do we regard the larger sheaf? The House of Shammai hold that the four-*qab* sheaf is regarded as if it were divided into four of one *qab* each; in part E, the House of Shammai make it explicit that where there are four, they belong to the householder. Part E looks like a secondary formulation, with more detail, of the brief lemma before us. The simplest formulation of the whole would be simply:

House of Shammai: Four
House of Hillel: Three.

Part C retains the same full formulation: Principle of law or problem, plus the Houses. Here the issue is: Is a sheaf lying near some recognizable object or some specific location regarded as *forgotten*? The House of Shammai hold that since the sheaf is in some place that may be specified, it eventually will be remembered. The House of Hillel hold the contrary (see below, Tos. Pe'ah 3:2).

Part D.2 then supplies a point of agreement. Here, however, it is the House of Hillel that come over to the position of the House of Shammai. In the cases of part D, there is evidence that the owner has not completely forgotten the sheaves. He has at the outset given some sign that he intends to dispose of them. Therefore the law of the Forgotten Sheaf does not apply. Obviously, the Shammaite lemma is repeated.

What is the difference between parts D and C? In the cases of part D some process has been undertaken, i.e. *gathering* the sheaves, or *moving* them, while in part C, nothing signifies, according to the Hillelites, the intention of *doing* something with the sheaf. It is merely lying in a place that can be specified, but no purpose in leaving the sheaf there can be discerned.

Part E spells out the Hillelite position: *Three* (of anything) are not regarded as forgotten, but *two* (of anything) are; the Shammaites say, *Four/three*. The cases are a full catalogue:

Sheaves
Olives or carobs

Stalks of flax
Grapes
Ears of corn

I see no reason that all the cases require specification. In any event the redactor has been careful to specify these are not formulations of the Houses, but rather follow their views: *according to the words* of the House of Hillel. The Shammaite opinion is tacked on with a connector-phrase: *Concerning all of them.* This too is not an attribution of direct discourse, but a summary of the *position* of the House of Shammai. But the content of the lemma represents what the House originally laid down:

Three for the poor
Four for the householder

What we do not have is the equivalent formulation of the House of Hillel, which, quite obviously, was

Two for the poor
Three for the householder.

The difference between these pericopae and the collection-form discussed above (pp. 44f.) is obvious. The collection form is introduced with a simple statement of the subject-matter: *concerning the meal.* No further superscriptions stating the topic or legal problem then intervene. Here, by contrast, the collection-superscription is absent, though one might have looked for it in part A, and therefore we are given superscriptions in parts B and C. Part E is a separate pericope, in which the brief lemmas originally issued by the Houses are given in great detail for each possible type of produce, all in the Hillelite formulation, with the Shammaite opinion tacked on at the end. We need not regard part E as a later development of Hillelites, for the Shammaite position is accurately represented. But it is a quite different way of stating matters, with the Houses in reverse order for redactional reasons.

The lemmas of the Houses are extremely brief and always balanced opposites:

Shammai	*Hillel*
HBQR LʿNYYM HBQR	ʾYNW HBQR
ʾYNW ŠKḤH	ŠKḤH
ŠLŠH [LʿNYYM] [W]	ŠNY [ŠKḤH] ŠLŠH [ʾYNN ŠKḤH]
ʾRBʿH LBʿL HBYT	

In effect, the Houses differ on whether or not the negative particle belongs, and on a numbers-sequence (two/three vs. three/four). In all other respects the sayings are either balanced or glossed; they are not developed, articulated, or expanded in significant detail, except as specified.

Note Epstein, *Mevoʾot*, pp. 102-3.

II.i.6.A. As to the grapes of a Fourth-Year Vineyard

The House of Shammai say, "The rules of the [Added] Fifth and of Removal do not apply to [the grapes of] a Fourth Year Vineyard (ʾYN LW ḤMŠ Wʾ'YN LW BʿWR)."

And the House of Hillel say, "They do apply (YŠ LW)."

B. The House of Shammai say, "The laws of grape-gleanings and of the defective cluster apply, and the poor redeem the grapes for themselves (YŠ LW PRṬ WYŠ LW ʿWLLWT, WHʿNYYM PWDYN LʿṢMM)."

And the House of Hillel say, "The whole yield goes to the winepress (KWLW LGT)."

[M. Pe'ah 7:6, trans. Danby, p. 18 (y. Pe'ah 7:5, b. Qid. 54b; M. M.S. 5:3, M. Ter. 3:9, Tos. Ter. 2:13, M. M.S. 5:10)]

Comment: See above, Sifra Qedoshim 3:7, p. 23, and M. ʿEd. 4:5b. The issue before us is whether or not the rules of Second Tithe apply, to the Fourth-Year Vineyard grapes. The House of Shammai hold that grapes of the Fourth Year Vineyard are not like the Second Tithe in every respect.

The form is a curious variation of the standard one. Here, the statement of law is followed by *two* sets of Shammai/Hillel opinions:

Grapes of the Fourth-Year Vineyard:

A.	House of Shammai:	No Fifth and no Burning [*Unlike* Second Tithe]
	House of Hillel:	Yes [Like Second Tithe]
B.	House of Shammai:	Grape-gleanings and Defective Cluster apply [*Like* Second Tithe]
	House of Hillel:	Laws of Second Tithe apply *in all respects.*

The Hillelite-opinion therefore is duplicated in the two segments of the pericope. What would an antecedent form have looked like? It seems to me the problem for the redactor is the complex Shammaite opinion. An ideal form would have been:

Grapes of the Fourth-Year Vineyard:

The House of Shammai say: Are like Second Tithe in some respects, and are not like Second Tithe in some respects: *like* Second Tithe in that (a) grape gleanings (b) poor redeem; *not* like Second Tithe in that (a) no Fifth and (b) no Burning.

The House of Hillel say: Are like Second Tithe *in all respects.*

Such a full statement of the Shammaite position apparently was not possible within the range of formal or redactional alternatives available in early times. It therefore was necessary to split up the opinions into the clumsy form before us, thus to suggest two separate pericopae existed, when in fact the whole is a single problem and susceptible of formulation in a single, unitary framework.

The language of the Mishnah compares with Sifra Qedoshim 3:7 as follows:

Sifra Qedoshim 3:7	*M. Pe'ah 7:6*
1. *All their fruit will be*— to *include* HPRṬ and H'WLLWT, according to the words of the House of Hillel.	1. *Grapes of the Fourth-Year Vineyard:* House of Shammai said, Do not have *Fifth* and do not have *Burning*. House of Hillel say, They do.
2. The House of Shammai say, YŠ LW PRṬ WYŠ LW 'WLLWT	2. ,, ,, ,,
3. And the poor redeem for themselves.	3. ,, ,, ,,
4. And the House of Hillel say, It is all for the winepress	4. ,, ,, ,,

We see that in place of the exegesis, M. Pe'ah gives a topical superscription.

In y. Pe'ah 7:5, Judah the Patriarch limits the disagreement to the Seventh Year.

Ideally, the mnemonic fundament would have consisted of the superscription + Shammaite rule followed by the Hillelite negative—pretty much as in M. Pe'ah 7:6.

Note Epstein, *Mevo'ot*, p. 103, who observes that elsewhere the dispute is on Fourth-year *planting* (NṬ').

II.ii.4. R. 'Ila'i' said, "I asked R. Joshua, 'Concerning what sheaves ('WMRYN) did the House of Shammai dispute?'

"He said to me, 'By this Torah! Concerning what sheaves? Those near a wall, a stack, oxen, or implements, and he forgot it.'

"And when I came and asked R. Leazar, he said to me, 'They agree concerning these that *Forgetting* does *not* apply.

" 'Concerning what did they dispute? Concerning the sheaf on which he took hold to bring to town, and he set it by the fence and forgot it.

" 'For the House of Shammai say, '*Forgetting* does not apply, because he has made acquisition of it.' And the House of Hillel say, '*Forgetting*.' "

"And when I came and I laid the matters out before R. Leazar b. 'Azariah, he said to me, 'By the Torah! These things were said from Sinai.' "

[Tos. Pe'ah 3:2, ed. Lieberman, p. 51, lines 13-19 (y. Pe'ah 6:2, M.'Ed. 4:4, y. Ket. 8:1)]

Comment: The Tosefta reenforces the estimate of the *terminus ante quem* for Houses-disputes; M. Pe'ah 6:2 (= II.i.5.C) came by the time of Joshua b. Ḥananiah. Leazar has things contrarywise. They agreed on the sheaf by the wall, but differed about the sheaf to be brought to town. This means that two versions of the dispute existed.

The version of Joshua and that of the M. Pe'ah 6:2 compare as follows

M. Pe'ah 6:2	Joshua: *Tos. Pe'ah 3:2*
1. The sheaf which is near the wall, stack, oxen, or implements, and he forgot it.	1. [These are the sheaves] near the wall, stack, oxen, or implements, and he forgot it.
2. House of Shammai say, Is not Forgetting.	2. „ „ „
3. And House of Hillel say, Forgetting.	3. „ „ „

In fact, except for the slight variation in the introductory clause, where, for obvious redactional reasons, M. Pe'ah omits *these are* of the colloquy ('YLW) and then puts the whole into the singular (H'MWR instead of H'WMRYN), the passages are identical, and M. Pe'ah looks like the tradition according to Joshua. Leazar says that *Forgetting* here *does* apply, therefore he has the Hillelites agree with the Shammaites. He claims they differ in another case entirely:

M. Pe'ah 6:2	Leazar: *Tos. Pe'ah 3:2*
1. The sheaf which a man took hold of to bring to the town and forgot it	1. [Concerning ('L)] the sheaf which a man took hold of to bring to the town *and he put it beside the fence* and forgot it
2. They agree that it is not *Forgetting* [the forgotten-sheaf-law does not apply].	2. [That] the House of Shammai say, The law of *Forgetting* does not apply because he made acquisition of it. And the House of Hillel say, The law of *Forgetting* does apply.

M. Pe'ah differs with Leazar's version in several respects, but is strikingly similar in others. In no. 1, a new detail is introduced into Leazar's version, in italics, perhaps a contamination from the antecedent case. As to no. 2, the House of Shammai has already received a gloss ("because he made acquisition"). Otherwise, however, nos. 2-3 of the Joshua version are repeated here without change. So what is confused is *not* the decisions of the Houses, but the case to which they pertain. Both masters have what must be the primary tradition, attributed to the Houses by all parties:

1. House of Shammai: No *Forgetting*
   House of Hillel: *Forgetting.*
2. And they agree.

The issue is, To what cases do these decisions and agreement pertain? Joshua assigns the disagreement to the sheaf by the wall (etc.), and the agreement to the sheaf to be brought to town. Leazar assigns the agreement to the sheaf by the wall, the disagreement to the sheaf to go to town, left by the wall, and then forgotten. R. Eleazar b. ʿAzariah then agrees with Leazar's version of matters, but Judah the Patriarch apparently preferred Joshua's.

Now since the Houses originally could not have said both opinions, and since the Tannaitic tradents were unclear on just what the Houses were talking about, we may assume the basis for the differences in the versions of Joshua and Leazar had to do with legal principles. What were these principles? As to the sheaf by the wall, stack, oxen, and implements, the point at issue is (as pointed out above) whether the fact that the sheaf is found lying near an identifiable location means it eventually will be remembered ("Oh, what did I do with the sheaf I left by the implements?"), while if it was left in the field, the owner will never afterward be able to call to mind that particular sheaf. Joshua holds the Houses differed on this principle. As to the sheaf set aside to be brought to town and then forgotten: Earlier, Hillelites held that *Forgetting* applied when the object was left by a specific location. However, in the second case, *Forgetting* does not apply, because in the latter situation there is clearcut evidence that the householder has not completely forgotten the sheaf but must eventually remember it, since he intended to do something with it ("bring it to town")—so Joshua. Leazar holds the House of Hillel says the law of *Forgetting* does apply, since the owner's actions reveal what was his real thought. He did not actually plan to take the sheaf to town at all, but merely to signify that, in leaving it, he did not intend that the law of *Forgetting* should apply. But the householder has *no* right to do so (following Lieberman, *Tosefta, brief commentary*, p. 51, n. to 1. 17; and *Tosefta Kifshuṭah*, pp. 162-5. [On the question of Joshua's relationship to M. Pe'ah, see p. 162-4, note to lines 14-5. I have been careful not to state a view of that question, by saying that Joshua's opinion before us merely "looks like" the Mishnah.]) Note also Epstein, *Mevo'ot*, p. 61, and compare M. Maksh. 1:3; also p. 102.

What seems to have happened, therefore, is that the opinions of the Houses have come down, along with some generalized traditions on the legal matters to which the opinions pertained. The "finished" pericope before the several Yavnean Tannaitic authorities apparently consisted *only* of the opinions of the Houses, as specified above: *forgetting/no forgetting/and they agree*, along with a generalized context to which the opinions pertained, or the Tannaim assumed the context on the basis of the gnomic opinions only. The Tannaitic authorities were able to differ as to the details. This strongly suggests that the form of the Houses-disputes at the outset consisted of completed opinions, perhaps organized according to legal topics. The next stage of editing supplied introductions or superscriptions to the disputes. This would account for the extreme brevity of the primary elements in the several pericopae already considered, i.e. simple numbers, such as *four/three*, *three/two*, or affirmative-negative syzygies, e.g. *forgetting/no forgetting*, or reversals of order, i.e. *wine/dav* vs. *day/wine*, and so on. These very soon thereafter were amplified, as evidenced by the tendency to supply topical superscriptions or other appropriate augmentations. The third stage was the combination of the amplified pericopae into organized collections or lists, as in M. Ber. 8:1-8 and elsewhere, or their inclusion in other settings entirely.

See Epstein, *Mishnah*, p. 5.

II.i.7. Sweet oil—
The House of Shammai declare liable.
And the House of Hillel declare exempt.

[M. Demai 1:3, trans. Danby, p. 21 (y. Demai 1:3)]

Comment: The issue is whether sweet oil purchased from an outsider (*'am ha'areṣ*) is liable to the laws of *demai*-produce or not. If it is, it must be tithed. The Hillelites say that since the oil is not to be eaten, it is exempt from the rule. The form is conventional: *Problem*, *House of Shammai*, *House of Hillel*. The opinions of the Houses, as often, are expressed in single roots, ḤYB, PṬR, in plural, intensive present participles. The pericope must be a unity, and no element is gloss. No later masters refer to the pericope, nor does it relate to its setting, except in theme: exemption from the rules of *demai*-produce. See Tos. Demai 1:26-7, below p. 65.

II.i.8.A. *Demai*-produce may be given to the poor and to billeted troops [or, guests] to eat.

B. Rabban Gamaliel used to give *demai*-produce to his laborers to eat.

C. [As to] Almoners (GB'Y ṢDQH)—

The House of Shammai say, "They give what has been tithed to them that do not give tithe and what is untithed to them that do give tithe; thus every man will eat of what is duly tithed (MTWQN)."

But the sages say, "[Almoners] collect [food] and distribute [it] regardless (ŚTM) [of the rules of *demai*-produce], and he who wants to tithe it [according to the rules of *demai*-produce] will tithe it."

[M. Demai 3:1, trans. Danby, p. 22 (b. Ber. 47a, y. Demai 3:1, b. Shab. 127b, b. 'Eruv. 17b, 31b, b. Pes. 35b, b. Suk. 35b)]

Comment: The pericope is a composite of three separate, but related elements: *Demai* and the *poor/workers/troops*. Part A is not a superscription for the rest, but an independent lemma, to which part B, a story about Gamaliel's practice, is attached. Part C is separate from the foregoing, as follows:

As to collectors of charity
The House of Shammai say, "They give what is tithed to him who does not tithe [and the reverse]."

Then comes an obvious gloss:

They will be found [that] each man eats what is in order (MTWQN).

And finally:

And the sages say, "They collect regardless (ŚTM) and distribute regardless (ŚTM), and he who wants to order [properly] (TQN) [= tithe], let him order."

The form exhibits the curious difference that in place of the Hillelites are the "sages." We do not know who those sages are. Clearly, the editor has followed the usual form; but, apparently not having a Hillelite attribution, he has inserted anonymous "sages." This might suggest that where Hillelite-materials were not available, they sometimes were not invented. We have no evidence as to the time of redaction; we do not know which Gamaliel is involved. No other named sages appear in context. He would seem to stand closer to the Hillelite position.

II.i.9.A. The House of Shammai say, "A man may sell his olives only to an Associate (ḤBR)."

The House of Hillel say, "Even to one that [only] pays Tithes."

B. And the more scrupulous (ṢNW'Y) of the House of Hillel used to behave according to the words of the House of Shammai.

(M. Demai 6:6, trans. Danby, p. 25)

Comment: The pericope is abbreviated, for we have no superscription to supply the topic or principle of law. This is included in the opening lemma, attributed to the House of Shammai, because it comes first. A balanced pericope would have given approximately the same number of words to both Houses:

As to selling olives:
The House of Shammai say, "Only to a *ḥaver*"
The House of Hillel say, "*Also* to one who tithes"

(but who cannot be relied upon to preserve the olives in a state of ritual cleanness). The pericope is therefore somewhat developed beyond what we should have anticipated as the primitive form.

The subscription that the scrupulous Hillelites followed the Shammaite rule looks like the gloss of a later authority who agreed with the Shammaite opinion, therefore approved those who followed it. Since by later times the law nearly everywhere followed the Hillelites, it was necessary to express disagreement by attributing to "the scrupulous" conformity to the more stringent view. The subscribed gloss does not necessarily derive from Shammaite tradents.

Albeck explains (*Seder Zera'im*, p. 87) that the Hillelites hold one need not take for granted that the purchaser is going to prepare the olives to receive uncleanness. He may consume them while they are still dry and therefore unable to receive uncleanness. This is consistent with other Hillelite rulings which give the benefit of the doubt to normally unreliable people, e.g. M. Shev. 5:8.

II.ii.5.A. As to sweet oil (ŠMN ʿRB)—
The House of Shammai declare liable.
And the House of Hillel declare free [of liability to the laws of *demai*].

B. R. Nathan said, "The House of Hillel declare free of liability [of the laws of *demai*] only the oil of rose (PLYṬWN)."

C. Others say in the name of R. Nathan, "The House of Hillel declare free of liability the oil of rose and iris (WWYRYNWN).

[Tos. Demai 1:26-7, ed. Lieberman, p. 67, lines 66-69 (y. Dem. 1:3)]

Comment: See above, M. Demai 1:3. Judah the Patriarch has dropped the qualifying remarks attributed by Nathan to the House of Hillel. We do not know how Nathan knew such a tradition. Lieberman explains (*ad loc.*) that these are special cases. No principle of law is involved. This contradicts the version of M. Demai 1:3. According to Nathan the dispute concerned the particular oils specified by him:

As to rose/iris oil
House of Shammai declare liable
House of Hillel declare free [of liability]

Judah the Patriarch has preferred a superscription of a far more encompassing sort:

As to [all] sweet oil

Clearly, the tradition of the Houses consisted only of *House of Shammai/Hillel... declare liable/not liable.* The later tradents then had to sort out the legal issues to which the tradition in abbreviated form was supposed to pertain. Another form for Nathan's opinion would be, *They disputed only concerning*, or even MWDYM—*they agree* + ʿL MH NḤLQW—*con-*

cerning what did they differ. But these formulae never occur in a Nathan-lemma.

II.ii.6. The excess (MWTR) of the *ʿomer*, and the two breads, and the showbread, and the remnants of the meal offerings, and the supplements (TWŚPT) of the first fruits—

R. Simeon b. Judah says in the name of R. Simeon,

"The House of Shammai declare liable.

"And the House of Hillel declare exempt."

(Tos. Demai 1:28, ed. Lieberman, pp. 67-8, lines 69-71)

Comment: Lieberman, *Tosefta Kifshuṭah* to *Zeraʿim*, pp. 206-7, refers to M. Zev. 9:5, 14:3: This is the *ʿomer* that comes from grain whose processing was completed by an *ʿam haʾareṣ*. The House of Shammai rule that things which are food are liable to the laws of *demai*, but edibles used for the Temple altar do not come under the laws of *demai*. R. Simeon holds that the House of Shammai disagreed on all matters listed in M. Demai 1:3. If the dispute is genuine, it means the Temple priests could not be trusted to keep the Pharisaic *demai*-rules even for the cultic table.

II.ii.6*. Tos. Demai 2:12 is discussed below, III.ii.38, b. Bekh. 30b.

III.i.1. WTNY: R. Simeon b. Judah says in the name of R. Simeon, "*Ḥallah*—

"The House of Shammai declare liable.

"And the House of Hillel declare exempt."

[y. Demai 5:1, repr. Gilead, p. 19b (Tos. Demai 1:28, ed. Lieberman, p. 67)]

Comment: The form is standard, and the pericope shows how readily later generations made use of it without necessarily having access to antecedent traditions. The issue is whether the law of *demai* applies to *ḥallah*. Earlier it is taught that the *ḥallah* of an *ʿam haʾareṣ* is free of the obligation of *demai*.

II.i.10. He who would lay out his field in plots (MŠR) each bearing a different kind [of crop]—

The House of Shammai say, "[Between each he must leave a space equal to] three furrows of ploughed land."

And the House of Hillel say, "The width of a Sharon yoke."

And the opinion of the one is near the opinion of the other.

[M. Kila'im 2:6, trans. Danby, p. 30 (y. Kil. 2:4)]

Comment: The law concerns planting mixed seeds in a vineyard, so that the distance between the various varieties is such as not to violate the taboo against sowing mixed seeds. The case before us concerns laying out furrows bearing different species. The "dispute" concerns the choice of language of the Houses' respective rulings, for, as the gloss makes explicit, the actual differences are not considerable. Since there is distinguishable ground between the furrows, the law of *Kila'im* does not apply. In M. Kila'im 2:9 we have a similar superscription, "He who wishes to lay out his field. . ." with no reference to the Houses. There Meir, the sages, and Eliezer b. Jacob participate.

It is difficult to imagine the original dispute of the Houses, if the only considerable difference was in word-choice. Perhaps, as the glossator says, there *was* no substantial difference between them at all, but rather, the Houses handed on pretty much the same measurement in varying language, and later on the differences in the language were set into dispute form. This seems to occur fairly often, particularly where measurements are concerned.

II.i.11.A. Vineyard patch (QRḤT HKRM)—
The House of Shammai say, "[At least] twenty-four cubits [square]."
And the House of Hillel say: "Sixteen cubits."
The outer space of a vineyard (MḤWL HKRM)—
The House of Shammai say, "[At least] sixteen cubits."
And the House of Hillel say, "Twelve cubits."

B. What is a 'vineyard patch'? [The part of] a vineyard that is bare of vines in its midst. If this is less than sixteen cubits [square], seed may not be sown there; but if it is [at least] sixteen cubits [square], they must allow the vines enough space for their tillage, and they may sow in what is left.

[M. Kila'im 4:1, trans. Danby, p. 32 (y. Kil. 4:1, b. 'Eruv. 3b, 93a)]

Comment: The purpose is to signify a baldspot (QRḤT) in the vineyard, where seeds may be sown without violating the taboo. What is striking is that the opinions of the Houses are kept in their primary form, then the gloss (part B) explains what the Houses are talking about. Thus

Vineyard patch
House of Shammai: twenty-four

House of Hillel: Sixteen

Outer space of vineyard
House of Shammai: Sixteen
House of Hillel: Twelve

Then comes *What is a vineyard patch?* And in M. Kela'im 4:2, the parallel, *What is the outer space of the vineyard?* The *what is* clauses serve as commentaries to the enigmatic language of the Houses. The glossator has followed the law according to the Hillelites (sixteen/twelve) when explaining the case and giving examples, which proves that the gloss is Hillelite and obviously comes later than the original Houses-pericope. In M. Kila'im 4:3, Judah b. Ilai disputes the glossator's definitions, but he does not touch on the opinions of the Houses one way or the other.

Where Hillelites inserted glosses, definitions or supplements into completed Houses-pericopae, they did not change the existing materials, but they naturally did refer to their own ruling. The cited example, therefore, will give the correct impression that the Hillelite view is law.

II.i.12.A. He who plants a [single] row of five vines—

The House of Shammai say, "[This counts as a] vineyard."

And the House of Hillel say, "[It does] not [count as a] vineyard, unless there are there two rows."

B. Therefore if he sows [within the] four cubits of the vineyard—

The House of Shammai say, "He rendered forfeit [Lit.: sanctified, QDŠ] one row."

And the House of Hillel say, "He rendered forfeit two rows."

[M. Kila'im 4:5, trans. Danby, p. 33 (y. Kil. 4:2, 3, 6)]

Comment: Part A is in standard form: *vineyard/not vineyard*, but with an important gloss. If it is a vineyard, one must plant seed no nearer than four cubits. If not, one may plant within six *tefaḥs*. The issue is, Is the collection of five vines regarded as a *vineyard* or not? The House of Shammai say, *Vineyard*. The House of Hillel say, *No vineyard*. Then comes the gloss, "Unless there are there two rows." How many plants are in the two rows? That is the crux of the matter. Since the superscription specifies five plants to begin with, we might have imagined that the Hillelites are talking about two rows of ten plants, and the difference between the Houses is *five/ten*. However, M. Kila'im 4:6, immediately following, takes for granted that three plants constitute one row for the purposes of defining a vineyard. Therefore the Hillelite view presumably is that *six* plants in *two* rows will constitute a vineyeard, but not *five* plants in *one* row. If so, the dispute ought to have read something like this:

He who plants a row of vines
House of Shammai say, *Five* [equal a vineyard]
House of Hillel say, *Six* [in two rows equal a vineyard].

The attribution to the Shammaites poses no problem in its present form. But the Hillelite lemma is ambiguous and awkward, *Not vineyard unless...* The simpler form has been broken and reconstructed so as to give the Shammaites the ruling, and to leave the Hillelites in the position of supplying an enigmatic saying, itself requiring a gloss.

The joining-word of part B, LPYKK, is also difficult. One is left to wonder whether a later authority has drawn the implications of the earlier dispute, now phrasing the whole as a direct attribution to the Houses. The rule concerns one who sows within the four *amot* (cubits) he must have for the tending of the vineyard. How much land does he have to forfeit? The language is QDŠ (as in Deut. 22:9); he has sanctified one row, according to the Shammaites, and two according to the Hillelites. Normally one should not sow within four *amot* of the vineyards. If he does, he gives up the outermost row of the vineyard, nearest the seed, for the Shammaites hold *one row* is called *vineyard*; and the Hillelites require both the outermost *and* that next to it, since they hold that *vineyard* means no less than two rows.

Surely it would have been possible to present the whole as a composite pericope:

He who plants a row of vines
House of Shammai: Five [equal a vineyard]
House of Hillel: Six
He who sows within four amot
House of Shammai: Loses (QDŠ) *one* row (five plants)
House of Hillel: Loses *two* rows (six plants)

It looks as if *therefore* is a joining word connecting two quite independent Houses-disputes. Alternatively, the Houses-disputes originally consisted only of the numbers *five/six*, *one/two*, and these have been broken down into two separate, but thematically related laws. Or perhaps in choosing LPYKK as the joining-word, the redactor wished to make it clear that it was he himself who drew the logical consequences of the former pericope, but no lemma attributing such opinions to the Houses themselves existed.

II.i.13.A. What is the 'trellised vine' ('RYŚ)?

If a row of five vines was planted beside a fence ten handbreadths high or beside a ditch ten handbreadths deep and four wide, four cubits are allotted for its tillage.

B. The House of Shammai say, "They measure the four cubits from the root of the vines toward the field [beyond the wall]."

And the House of Hillel say, "From the wall [itself] toward the field."

C. R. Yoḥanan b. Nuri said, "All err that say so; but [the House of Hillel said that] if there was a space of four cubits from the root of the vines to the wall, space enough is allotted for its tillage, and seed may be sown over what is left."

D. And how much is the space needful for the tillage of the vine? Six handbreadths in every direction.

R. ʿAqiba says, "Three."

[M. Kila'im 6:1, trans. Danby, pp. 34-5 (y. Kil. 6:1)]

Comment: As above, we have a definition (part A) serving as a gloss for a Houses-dispute. But A is ignored, not answered. Albeck explains (*Seder Zeraʿim*, p. 366), that the question "What is the trellised vine" is to be interpreted not as a definition of such a vine—"which everyone well knew"—but rather, What is *the* trellised vine whose law follows that of the vineyard, to which one gives four cubits as tillage. The cubits to which reference is made come between the plants and the wall, not on the other side of the wall.

Then (part B) the Houses dispute about it. One sets aside the ground necessary for working the trellised vine (etc.) and may sow further back. While earlier (M. Kil. 4:5) the House of Hillel held that the vineyard must mean two rows, they agree concerning the trellised vine that even one row is judged as if it were a vineyard. The House of Shammai held that one measures back from the roots toward the field, the House of Hillel, from the wall itself. The primary language of the original tradition obviously would conform to the formula now attributed to the Hillelites:

House of Shammai:	[From the] root
House of Hillel:	[From the] wall

The rest (*The four cubits need be measured only*) has been added, and since the House of Shammai comes first, its saying has necessarily been augmented for the sake of completeness and clarity.

The foregoing account presupposes the agreement of the Houses that, with reference to the trellised vine, even one row is judged like a vineyard. Yoḥanan b. Nuri (part C), however, revises the dispute. Even in connection with the trellised vine, one row is *not* regarded by the House of Hillel as a vineyard, and one does not concede to it four *amot*. If between the trellised vine and the wall are four cubits, one allows for its tillage six *tefaḥs*, just as for a row of single plants, and one may then sow the rest. But if there are not four *amot* between the wall and the plants, it is prohibited to sow between the wall and the plants, even though their law is not as that of the *vineyard*. Yoḥanan thus has completely ignored the Shammaite position, rejected the antecedent version of the dispute, and supplied his own. Albeck comments (*Seder Zeraʿim*, p. 366) that the tradition of Yoḥanan b. Nuri must have been, "As to the trellised vine, one separates from it four cubits and provides it with its tillage."

Tos. Kil. 4:1 reads, "Rabban Gamaliel and his court ordained that one separates four cubits from the root of the vines to the wall." This follows Yoḥanan b. Nuri's tradition, that if there are not four cubits in the trellised vine, it is prohibited to sow there.

II.i.14. As for the weasel, R. Yosi says, "The House of Shammai say, 'An olive's bulk conveys uncleanness by carrying, and a lentil's bulk by contact'."

[M. Kila'im 8:5, trans. Danby, p. 37 (y. Kil. 8:4)]

Comment: R. Yosi presents the Shammaites' view, that the weasel is in the category of a "doubtful beast" since it *may* be a wild animal. The House of Shammai hold that one who carries as much as an olive's bulk of the weasel, as of the corpse of any wild beast, even though he does not touch it, is unclean; *and* because the weasel may be regarded as an insect, one who touches as much as a lentil's bulk is unclean, but the insect does not render unclean by carrying. So the stringencies of both categories apply.

It is difficult to ascertain the source of Yosi b. Ḥalafta's ruling for the Shammaites. No equivalent Hillelite opinion occurs.

II.ii.7. [As to] the caper-bush (ṢLP)—

The House of Shammai say, "[It constitutes] mixed seeds in the vineyard."

And the House of Hillel say, "[It does] not [constitute] mixed seeds."

And both ('YLW W'YLW) agree that it is subject to the law of *'orlah*.

[Tos. Kila'im 3:17, ed. Lieberman, p. 217, lines 60-1 (b. Ber. 36a, y. Maʿaserot 4:4, y. Kil. 5:8)]

II.ii.8. "The young shoot that passes over a stone, even though there are only two fingers' [depth] of dirt on it—one may sow on it," the words of R. Meir.

R. Yosa says, "Three fingers."

Rabban Simeon b. Gamaliel says, "The House of Shammai say, 'Ten *tefaḥs*.'

"And the House of Hillel say, 'Six *tefaḥs*.' "

(Tos. Kila'im 4:11b, ed. Lieberman, p. 220, lines 41-4)

Comment: II.ii.7 is a completely conventional pericope. *In the vineyard* serves both Houses' lemmas. y. Kil. 5:8 adds a second element on which the Houses agree: It is "not mixed seeds among seeds" (ZR'YM). Then, *all agree...*

II.ii.8 is still another instance in which the generation of Usha and other, later Tannaim supply opinions in the name of the Houses. The issue between them is what measurement pertains to the vine below the ground. The House of Hillel, which earlier permitted six *tefaḥs* for the explosed plant (above, M. Kil. 6:1.C-D, following Yoḥanan b. Nuri), maintain (or, are given) the same position here. The House of Shammai hold that the law of the vine planted in the ground is the same as the law of the exposed vine, and a space of ten is required (Lieberman, *Tosefta Kifshuṭah, ad loc.*, p. 644, to lines 42-3). Once again we are left to wonder at Simeon b. Gamaliel's source for the dispute of the Houses. M. Kil. 7:1 holds that if there are not three *tefaḥs* of dirt on it, one may not plant seed there. Judah the Patriarch therefore has ignored the alleged dispute of the Houses; but he must have known it.

II.i.15. Until what time do they plough a tree-planted field in the year before ('RB) the Seventh Year?

The House of Shammai say, "So long as this benefits the produce [of the sixth year]."

The House of Hillel say, "Until Pentecost."

And the opinion of the one is near the opinion of the other.

[M. Shev. 1:1, trans. Danby, p. 39 (y. Shev. 1:1, b. M.Q. 3b)]

Comment: The context is the additional Sabbatical months added to the year before the actual Sabbatical Year. Work must not be done then to benefit the produce of the Seventh Year. The Houses say much the same thing, but in different language. The principle is not disputed. The gloss again says no actual disagreement between the Houses existed; each phrased its opinion in its own way. Both preserved their own word-choices, later on combined in what apparently was the only form available for that purpose: the dispute.

M. Shev. 1:2 then provides a necessary gloss, defining "a tree-planted field." No dispute between the Houses centers on that definition. It is difficult to assign responsibility for the gloss. It is neutral, but not necessarily early.

See Epstein, *Mevo'ot*, p. 228.

II.i.16.A. A field that has been cleared of thorns [in the Seventh Year] may be sown in the eighth year (MWṢ'Y ŠBY'YT). [But one] that has been prepared, or used by cattle, may not be sown in the eighth year.

B. A field that has been prepared—

The House of Shammai say, "They do not eat its produce in the Seventh Year."

But the House of Hillel say, "They eat."

C. The House of Shammai say, "They do not eat produce of the Seventh Year if it is by favor [of the owner]."

The House of Hillel say, "They eat it whether by favor or not by favor."

D. R. Judah says, "The rule is to the contrary; this is one of the lenient rulings of the House of Shammai and the stringent rulings of the House of Hillel."

E. He who thins out (HMDL) olive trees [in the Seventh Year]—

The House of Shammai say, "He razes them to the roots (YGM)."

The House of Hillel say, "He uproots them (YŠRŠ)."

F. But they agree concerning one who levels his field [that he may only] raze [the trees to the roots].

G. Who is he that 'thins out'? [He that removes but] one or two. And he that 'levels'? [He that removes at least] three [growing] side by side. This applies to what grows within a man's own domain; but within the domain of his fellow he that levels may also uproot.

[M. Shev. 4:2, 4, trans. Danby, p. 43 (y. Shev. 4:2, 4, 9:6)]

Comment: The issue is, What work is permitted in the Seventh Year? And what to do with the produce thereof? M. Shev. 4:2, given in parts A-D, is a composite.

Part B concerns the disposition of the produce of a field which in the Seventh Year has been improved or used by cattle, therefore fertilized. The House of Shammai hold one may not consume the produce of such a field in the Seventh Year, even though it may have grown without the farmer's cultivation. The House of Hillel say it may be eaten. The form is standard:

Fruit of a field that has been improved in the Seventh Year:
House of Shammai: They do not eat
House of Hillel: They eat.

The Shammaite-opinion has been augmented with an explanatory clause, *its fruit in the Seventh Year*. The unglossed opinions of the Houses originally would have been *not eat/eat*.

Part C lacks a topic-sentence or superscription but is perfectly clear because of the conventional augmentation of the opening clause, the Shammaite saying. The issue is, Are the fruits of the field ownerless property? The Shammaites hold that the produce is regarded as ownerless property; therefore if the owner's permission is needed or granted, then the produce may not be consumed. The Hillelites hold that the produce may be consumed whether by favor or otherwise. In part D Judah b. Ilai reverses matters, on the principle that this matter of law should have the Shammaites in the lenient position, therefore the Shammaites must be given the opinion that one may eat the fruit whether or not by the owner's favor, and the Hillelites, only if it is *not* with the owner's favor. See Sifra Behar, 1:5, and M. 'Ed. 5:1. Judah the Patriarch has ignored Judah b. Ilai's tradition. Obviously, Judah b. Ilai had, or would have fabricated, something like the following:

As to fruits of the seventh year
The House of Shammai: [They eat them] by favor or not by favor.
The House of Hillel: [They eat them only] not by favor [Or: they do not eat them by favor].

The primary language before all authorities therefore was simply:

By favor—not by favor/not by favor.

Clearly, to keep matters straight, various sorts of mnemonic devices must have circulated, helping the tradent to assign the correct opinion to the correct House. This further implies that the original tradition left matters unclear, and consisted, as we have several times noticed, of a few gnomic words, later on spelled out, assigned to the Houses, and glossed (as in M. Shev. 1:2 above, for one instance, were the 'tree-planted field' of which the Houses spoke is carefully defined).

M. Shev. 4:4, parts E, F, and G, above, contains in part G the same sort of extended gloss of the Houses' opinions.

Part E concerns what work may be done in connection with thinning out olive trees. The Shammaites hold one may cut down the trees to the roots, but may not pull up the roots, since that would appear to be improving the field. The Hillelites concede (part F) that in leveling the field—therefore not merely thinning out the trees—the farmer may not pull up the roots. Part G then supplies a definition for the foregoing rules: thinning out is removing one or two, but leveling is pulling up three together. Part G applies to both Houses, merely a philological gloss.

The form of M. Shev. 4:4 is standard. The only variation is in the selection of different words for the opinions of the Houses, rather than using affirmative/negative versions of the same verbal root; the Shammaites say YGM, he may raze, the Hillelites, YŠRŠ, he may uproot, both in the affirmative. In fact, the difference between razing and uprooting is the point of the dispute. The form looks suspiciously like a difference merely in word-choices for saying pretty much the same thing (e.g. M. Shev. 1:1). It is possible that no dispute originally existed between the Houses, but rather different verbal traditions persisted. In this case both Houses held one *may* indeed thin out the olive trees. In preserving the two traditions in a single pericope, it became important not only to keep the language used by the Houses, but also to stress that a dispute, or difference, actually separated them. Here, unlike M. Shev. 1:1, a substantive difference could be attached to the words chosen by the Houses. But a different gloss, *the opinion of one is near the opinion of the other*, would have served almost as satisfactorily. This is all the more evident in part F, where the range of disagreement is narrowed still further: *two* vs. *three* trees.

y. Shev. 4:2 has Ṭarfon follow the House of Shammai, with the same result as M. Ber. 1:3B. If *not with permission, as the House of Shammai* is not a later gloss, then Ṭarfon supplies both the *terminus ante quem* and the refutation of Judah b. Ilai, part D. See Epstein, *Mevo'ot*, p. 94; *Mishnah*, p. 58.

II.i.17.A. After what time is it forbidden to cut down a tree in the Seventh Year?

The House of Shammai say, "Any tree [may not be cut down] after it puts forth [leaves]."

The House of Hillel say, "Carob trees—after their branches begin to droop; vines—after they produce berries; olive trees—after they blossom; and any other tree—after it puts forth [leaves]."

B. Any tree that has reached the season, when it is liable to tithes, may be cut down.

[M. Shev. 4:10, trans. Danby, p. 44 (b. Pes. 52b)]

Comment: Produce in the Seventh Year may only be eaten, not destroyed, according to M. Shev. 8:2:

> The produce of the Seventh Year is for eating, drinking, (etc.)—and not for destruction.

The pericope before us presupposes and follows the general rule, though not necessarily in its present form. The Shammaite rule applies overall. The Hillelites supply definitions for various trees, ending with the definition of the Shammaites. Thus:

After what time is it forbidden to cut down trees?
House of Shammai: Every tree—*after in puts forth*
House of Hillel: Carobs, vines, olive trees etc. [*And*] every tree—*after it puts forth.*

The rule for carobs, vines, and olives differs from that for the remainder. It depends in these instances not on leaves but on other phenomena. At issue, therefore, is whether specific rules pertain to these three or not. Perhaps, once again, the real difference is in the style of formulating the Houses' respective opinions. The Shammaites may have advanced a general principle. The Hillelites obviously did not differ about the general principle, but provided a number of specific illustrative instances. It all comes down to the same thing. So the dispute-form required the specification of distinctions where no real differences separated the substance of the Houses' opinions.

II.i.18. When arum (LWP) remains from the sixth year until the Seventh Year, so, too, with summer-onions and madder from good soil—

The House of Shammai say, "They may only be dug up with wooden rakes."

The House of Hillel say, "With metal spades."

But they agree that madder from stony soil may be dug up with metal spades.

[M. Shev. 5:4, trans. Danby, p. 45 (y. Shev. 5:2)]

Comment: The form is standard and poses no problems. The specified produce has ripened in the sixth year. Normally, one uproots them with spades, not merely pulls them up. The House of Shammai require a change in the normal procedure so that the process will not appear to be working the land in the Seventh Year. The Hillelites hold one may do so in the ordinary way. As to the agreement on madder, it is because one simply cannot do it any other way (so Albeck, *Seder Zera'im*, p. 152). The Houses' opinions are balanced, except *they uproot them:*

M'RWPWT ŠL'Ṣ
QRDWMWT ŠLMTKT

But here the issue is not mere word-choice, but a substantive difference.

II.i.19.A. The House of Shammai say, "He should not sell him a ploughing heifer in the Seventh Year."

And the House of Hillel permit it, since he can slaughter it.

B. One may sell him produce even in time of sowing; even if it is known that he has a threshing-floor, one may lend him a *seah*-measure; and one may give him small money in change even if it is known that he employs laborers. But if [it is known that these things are required] expressly [to transgress the Seventh Year law], they are forbidden.

[M. Shev. 5:8, trans. Danby, p. 45 (y. Shev. 5:3, b. A.Z. 15b)]

Comment: The pericope supplies full, unbalanced statements to both Houses. This is unusual; especially unexpected is attaching the reason to the Hillelite ruling. Part B adds further examples of the Hillelite view, presumably from the same glossator, ending with the restrictive aspect of the Hillelite ruling. The pericope is apt to be a highly developed *summary* of a primary dispute that would have looked something like this:

As to selling a ploughing heiferi n the Seventh Year to one suspected of not observing the law:
House of Shammai: Prohibit
House of Hillel: Permit

Everything else is a Hillelite gloss. As in earlier instances the redactor has given a full account of the dispute in the Shammaite part of the pericope, then preserved the Hillelite part in its primary form: *permit.*

The law in question concerns selling to someone who may not scrupulously observe the Sabbath-year. M. Shev. 5:7 supplies the antecedent of *him*: a gentile in Palestine and a Jew abroad. To the Hillelites is attributed the more lenient view. Since the heifer does not give milk, the Shammaites imagine it can only be used for ploughing, thus violating the law. The Hillelites take account of an unlikely possibility and so permit the sale. The context is laws concerning sales in the Seventh Year. Immediately preceding is a general rule: "Any implement is forbidden [for sale] whose *sole* use is one that transgresses [Seventh Year law]. But it is allowed if its use may be either one forbidden or one permissible" (M. Shev. 5:6). The general rule therefore is formulated on the basis of the Hillelite principle. The Shammaites would not have used *sole*, rather *general*, or something similar. The pericope before us ought to antedate the general rule.

Tos. Shev. 4:5b has the same dispute in principle, this time about selling land; and Tos. Shev. 6:19 has a less exact parallel.

II.i.20.A. Seventh Year produce may not be sold, whether by bulk, weight or number; even figs [may not be sold] by number or vegetables by weight.

B. The House of Shammai say, "Nor even ('P) in bundles."

And the House of Hillel say, "What is usually tied up in bundles in the house may be tied up in bundles in the market; like, for example, leeks and asphodel."

(M. Shev. 8:3, trans. Danby, p. 48)

Comment: The general rule is given in M. Shev. 7:3:

...none may do business with Seventh Year produce, or with Firstlings, or with Heave-offering, or with carrion, or with what is *ṭerefah*, or with forbidden beasts and creeping things.

[In the Seventh Year] a man may not gather wild vegetables and sell them in the market; yet he may collect them, and his son may sell them for him in the market. If he had gathered them for his own use and anything remains, he may sell it.

The general rule in part A above amplifies the foregoing. One may not sell even what one *is* allowed to sell in the Seventh Year in such a way that it looks like doing business in the normal fashion.

To this general rule, the House of Shammai now add a detail: One may not even make up bundles, as is normally done. The House of Hillel say one makes minor changes in the ordinary manner of doing things and may therefore bind up in the market rather than at home, with the gloss's supplying examples. It is difficult to imagine the brief pericope of which this is an amplification. Perhaps:

[General rule: One does not sell by bulk, weight, number]

As to making bundles

House of Shammai: Prohibit
House of Hillel: Permit.

This, however, is manifestly unsatisfactory, for it fails to find a place for the exact opinion of the Hillelites, which one can hardly reduce to a simple one or two-word formula. If one added *as usual at home*, the Shammaites would be misrepresented, for they prohibit under all curcumstances.

II.ii.9. One may water the plants until the New Year.

R. Yosa b. Kifar says in the name of R. Leazar, "The House of Shammai say, 'One waters the foliage, and it drips on to the root.'

"The House of Hillel say, '[One waters both] on the foliage and on the root.'

"The House of Hillel said to the House of Shammai, 'If you permit him part, permit him all. If you do not permit him all, do not permit him part.' "

[Tos. Shev. 1:5, ed. Lieberman, p. 166, line 19—p. 167, line 23 (y. Shev. 2:4)]

Comment: M. Shev. 2:4 has the Shammaite opinion in the name of Eliezer b. Ṣadoq, "A man may even water the foliage in the Seventh Year itself, but not the roots." The Leazar here is, however, Eliezer b. Shammuʿa, so Lieberman, *Tosefta Kifshuṭah*, p. 488, to lines 19-20.

I see no difficulty with the logia attributed to the Houses, though the Shammaite one in primary form ought to have begun, "Foliage, not root," corresponding in form to the Hillelite one. The colloquy however is truncated; the expected Shammaite response is not given. This suggests that the colloquy's unanswered question is a Hillelite gloss, deriving from circles other than those responsible for the Hillelite-Shammaite exchanges seen earlier. The Hillelite tendency elsewhere is to point up Shammaite inconsistences, e.g. in connection with picking olives and grapes, above, I, pp. 318-321.

II.ii.10. Rabban Simeon b. Gamaliel said, "The House of Shammai and the House of Hillel did not differ concerning that which was complete, that it [is assigned to] the past [year], and concerning that which has not blossomed, that it [is assigned to] the coming one.

"Concerning what did they differ? Concerning the pod (TWRML),

"For the House of Shammai say, '[It is assigned] to the past [year].'

"And the House of Hillel say, '[To the] coming [one].' "

[Tos. Shev. 2:6, ed. Lieberman, p. 170, lines 21-25 (y. Shev. 2:8, Tos. Ma. 1:5)]

Comment: The dispute relates to M. Shev. 2:7-8. M. Shev. 2:7 specifies that if various species, e.g. rice and sesame, have taken root before the New Year, they are tithed after the manner of the past year; i.e. if the past year was liable for First and Second Tithe, it is given; if for First and Poorman's Tithe, that is given. But if not, they are forbidden in the Seventh Year, and then are to be tithed after the manner of the coming year. As to Egyptian beans, Simeon of Shezur assigns to them the same rule if they are sown for seed. Simeon says, "If they are large beans." Eleazar says, "Large beans are treated in like manner only if they have formed pods before the New Year." As to shallots and Egyptian beans not watered within thirty days of the New Year, they are tithed after the manner of the past year and are permitted in the Seventh Year (M. Shev. 2:9). Otherwise they are forbidden in the Seventh Year and are tithed after the manner of the coming year.

Simeon b. Gamaliel now introduces the issue of a dispute of the Houses, and holds it concerns whether pods have formed—a case between a completed growth-cycle and a growth-cycle not yet begun. In such an intermediate, ambiguous situation the Houses take the two possible positions. We do not know how Simeon b. Gamaliel knew the tradition on the Houses-dispute, which is absent in the corresponding Mishnahs, and for which we have no chain of tradition or earlier allusions. But a parallel problem is in Tos. Shev. 4:21.

The simplest possible form is before us:

The pod

House of Shammai:	To the past [year] (LŠ'BR)
House of Hillel:	To the coming [one] (L'TYD LB').

While, therefore, the form is simple and conventional, understanding its substance would have required considerable information. But this is generally the case and provides no criterion in evaluating the likely authenticity of the attribution to the original Houses. One may theorize that here the Houses serve as convenience-names, to which to attribute the two possible opinions on an intermediate or ambiguous stage of an issue. Simeon may on his own have fabricated the Houses-dispute, in conformity with a prevailing literary convention.

II.ii.11. [One may not sell produce of the Seventh Year to one suspected concerning the observance of the Seventh Year. . .]

The House of Shammai say, "One may not sell him a field in the Seventh Year."

And the House of Hillel permit [it].

[Tos. Shev. 4:5b, ed. Lieberman, p. 180, lines 10-13 (b. A.Z. 15b)]

Comment: The same pattern was evident in M. Shev. 5:8. Here the dispute is extended to the sale of a field. The Hillelites depend on the unnatural assumption that the Seventh Year violator bought the field intending to plant it *after* the Seventh Year. The form follows that of M. Shev. 5:8: House of Shammai say, "One may not sell. . .," and House of Hillel *permit*. The difference is that here the superscription is not inserted into the Shammaite opinion as explanatory matter, because it does not pertain, but stands before, and independent of, the Shammaite lemma, as one would expect, since it speaks of produce, not a field. The superscription therefore has merely given an antecedent to *him*, such as is lacking in M. Shev. 5:8. The Hillelite position here lacks the gloss "since he may perchance. . ." Dropping the glosses, the whole pericope therefore follows M. Shev. without significant change of form. That means available Houses' opinions have been assigned to a new legal issue. But these opinions, consisting—in effect—of *prohibit/permit*, are standard and not intrinsically related to the superscription to which they are assigned.

II.ii.12. (M'SH B) R. 'Aqiba (Š) picked an *etrog* on the first day of Shevaṭ and treated it according to the words of the House of Shammai *and* according to the words of the House of Hillel.

[Tos. Shev. 4:21, ed. Lieberman, p. 185, lines 71-2 (b. R.H. 14a-b, y. Bik. 2:5, y. R.H. 1:2, b. 'Eruv. 7a, b. Yev. 15a; compare Tos. Shev. 2:6)]

Comment: The story is simple, the background complex. Lieberman explains: The first of Shevaṭ pertains to the third or sixth year of the seven-year cycle. R. 'Aqiba agrees with R. Gamaliel (M. Bik. 2:6) that the *etrog* when it is picked is to be tithed. The House of Shammai (M. R.H. 1:1) hold that the first of Shevaṭ is the New Year for trees, so it is already the third (or sixth) year of the cycle, and Poorman's Tithe must be given. The House of Hillel place the New Year on the fifteenth of the same month, so it is still the second or fifth year of the cycle, and the *etrog* is liable for Second Tithe. R. ʿAqiba has separated the Second Tithe and both redeemed it *and* given it to the poor, therefore satisfying the opinions of both Houses (Lieberman, *Tosefta Zeraʿim*, p. 185, note to l. 71).

For our purpose the story is valuable in indicating, first, a *terminus ante quem* for the rulings of M. R.H. 1:1 (below), second, an attitude of respect for the Shammaites one would not have expected on the basis of the Ṭarfon/Ishmael stories in connection with the *Shemaʿ*.

II.ii.13. The House of Shammai say, "They do not sell the produce of the Seventh year for coins, but for produce, so that he will not purchase for them [the coins] a spade."

And the House of Hillel permit [it].

(Tos. Shev. 6:19, ed. Lieberman, p. 192, lines 33-5)

Comment: The problem is that the man may buy something which is not for eating, as in M. Shev. 8:2, "Seventh Year produce is intended for use as food, drink, or unguent. . ." The positions are consistent with Tos. Shev. 4:5b. The remarks on the form of that pericope pertain here as well.

II.i.21.A. Heave-offering may not be given from olives instead of from oil, or from grapes instead of from wine.

B. If they gave Heave-offering—

The House of Shammai say, "[It may still be deemed] Heave-offering of the olives or of the grapes themselves (TRWMT ʿṢMN BHM)."

And the House of Hillel say, "Their Heave-offering is not Heave-offering."

[M. Ter. 1:4, trans. Danby, p. 52 (y. Ter. 1:2, 5; 4:4; M. ʿEd. 5:2, b. Ḥul. 163a)]

Comment: The issue is set in part A, which necessarily comes before part B; the Houses here differ only on secondary matters. The presumption is that the law-code existed in its final form before the Houses discussed the problem before us, as is often the case.

The rule is, One does not give Heave-offering from produce whose preparation is completed for produce whose preparation is incomplete (M. Ter. 1:10). The House of Shammai hold (Albeck, *Seder Zeraʿim*, p. 179n) that the Heave-offering he is liable to separate from the olives and grapes themselves inheres in the olives and grapes which he has already separated, but what he has separated from them for the olive-oil or wine is not Heave-offering. Therefore the law of the olives and grapes which he has separated is like the law of a mixture of Heave-offering with unconsecrated food. If the unconsecrated food contains one hundred times more than the quantity of the Heave-offering, it *is* neutralized and does not have the status of a mixture (M. Ter. 4:7). If not, the mixture is to be sold to priests, who are allowed, of course, to use it.

The House of Hillel say, "Since he intended to give Heave-offering *also* for the oil and the wine, Heave-offering is simply *not* present here at all." So the dispute concerns the legal force of intention. Albeck adds that since it was common to give Heave-offering from olives for olive oil and from grapes for wine, the House of Hillel ruled stringently: even though one *has* given the Heave-offering, in no way has he carried out his obligation in the matter.

The form is standard:

If they gave Heave-offering:
House of Shammai: Their own Heave-offering is in them (TRWMT 'ṢMN BHM)
House of Hillel: Their Heave-offering is not Heave-offering ('YN TRWMTN TRWMH)

The sayings, though metrically balanced, are not quite syzygies. On the other hand, the choice before the House of Shammai did not include the ruling *Their Heave-offering is Heave-offering*, which would have been the logical and formal opposite of the Hillelites' negative. The Shammaite ruling still is brief and simple in form, matching the Hillelites' in the number of syllables.

See Epstein, *Mevo'ot*, p. 436; *Mishnah*, p. 399.

II.i.22. The proper measure of Heave-offering, if a man is liberal, is one-fortieth part.

The House of Shammai say, "One-thirtieth."

If he is liberal in medium degree, one-fiftieth part; if he is mean, one-sixtieth part. [M. Ter. 4:3, trans. Danby, p. 56 (y. Ter. 4:3)]

Comment: The gloss containing the House of Shammai's opinion takes for granted the existence of the structure into which it is inserted. Otherwise, the Shammaite ruling would have to be that one gives one-thirtieth under all circumstances, which is impossible.

The Tosefta version must be introduced for comprehension of the Shammaite lemma:

The proper measure of Heave-offering:

The House of Shammai say, "If a man is liberal [Lit.: good eye], [One] of thirty; if he is liberal in the medium degree [Lit.: intermediate], [one] of forty; and if he is mean [Lit.: evil], [one] of fifty."

The House of Hillel say, "If a man is liberal, one of forty; if he is liberal in the medium degree, one of fifty; and if he is mean, one of sixty."

(Tos. Ter. 5:3, ed. Lieberman, p. 129, lines 9-12)

The Mishnaic pericope therefore is identical with, and follows, the Hillelite position, but it is not so labeled. Rather, the Shammaite view is interpolated into the Hillelite position, which is presented anonymously. The fact that the Shammaites held a contrary, or different, view would not have been revealed without the gloss. Otherwise, the whole Houses-pericope would have been preserved, as is ordinarily the case.

The primary form of the pericope clearly must have been the numbers:

Measure of Heave-offering:
House of Shammai: 30/40/50
House of Hillel: 40/50/60

The meaning would have been readily apparent, and no difficulty could have inhered in assigning the tradition to a particular legal problem, or —given the principle that the Hillelites normally are more liberal—the right opinion to the right House.

M. Ter. 4:3 therefore looks like a defective tradition, for either the Shammaites should have been dropped altogether, or the Hillelites should have been included by name. For formal reasons the Mishnah either is a secondary development and shows us that Shammaite opinions could have been (and, in who knows how many instances, *were*) suppressed, *or* it is garbled. We have other instances of the garbling of just this sequence, best, medium, worst, below, b. R.H. See Epstein, *Mishnah*, p. 1008.

II.i.23.A. [If] one *se'ah* of unclean Heave-offering fell into a hundred *se'ahs* of clean Heave-offering—

The House of Shammai forbid.

And the House of Hillel permit [it].

B. The House of Hillel said to the House of Shammai, "Since clean [Heave-offering] is forbidden to non-priests, and also ('P) unclean is forbidden to priests, if the clean can be neutralized, cannot the unclean be neutralized also?"

The House of Shammai said to them, "No! If common produce (ḤLYN), to which leniency applies and which *is* permitted to non-priests, neutralizes what is clean, should Heave-offering, to which stringency does apply and which is forbidden to non-priests, neutralize what is unclean!"

C. *After they had agreed*—

R. Eliezer says, "It should be taken up and burned."

But the Sages say, "It is lost through its scantness ('BDH BM'WṬH)."

[M. Ter. 5:4, trans. Danby, p. 58 (y. Ter. 5:2)]

Comment: The issue is, Is the unclean Heave-offering neutralized in the clean? The Shammaites prohibit it, and the House of Hillel permit it. According to the Shammaites it must be left to rot; the priests cannot use it ("prohibit").

The argument of the Hillelites (part B) is this: Clean Heave-offering is prohibited to non-priests, and unclean is prohibited to priests. Since clean Heave-offering *is* capable of being neutralized when it falls into one hundred times its quantity of unconsecrated food, so the unclean should be neutralized in clean Heave-offering.

The Shammaites reply that common produce can indeed serve to neutralize what is clean. But clean Heave-offering, to which more stringent rules apply, cannot serve to neutralize unclean.

Part C begins with the *agreement*-form, but does not specify who agreed with whom. Normally, part B would have ended the argument. The Shammaites would have the last word and win. Later masters assume that the House of Shammai agreed with the House of Hillel. As it stands, *after they agreed* serves as a joining-formula, to tie R. Eliezer b. Hyrcanus's opinion—in the present tense!—to the antecedent elements.

Part C is a separate pericope, awkwardly tied to the superscription of the whole:

[If] one se'ah of unclean Heave-offering fell into hundred se'ahs of clean Heave-offering:

R. Eliezer says, "It should be taken up and burned."

The sages say, "It is lost [= neutralized] through its scantiness."

The word-choices differ from the foregoing, but the positions are the same:

Eliezer = House of Shammai
Sages = House of Hillel

That is, the man must take up a *se'ah* and give it to the priest, as in the case of clean Heave-offering that is neutralized, but the *se'ah* is not to be eaten, rather to be burned like unclean Heave-offering (M. Tem. 7:5). Hence Eliezer forbids the unclean Heave-offering to the priest, just as do the House of Shammai. The sages' position, that it is lost (= neutralized) through its scantiness, is identical with the Hillelite position. There is no necessity to supply further Heave-offering. The whole is regarded as Heave-offering, and the priests consume it in a state of cleanness. The substance of part C, excluding the curious redactional formula, *after they had agreed*, is a separate and complete pericope, which duplicates or is duplicated by part B. The differences are in word-choice, but the law is the same.

Eliezer's position is consistent in the following rulings: in M. Ter.

5:2, If one *se'ah* of unclean Heave-offering fell into a hundred *se'ahs* of common produce; M. Ter. 5:5, If one *se'ah* of Heave-offering fell etc., and was lifted out and *again* fell; M. Ter. 5:6, If one *se'ah* of Heave-offering fell into *less* than a hundred. The whole constitutes a veritable repertoire of Eliezer rulings on pretty much the same legal issue, spelled out in closely related cases.

The commentaries, which suppose that the Houses came to an agreement in conformity with the Hillelite position and that *afterward* Eliezer disagreed, take for granted the existence of a unitary text. They therefore hold that Eliezer's position remains consistent with the Shammaites' original one, and the issue therefore becomes this: Does the man have to take up a *se'ah* as Heave-offering for the priest, as in the case of clean Heave-offering? He does—*but* then it is to be burned. This, I have argued, still is in effect the Shammaite position at the outset ("prohibit"), therefore no different in substance from before. The sages' enigmatic saying is that the whole is annulled, and the commentaries see the issue as whether Heave-offering now has to be taken up. The sages' view is that it does *not* have to be taken up because the *whole* has been made Heave-offering and the priests get to consume it in a state of ritual purity (etc.) as explained above.

Seeing the pericope as a complex of two versions of the same dispute, with corresponding positions taken by the Houses and the later masters, we do not have to introduce the issue of whether Heave-offering is *further* to be taken up. Both versions stand in direct relationship to the opening problem as given in the superscription:

> *A se'ah of unclean Heave-offering that has fallen into hundred se'ahs of clean Heave-offering.*

Which version comes first? The word-choices of the Houses-opinions are curiously inappropriate to the argument: *prohibit/permit.* They have no direct bearing on the facts of the case. One has to know that "prohibit" will mean that the unclean Heave-offering is not neutralized in the clean Heave-offering, therefore is "prohibited" for priestly use. By contrast, Eliezer's language is entirely appropriate: *It should be raised up and burned.* This specification of the fate of the unclean Heave-offering answers the problem set in the topic-sentence: A *se'ah* of *unclean Heave-offering that fell into a hundred se'ahs of clean Heave-offering.* Likewise the Hillelite language—*permit*—is generalized and irrelevant to the immediate context, while the sages' language, *It is lost through its scantiness*, completes the topic-sentence. On the face of it, therefore, the Houses-dispute looks like an interpolation in the Eliezer-sages pericope; if one dropped the Houses, the whole would be lucid and tightly-organized.

Two separate versions have been awkwardly combined, the Houses' dispute and argument, and the Eliezer-sages' formally conventional ruling (Statement of the problem, Rabbi X rules, Sages [Rabbi Y] rule). Since the latter renders more precise and clear what the former leaves generalized and unclear, it seems to me likely that the latter improves upon, and comes later than, the former. But this is merely a suggestion. Yavneh surely supplies the *terminus ante quem*.

Note Epstein, *Mevo'ot*, p. 61 n. 20; *Mishnah*. p. 708.

II.ii.14. [If a man] had black and white figs in his house, and so two kinds of wheat, they give Heave-offering and Tithe from one for the other.

R. Isaac says in the name of R. Eleazar, "The House of Shammai say, 'One does not give Heave-offering.'

"And the House of Hillel say, 'One does give Heave-offering [in such a circumstance, from one for the other].' "

[Tos. Ter. 2:5, ed. Lieberman, p. 112, lines 10-12 (y. Ter. 4:7 = Eliezer and Joshua; b. Ḥul. 136b)]

Comment: The rule is that one may not tithe or give Heave-offering for differing species. But all kinds of wheat, nuts, pomegranates, and so forth are respectively regarded as single species. The issue before us therefore is the rule as to Heave-offering. The antecedent rule (Tos. Ter. 2:4) follows the Hillelite view that one gives both Heave-offering and Tithes from two kinds of wheat (presumably, also figs etc.). The named authorities are responsible for a version of the Houses-disputes. We should have expected

As to two kinds of figs/wheat (etc.)

House of Shammai:	They do not give Heave-offering [from one for the other]
House of Hillel:	They do give Heave-offering [from one for the other].

We may therefore suppose that some other disputes following the conventional form such as given here would have been shaped by named Tannaitic authorities, and that the final versions, dropping reference to the authorship of later authorities, would represent a later development. This is contrary to the normal procedure alleged to have been followed by Tannaim, that those responsible for pericopae are named, and the names are carefully preserved. Many Houses-pericopae are assigned to later authorities.

Lieberman notes (*Tosefta Kifshuṭah*, p. 310, to p. 112 lines 11-12) that b. Ḥul. 136b gives R. Ilai. The change from 'Ele'azar to 'Ele'a'y is in the last two letters only. b. Ḥul. 136b, whose reading Lieberman calls "certain", reverses matters:

If he had two kinds of figs, black and white, and so two kinds of wheat, they do not give Heave-offering and tithe from this for that.

R. Isaac says in the name of R. Ilai, "The House of Shammai say, 'One does *not* give Heave-offering.'

"And the House of Hillel say, 'One gives Heave-offering.' "

So the superscription in this version follows the Shammaite opinion. The substance of the Houses-opinions is the same.

II.ii.15.A. When do they make it [the vat for winepressing] unclean?

The House of Shammai say, "After the First Tithe is taken."

The House of Hillel say, "After the Second Tithe is taken."

B. R. Judah said, "The law is according to the words of the House of Shammai, but the majority (HRBYM) behave according to the words of the House of Hillel."

C. And the sages say, "They remove the Heave-offering of the tithe and forthwith render the vat unclean."

[Tos. Ter. 3:12, ed. Lieberman, pp. 118-9, lines 43-47 (y. Ter. 3:2, Tos. Ṭoh. 11:4)]

II.ii.16.A. They may not give Heave-offering of oil for crushed olives, and not of wine for trodden grapes, and if he gave Heave-offering, it *is* Heave-offering, but he goes and gives Heave-offering again. . .

B. R. Yosa says, "The House of Shammai say, 'They give Heave-offering.'

"And the House of Hillel say, 'They do not give Heave-offering.'

"They agree that if he gave Heave-offering, he needs [y. Ter. 1:5: *not*] to give Heave-offering a second time."

[Tos. Ter. 3:14, ed. Lieberman, p. 119, lines 50-54 (y. Ter. 1:5,8; M. 'Ed. 5:2)]

Comment: According to Tos. Ter. 3:12 the householder sets aside a place for the tithe and takes out the Heave-offering of the tithe, but he does not have also to take out the tithe, for it does not matter that he gives unclean tithe to the Levite, *if* the Heave-offering of the tithe has already been removed from the tithe. Lieberman explains (*Tosefta Kifshuṭah*, p. 329, to lines 44f.) that it was customary intentionally to render the vat unclean so that there would be no doubt of the matter. If it is rendered unclean, people will be more careful not to allow clean things to touch it (as in M. Ter. 3:4). The Palestinian version reverses the opinions of the Houses. Lieberman observes that this is not listed among the lenient rulings of the Shammaites (M. 'Ed. 5:1-2). The form of the Houses-dispute poses no difficulty.

As to II.ii.16, the issue is whether the crushed olives are regarded as olives or as olive-oil. Clearly, it would be more logical to regard them as olives. The superscription is Hillelite: one does *not* give Heave-offering. R. Yosa's version has the Hillelites prohibit the matter, lest, from the case of crushed olives, people assume that olive-oil is likewise given for olives, which is contrary to the law. The Hillelites are again in the more stringent position. The parallel is M. Ter. 1:4, above, p. 81. For further discussion, see Lieberman, *Tosefta Kifshuṭah*, pp. 331-2. Epstein, *Mevo'ot* p. 436, notes that it is Meir who is the authority for the contrary view, that the Shammaites are in the stringent position, y. Ter. 1:5. See also Epstein, *Mishnah*, p. 399.

II.ii.17.A. He who gives Heave-offering of grapes for the market [= eating] but eventually makes them raisins; figs, but eventually makes them dried figs; pomegranates, but eventually makes them into split and dried (PRD) pomegranates—it is Heave-offering [even though this is produce whose preparation has been completed eventually, serving as Heave-offering for produce whose preparation has not been completed], and he does not have to give Heave-offering a second time.

B. R. Eliezer says, "The House of Shammai say, 'He does not have to give Heave-offering a second time.'

"And the House of Hillel say, 'He has to give Heave-offering a second time.'

C. "The House of Hillel said to the House of Shammai, 'Lo, it is said (Num. 18:27) *[And your offering shall be reckoned to you as though it were the grain of the threshing floor and] as the fulness of the wine press.* This one has *not* given Heave-offering from the winepress.'

"The House of Shammai said to them, 'Lo, it says (Lev. 27:30) *All the tithe [of the land, whether of the seed of the land or of the fruit of the trees is the Lord's; it is holy to the Lord].* If you say that he needs to give Heave-offering a second time, this one has not carried out also *it is holy to the Lord.*' "

(Tos. Ter. 3:16, ed. Lieberman, p. 120-1, lines 61-7)

Comment: What is striking is the attribution to R. Eliezer of the *entire* Houses-dispute, including the conventional debate. Since, as we have observed, Eliezer's opinions and those of the Shammaites sometimes coincide, so that he was called *the Shammaite*, it is of interest to find pericopae attributing the Houses-form to the authority of Eliezer. On that basis, we obviously cannot attribute *all* of the Houses-materials following what we have called conventional form to Eliezer, but we do have *prima facie* evidence that the conventional form of disputes does derive from early Yavneh. Clearly, it later on was copied.

Part A anonymously presents *verbatim* the Shammaite rule.

The pericope supplements and explains M. Ter. 1:9-10 (trans. Danby, p. 53) (and see M. Ter. 1:4, above, p. 81):

> Heave-offering may be given from oil instead of from olives that are to be preserved, or from wine instead of from grapes that are to be made into raisins.
>
> If a man gave Heave-offering from oil instead of from olives intended for eating, or from [other] olives instead of from olives intended for eating, or from wine instead of from grapes intended for eating, or from [other] grapes instead of from grapes intended for eating, and he afterward determined to press them, he need not give Heave-offering afresh.
>
> Heave-offering may not be given from produce whose preparation is finished instead of from produce whose preparation is unfinished, or from produce whose preparation is unfinished instead of from produce whose preparation is finished, or from produce whose preparation is unfinished instead of from [other] produce whose preparation is unfinished.
>
> But if this is done, the Heave-offering is valid.

R. Eliezer here contributes the dispute of the Houses. If he has trodden the grapes (or carried out the other procedures listed), then *retroactively* it becomes clear that he has not given Heave-offering. The Shammaite argument is that when he gave the Heave-offering, since he had not yet given thought to treading the grapes, he *already* has sanctified the Heave-offering and has already carried out *holy to the Lord*: "If you say that he has to give Heave-offering a second time, you annul what is already *holy unto the Lord*."

It is noteworthy that Eliezer's version follows the simplest mnemonic style; the Houses-opinions differ only as to the inclusion of the negative, but otherwise are identical. It is clear that the mnemonic marks do not in themselves prove a pericope is "very old." What it does suggest is that Yavnean materials in many instances were shaped so as to facilitate memorization. The Houses-debate of part C is another matter, but, reduced to the Scriptural citations and brief exegesis of them, the debate would not greatly alter the form for easy memorization.

II.ii.18. Tos Ter. 5:3, see above, p. 83.

II.ii.19.A. [If] A *se'ah* of unclean Heave-offering (that) fell into a hundred *se'ahs* of clean Heave-offering—

The House of Shammai prohibit.

And the House of Hillel permit.

B. The House of Hillel said to the House of Shammai, "Clean [Heave-offering] is prohibited to outsiders (ZRYM) [non-priests], and unclean [Heave-offering] is prohibited to priests. If clean [Heave-offering] can be neutralized, so the unclean also can be neutralized."

The House of Shammai said to them, "No! If you say so concerning clean [Heave-offering], which is neutralized by [a sufficient quantity of] unconsecrated food so as to be given to priests to eat, will you say so of unclean [Heave offering], which is not neutralized [in a sufficient quantity of] unconsecrated food so as to be given to priests to eat [but is burned, M. Ter. 5:2]?"

C. The House of Hillel said to them, "Lo, unclean [Heave-offering] which fell into the unconsecrated [food] will prove [the point], for it does not become neutralized by the unconsecrated food so as to be given to outsiders to eat, yet it *is* neutralized."

The House of Shammai said to them, "No, if you say so concerning unconsecrated food, whose permissibility is considerable [for outsiders eat it], will you say so of Heave-offering, whose permissibility is not considerable [for it is limited to priests]?"

D. The House of Hillel said to them, "And concerning which is the Torah more stringent? For outsiders or priests who eat Heave-offering?

"[And] concerning outsiders who eat Heave-offering: a clean person who ate clean [Heave-offering], and a clean person who ate unclean, an unclean person who ate clean, and an unclean person who ate unclean—all of them are punished by death.

"But as to priests who eat Heave-offering: the clean [priest] who ate clean [Heave-offering] did as he was commanded [to do]. The clean [priest] who ate unclean [Heave-offering transgresses] a positive commandment. And the unclean [priest] who ate clean [Heave-offering] and the unclean priest who ate unclean [Heave-offering all transgress] a negative commandment.

"And is it not an argument *qal veḥomer*: Now in a situation in which the Torah dealt stringently, namely with outsiders who ate Heave-offering, lo, it *is* neutralized by unconsecrated food so as to be eaten by outsider—in a situation in which the Torah dealt leniently, namely with priests who eat Heave-offering, is it not logical that the unconsecrated food should neutralize it so as to be eaten by priests?"

E. After they had agreed [that the unclean is neutralized and not forbidden], R. Eliezer says [*sic*], "It should be taken up and allowed to rot."

And the sages say, "It is lost through its scantiness."

[Tos. Ter. 6:4, ed. Lieberman, pp. 137-8, lines 14-31 (y. Ter. 5:4, y. Suk. 2:8, y. Bik. 2:1, Tos. Zev. 12:17, Tos. Ker. 1:5)]

Comment: Let us first compare the two versions:

M. Ter. 5:4	*Tos. Ter. 6:4*
1. A *se'ah* of unclean Heave-offering that fell into a hundred *se'ahs* of clean Heave-offering	1. ,, ,, ,,
2. The House of Shammai prohibit	2. ,, ,, ,,
3. And the House of Hillel permit	3. ,, ,, ,,
4. The House of Hillel said to the House of Shammai	4. ,, ,, ,,
5. Since clean is prohibited to strangers and unclean is prohibited to priests, just as clean is neutralized [Lit.: comes up ('WLH)], so unclean should be neutralized.	5. Clean is prohibited to strangers and unclean is prohibited to priests. Just as clean is neutralized [Lit.: will come up], so unclean should be neutralized.
6. The House of Shammai said to them, No, if the light, unconsecrated food (ḤLYN QLYN), which is permitted to strangers, neutralized the clean, should heavy Heave-offering (TRWMH HḤMWRH), which is prohibited to strangers, neutralize the unclean?	6. The House of Shammai said to them, No, if you say so concerning the clean, which is neutralized in the unconsecrated to be eaten by priests
	[Part C—no equivalent in Mishnah to Hillelite argument. Lieberman says the Shammaite answer *re* "permissibility is considerable" corresponds to M. Ter. no. 6, *permitted to strangers*.]
7. —	7. [Part D]
8. After they agreed	8. ,, ,, ,,
9. Rabbi Eliezer says, Let it be raised up (TRWM) and burned.	9. ,, ,, ,, and *allowed to rot*
10. And the sages say, It is lost in its minuteness ('BDH BM'WṬH).	10. ,, ,, ,,

We see that the argument of the Hillelites in no. 5 recurs nearly *verbatim*, with the mere addition of *since* in M. Ter. M. Ter. no. 6 is considerably more complex than Tos. Ter. no. 6, and has added an allusion to the argument in Part C of Tos. Ter. (following Lieberman). Tos. parts C and D have no close equivalent, part D none at all, in M. Ter.

Tos. Ter. thus supplies three Hillelite and two Shammaite arguments:

I. Hillel: Clean Heave-offering is prohibited to outsiders but can be neutralized; unclean, which is prohibited to priests, also should be neutralized.

Shammai: No. Unclean Heave-offering cannot be neutralized by unconsecrated food so that priests can *ever* eat it [therefore the argument *a forteriori* is based on false premises about which is the lesser (lighter) category].

II. Hillel: Unclean which fell into unclean does not become neutralized by the unconsecrated food so as to be given to outsiders to eat, yet it *is* neutralized.

Shammai: No, unconsecrated food can be eaten by outsiders, but Heave-offering can be eaten only by priests.

III. Hillel: Torah is more stringent on outsiders who eat Heave-offering. It is an argument *a forteriori:* In a situation in which the Torah dealt stringently—outsiders who eat heave-offering—it *is* neutralized by unconsecrated food so as to be eaten by outsider. In a situation in which the Torah dealt leniently—priests who eat Heave-offering—is it not logical that unconsecrated food *should* neutralize it so as to be eaten by priests?

Argument III looks like an elaborated version of argument I. I do not see why the Shammaite response in argument I could not have served as well, perhaps in more pretentious form, in argument III. Clearly, the dispute-form is preserved in part A. Parts B and C follow the form normal for debates: Hillel-Shammai, with Shammai's House getting the last word and winning the argument. It is part D that breaks the form, clearly a Hillelite (or later) supplement to the whole. I take it for granted that the earlier argumetns were already shaped and could well have reached something like their final form before the crucial Hillelite argument of part D was added. This then leaves no ambiguity. The Shammaites now are represented as agreeing with the Hillelites, and Eliezer's opinion follows, naturally, along Hillelite lines. But then the substance of his opinion requires a different explanation from the one offered earlier.

For an account of the position of Eliezer in the presumption of a unitary text, see Lieberman, *Tosefta Kifshuṭah*, *ad loc.*, pp. 382-3, to line 30. Lieberman demonstrates that "the House of Shammai *did* agree with the House of Hillel," and it seems to me that that is how the passage was understood in Amoraic times. Epstein, *Mishnah*, p. 708, has the same view.

III.ii.4. TNY': A cask of Heave-offering wine which was made unclean—

The House of Shammai say, "It must be poured out forthwith.

And the House of Hillel say, "It may be used for sprinkling."

(b. Pes. 20b = b. B.Q. 115b-116a)

Comment: R. Ishmael b. R. Yosi comments on the pericope, therefore supplying a *terminus ante quem:* ca. 200, the generation of Judah the Patriarch.

III.i.2. TNY: R. Judah said, "The House of Shammai and the House of Hillel did not disagree concerning clean Heave-offering, that it is prohibited to burn it, and concerning unclean Heave-offering, that it is permitted to burn it.

"Concerning what did they dispute?

"Concerning the doubtful [Heave-offering], for

"The House of Shammai say, 'They do not burn.'

"And the House of Hillel say, 'They burn.'

"The House of Shammai said to the House of Hillel, 'Do you not say concerning the clean that it is not to be burned? But I say, perhaps a priest may spend the Sabbath within the limit, and he may come and eat it on the Sabbath. So also the doubtful should not be burned, for I say, perhaps Elijah may spend the Sabbath on Mount Carmel, and he may come and testify concerning it on the Sabbath that it is clean.'

"The House of Hillel said to them, 'We are positive that Elijah comes neither on Sabbaths nor on the festivals.' "

(y. Pes. 3:6)

Comment: The disagreement may be genuine, but the little debate cannot be. The issue is discussed frivolously, and leaves the Shammaites in a silly position. That the form is unconventional is the least problem. Epstein, *Mevo'ot*, p. 61, shows that Judah's *Houses* are in fact the Eliezer and Joshua of b. Pes. 13a.

II.i.24. A basket of fruit intended for the Sabbath—
The House of Shammai declare exempt [from Tithes].
But the House of Hillel declare it liable.

[M. Ma'aserot 4:2, trans. Danby, p. 71 (y. Ma'aserot 4:2)]

Comment: The issue is, Is the produce picked for the Sabbath liable to tithes if eaten before the Sabbath? The House of Shammai say that it is permitted to eat of the fruit at random before the Sabbath, since random-nibbling does not render the fruit intended for the Sabbath to be liable to the various tithes. The House of Hillel require tithing, since, while set aside for the Sabbath, the fruit forthwith was liable for the tithes, and it is prohibited to eat it at random before the Sabbath without tithing (Albeck, *Seder Zera'im*, p. 234).

The form is simple and the opinions of the Houses are phrased in standard language:

Fruit of the Sabbath

House of Shammai:	Declare exempt
House of Hillel:	Declare liable

Here too it looks as if the House of Shammai has taken the more lenient position.

Hillel's rulings in Tos. Ma. 3:3-4, above, I, p. 229-231, are consistent.

II.ii.20. Tos. Maʿaserot 1:5, ed. Lieberman, p. 228, lines 15-17.

Comment: See above, Tos. Shev. 2:6, p. 79. The only change here is that the dispute concerns not the pod but hyssop (ʾYBWN/YYBWN), so Lieberman).

II.ii.21. R. Simeon b. Leazar said, "The Houses of Shammai and Hillel did not differ concerning one who sifts (BRR) on the ground, that he is free [of liability]; or concerning one who sifts with a vessel, that he is liable.

"Concerning what did they differ? Concerning one who sifts by hand for (Š)

"The House of Shammai declare liable.

"And the House of Hillel declare exempt."

[Tos. Maʿaserot 3:10, ed. Lieberman, pp. 239-240, lines 29-32 (M. Beṣ. 1:8)]

II.ii.22. R. Simeon b. Gamaliel said, "The Houses of Shammai and Hillel agree that a man should sell [large quantities, e.g.] a stack of grain, a basket of grapes, and a vat of olives only to a fellow (ḤBR) *and* to one who works in cleanness.

[Tos. Maʿaserot 3:13, ed. Lieberman, p. 240, lines 40-42 (y. Demai 6:7, Tos. Ma. 5:4)]

Comment: The issue of Tos. Maʿaserot 3:10 is whether the man is liable for tithes if he sifts or selects by hand. The Shammaite position is consistent with their ruling in M. Beṣ. 1:8. The Houses-pericope is attached to the foregoing with Š.

Tos. Maʿaserot 3:13 appears in y. Demai 6:7 without the attribution to Simeon b. Gamaliel. M. Maʿaserot 5:4 has a similar law:

> A man may not sell his straw or olive-peat or grape-residue to the one that is not trustworthy in what concerns tithes for him to extract the juices therefrom. . .

Here, the converse, concerning cleanness, is stated in the affirmative. The issue is, May one sell to him who is reliable for tithes but *not* for preserving the cleanness of the food? M. Demai 6:6 (above, p. 64) has the following:

The House of Shammai say, "A man may sell his olives only to a fellow (ḤBR)."

And the House of Hillel say, "Even to one that [only] pays tithes."

The Hillelites permit the sale only of olives, since the unreliable purchaser may eat them whole and not crush them; the olives therefore are not yet susceptible to receive uncleanness. But if the man states he plans to crush them for the oil, even the Hillelites forbid the sale to him.

Simeon b. Gamaliel here adds that all agree that one may not sell to one who is not a fellow (ḤBR) *large quantities* of wheat, grapes, and olives, for he will certainly make them liable to receive uncleanness, therefore they will become unclean, so Lieberman, *Tosefta Kifshuṭah*, p. 705.

The form is standard, which shows that once it was available, later authorities (Simeon) made use of it for their *own* glosses of earlier materials. The position of the Hillelites is at issue; the Shammaites had already prohibited such a sale. Simeon b. Gamaliel presumably could not state on his own authority a position apparently contrary to that of the Hillelites, but he could have the Hillelites "agree" with the Shammaites, therefore come out in favor of the law he wanted to advance. Still later, the superscription attributing the whole to Simeon was dropped, leaving the Houses-dispute in the form one would have imagined to be primary. Once again, therefore, we observe that Houses-materials at the outset were shaped by later masters, and not only in the setting of pre-destruction Jerusalem or early Yavneh. The forms apparently were so widely known and conventional that they would be used even for what amounted to new material. The attestations that Yavnean masters knew Houses-disputes therefore become all the more important in helping us to separate possibly authentic from certainly fabricated materials attributed to the Houses.

II.i.25.A. Second Tithe of fenugreek may be consumed only in its green condition.

As for Heave-offering [of fenugreek]—

The House of Shammai say, "Whatsoever concerns it [is done] in cleanness, save combing [the head] therewith."

And the House of Hillel say, "Whatsoever concerns it [is done] in uncleanness, save the soaking of it."

B. Second Tithe vetches may be consumed only in their green condition and may be brought up to Jerusalem and taken out again.

If they have contracted uncleanness, R. Ṭarfon says, "They should be divided among lumps of dough."

But the sages say, "They should be redeemed.

C. As for Heave-offering [vetches]—

The House of Shammai say, "They soak and rub in cleanness, but they give as food in uncleanness."

And the House of Hillel say, "They soak in cleanness, but they rub and give as food in uncleanness."

Shammai says, "They must be eaten dry."

R. ʿAqiba says, "Whatsoever concerns them [may be done] in uncleanness."

II.i.26.A. The House of Shammai say, "A man may not change his *śelas* for golden *denars*."

And the House of Hillel permit [it].

B. R. ʿAqiba said, "I changed silver for golden *denars* for Rabban Gamaliel and R. Joshua."

C. If a man changes a *śela's* worth of Second Tithe money [outside of Jerusalem]—

The House of Shammai say, "He may change it for a whole *śela*."

And the House of Hillel say, "A *sheqel*'s worth of silver and a *sheqel's* worth in copper coins."

D. R. Meir says, "They may not change silver and produce [together] into [other] silver."

But the sages permit it.

E. If a man would change a *śela* of Second Tithe money in Jerusalem—

The House of Shammai say, "He must change the whole *śela* into copper coins (MʿWT)."

And the House of Hillel say, "He may take one *sheqel's* worth of silver and one *sheqel's* worth in copper coin."

They that made argument before the sages say, "Three *denars'* worth of silver and from the fourth [*denar*] a quarter in copper coin."

R. Ṭarfon says, "Four *aspers* in silver."

Shammai says, "Let him deposit it in a shop and [gradually] consume its value (WY'KL KNGDH)."

[M. M.S. 2:3,4,7,8,9, trans. Danby, p. 75-6 (y. M.S. 2:2,3,4; y. Ter. 3:3; b. B.M. 44b-45a)]

Comment: Before us are discrete pericopae, not a collection. *II.i.25.A* (M. M.S. 2:3) exhibits standard form:

[Fenugreek] heave-offering
House of Shammai say, All its works (MʿSYH) in *cleanness*, except its *combing* (ḤPYPTH)

House of Hillel say, All its works in *uncleanness*, except its *soaking* (ŠRYYTH)

The sayings are thus evenly matched in all respects and the rhythm is identical. Only word-order changes.

The House of Shammai say it is prohibited to make Heave-offering unclean. One must therefore preserve ritual purity in dealing with Heave-offering of *fenugreek*, for it may serve as food. When small and properly cooked, it can be eaten; when full-grown and hardened, it is not eaten, but used as a comb. It would therefore not be subject to the laws of Second Tithe, but Heave-offering still would be given from it. It represents the sort of intermediate situation on which the Houses are apt to dispute—the sort of pattern to suggest that the Houses here serve as (imaginary) authorities to which conveniently to assign the two theoretically possible, diametrically opposed positions.

The Shammaite position is that *only* when the fenugreek is used for combing is it no longer going to be eaten; therefore it need not then be preserved in a state of ritual purity. The House of Hillel regard it as *not* in the category of food *except* when soaked in preparation for eating. The dispute is clear: Is fenugreek to be treated as food, except when it clearly is *not* suitable for eating? Or is it to be treated *not* as food, except when it clearly is suitable for eating? There are no other possible positions. See Tos. M.S. 2:1, below, p. 108.

II.i.25 part B-C (M. M.S. 2:4) is a similar dispute (see above, I, p. 189); here the issue again concerns Heave-offering, this time of vetches. The form is identical:

[Vetches] *Heave-offering*

House of Shammai say: Soaked and rubbed in cleanness, and given as food in uncleanness

House of Hillel say: Soaked in cleanness, and rubbed and given as food in uncleanness.

Vetches may be eaten when soft, but once fully grown, they are fed to cattle. One does not feed Second Tithe to cattle, but Heave-offering may be so used. The Houses once again take the two possible, opposing positions. Since the vetches are not *yet* given to cattle to eat, the Shammaites hold they must be preserved in a state of ritual purity, like other food. Only when given to cattle may they be unclean. The Hillelites rule that only the first stage is in cleanness, the rest in uncleanness. The sayings match in every detail except word-order; the position of *in cleanness* is the sole formal difference.

II.i.26 parts A-B (M. M.S. 2:7) concern changing Second Tithe into coins for the journey to Jerusalem. The Shammaites hold one may not change them for golden *denars*. The Hillelites say the opposite. The form is somewhat complex, for the opinions not only are not matched, but also are not readily reconstructed as a syzygy:

[As to changing] *selas* [of Second Tithe] *to denars of gold:*
House of Shammai: Prohibit
House of Hillel: Permit

But the transition from the language now attributed to the Shammaites to the above is not simple. Normally it is easy to extract the general rule from the first House's opinion [Shammaites] and to restore it as a superscription. But here one must drop *a man may not change*, which is part of the substance of the Shammaite position, and it is difficult to imagine the rest without it.

Part B, the testimony of ʿAqiba, tells us that the early Yavneans followed Hillelite practice. Is Shammaite practice so widespread that the deeds of the early authorities supply important contrary evidence? Unlikely, since no one made the pilgrimage any more. Does ʿAqiba intend to make it clear that the early Yavneans followed Hillelite practice? But who suspected the contrary? Everyone "knew" that the law follows the Hillelites. Perhaps the chronological order of the pericope's elements therefore ought to be reversed. Possibly, opinions of the Houses survived, but no one was quite sure which opinion was to be attributed to which House. ʿAqiba's testimony made it clear that the dominant—Hillelite—opinion was that one *may* change silver for golden *denars*. Then comes the formulation of the dispute. The record of part B was preserved, owing to the conservatism of the tradents, along with part A, which must, therefore, postdate ʿAqiba. It is also possible that no opinions of the Houses derived from pre-ʿAqiban times, but that those holding the opposite opinion from his were relegated to the position of the House of Shammai, in a redaction of the matter in the form of a (fictitious) Houses-dispute. The former alternative seems to me somewhat more likely.

Parts C-D (M. M.S. 2:8) is a related, but separate, pericope. The exchange is copper coins of Second Tithe for a *śela* of silver for the journey to Jerusalem. If the man has copper coins worth a whole *śela*, he is permitted to make the exchange, according to the House of Shammai. But if he has copper coins for only half a *śela*, and for the other half he has a *sheqel*, that is, half a *śela*, of silver of Second Tithe, he may not exchange them all together for a whole *śela* of silver, for one may not exchange the silver of Second Tithe for silver (Albeck, *Seder Zeraʿim*, pp. 252-3). The House of Hillel say one may indeed exchange a *sheqel* of silver and a *sheqel* of copper coins for a *śela* of silver; since he is giving copper coins for half, it is permitted to change the silver as part of the transaction.

The dispute of Meir and the sages is along the same lines, only now it is silver and produce for a *śela*; the Hillelite ruling applied only to copper coins and silver, not to produce and silver. The sages extend the Hillelite leniency even further.

Part E (M. M.S. 2:9) brings the repertoire to a conclusion. Now the man is in Jerusalem with his large coin, and requires small change again. The House of Shammai say he must change the whole thing to copper coins, since one may exchange in Jerusalem only silver for copper, but not copper for silver, and not silver for silver. The House of Hillel say that since he is changing silver for copper, he may also change silver for silver as part of the transaction. The other positions are of no interest here. Parts C and E (M. M.S. 2:8 and 9) follow the same form:

If a man changes a coin's worth of Second Tithe money
House of Shammai say: All the *ṡela*—coins
House of Hillel say: A *sheqel* of silver, and a *sheqel* of coins.

If a man would change a ṡela of Second Tithe in Jerusalem
House of Shammai say: All the *ṡela*—coins
House of Hillel say: A *sheqel* of silver and a *sheqel* of coins.

Thus in both instances, the Houses are given the same opinions, phrased in exactly the same words. If the Houses' opinions are accurately represented, they then are placed into the context of two different disputes. It again seems that the tradents had difficulty not only in attributing the right opinion to the right House, but also in figuring out to what legal problem the opinions actually pertained.

Part D is added to part C. The later opinions of part E are all tacked on as well. That does not mean that the several authorities (including Shammai, above, I, p. 190) came later than the Houses, knew their opinions, and disregarded them. On the contrary, it would suggest that the Houses' opinions had not yet been redacted and may not have existed. One can hardly fix the rule that where later masters differ from Houses' rulings, it was because they did not know those rulings, and therefore the rulings presumably did not exist, but were formulated afterward and attributed to the Houses. This would, however, seem likely when, as in this instance, the masters not only make no reference to the Houses' opinions, but also use quite different language for their own. It further conforms to my suggestion about the formulation of the Houses' opinions *after* ʿAqiba.

If so, one must wonder why the laws about bringing Second Tithe money to Jerusalem were under debate when Jews could not make the pilgrimage to the Temple in Jerusalem. Was there no earlier tradition on the subject? Why formulate the law now that it was no longer a serious consideration? As to the former, it looks either as if the earlier common law was unknown to the rabbis (highly unlikely), or as if there was no law on the subject at all. As to the latter, the rabbis certainly expected Jerusalem to be rebuilt and the rite of pilgrimage with Second Tithe money to be restored, so they legislated for that time, which, they fully expected, could not be long postponed. It was part of their broader effort to ensure through proper observance of the whole Torah that the future Temple would not suffer the fate of the last one, when, manifestly, the whole Torah had not been observed.

On M. M.S. 2:8-9, Epstein, *Mevo'ot*, pp. 76-77, 216; on M. M.S. 2:4, p. 273: p. 73: ʿAqiba's Hillelites of Tos. M.S. 2:1 are in M. M.S. 2:4 as the anonymous authority. See also Epstein, *Mishnah*, p. 487.

II.i.27.A. Produce that was fully harvested and passed through Jerusalem, the Second Tithe thereof must be brought back again and consumed in Jerusalem.

B. If it was not yet fully harvested, [such as] grapes [that are carried] in baskets to the winepress, or figs in baskets to the drying-place)—

The House of Shammai say, "The Second Tithe thereof must come back and be consumed in Jerusalem." (MS Kaufmann: YḤZWR *WYTRWM* M'SR ŠNY ŠLHM WY'KL. . . = *He* should return and *raise up* their Second Tithe etc.).

And the House of Hillel say, "It may be redeemed and eaten anywhere."

C. R. Simeon b. Judah in the name of R. Yosi says, "The House of Shammai and the House of Hillel did not dispute about produce that was not fully harvested, whose Second Tithe can be redeemed and eaten anywhere. But about what did they dispute?

"About produce that *was* fully harvested—

"For (Š) the House of Shammai say, 'The Second Tithe thereof must come back and be consumed in Jerusalem [= part A].'

"And the House of Hillel say, 'It may be redeemed and eaten anywhere.' "

And *demai*-[produce] may be brought in and taken out again and may be redeemed.

D. [If] a tree stands within [the wall of Jerusalem] and [its boughs] stretch outside, or stands outside and [its boughs] stretch within, [the part of the foliage] directly above the wall and inwards is deemed within [Jerusalem], and the part directly above the wall and outwards is deemed outside.

E. [If] the entrances to olive-presses [in the city wall] were within [Jerusalem] and their contained space (ḤLLN) outside, or their entrances outside and their contained space within [Jerusalem]—

The House of Shammai say, "The whole [is deemed] as within [Jerusalem]."

And the House of Hillel say, "The part directly above the wall and inwards [is deemed] as within and the part directly above the wall and outwards [is deemed] as outside."

II.i.28. If Second Tithe was brought into Jerusalem and contracted uncleanness, whether from a Father of Uncleanness or from an Offspring of Uncleanness, whether within or without [the wall of Jerusalem]—

The House of Shammai say, "All should be redeemed and consumed within [the walls], excepting only what was rendered unclean by a Father of Uncleanness—without [the walls]."

And the House of Hillel say, "All should be redeemed and consumed outside [the walls], excepting only what was rendered unclean by an Offspring of Uncleanness—within [the walls]."

II.i.29. The House of Shammai say, "[If he would give Heave-offering from one on behalf of all after he has sealed them up], he opens [the jars] and empties [them] into the winepress."

And the House of Hillel say, "He opens [them], but he need not empty them."

[M. M.S. 3:6,7,9,13, trans. Danby, pp. 77-8 (y. Maʿaserot 3:4; y. M.S. 3:3,4,5,6; b. Mak. 20a)]

Comment: II.i.27: Parts A, B, C, (M. M.S. 3:6), concern bringing back to Jerusalem for consumption in the city Second Tithe which once has passed through. The produce now cannot be redeemed for coins.

The first version of the Houses' dispute concerns produce which was *not* fully harvested and passed through Jerusalem, for instance, grapes brought to the vat and olives to the press. The House of Shammai say that the Second Tithe must be brought back and eaten in Jerusalem, and the House of Hillel say that the Second Tithe may be redeemed for coins and consumed anywhere, and (of course) the coins must be brought back to the city. The dispute therefore places the Houses at the two possible, opposing poles. What is the rule for produce whose harvest procedures are still in progress? It is either like produce whose procedures have been completed (Shammaites), or like produce whose harvest procedures have *not* been undertaken, so far as the trip through Jerusalem is concerned (Hillelites). The form poses no difficulties:

Produce not fully harvested: The Second Tithe in it

House of Shammai: *Returns* and eaten in *Jerusalem.*
House of Hillel: Is *redeemed* and eaten *anywhere.*

The rulings can be restored to the form of balanced opposites, in the conventional form (1) ḤZR (2) ʾKL (3) BYRWŠLM vs. (1) PDH (2) ʾKL (3) BKL MQWM. Thus (1) is a matched opposite, also (3); in both instances we find the same number of syllables. (2) is the same in both parts. (MS Kaufmann adds YTRWM to the Shammaite ruling, but this does *not* recur in its version of Yosi's Shammaites.)

In part C, R. Yosi, as before, supplies a quite different version of the dispute. Both Houses agree that the produce is treated like ordinary fruit outside of the city—that is, they agree on the Hillelite position. They differ as follows:

Produce that has been *fully harvested: The Second Tithe in it*—
House of Shammai: *Returns* and is eaten in *Jerusalem*
House of Hillel: Is *redeemed* and eaten *anywhere.*

So Yosi has repeated the same rulings, but attached them to a different superscription. Yosi's superscription now serves for the whole pericope, according to the antecedent (anonymous) tradent, as part A. Following him, the parties agree on the position attributed by Yosi to the Shammaites; he thus has made the Hillelites into Yosi's Shammaites.

The difference between Yosi and the anonymous tradent concerns whether the word *not* occurs in the superscription of the Houses-dispute. Otherwise—excluding the gloss about grapes and olives—the two versions are identical, both in superscriptions and in the body of the Houses-dispute. Yosi's tradition obviously did not include *the Houses did not dispute*—that is his own. It consisted, as I said, of a slightly different superscription, but of identical opinions. The anonymous tradition (parts A-B) comes before Yosi. Whether he himself then revised it for reasons of his own, or whether he actually had a tradition such as we have reconstructed, of course no one can say (see Tos. M.S. 2:11). Middle-second-century masters were quite well prepared to revise Houses-materials according to their own understanding of either the law or of "history," probably the former, and to present as authentic Houses' disputes what in fact were their own fabrications.

II.i.29: Parts D and E (M. M.S. 3:7) present legal issues that could not have affected many people even while Jerusalem flourished. They are the kind of legal theorizing about intermediate, ambiguous categories, of which the sages seemed so fond. The rule of part A is clearcut and decisive; all parties agree. The tree is regarded as entirely within Jerusalem; therefore one must eat the produce in Jerusalem and may not redeem it for coins. The Houses-dispute then introduces a more difficult matter, namely, olive presses in a similar state. The practical difference is whether the olive-oil must be consumed in the city or may be redeemed for coins.

The theoretical problem obviously is going to be more interesting. It concerns a crop, work on which is completed (therefore making it liable to tithes) *partly* in Jerusalem and *partly* outside the city—the third possible state already introduced in II.i.25, parts A-B:

A. Fully harvested and passed through Jerusalem
B. Not yet fully harvested and passed through Jerusalem
C. Not yet fully harvested and not fully through/in Jerusalem when the work is completed.

—that is, the most ambiguous situation of all.

The Shammaite ruling (following the formulation of parts A-B) is that the whole is regarded as having been done in Jerusalem; therefore the laws of Jerusalem apply. This remains their position throughout. The Hillelites rule that one must determine which part of the crop will be subjected to which law. The language of the House of Hillel is identical with the tree-ruling of part D. Had a ruling been preserved, the House of Shammai would have ruled that the tree should be seen as unambiguously within Jerusalem, because part of it was there. M. M.S. 3:8 thus stands within the Hillelite tradition.

The whole complex looks suspicious. To be sure, the historical Houses may indeed have debated such theoretical legal problems. But the reappearance of the same words in opinions on quite different matters, the fabrication by later authorities of revised versions of the entire dispute, and the absence of a Houses-dispute on part D, where the appearance of the Hillelite opinion of part E *verbatim* would suggest the Shammaite contrary opinion, also *verbatim*, ought to have been given—all suggest that what we have is a fabrication in the Houses' names (and not fully worked out) of a later, theoretical dispute. This further points to the persistence of the Houses-form after the Houses ceased to exist.

II.i.28, M. M.S. 3:9, continues the theme of Second Tithe in Jerusalem. The tithe has come to the city but has been made unclean. The dispute now is complicated by two different degrees of uncleanness. The Father of Uncleanness is an insect or a corpse. An Offspring of Uncleanness is something made unclean by touching a Father of Uncleanness, therefore itself of lesser uncleanness. As in Sifra the superscription is impossible, since it announces that the Houses will *not* make such distinctions, and these distinctions then constitute the heart of their disagreement.

The distinction on where the uncleanness took place—en route to Jerusalem or in the city—does not figure in the Houses' dispute, so that element of the superscription is accurate. But not entirely so, since the superscription begins, . . .*entered Jerusalem and made unclean* and then adds the qualification, *whether within or without*. It looks to me as if the superscription has been doctored. Let us present what might have been the earliest version of the dispute:

Second Tithe that entered Jerusalem and was made unclean (in Jerusalem)
House of Shammai: [All is redeemed, and consumed] *inside* [the city]
House of Hillel: [All is redeemed and consumed] *outside* [the city].

The Houses-dispute therefore resolves itself into the words *inside/outside*. Nothing more is required. The place and source of the uncleanness play no role whatever. The *whether*-clauses are an accurate gloss on the foregoing. The Houses-rulings are simple and unambiguous, no matter the circumstances.

Our earlier discomfort at the contradiction of the *whether inside/outside*, *whether Father/Offspring*, however, was not without cause, for *inside/outside* is either redundant of the simple *was made unclean*, or contradicts it. The *whether*-clauses therefore must be glosses supplied after the revision of the Houses-sayings themselves, to represent the dispute as it originally had taken place, contrary to the intrusions of the later glossator; so comes the second stage:

Second Tithe that entered Jerusalem and was made unclean
House of Shammai: All redeemed and eaten *inside* + (except that which was made unclean by a Father of Uncleanness [which is eaten] outside)

House of Hillel: All redeemed and eaten *outside* + (except that which was made unclean by an Offspring of Uncleanness [which is eaten] inside).

The issue has not only been made more complex, but new problems have been introduced. The Houses-positions preserve fixed differences throughout.

As to the position of the Shammaites, Second Tithe which has been made unclean is redeemed even in Jerusalem. It nonetheless is prohibited to bring in the food which has been redeemed outside of the city. But food made unclean by a major source of uncleanness *and* which has entered Jerusalem may be taken out again and eaten outside (so Albeck, *Seder Zera'im*, p. 257). So the intrusion of *Father/Offspring* has necessarily required the introduction of *unclean* + *inside/outside*. The Hillelite position is that the whole is redeemed and taken outside, except what is made unclean by an Offspring of Uncleanness in *Jerusalem* —thus introducing *in the city* to go along with *Offspring*. And the rest follows: he eats in Jerusalem and may not take it out.

Thus the distinction of *Father/Offspring* brings in its wake the distinction about *where* the uncleanness happened. The contradictory superscription is then completed and added to the whole, denying that the Houses had made such distinctions! Presumably the authority who glossed the superscription would also have dropped the *except*-clauses. Some sort of compromise or misunderstanding preserved both the gloss and the *except*-clauses. And that is how it comes down to us.

Did the Houses originally rule on the matter? Or was the whole the creation of the later legal theorists? Tos. M.S. 2:16 definitively answers the question: Judah b. Ilai is the source. The brevity of the Houses' language and the ease with which we could recognize the original dispute do not constitute probative evidence of an authentic attribution to the Houses themselves, since, as we have seen several times, the later tradents were quite capable of making disciplined use of the form for their own fabrications.

II.i.29 (M. M.S. 3:13) has Houses-opinions but no explanatory matter. This is supplied by Danby, in brackets added to the Shammaite opinion. The antecedent case, in which the Houses do not appear, is taken for granted:

> If wine was designated Heave-offering before the jars were sealed up [and they were confused with others], they are neutralized in a hundred and one. But if they were later sealed up, they render holy [others with which they are confused] in any quantity whatsoever.
>
> Until he has sealed them up, he may give Heave-offering from one on behalf of all; but after he has sealed them up, he must give Heave-offering from each singly.
>
> (M. M.S. 3:12b, trans. Danby, p. 78)

Now the Houses-dispute appears. If the man has sealed them and then wants to give Heave-offering, how does he give Heave-offering from each? The House of Shammai say he has to open the jars and empty them all back into the winepress. The House of Hillel say he must open them but need not empty them. The Houses' language is as follows:

House of Shammai:	Open and empty into vat
House of Hillel:	Open but *does* not *need* to empty

The language seems to me to conform to convention; it is abbreviated and preserves the difference between the Houses in a brief clause. Perhaps the Hillelite form might be simplified: Open, but does *not* empty; and the Shammaites' language might be simplified by dropping *into vat*. But these little glosses (*need*, *into vat*) do not make much difference.

What is difficult is the reconstruction of an appropriate superscription. The issue is not set by the foregoing, which concerns a mixture of Heave-offering with other *jars*. Perhaps the final clause of M. M.S. 3:12 would serve:

After he has sealed them, he gives Heave-offering from each one [with *how does he do so* being understood]:

House of Shammai:	He opens and empties [them] (into the vat).
House of Hillel:	He opens and does not need to empty [or, he opens and *does not empty*, dropping ṢRYK)

If so, the editors (or scribes) have erred in splitting the Houses-dispute from the foregoing paragraph.

II.i.30.A. If a man set aside one *issar* [as Second Tithe redemption-money] and in virtue of this consumed half its value and then went elsewhere where it was worth a *pondion*, he can still consume another *issar's* worth.

If he set aside one *pondion* and in virtue of this consumed half its value and then went elsewhere where it was worth [only] one *issar*, he may consume only another half-*issar's* worth.

If he set aside one *issar* as Second Tithe redemption money, he may in virtue of this consume up to one-eleventh of an *issar's* worth [if it was *demai*-produce] and one-hundredth of an *issar's* worth [if it was produce certainly untithed].

B. The House of Shammai say, "In either case one-tenth (HKL ʿSRH)."

And the House of Hillel say, "One eleventh [if it was produce] certainly untithed, and one-tenth if it was *demai*-produce (BWDʾY ʾḤD ʿSR, WBDMʾY ʿSRH)."

[M. M.S. 4:8, trans. Danby, p. 79 (y. M.S. 4:5)]

Comment: Albeck (*Seder Zera'im*, p. 261) explains that the variation in the value of the coin imposes the necessity of adding when consuming the food. The House of Shammai say there is no need to add. The House of Hillel say, as in the anonymous rule, one adds one-eleventh or one-tenth, depending on the state of the produce. So part A anonymously presents the Hillelite view, which then, in part B, occurs in dispute-form.

II.i.31.A. The House of Shammai say, "The rules of the [Added] Fifth and of Removal do not apply to [the grapes of] a Fourth Year Vineyard."

And the House of Hillel say, "They do apply."

B. The House of Shammai say, "The laws of grape-gleanings and of the defective cluster apply, and the poor redeem the grapes for themselves."

And the House of Hillel say, "The whole [yield goes] to the winepress."

II.i.32. [On the eve of the first Festival-day of Passover in the fourth and seventh years the duty of Removal was fulfilled. Thus Heave-offering and Heave-offering of Tithe were given to whom they were due, and the First Tithe was given to whom it was due, and the Second Tithe and the First-fruits everywhere were removed. R. Simeon says, "The First-fruits like the Heave-offering were given to the priests."]

Cooked food—

The House of Shammai say, "One must remove it."

And the House of Hillel say, "It is accounted a thing removed [already]" (ṢRYK LB'R vs. HRY HW' KMB'R).

II.i.33. If a man had produce at this time and the season (Š'T) came for Removal—

The House of Shammai say, "He must redeem it with money (ṢRYK LḤLLN 'L HKŚP)."

And the House of Hillel say, "It is all one whether it is in the form of produce or of money ('ḤD ŠHN KŚP W'ḤD ŠHN PRWT)."

[M. M.S. 5:3,6,7, trans. Danby, p. 80-1 (y. M.S. 5:2,3)]

Comment: II.i.31, M. M.S. 5:3—see above, p. 59.

*II.i.*32, M. M.S. 5:6, adds a Houses-dispute to a minor detail in connection with the duty of Removal. The form is nearly perfect, statement of law, Houses opinions:

As to cooked food [of Second Tithe]
House of Shammai say, He needs to remove
House of Hillel say, Lo, it is as if it were removed.

Actually, we should have expected the Hillelite language to be a counterpart to the Shammaite:

House of Hillel: He does *not* need to remove.

This *is* the language of y. M.S. 5:3 (ed. Gilead, p. 62). The lemma before us thus takes for granted that ruling and explains it, therefore is a secondary development: He does not need to remove it *because* it is as if it were removed: the fruits are no longer before us in their original form.

II.i.33, M. M.S. 5:7, follows the same form, and the language is similarly not quite balanced. After the Temple was destroyed, Second-Tithe produce could no longer be brought to, and eaten in, Jerusalem. What to do with it at the time of removal? The House of Shammai rule that one has to exchange it for coins. But this does not solve the matter, for the coins will remain in his hand. The House of Hillel rule that whether they are coins or produce, the Second Tithe is under the same law: The man does not need to exchange the produce for money, but he removes the fruit from the house and leaves it until it rots. This is the same ruling as M. M.S. 1:5, "If no sanctuary, they are left to rot," a ruling given for produce that for *any* reason cannot be brought to Jerusalem.

The classic form is followed, but the traditions of the Houses do not compare to one another:

He who has produce in this time and the hour or removal has come—
The House of Shammai say, He needs to profane them by money
The House of Hillel say, It is all the same [Lit.: One that they are] for money and produce.

The opinions therefore are not matched, and the problem of what to do *with the money* is not solved.

The Houses in their pre-Destruction form presumably did not persist for long at Yavneh. But this issue ought to have come up at once. On the other hand, Yoḥanan b. Zakkai ignores the problem. Simeon b. Eleazar alleged that Yoḥanan b. Zakkai annulled the practice of setting aside a quarter-coin for the proselyte's offering, on the basis of M.M.S. 5:2: "One does not declare holy, or to be evaluated, or declare *ḥerem*, or raise up Heave-offering and Tithes. . ." M. Yad. 4:3 raised the question of the tithes to be given by Ammon and Moab in the Seventh Year. The participants are Ṭarfon, Eleazar b. ʿAzariah and Ishmael. The vote is taken that the countries should give Poorman's Tithe in the Seventh Year, rather than Second Tithe. Then Eliezer b. Hyrcanus announces that Yoḥanan b. Zakkai taught him a tradition, deriving from Sinai, that Ammon and Moab give Poorman's Tithe in the Seventh Year. It is quite clear, therefore, that the later Yavneans supposed tithes would continue to be separated, not only in Palestine, and that Yoḥanan b. Zakkai similarly supposed the destruction had made no difference. This seems to me decisive evidence that the dispute of the Houses follows a period in which it was unanimously assumed tithes would continue to be given. The Shammaites of II.i.30-31, who assume the law continues to apply, represent the earliest view of the Yavneans. The Hillelites, who regard the various laws of tithing as annulled, take a position that became dominant only later on, and is now represented by M. M.S. 5:2. So the dispute must formulate in the names of the Houses opinions which only afterward were accepted.

Why should Yavneans and Ushans have continued to make use of the dispute-form? Perhaps in the very earliest period no other seemed appropriate. Contrasting opinions of living masters, rather than of the old Houses, required the recognition both that the new masters had the authority to differ on their own, not merely pseudepigraphically in the names of the ancient authorities; and that the authority of the Shammaites would no longer be recognized, so anyone who hoped to be taken seriously had better not attribute his opinion to the Shammaite House at all. At the outset the masters persisted in using the forms they knew from Jerusalem, but later on abandoned sole reliance on them, as either outdated or inappropriate, and alongside the old forms developed new ones. The necessity to attribute opinions to established Houses or parties diminished, and the practice of giving opinions to named authorities began.

The facts that as late as the middle of the second century new Houses-disputes were still being fabricated and that the form was still in use suggest that, despite the predominance of Hillelites, the old forms, reflecting a quite different state of affairs, continued to serve the purposes of tradents.

On M. M.S. 5:3, see Epstein, *Mevo'ot*, p. 103, and compare M. Ter. 3:9, Tos. Ter. 2:13—*Vineyard* becomes *planting*.

II.ii.23.A. [Fenugreek] of Heave-offering—

"The House of Shammai say, 'Whatsoever concerns it must be done in cleanness.'

"And the House of Hillel say, 'Whatsoever concerns it may be done in uncleanness, except for combing [the head] therewith' "—

the words of R. Meir.

B. R. Judah says, "The House of Shammai say, 'Whatsoever concerns it must be done in cleanness, except for combing [the head] with it.'

"And the House of Hillel say, 'Whatsoever concerns it must be done in uncleanness, except for soaking it.' "

C. [Vetches] of Heave-offering—

"The House of Shammai say, 'They are soaked in cleanness, and rubbed and given as food in uncleanness.'

"And the House of Hillel say, 'They must be soaked and rubbed in cleanness, and given as food in uncleanness' "—

the words of R. Judah.

D. R. Meir says, "The House of Shammai say, 'They must be soaked and rubbed in cleanness, and given as food in uncleanness.'

"And the House of Hillel say, 'Whatsoever concerns them must be done in uncleanness.' "

E. R. Yosi said, "This is the Mishnah of R. 'Aqiba. Therefore he says, 'They are to be given to any priest [even an unobservant one].'

"And the sages did not agree with him."

[Tos. M.S. 2:1, ed. Lieberman, pp. 248-9, lines 3-10 (y. M.S. 2:2)]

Comment: See above, M. M.S. 2:3-4, II.i.23A-C. Judah the Patriarch evidently had the versions supplied by Judah and Meir, and chose Judah's for M. M.S. 2:3, but the version of neither for part B. Judah gives the opinion of the House of Hillel as that of Shammai's House in Part C, and the opinion of Shammai's House as that of the House of Hillel. Meir in part D gives the opinion of Shammai as Judah the Patriarch does in M. M.S. 2:4, but then Meir's view of the Hillelite position is rejected by Judah the Patriarch:

M. M.S. 2:3 *Judah the Patriarch*	*Tos. M.S. 2:1* *Meir*	*Tos. M.S. 2:1* *Judah b. Ilai*
Shammai: All in cleanness except combing	All in cleanness	All in cleanness except combing
Hillel: All in uncleanness except soaking	All in uncleanness, except combing	All in uncleanness except soaking
M. M.S. 2:4		
Shammai: Soaked and rubbed in cleanness, and fed in uncleanness	Soaked and rubbed in cleanness, and fed in uncleanness	Soaked in cleanness, rubbed and fed in uncleanness
Hillel: Soaked in cleanness, and rubbed and fed in uncleanness	Whatsoever concerns it must be done in uncleanness	Soaked and rubbed in cleanness, fed in uncleanness.

So, as I said, in M. M.S. 2:3 Judah the Patriarch has given the version of Judah b. Ilai. In M. M.S. 2:4, he has given Meir's version of Shammai's opinion and Judah's view of Shammai's opinion as *Hillel's* ruling! Judah and Meir have diametrically opposite views of the opinions of the Houses on the heave-offering of vetches.

The foregoing proves that the Houses' disputes in this connection are based upon dubious traditions, if any. What seems likely is that no one knew precisely what the Houses had said. Each party formulated the extremes as he saw them and attributed them to the Houses. That no authorities had accurate traditions on the matter is probably because the Houses never produced any.

See Epstein, *Mevo'ot*, pp. 73, 90, 303.

II.ii.24.A. R. Simeon b. Judah said in the name of R. Yosah, "Thus the House of Hillel said to the House of Shammai, 'Do you not agree about produce that was not fully harvested, that, if the Second Tithe is redeemed, it should not be eaten in any place [but only in Jerusalem]? Also produce whose harvest has been completed is like it (Lit.: them).' "

B. "The House of Shammai said to them, 'No, if you say so concerning produce whose harvest has not been completed, [it is] because he can declare them ownerless property to remove them [entirely] from the [obligations for] Heave-offering and Tithes [since they are not yet liable]. [y. M.S. 3:3:] Will you say so of produce whose harvest has been completed, which he cannot declare ownerless and so free from Tithes?'

C. "The House of Hillel said to them, 'Also produce whose harvest *has* been completed—he can make it [them] Heave-Offering and Tithes for [produce in] another place.' [y. M.S. 3:3: He can declare them ownerless and free them from Tithes.]

D. " 'Another matter: They are not liable for Heave-Offering and Tithes until they have been lifted up.' "

[That is, until the Tithes have been removed, the owner has no liability whatsoever and can burn the crop if he wants, and therefore the walls of Jerusalem have not affected the Tithes inhering therein one way or the other, there being no *present* obligation for such Tithes.]

[y. M.S. 3:3: The House of Shammai said to them, "No, if you say so concerning produce whose harvest has not been completed, for which he can bring out Second (Tithe) from another place, will you say so of produce whose harvest has been completed, for which he cannot (etc.)?"]

[Tos. M.S. 2:11, ed. Lieberman, pp. 252-3, lines 55-62 (y. M.S. 3:3,6)]

II.ii.25.A. Olive presses whose doors open inward [in the city] and their contained space outside, or whose doors open outward and contained space inward—

B. The House of Shammai say, "They do not redeem in them Second Tithe, as if they were within, and they do not eat in them lesser sanctities, as if they were outside."

And the House of Hillel say, "The part directly above the wall and inwards is deemed within, and the part directly above the wall and outwards is deemed outside."

C. R. Yosah said, "This is the Mishnah of R. ʿAqiba.

"The first Mishnah:

"The House of Shammai say, 'They do not redeem in them Second Tithe as if they were within, and they do not eat in them lesser sanctities, as if they were outside.'

"And the House of Hillel say, 'Lo, they are like the [Temple] chambers. That whose door opens inward is deemed inside, and that whose door opens outward is deemed outside.' "

[Tos. M.S. 2:12, ed. Lieberman, pp. 253-4, lines 65-72 (Tos. ʿArakh. 5:15)]

Comment: II.i.24, Tos. M.S. 2:11, relates to M. M.S. 3:6, and II.i.25, Tos. M.S. 2:12, to M. M.S. 3:7, above, pp. 100-105.

In M. M.S. 3:6, Simeon b. Judah alleges in R. Yosi's name that the Houses did not dispute concerning produce whose harvest was not completed. All agreed, he said, that the Second Tithe inhering in them should be redeemed and the produce might be eaten anywhere. Now we have Simeon's expansion of the version of the dispute he presents in the Mishnah: produce whose harvest *has* been completed. The Shammaites hold that the Second Tithe must be brought back to Jerusalem, and the Hillelites, that it may be redeemed for money and eaten anywhere (and the money must be brought to Jerusalem, as usual).

The argument of Hillelites in part A is that just as the coins exchanged for the produce *not* fully harvested must be brought to Jerusalem, and the produce may be eaten anywhere (on which Simeon and Yosi allege the House agree), so the same rule pertains to produce *fully* harvested. The Hillelites' argument is rejected by the Shammaites, who introduce a distinction (part B) to show why the same rule cannot pertain to the harvest in both circumstances. That which has not been completed may in the end *never* be subject to the agricultural tithes, while that which has been completed is thereby already subject to the Tithes. Lieberman (= y. M.S. 3:3) supplies the following text for part C:

"Also produce whose harvest has been completed—he can declare them ownerless property."

'Another matter: The House of Shammai said to them, 'No, if you say so concerning produce whose harvest has not been completed, that he can declare them Heave-offering and Tithes for [produce in] another place, will you say concerning produce whose harvest has been completed that he declare them Heave-offering and Tithes for [produce in] another place?' "

As to the argument of part D, Lieberman explains (*Tosefta Kifshuṭah*, p. 739 to line 62) that the owner is not liable to the priest and Levite for Heave-offering and Tithes until he raises up and separates from the untithed mass the Heave-offering and Tithes. The owner can burn the wheat, without profiting from it, if he wishes.

For our purposes, it suffices to note that Simeon and Yosi have supplied a fabricated colloquy to spell out what is at issue in the Mishnaic passage. Judah the Patriarch selected the substitute version for the Mishnah, and left for the supplementary collection, without the appropriate superscription, the remaining elements of the Simeon-Yosi fabrication.

II.ii.25 corresponds to M. M.S. 3:7:

If the entrance to olive-presses in the city wall was within, and the contained space outside, or vice versa—

House of Shammai: The whole is deemed within

House of Hillel: The part directly above the wall and inwards is deemed within, the part directly above the wall and outwards is deemed outside.

According to part B the opinion of the Hillelites is the same as in the Mishnah. But that of the Shammaites here is much more complex.

The Tosefta explains the opinion of the House of Shammai. They did not say that all is deemed as within *except* to effect the more stringent of the possible rulings. One may not redeem Second Tithe therein, just as in Jerusalem one may not do so. But one may not eat lesser sanctities therein, just as outside of Jerusalem one may not do so. The Hillelite ruling is therefore clarified: What is like Jerusalem enjoys the prerogatives of Jerusalem in all respects, and contrarywise as well. Therefore one may eat lesser sanctities and Second Tithe. What is not like Jerusalem is likewise not like Jerusalem in all respects: one may there redeem Second Tithe.

R. Yosah then tells us that this is the version of ʿAqiba. Before him, we had a somewhat different form. In it the House of Shammai's opinion is unchanged. But that of the Hillelites comes in quite different language, although the meaning seems the same. That is, what is deemed inside still enjoys all the prerogatives of being in the city, and what is deemed outside likewise. This follows M. M.S. 3:8:

In the chambers built in the Temple and opening into ground that was not holy, no sanctity attached to the space within them, but their roofs are deemed to be within holy ground.

. . .in those built both within the Temple court and on ground that was not holy and opening both into the Temple and into ground that was not holy, [then in what concerns] the space within them and their roofs, directly above the Temple [court] and inwards toward the Temple is holy, and directly above the Temple and outward toward ground that is not holy is not holy.

(M. M.S. 3:8, trans. Danby, p. 77)

Accordingly, one follows the direction of the door and contained space. If the door (etc.) is toward one direction, the law of the place follows that side in all respects. Thus the Hillelite rule remains the same, but the language in which it was framed is different.

Once again we have a *terminus ante quem* for a tradition. But the forms of the tradition are various and complicated. Clearly, a Houses-dispute was set by the time of R. ʿAqiba. But the *form* of ʿAqiba is somewhat different from that of M. M.S. 3:7. The House of Shammai is unchanged in the two versions—and *different* from the opinion attributed to them in the Mishnah! The House of Hillel is changed in form, though not in substance, and also differs in form, though not in substance, from the Mishnah in the latter version. For the House of Hillel, Judah the Patriarch has selected the ʿAqiban version. But we do not know where he got his version of the Shammaites' opinion. What came before ʿAqiba? It is difficult to say. My guess is that this is not the sort of pericope one can readily date to pre-70 times. First, it is complex in form. Second, in the face of attributions to later authorities, one had best not seek earlier sources, surely not among pre-Yavnean traditions. It once again looks as if an existing form has been used for new materials.

Note Epstein, *Mevo'ot*, p. 78.

II.ii.26.A. Second Tithe which entered Jerusalem and became unclean, whether it was made unclean by a Father of Uncleanness or by an Offspring of Uncleanness, whether within the city or outside—

B. "The House of Shammai say, 'All will be redeemed and eaten within.'

"And the House of Hillel say, 'All will be redeemed and eaten within, except for that which has been made unclean by a Father of Uncleanness [and which is eaten] outside' "—

The words of R. Meir.

C. R. Judah says, "The House of Shammai say, 'All will be redeemed and eaten within, except for that which is made unclean by a Father of Uncleanness [which is eaten] outside.'

"And the House of Hillel say, 'All will be redeemed and eaten outside, except for that which is made unclean by an Offspring of Uncleanness [which is eaten] inside.' "

D. R. Leazar says, "If it was made unclean by a Father of Uncleanness, whether inside or outside, it will be redeemed and eaten outside. If it is made unclean by an Offspring of Uncleanness, whether inside or outside, it will be redeemed and eaten inside."

E. R. ʿAqiba says, "If it is made unclean outside, whether by a Father of Uncleanness or by an Offspring of Uncleanness, it will be redeemed and eaten outside. If it is made unclean within, whether by a Father of Uncleanness or by an Offspring of Uncleanness, it will be redeemed and eaten within."

F. R. Simeon b. Leazar said, "The House of Shammai and the House of Hillel did not dispute concerning that which was made unclean by a Father of Uncleanness outside, that it should be redeemed and eaten outside.

"And concerning that which was made unclean by an Offspring of Uncleanness within, that it should be redeemed and eaten within.

"Concerning what did they debate?

"Concerning that which was made unclean by a Father of Uncleanness inside, and concerning [that which was made unclean] by an Offspring of Uncleanness outside, for

"The House of Shammai say, 'It will be redeemed in the place [where it was made unclean] and eaten in the place [where it was made unclean].'

"And the House of Hillel say, 'It is redeemed in the place and eaten in *every* place.' "

(Tos. M.S. 2:16, ed. Lieberman, pp. 255-6, lines 87-101)

Comment: The relationship to M. M.S. 3:9 is clear:

Judah the Patriarch (M. M.S. 3:9)	*Meir*	*Judah b. Ilai*	*Leazar*	*ʿAqiba*	*Simeon b. Leazar*
1. Whether made unclean by a Father of Uncleanness or by an Offspring of Uncleanness	1. „ „ „	1. —	1. — Unclean by Father of Unleanness	1. — Unclean outside	1. Father/outside—outside. Offspring/inside—inside
2. Whether within or without	2. „ „ „	2. —	2. „ „ „	2. — Whether by Father of Offspring	2. —

Judah the Patriarch	*Meir*	*Judah b. Ilai*	*Leazar*	*'Aqiba*	*Simeon b. Leazar*
3. House of Shammai: All will be redeemed and eaten inside	3. „ „ „	3. „ „ „	3. —	3. —	3. —
4. Except what is made unclean by a Father of Uncleanness outside [that it is eaten outside]	4. —	4. „ „ „	4. —	4. —	4. Father/inside and Offspring/outside
4.*—	4.*—		4.* Redeemed and eaten outside	4.* „ „ „	4.* Shammai: Redeem in the place [Jerusalem] and eat in the place. Hillel: Redeem in the place and eat anywhere.
5. And House of Hillel: All redeemed and eaten outside	5. „ „ „ *inside*	5. „ „ „	5.—	5. —	5. —
6. Except what is made unclean by an Offspring of Uncleanness inside [to be eaten inside]	6. Except unclean by Father of Uncleanness —outside.	6. „ „ „	6. —	6. —	6. —
7.	7. —	7. —	7. By an Offspring, whether in or out eaten within	7. Unclean inside, whether Father or Offspring, eaten inside	7. —

Judah the Patriarch's version derives from Judah b. Ilai. But he has taken the superscriptions of Meir, nos. 1 and 2, then the substance of Judah b. Ilai, nos. 3, 4, 5, and 6 (!). Strikingly Leazar and 'Aqiba do not even *bother* to frame their opinions in the form of Houses-disputes, but speak in their own names. Simeon b. Leazar has complicated matters still more by denying the dispute concerned what all the others supposed, then by giving completely new substance to the dispute, with new legal forms and rulings (no. 4*).

The legal issues are no longer of much consequence. Our earlier conclusion applies here as well.

II.ii.27. R. Simeon b. Leazar said, "The House of Hillel and the House of Shammai did not disagree concerning one who stamps with his finger on the jar [and in this connection, the wine was never in the vat, for with his finger he stamped and pressed out the grapes in the bottle and afterward stopped it up], that he opens but does not have to empty [out the wine into the vat, for it is sufficient if he opens the bottle and restores it to its former condition, and even the House of Shammai agree in this matter].

"Concerning what did they differ?

"Concerning him who tramples [the grapes] in the vat, for

"The House of Shammai say, 'He opens and empties into the vat.'

"And the House of Hillel say, 'He opens but does not need to empty.' "

[Tos. M.S. 2:18, ed. Lieberman, p. 256, lines 111-113 (y. M.S. 2:10)]

Comment: In M. M.S. 3:13 the House of Shammai say that if the bottles are sealed and the man wants to give Heave-offering from one on behalf of all, he must open the jars and empty them into the wine-press. The House of Hillel say, "He must open them but need not empty them." Simeon b. Leazar's supplement specifies that the dispute pertains only to wine which has originally come from the vat. Judah the Patriarch was unclear on this point. All he preserved of the Houses was their ruling, but not the case to which it applied.

II.ii.28.A. They redeem (ḤLL) produce with coins in Jerusalem in this time—

The House of Shammai say, "This and this are Second Tithe."

The House of Hillel say, "The coins are as they were, and the produce is as it was [= not holy but profane]."

B. The House of Hillel say, "A man separates First Tithe of *Demai* and lifts its Heave-offering and eats it [the rest], and does not need to separate Second [Tithe]."

The House of Shammai say, "He needs to separate Second [Tithe], for I say, 'If the Second is raised up, the First is raised up; if the First is raised up, the Second is not raised up.' "

And the law is according to the words of the House of Shammai.

[Tos. M.S. 3:14-15, ed. Lieberman, pp. 260-1, lines 48-53 (y. M.S. 1:3)]

Comment: Part A is the counterpart of M. M.S. 5:7, above, p. 106. The Hillelites hold he has done nothing at all, and both the produce and the coins are as they were. In other words the law is now in abeyance.

In part B the man does not have to take into account the possibility that a non-observant person has separated First Tithe and not separated Second Tithe, so the Tithe of the fellow (ḤBR) is still to be tithed for Second Tithe, since we assume that if a non-observant person normally separates First Tithe, he will also separate Second Tithe. The Shammaites give the same opinion as Leazar, (y. M.S. 4:8, cited by Lieberman, *Tosefta Kifshuṭah*, p. 761, to line 52): "He who is reliable for Second Tithe is reliable for First Tithe."

II.ii.29A. Fruit of the Fourth-Year Vineyard—

"The House of Shammai say, 'It has no Added Fifth, and it has no Removal.'

"And the House of Hillel say, 'It has the Added Fifth, and it has Removal.'

"Under what circumstances? In the Seventh Year, but in the rest of the years of the seven, it has the Added Fifth and it has Removal"—the words of Rabbi.

Rabban Simeon b. Gamaliel says, "It is all the same whether it is the Seventh Year or the rest of the years of the seven. The House of Shammai say, 'It has no Added Fifth, and it has no Removal.'

"And the House of Hillel say, 'It has the Added Fifth, and it has Removal.' "

B. The House of Shammai say, "They do not cut it down (GMM)."

And the House of Hillel say, "They cut it down."

C. The House of Shammai say, "They do not redeem it as grapes but as wine."

And the House of Hillel say, "[As] wine *and* grapes."

But all agree that they do not redeem that which is attached to the soil [since it cannot be accurately evaluated].

D. The House of Shammai say, "They do not plant it in the fourth year, for the fourth year [next] will fall in the Seventh Year."

And the House of Hillel permit.

(Tos. M.S. 5:17-20, ed. Lieberman, p. 272, lines 54-62)

Comment: The words of the Houses are constant. Rabbi has omitted in the Mishnah reference to the dispute between himself and his father with regard to the limitations specified in the superscription.

Lieberman explains that the House of Hillel compare the Fourth Year fruits to Second Tithe. Just as Second Tithe is not given in the Seventh Year, so the law of the Fourth Year fruits does not apply in the Seventh Year. This is made explicit in part D, which draws the same conclusion.

Part A therefore limits the Shammaite ruling to the Seventh Year. For the rest of the years of the cycle, the House of Shammai is represented as agreeing with the House of Hillel: Fourth Year fruits do have the Added Fifth and Removal, just as does Second Tithe. Compare Sifra Qedoshim 3:8. Simeon b. Gamaliel says that the House of Shammai do not compare Fourth Year fruits to Second Tithe. Scripture (Lev. 19:24) contains no hint that the Fourth Year fruits have the Added Fifth and Removal.

For further comment, see Lieberman, *Tosefta Kifshuṭah* to *Zera'im*, pp. 785-7.

II.i.34.A. Flour-paste is exempt according to the House of Shammai. According to the House of Hillel it is liable.

B. Dumplings are liable according to the House of Shammai. According to the House of Hillel they are exempt.

[M. Ḥallah 1:6, trans. Danby, p. 83 (y. Ḥal. 1:4, b. Pes. 37b)]

Comment: Danby's translation obscures the form:

The flour-paste
House of Shammai declare it exempt [of *Ḥallah*]
House of Hillel declare it liable.

The dumplings
House of Shammai declare liable
House of Hillel declare exempt.

No logical reasons are given in the commentaries (e.g. Albeck, *Seder Zera'im*, p. 276) for the rulings of the Houses. Epstein, *Mishnah*, pp. 2-3, holds A and B are on the same species of food, and the Tanna of A, R. Yosi (M. 'Ed. 5:2), differs from that of B, R. Meir. He cites *Tarbiṣ* 7, pp. 143, 156-7.

II.i.35.A. Whatsoever is leavened, flavored, or mingled with Heave-offering, '*Orlah*-fruit, or Diverse Kinds of the Vineyard, is forbidden.

The House of Shammai say, "It can also convey uncleanness."

And the House of Hillel say, "It can never convey uncleanness unless it is an egg's bulk in quantity."

B. Dositheus of Kefar Yatmah was one of the disciples of the House of Shammai, and he said, "I have heard a tradition from Shammai the Elder, who said, 'It can never convey uncleanness unless it is an egg's bulk in quantity.' "

[M. 'Orlah 2:4-5, trans. Danby, p. 90 (y. 'Orlah 2:3)]

Comment: The prohibition concerns whether produce that conveys a marked flavor can be neutralized (in a hundred and one). It cannot.

The House of Shammai say that if it is unclean, even though less than an egg's bulk, which is the quantity that conveys food-uncleanness, it also conveys uncleanness. The House of Hillel rule it can convey uncleanness only in the usual quantity. The rulings of the Houses gloss the foregoing:

And House of Shammai say, *Also* ('P) renders unclean
House of Hillel say, Never renders unclean, unless there is in it as [much as] an egg.

The form of the Houses' rulings is complex. Since the Shammaite ruling is *also makes unclean*, without further qualification as to quantity, it carries the implication that less than an egg's bulk is sufficient. The Hillelite ruling therefore could not have been *does not make unclean*, under *any* circumstances. The issue would thereby have been obscured. Hence the gloss, *unless. . . an egg*, makes things entirely clear. But had the Shammaite ruling read:

House of Shammai say, Less than an egg's bulk renders unclean

then the Hillelite lemma would have been:

House of Hillel say, Less than an egg's bulk does *not* render unclean.

That would have been the simplest form. Why was it not used? Perhaps the pericope is highly developed. But the development included dropping the operative words *less than egg's bulk* from the primary Shammaite lemma—and that would not serve any editorial purpose. Perhaps, therefore, the Houses-dispute originally stood by itself, as follows:

Less than an egg's bulk
House of Shammai say: Renders unclean
House of Hillel say: Does *not* render unclean.

The referent is omitted. The pericope was attached to the foregoing. All that was augmented in the Shammaite version was the addition of *also*, the necessary joining-word. Then the Hillelite saying was completely revised; the superscription was included in *its* lemma, and the whole was rephrased as *never. . . until. . .* Normally, superscriptions are read into the first, Shammaite clause. Still, this seems the more satisfactory theoretical form.

Part B is quite another matter. Here Shammai is curiously represented as saying the words of the House of Hillel, *verbatim*. We are supposed to believe that the House of Shammai did not know the ruling of the master (above, I, pp. 192-193). It was a disciple of that very House who did know what Shammai had said. These were not told—or, incredibly, *were* told and did not accept the tradition. Then the Hillelites took it over. This seems on the face of it a Hillelite fabrication. But what if the tradition was an accurate report? Then what has been fabricated is not Shammai's opinion, but the position of the *House* of Shammai. On that basis, the Hillelite position in part A should be exchanged with the Shammaite one. But to do so, it would be necessary to reverse the order of the Houses—highly irregular!—or to reverse the opinions attributed to them. Form-critical considerations suggest this too is difficult:

> House of Shammai say, "It can *never* convey uncleanness *unless* it is an egg's bulk in quantity."
> House of Hillel say, "It can (*also*) convey uncleanness."

Without knowing the position of the Hillelites, that of the Shammaites is incomprehensible. Why say *never*. . . *unless*. . ., not as a contradiction to an antecedent opinion, but as an independent lemma, first in sequence? Normally *never*. . . *unless*. . . serves as the negative-intensive for the second, contrary opinion. It would have been adequate for the Shammaite position to read as follows:

> House of Shammai: An egg's bulk conveys uncleanness.
> House of Hillel: Even less than an egg's bulk conveys uncleanness.

The language of the House of Hillel obviously has been given to Shammai. If Shammai had shared the opinion of the House of Hillel, it would not likely have been phrased in the form necessary for a Houses-dispute. And Dositheus is not accurately represented.

II. MOʿED

II.i.36.A. (And) these are among the laws which the sages said in the upper room of Ḥananiah b. Ḥezeqiah b. Gurion. When they went up to visit him, they voted, and the House of Shammai outnumbered the House of Hillel.

Eighteen things did they decree on that day.

B. The House of Shammai say, "They do not soak ink, dyestuffs, or vetches [on a Friday], unless there is (ʾLʾ KDY Š) [time] for them to be [wholly] soaked while it is still day (MBʿWD YWM)."

And the House of Hillel permit.

C. The House of Shammai say, "They do not put bundles of flax into an oven, unless there is time for them to steam off while it is still day; nor wool into a [dyer's] cauldron, unless there is time for it to absorb the color while it is still day."

And the House of Hillel permit.

D. The House of Shammai say, "They do not spread nets for wild animals, birds, or fishes, unless there is time for them to be caught while it is still day."

And the House of Hillel permit.

E. The House of Shammai say, "They do not sell [aught] to a gentile or help him to load his beast or raise [a burden] on his shoulders, unless there is time for him to reach a place nearby."

And the House of Hillel permit.

F. The House of Shammai say, "They do not give hides to a [gentile] tanner nor clothes to a gentile washerman, unless there is time for [the work to be] done while it is still day."

G. And all these the House of Hillel permit such time as the sun is up (ʿM HŠMŠ).

H. Rabban Simeon b. Gamaliel said, "In my father's house they used to give white clothes to a gentile washerman three days before Sabbath."

I. Both [the House of Shammai and the House of Hillel] agree that men may lay down the olive-press beams or the winepress rollers.

[M. Shab. 1:4, 5, 6, 7, 8, 9, trans. Danby, pp. 100-101 (y. Shab. 1:4, 5, 6, 7, 8, 9, b. Shab. 13b, 17b, 18a-b, b. A.Z. 36a-b)]

Comment: The legal problem concerns beginning on the eve of the Sabbath (Friday) work which will be completed on the Sabbath. The Shammaites say that one must not begin such work; the Hillelites, that one may begin it. We have already seen the same dispute attributed to Shammai and Hillel, I, pp. 324-325, 157, 196-197.

The first problem is the referent of part A. The accepted explanation is that it pertains to the foregoing paragraphs, which are as follows:

A man should not sit down before the barber near to the time of the afternoon *Tefillah*, unless he has already prayed; a man should not enter a bath-house or a tannery, nor should he [begin to] eat a meal or decide a suit, though if any have begun [a like deed] they need not interrupt it. They must interrupt [their doings] to recite the *Shemaʿ*, but they need not interrupt them for the *Tefillah*.

A tailor should not go out with his needle [on Friday] near to nightfall, lest he forget and 'go out,' nor should a scrivener [go out then] with his pen; nor should a man search his clothes [for fleas] or read by lamplight.

Rightly have they said, "A school-master may look where the children are reading, but he himself may not read."

In like manner a man that has a flux may not eat with a woman that has a flux, since it lends occasion to transgression.

(M. Shab. 1:2-3, trans. Danby, p. 100)

The greater number of readings is, *These are*, meaning *the foregoing*, though some readings have *And these are*, meaning, the *following* (b. Shab. 13b). Albeck (*Seder Mo'ed*, p. 406, to 1:4) prefers the first, though he notes that even *These are* serves both to introduce, as well as to complete, a pericope. He admits that there is no decisive evidence, one way or the other. See Epstein, *Mishnah*, p. 426.

The further problem is, What are the *eighteen things?* In the antecedent paragraphs, we find the following issues: 1. barber; 2. bath-house; 3. meal; 4. law-suits; 5. tailor; 6. scribe; 7. fleas; 8. read. However, one counts, we do not have eighteen. Nor do eighteen follow. Albeck further reviews the traditional commentaries on this point.

Part A, M. Shab. 1:4, is an independent lemma, attached as a superscription for the following collection. It mentions the Houses, and since the Houses do not occur in the antecedent materials, it seems to me unlikely that the editor meant M. Shab. 1:2-3.

The little story about the superiority of the Shammaites joins the several (*sword*, *Hillel in Temple*) in which the temporary predominance of the Shammaites is explained. The story is composed of several phrases:

1. These are [some] of the laws which they said in the upper chamber of Ḥananiah b. Ḥizqiyahu b. Gurion
2. When they went up to visit (BQR) him
3. They voted, and the House of Shammai were more numerous than the House of Hillel
4. [and] eighteen things they decreed
5. on that day.

The function of no. 2 is a little problem. It may be assigned as the conclusion of no. 1, or as the beginning of no. 3; my guess is that it serves as a joining-phrase, a later gloss, for one could proceed from no. 1 to no. 3 without it.

As to no. 1, we have already seen material of the same sort in connection with the question of why Hillel did not receive the holy spirit. There the sages were assembled as follows: Tos. Soṭ. 13:3: house of *Guryo* in Jericho; y. Soṭ. 9:13, same, but *GDY'*; b. Sanh. 11a, once they were *reclining* in the *upper room* of *Guryo*; b. Soṭ. 48b = b. Sanh. 11a; y. A.Z. 3:1 = y. Hor. 3:5 has *upper room* of *GDYY'*. The combination of the Houses (Hillel), *upper room* and *Guryo/Gedya* looks suspicious. We may readily recognize *when they went up to visit him* as a gloss of no special interest. But what shall we make of *upper room* of Ḥananiah

b. Ḥizqiyahu b. *Gurion*? Perhaps someone supposed this is Guryo's (Gedya's) grandson? That seems to me implausible. What appears more likely is that a garbled tradition has been straightened out and used for another meeting of the sages, this time not for the purpose of receiving heavenly messages or of discussing why they were not receiving them, but to make decrees. Since the *holy-spirit*-materials derive from Samuel the Small-Judah b. Baba, we had best suppose that the whole was doctored sometime after ca. 150.

No. 3 is the operative clause: the Shammaites outnumbered the Hillelites. We have seen this theme earlier, in connection with the Shammai-Hillel debate about vintaging grapes and crushing olives in cleanness, also Hillel in the Temple. There Hillel is silenced by a sword—or by the mob—and the Shammaites outvote the Hillelites anyhow. Now it is unambiguous that one time the Shammaites were more numerous. y. Shab. 1:4 supplies the missing violence: it has the Shammaites murder Hillelite voters.

No. 4 obviously is a formal lemma, which can serve any sort of list. The *eighteen things* tradition perhaps began in some sort of collection, arranged for mnemonic purposes, much like the Ushan ones (M. ʿEd., below). It has been taken up and set into narrative form.

No. 5 surely comes together with no. 4. *On that day* also serves as a formula to introduce or conclude stories connected with the deposition of Gamaliel II. Here, however, I doubt that it means more than it says: *then*. I hear no echo of the Gamaliel-deposition.

The pericope need not be regarded as a composite, in the sense that a final editor has put together existing, completed materials. Apart from no. 2, nothing seems to me either superfluous or redundant. I see no other glosses. It looks to me like a little story, much like the *holy spirit*-stories and the *sword-in-the-school-house* fable, composed of existing themes, or key-words and episodic phrases, but not put together part by part, as elsewhere. It surely comes at the end of a long history of transmission of inchoate and unfinished materials. No. 4 can be no earlier than other collection-forms, therefore not much before the middle of the second century. It certainly is more elaborate than other collection-superscriptions, which consist of numbers plus key-words (stringencies/leniencies), and represents a considerable literary improvement.

The form of parts B, C, D, E, F is rigidly fixed and consistent:

> The House of Shammai say, *They do not. . . except in order to* (’L’ KDY Š). . .
> And the House of Hillel *permit*.

The laws are as follows:

Part B: They do not soak ink, and dyes, and vetches, except in order that they may be wholly soaked while it is still day

Part C: They do not place bundles of flax in the oven, except in order that they may steam off while it is still day

Part D: They do not spread nets of beast, birds, and fish, except in order that they may be trapped while it is still day
Part E: They do not sell to the gentile and carry with him and they do not raise up on him, except in order that he may reach a near place [Omits: *while it is still day*]
Part F: They do not give hides to the tanner, and not vessels to the gentile laundryman, except in order that they may be done while it is still day.

Part G then serves as a summary-subscription for the whole, as well as for part F:

And in all of them the House of Hillel permit *with the sun.*

The Hillelite stock-phrase of the foregoing is augmented fore and aft. The glossator provides an appropriate summary; at the end, a new element is introduced, which is redundant: *with the sun* (while it is still day = with the sun, as long as the sun is shining). The expected Hillelite lemma, with appropriate editorial glosses (in italics), completes the collection. Epstein, *Mevo'ot*, p. 282, does not see these as glosses.

The laws are closely related to one another. Parts B, C, and D concern Jews only. Parts E and F pertain to what one may ask a gentile to do. The form of part E is slightly defective, as I pointed out, but the change is not consequential. Albeck (*Seder Mo'ed*, p. 20) explains that the Shammaites hold all one's work must be done at the end of the sixth day. The Hillelites say that if the work is completed on the Sabbath, it is permissible, since inanimate objects, but neither man nor beast, are involved. The Shammaites prohibit imposing on the gentile, lest it appear that the gentile is doing the work of an Israelite, as his agent, on the Sabbath.

Part H tells us that Simeon b. Gamaliel's father's house followed the Shammaite ruling. We do not know whether this is Gamaliel I or Gamaliel II, though the state of the Simeon b. Gamaliel I materials is such that the much greater likelihood is Gamaliel II. If so, then once again the Yavnean Gamaliel is represented as a Shammaite. I see no hostile polemic in his son's report. On the contrary, it is probably as firm historical evidence as we are likely to have. Had he not said it, given the conditions governing the formation of Hillelite traditions, no one would likely have invented it; and he did not say it to prove a case ("father was a Shammaite"), but told it in innocence. Perhaps no one later on (in Judah the Patriarch's day) was much disturbed, since the House-disputes had long since become a matter of legal theory (as asserted in M. Yev. 1:4) for Hillelite heirs to work on.

Part I comes at the end and seems to me not part of the foregoing list, but a later addition. One may begin the process of crushing olives and grapes. The placing of the weights (beams, rollers) may be done before the Sabbath, since the primary pressing is thereby completed. The issue of parts B-D therefore does not apply.

The form before us is exceptional. We should have expected:

As to soaking ink(before/and) on the Sabbath
House of Shammai: Prohibit
House of Hillel: Permit

This would have covered all aspects of both opinions. The ʾLʾ KDY Š form is an awkward circumlocution. Some affirmative formulation of the issue must have been possible; the one proposed above is hardly adequate. That the Shammaite lemmas before us are all highly developed and carefully glossed (*while it is still day*), the persistence of the glosses, and the ʾLʾ KDY Š clauses prove that a developed form has taken the place of a primitive one. But why? My guess is that the authority behind the collection is also responsible for its form and structure. He has preferred a smoother set of legal cases, not separated by superscriptions or other topical phrases, and therefore has turned whatever explanatory matter he had into integral parts of the Shammaite part of the pericopae. But even as it stands the collection follows an obvious mnemonic pattern.

Note Epstein, *Mevoʾot* p. 145, 282-6, 423. He assigns the whole of 1:5-7 to ʿAqiba, by reference to b. Shab. 18b.

III.i.3. R. Joshua Onia taught (TNʾ), "The disciples of the House of Shammai took up positions for themselves downstairs and would slay the disciples of the House of Hillel."

TNY: Six of them went up and the rest stood with swords and spears.

(y. Shab. 1:4, ed. Gilead, p. 9a)

Comment: The traditions supply details of the *spear in the school house* story to expand this one.

II.i.37.A. A stove (KYRH) which had been heated with stubble or straw—cooked food may be set on it. But if with peat or wood, cooked food may not be set on it until it has been swept out or covered with ashes.

B. The House of Shammai say, "Hot water but not cooked food [may be set thereon]."

And the House of Hillel say, "Hot water *and* cooked food."

C. The House of Shammai say, "They remove [on the Sabbath] but do not put back."

And the House of Hillel say, "They also put back."

[M. Shab. 3:1, trans. Danby, p. 102 (y. Shab. 3:1, 4; b. Shab. 36b-37a)]

Comment: The dispute of the Houses pertains to the second clause of the foregoing rule: a stove heated by fuel that produces coals likely to burn for some time. The possibility is that he may stir the coals. In part B the Shammaites rule that even after it is swept out, one cannot put food on such a stove, but only hot water. One may not put food back on it either. The Houses-dispute glosses the foregoing. Without it we should have assumed no distinction is made between hot water and food, or between removing food and putting it back. The form is brief and elliptical:

B. House of Shammai: Hot water *but not* food.
House of Hillel: Hot water *and* food.
C. House of Shammai: Take but not return.
House of Hillel: *Also* return.

The first pair is perfectly balanced, and the sole difference is the negative particle. The second pair makes the Hillelite opinion dependent on the Shammaite one. It should have been *take* and *return*. The latter pair therefore looks like a gloss on the former, extending the ruling of the Houses to a separate, but related case.

See Epstein, *Mishnah*, p. 455-6.

II.i.38. The House of Shammai say, "They take up bones and shells from the table (ŠLḤN) [on the Sabbath]."

And the House of Hillel say, "He takes the entire table (ṬBLH) and shakes it (MN'RH)."

[M. Shab. 21:3, trans. Danby, p. 118 (b. Shab. 143a, 157a, b. Beṣ. 2a)]

Comment: The Houses opinions are not balanced, but separate:

House of Shammai: *They* raise up from the table (ŠLḤN) bones and shells
House of Hillel: *He* take*s* the whole tablet (ṬBLH) *and shakes* it.

The verbs are neither the same root nor in the same person; the noun of the predicate changes. The two thus look more like separate rulings which have been juxtaposed, than a standard dispute on the same matter in the same language and forms. Tos. Shab. *reverses* the Houses' positions, but preserves the anomalies of form and word choice. This makes it all the more curious. MS Kaufmann has the following:

The House of *Hillel* say, "They *remove* ('BR) from on the table (ŠLḤN) shells and bones."

And the House of *Shammai* say, "He *takes away* (ŠLQ) the whole tablet (ṬBLH) and shakes it (WMN'RH)."

The order is Tosefta's, and so are the word-choices. See Epstein, *Mevo'ot*, p. 297; *Mishnah*, pp. 357-8, for a full explanation.

II.ii.30.A. R. Simeon b. Leazar said, "...they said a male should not eat with a female *Zab* [= one afflicted with gonorrhaea] on account of becoming accustomed to transgression.

"For(Š) the House of Shammai say, 'A Pharisee-*Zab* should not eat with an outsider-*Zab*.'

"And the House of Hillel permit."

[Tos. Shab. 1:14 (end)-15, ed. Lieberman, p. 4, lines 34-5 (y. Shab. 1:3, b. Shab. 13a)]

B. These are among the laws which they said in the upper chamber of Ḥananiah b. Ḥizqiyahu b. Garon when they went up to visit him.

And they counted, and the House of Shammai were more numerous than the House of Hillel.

Eighteen thing[s] they decreed on that very day.

And that day was as hard for Israel as the day on which the [golden] calf was made.

(Tos. Shab. 1:16, ed. Lieberman, p. 4, lines 36-8)

C. On that day they said, "All things which are carried bring uncleanness with the thickness of an ox-goad (MRDʿ)."

And they counted and the House of Shammai were more numerous than the House of Hillel.

[Tos. Shab. 1:18, ed. Lieberman, p. 4, lines 40-41 (b. Shab. 16b-17a, M. Oh. 16:1)]

D.1. On that day they said, "He who forgets vessels on the Eve of the Sabbath at darkness under the water pipe."

2. And they counted, and the House of Shammai were more numerous than the House of Hillel.

[Tos. Shab. 1:19, ed. Lieberman, p. 4, lines 42-3 (M. Miq. 4:1, b. Shab. 16b assigns D.2 to Meir)]

E. The House of Shammai said to the House of Hillel, "Do you not agree that they do not roast meat, onion[s] and egg[s] on the Eve of the Sabbath except so that (ʾLʾ KDY Š) they may be roasted [while it is still day]? Also it suffices for dyestuffs and vetches [to be] like them."

The House of Hillel said to them, "Do you not agree that they lay down the olive-press beams and the winepress rollers on the Eve of the Sabbath at darkness? Also it suffices for dyestuffs and vetches [to be] like them."

F. These stood in their answer, and these stood in their answer, but that ('L' Š)

The House of Shammai say, "*Six days will you labor and do all your work* (Ex. 20:9)—that *all* your work should be finished by the eve of the Sabbath."

And the House of Hillel say, "*Six days will you labor*—you do work all six days."

[Tos. Shab. 1:20-21, ed. Lieberman, pp. 4-5, lines 43-49 (y. Shab. 1:5, b. Shab. 18b)]

G. The House of Shammai say, "One does not sell to the gentile or carry with him or lift up on him [a burden] unless there is time ('L' KDY Š) for him to reach a near place."

H. What is a near place? Until he reaches a house near the wall.

R. ʿAqiba says. . .

I. R. Leazar b. R. Ṣadoq said, "[Those] of (ŠL) the House of Rabban Gamaliel would bring their washing to the gentile washerman three days before the Sabbath, and dying on the eve of the Sabbath. . ."

[Tos. Shab. 1:22, ed. Lieberman, p. 5, lines 49-55 (b. Shab. 19a has R. Ṣadoq)]

Comment: Part A: Lieberman explains (*Tosefta Kifshuṭah* p. 13) that the Hillelites, even though they permit the Pharisaic *Zab* to eat with the non-Pharisaic *Zab*, agree with the foregoing rule, that a male and female *Zab* should not eat together. Other texts, however, present the Houses-dispute as a new and separate item.

Part B: The superscription of the eighteen things, M. Shab. 1:4, is somewhat different: M. Shab. *Gurion* becomes *Garon*. The gloss *and that day*, which we saw above in connection with the humiliation of Hillel (b. Shab. 17a, I, p. 318), fits as well here as it does there, and for the same reason: It is the Hillelite comment on the affair. (See Lieberman's extended comments, *Tosefta Kifshuṭah*, pp. 14-16.) But the comment itself is a stock phrase, which can be attached pretty much anywhere.

Part C: Now we have a new form,

On that day they said
Law
And they counted and the House of Shammai were more numerous than the House of Hillel.

The form is sound, but the statement of the law is in several places truncated; the Hillelite opinion is omitted. Thus in part C, we do not have the opposing opinion, (presumably) that even less than the thickness of a staff suffices. See M. Oh. 16:1:

> Any movable object conveys the uncleanness if it is as thick as an ox-goad.
> R. Ṭarfon said, "May I bury my children if this is not a perverted *halakhah*, which the hearer heard wrongly:
> "When a husbandman passed by [a tomb] with the ox-goad over his shoulder and one end of it overshadowed the tomb, they declare him unclean by virtue of the law of 'vessels which overshadow a corpse.' "
> R. 'Aqiba said, "I will amend [it] so that the words of the sages shall remain valid:
> "Any movable object conveys uncleanness to him that carries the object if it is as thick as an ox-goad, and the object conveys the uncleanness to itself whatsoever its thickness, but to other men and vessels only if it is a handbreadth wide."
> (M. Oh. 16:1, trans. Danby, p. 672)

We therefore have here the unaltered law, before 'Aqiba's emendation.

Part D presents the same strange form, in which the law is stated without the opposing opinion. This time it concerns one who leaves vessels under the water-pipe on the Sabbath Eve at darkness—now, however, without the pertinent law, let alone a conflicting opinion! It obviously is an abbreviated allusion to existing materials.

Lieberman explains that the man has left the objects intending to bring them into his house, but has forgotten to take them in. Meanwhile rain fell, and the water pipe filled up, so the vessels are filled as well. The water is not regarded as drawn water, according to the House of Hillel, since the man did not leave the vessels *intending* to fill them up. We shall see other versions of the same situation, in which the *Sabbath* is not the issue at all. What we have here, therefore, is an apocopated lemma, in which reference is made to a case without the legal details and outcome.

Parts E-F supply an argument for M. Shab. 1:5 (II.i.34.B), and make reference as well to M. Shab. 1:9 (II.i.34.I). See Mekhilta deR. Simeon b. Yoḥai, ed. Epstein-Melamed, p. 149, cited above, I, pp. 185-187. Lieberman explains the Hillelite exegesis: "You work all six days, and the rest of your work will be done of itself on the Sabbath (without your own efforts)." The legal exegesis is joined by the awkward ʾLʾ Š, the Š being a common joining-particle.

Part G = M. Shab. 1:7: M. Shab. gives Lʾ, Tos. Shab., ʾYN, for the negative particle. Otherwise there are no changes.

Part H is of interest in supplying a *terminus ante quem* for the antecedent paragraph: R. 'Aqiba and others of his generation (b. Shab. 18b).

Part I compares to M. Shab. 1:9:

M. Shab. 1:9	*Tos. Shab. 1:22*
1. Rabban Simeon b. Gamaliel said	1. R. Leazar b. R. Ṣadoq said,
2. The House of Abba were accustomed (NWHGYN HYW)	2. *Those of* (D) the House of *Rabban Gamaliel would bring* (HYW MWLYKYN) *their*
3. that they would give white garment (KLY LBN) to the gentile laundryman three days before the Sabbath.	3. white garment to the gentile laundryman three days before the Sabbath.

The differences in no. 1 are striking indeed. Instead of a first-hand report, we have the recollection of Leazar b. R. Ṣadoq. No. 2 of Tos. drops *were accustomed*, and supplies *would bring their* for *would give*, but otherwise, the passages are identical, and strikingly, *verbatim* in the operative clause: *white garment/gentile laundryman/three days before Sabbath*. We have a single lemma, which has come down in one form, but with differing superscriptions. Judah the Patriarch has preferred the version of his father. It is difficult to understand how a first-person recollection in direct discourse could have produced a third-person-narrative in indirect discourse. It seems more likely that someone dropped Eleazar b. R. Ṣadoq and reframed the story in the first person, supplying the name of Simeon b. Gamaliel. It is hard to believe someone would have suppressed the name of the *nasi* and inserted that of a subordinated sage, especially in a matter pertaining to the household of the earlier *nasi*. Therefore the Eleazar-attribution must be authentic. And note b. Shab. 19a:

> R. Ṣadoq said, "This was the practice of those of the House of R. Gamaliel: They would give white garments to the fuller three days before the Sabbath, but colored garments even on the eve of the Sabbath."

See also Epstein, *Mevo'ot*, p. 278, 286, 507; *Mishnah*, p. 426.

II.ii.31A. . . .What do they keep on it [stove]?

"The House of Shammai say, 'One may not keep (QYM) *anything* at all on it.'

"The House of Hillel say, 'Hot water, but not food.'

B. "[If] he has removed ('QR) the kettle, all agree that he should not put back," the words of R. Meir.

R. Judah says, "The House of Shammai say, 'Hot water, but not food.'

"And the House of Hillel say, 'Hot water and food.' "

C. He removed [the kettle]—

The House of Shammai say, "He does not put [it] back."

And the House of Hillel say, "He puts [it] back."

[Tos. Shab. 2(3):13, ed. Lieberman, pp. 9-10, lines 42-46 (y. Shab. 3:1,4 [hot/cold water], b. Shab. 36b-37a, 42a [hot/cold water])]

Comment: The synopsis is as follows:

M. Shab. 3:1	*Tos. 2:13 (Anon.)*	*Meir*	*Judah*
1. [Stove heated with peat or wood], cooked food may not be set on it until it has been swept out or covered with ashes.	1. What do they keep on it? House of Shammai: *They do not keep anything on it.* House of Hillel: *Hot water, but not food.*	1. —	1. —
2. House of Shammai say: Hot water but not food	2. —	2. If he removed the kettle, all agree that he should not put it back.	2. —
3. House of Hillel say, Hot water and food.	3. —	3. —	3. R. Judah says, House of Shammai say, Hot water but not food. House of Hillel say, Hot water and food.
4. House of Shammai say, They take off but do not put back.	4. —	4. —	4. —
5. House of Hillel say, They also put back.	5. —	5. —	5. —
6. —	6. —	6. —	6. He removed—House of Shammai say, He does not put back. House of Hillel say, He puts back.

Judah the Patriarch has taken Judah b. Ilai's version of the opinions of the Houses, dropped the superscription, put the whole into the plural (*they/he*), and assigned the rulings to a new situation entirely. M. Shab. nos. 2-3 are the same as Judah no. 3; nos. 4-5 = Judah no. 6. Here the form of the Houses-sayings is so abbreviated that one can well understand how the second-century authorities would have had difficulty in knowing to what legal problem the sayings pertained. It is the sort of lemma one would be inclined to assign to the earliest stratum of the Houses' sayings.

II.ii.32. [As to carrying certain objects on the Sabbath]—

R. [Simeon b.] Leazar says, "The House of Shammai say, 'They are not handled (NYṬLYN) except in case of need.'

"And the House of Hillel say, 'In case of need and not in case of need.' "

[Tos. Shab. 14(15):1, ed. Lieberman, p. 64, lines 5:7 (Tos. Beṣ. 1:11, y. Shab. 17:4)]

Comment: The form is a standard, developed exemplum, with the insertion of the explanatory matter into the opinion of the House of Shammai:

Handling
House of Shammai say, Only in case of need
House of Hillel, In case of need and not in case of need.

Simeon b. Leazar followed the form that seems to have come early in the formation of the Houses-materials. We therefore can hardly assign all such materials in conventional form to the time of the Houses themselves. We shall see further disputes about the same principle. For the legal issues, see Lieberman, *Tosefta Kifshuṭah* to *Mo'ed*, p. 226.

Note also b. Shab. 124a-b:

DTNN: The House of Shammai say, "One may not [on festivals] carry out an infant, *lulav*, or scroll of Torah into the street."
And the House of Hillel permit.

See Epstein, *Mevo'ot*, p. 279.

II.ii.33. R. Simeon b. Leazar said, "The House of Shammai and the House of Hillel did not dispute concerning one that was born circumcized, that one needs to draw from him a drop of blood [in observance] of the covenant, because it is a tucked-in foreskin ('RLH KBWŠH).

"Concerning what did they dispute? Concerning a proselyte who converted when already circumcized, for (Š)

"The House of Shammai say, 'One needs to draw from him a drop of blood [in observance] of the covenant.'

"And the House of Hillel say, 'One does not need to draw from him a drop of blood [in observance] of the covenant.' "

[Tos. Shab. 15(16):9, ed. Lieberman, pp. 71-2, lines 43-7 (y. Shab. 19:2, b. Shab. 135a, y. Yev. 8:1, Sifra Tazri'a 1:6)]

Comment: See Sifra Tazri'a 1:6. There the issue is whether the circumcision may be done on the Sabbath. The Shammaites hold it may, the Hillelites that it may not. The primary form clearly was phrased in negative/affirmative terms:

[Concerning drawing a drop of blood in observance of the covenant from one who was] born circumcized:
House of Shammai: They do draw blood
House of Hillel: They do not draw blood.

Again, the superscription has been inserted into the House of Shammai's lemma. The original Houses-lemma certainly consisted of *one born circumcized* + *draw blood* +/— negative. This was then assigned to the Sabbath- or conversion-circumcision of one born circumcized. But before both versions comes the dispute rejected by Simeon: *one born circumcized*, for this is the only issue to which the actual Houses-rulings really pertain.

II.ii.34.A. The House of Hillel say, "They lift up from (M'L) the table (ŠLḤN) bones and shells."

The House of Shammai say, "He removes (ŚLQ) the tablet (ṬBLH) entirely and empties it out."

B. Zekhariah b. Avqilas did not behave according to either the words of the House of Shammai or the words of the House of Hillel, but he took and threw [it] behind the couch.

C. R. Yosah said, "The modesty of Zekhariah b. Avqilas is what burned the Temple."

[Tos. Shab. 16(17):7, ed. Lieberman, pp. 76-7, lines 14-17 (b. Shab. 142b-143a, 157a, b. Beṣ. 2a)]

Comment: M. Shab. 21:3 has it in reverse, but the words of the Houses' opinions are nearly identical. What has been changed is the order of the Houses, Hillel first, then Shammai. See Lieberman, *Tosefta Kifshuṭah*, p. 268, Epstein, *Mevo'ot*, p. 247.

II.ii.35.A. R. Simeon b. Leazar says, "'The House of Shammai say, 'They do not kill a louse (M'KWLT) on the Sabbath.'

"And the House of Hillel permit."

B. And so Rabban Simeon b. Gamaliel would say, "The House of Shammai say, 'They do not distribute charity to the poor on the Sabbath in the synagogue, even to pay the costs of the marriage of an orphan boy and an orphan girl, and they do not make a match between a man and his woman, and they do not pray concerning the sick person on the Sabbath.'

"And the House of Hillel permit."

[Tos. Shab. 16(17):21-22, ed. Lieberman, pp. 79-80, lines 47-51 (b. Shab. 12a; y. Shab. 1:3)]

Comment: The second-century masters here tend to follow the more developed form, in which the Shammaites' lemma carries the superscription. However, as we observed above, it was quite possible for them to make use of the more primitive form, and we cannot assign precedence to one over the other.

The Shammaite view is attested by Eliezer b. Hyrcanus, Epstein, *Mevo'ot*, p. 279.

III.ii.5.A. TNW RBNN: They do not send a letter by the hand of a gentile on the eve of the Sabbath, unless he stipulated the cost—

The House of Shammai say, "So that he may reach his home."

And the House of Hillel say, "So that he may reach the house nearest the wall."

(b. Shab. 19a)

Comment: The *beraita* is parallel to II.i.36.E. but with a new superscription, and the Hillelite opinion is different.

IV.i.1. They do not send letters by a gentile either Friday or Thursday.

The House of Shammai prohibit even on Wednesday.

And the House of Hillel permit.

(y. Shab. 1:9, repr. Gilead, p. 13a)

Comment: The above is not attributed to Tannaitic authorities.

III.ii.5.B. TNW RBNN: The House of Shammai say, "On the first day [of Ḥanukkah] he lights eight [candles], from then on he proceeds to reduce [the number]."

And the House of Hillel say, "On the first day he lights one, and from then on he proceeds to augment [the number]."

(b. Shab. 21b)

Comment: The form is standard. The primary form would have been *eight/one* (which could have been merely *all/not all*, or *all/one*). The superscription, *on the first day he lights*, is inserted into the lemma of each House, and then both are glossed with the obvious consequent ruling, *from then on* etc.

II.i.39.A. To render [such] an alley-entry valid (HKŠR HMBWY): The House of Shammai say, "[It must have both] side-post *and* cross-beam."

And the House of Hillel say, "Side-post *or* cross-beam."

R. Eliezer says, "There should be two side-posts."

B. In the name of R. Ishmael a disciple stated before R. ʿAqiba, "The House of Shammai and the House of Hillel did not dispute about an entry less than four cubits [wide], which is valid if it has either side-post or cross-beam.

"About what did they dispute?

"About one whose width was from four to ten cubits, for (Š)

"The House of Shammai say, '[It must have both] side-posts and cross-beam.'

"And the House of Hillel say, '*Either* side-post *or* cross-beam.' "

R. ʿAqiba said, "They disputed about both cases."

[M. ʿEruv. 1:2, trans. Danby, pp. 121-2 (b. Shab. 117a; y. ʿEruv. 1:2, b. ʿEruv. 2b, 11b-12a)]

Comment: The law concerns what must be done to mark an alley so that its residents may carry therein. The House of Shammai say the alley must have both a side-post and a crossbeam. The House of Hillel require one or the other, not both. Eliezer b. Hyrcanus wants two sidebeams. Part A is in standard, primitive form:

Preparation (HKŠR) of the alley-entry (MBWY):
House of Shammai say, Side beam *and* cross-beam
House of Hillel say, Side-beam *or* cross beam.

That this primitive form also comes very early in the formation of the tradition is proved by the dispute of the Ishmaelean and ʿAqiba. The disciple reports identical language for the Houses, but assigns it to another circumstance:

Concerning [an alleyway] wider than four cubits to ten
[beyond that, all agree it must have both side and cross-beam]:

House of Shammai say, Side-beam and cross-beam.
House of Hillel say, *Either* side-beam *or* cross-beam.

Thus, as I said, the disciple of the Ishmaeleans has made the Hillelites agree, taken the words of the original dispute, and given them a different superscription. ʿAqiba says the dispute pertains to an alleyway of any width, which means he has the same superscription as is before us in part A. The second version makes a minor stylistic improvement by adding *either* (ʼW).

See Epstein, *Mevoʼot*, pp. 79, 119; *Mishnah*, p. 1064: The authority is Judah b. Ilai.

III.ii.6. TNW RBNN: How is a road through the public domain to be provided with an *ʿeruv*?

The shape of a doorway is made at one end, and a side-post and cross-beam are fixed at the other.

Ḥananiah said, "The House of Shammai say, 'A door is made at one end as well as at the other, and it must be locked when one leaves or enters.'

"And the House of Hillel say, 'A door is made at one end and a side-post and a cross-beam at the other.' "

[b. ʿEruv. 6a (y. ʿEruv. 1:1, repr. Gilead, p. 69)]

Comment: The anonymous rule of part A is that of the House of Hillel in Ḥananiah's tradition. The form is not standard, but we are accustomed to the development of Houses-disputes by later masters. The Ḥananiah is Ḥananiah nephew of R. Joshua, following y. ʿEruv. 1:1.

II.i.40.A. Rabban Gamaliel said, "(MʿSH B+Š) A Sadducee lived with us in the [same] alley in Jerusalem. Father said to us, 'Hasten and put out all the [needful] vessels in the alley before he brings out [his vessels] and [so] restricts you.' "

B. When do they give right of access?

The House of Shammai say, "While it is yet day."

And the House of Hillel say, "After it has become dark."

C. If five companies (ḤBWRWT) kept the Sabbath in the same eating-hall (ṬRYQLYN), the House of Shammai say, "An *ʿeruv* [is needful] for each company (ḤBWRH)."

And the House of Hillel say, "One *ʿeruv* [suffices] for all."

[But] they agree that if some of them occupied rooms or upper chambers, an *ʿeruv* is needful for each company.

[M. ʿEruv. 6:2, 4a, 6, trans. Danby, pp. 129-130 (y. ʿEruv. 6:3-4, 6; b. ʿEruv. 48b-49a, 68b, 69b, 71a, 72a-b)]

III.i.4. The House of Shammai say, "They do not prepare an *ʿeruv* for a man unless his utensils are there."

[y. ʿEruv. 3:1 (b. ʿEruv. 30b)]

III.ii.7. TNY': If five residents [of the same courtyard] collected their *'eruv* and deposited it in two receptacles —

The House of Shammai rule, "Their *'eruv* is not an *'eruv* ('YN 'RWBN 'RWB)."

The House of Hillel rule, "Their *'eruv* is an *'eruv* ('RWBN 'RWB)."

(b. 'Eruv. 48b)

Comment: Part A (M. 'Eruv. 6:2) is discussed above, I, p. 379, and synopsis, I, p. 384. It makes Simeon b. Gamaliel follow the Shammaite view.

Part B (M. 'Eruv. 6:4) pertains to M. 'Eruv. 6:3:

> If one of them that lived in the courtyard forgot to take part in the *'eruv*, his house is forbidden both to him and to them... but their houses are permitted both to him and to them.
>
> If they had given him right of access to their houses, he is permitted [to take aught in and out of his house and the courtyard], but they are forbidden...
>
> (M. 'Eruv. 6:3A, trans. Danby, p. 129)

The man who forgot renders his property a different domain from that of the others and may not carry in or out of it on the Sabbath. When can they give him right of access, as specified here? The House of Shammai say it must be done before sunset on Friday, since one cannot do so on the Sabbath itself. The House of Hillel say, *After it gets dark*. Some MSS (plausibly) read, *also*, a good gloss.

y. 'Eruv. 6:4 contains the following:

> The House of Shammai say, "They do not annual the right after it gets dark."
>
> And the House of Hillel say, "They do annul the right after it gets dark."

This is the simplest possible version of the dispute, and all the tradent needed to know was that a Houses' dispute about the matter existed. He could then reconstruct the dispute and supply the proper opinion to the right House on the basis of the general principle that the Shammaites were strict, the Hillelites lenient.

The problem of *part C* (M. 'Eruv. 6:6) concerns five companies who spend the Sabbath in a single room, but remain as separate groups within it. The House of Shammai say that each group must supply its own *'eruv* with others in the same courtyard; the House of Hillel say that one serves for all five, for the room joins the five groups to one household. The form of part B poses no problems:

When do they give right of access?
House of Shammai: While it is still day
House of Hillel: [While it is still day and] *also* after it gets dark.

Part C likewise has similar form, though the opinions of the Houses are somewhat developed:

If five companies—same eating-hall
House of Shammai: [An] *'eruv* for each (KL) *company and company*
House of Hillel: *An 'eruv* for all (KWLN) *of them*

The differences are the italicized words. The Hillelite opinion depends upon the Shammaite one and could not have stood separately. The same is so in part B. The original words of the Hillelites therefore cannot be before us, though the changes in the earlier form need not have been substantial. The lemmas are not neatly matched:

'RWB LKL ḤBWRH WḤBWRH
'RWB 'ḤD LKWLM

We should have expected for the Shammaites

['RWB] LKL 'ḤD [W'ḤD]

Thus, as above (p. 55) 1,2-2,1. The same principle is debated by the Houses in Tos. Ber. 5:30, above, p. 51.

See Epstein, *Mishnah*, pp. 460, 1200; Simeon b. Gamaliel follows the Shammaite view.

II.i.41.A. [If there was] a cistern between two courtyards [which had not made *'eruv*], they may not draw water therefrom on the Sabbath unless they had made for it a partition ten handbreadths high, either above, or below or [only] within its rim.

B. Rabban Simeon b. Gamaliel says,
"The House of Shammai say, 'Below.'
"And the House of Hillel say, 'Above.' "

[M. 'Eruv. 8:6, trans. Danby, p. 132 (y. 'Eruv. 8:6, b. 'Eruv. 86a, b. Suk. 16a-b)]

Comment: Part A ignores the dispute of the Houses. That does not tell us whether it comes before or afterward. The Houses-sayings contain nothing to join them to the foregoing case. It is Simeon b. Gamaliel who has supplied that connection. Otherwise we should not have known about what the Houses disputed. As it is, all we know is that Simeon b. Gamaliel alleges the Hillelites took a lenient position, allowing the partition to stand *above* the whole. But the law does not in this instance follow either House.

See Epstein, *Mishnah*, pp. 358-9.

III.ii.8.A. DTNY': Ḥananiah says, "The House of Shammai say, 'One may bake only if he set an *'eruv* of bread, and one may cook only if he set an *'eruv* of cooked food, and one may store only if he had already warm water stored on the eve of the Festival.'

"And the House of Hillel say, 'One may set an *'eruv* with one dish and prepare all his requirements [in reliance] thereon.' "

(b. Beṣ. 17b)

Comment: The issue is whether one must prepare an *'eruv* for each sort of food-preparation one plans to do. The Houses take the positions one would expect. Ḥananiah's form for the dispute is conventional, but that proves nothing about the authenticity of his tradition.

III.ii.9. An *'eruv* may be prepared for a Nazirite with wine etc. Our Mishnah does not represent the view of the House of Shammai.

For it was taught:

The House of Shammai say, "No *'eruv* may be prepared for a Nazirite with wine or for an Israelite with *Terumah*.

And the House of Hillel say, "An *'eruv* may be prepared for a Nazirite with wine or for an Israelite with *Terumah*."

B. The House of Hillel to the House of Shammai, "Do you not agree that an *'eruv* may be prepared for an adult in connection with the Day of Atonement?"

They said to them, "True ('BL)."

They said to them, "Just as an *'eruv* may be prepared for an adult in connection with the Day of Atonement, so may an *'eruv* be prepared for a Nazirite with wine or for an Israelite with *Terumah*."

III.ii.10. For it was taught: Ḥananiah stated, "The House of Shammai did not admit the very principle of *'eruv* unless the man takes out thither his bed and all the objects he uses."

(b. 'Eruv. 30a-b)

Comment: The form is reminiscent of b. Beṣ. 17b, above, in that we have the specification of several items on which the Houses take consistent positions. The Houses' opinions are carefully balanced:

1. *'YN* M'RBYN LNZYR BYYN
2. WLYSR'L BTRWMH
1. M'RBYN LNZYR BYYN
2. WLYSR'L BTRWMH

The only difference is the negative ('YN), assigned to the Shammaites.

The dispute of part B is not conventional; indeed, the Shammaites say practically nothing and are made to concede the correctness of the Hillelite position. The Hillelites *Do you not agree* is followed not by a distinction or counter-argument, but merely 'BL, true. Then the

Hillelites draw the obvious consequence of that agreement: the principle is identical, therefore just as one prepares what is theoretically prohibited for use on the Day of Atonement, so one prepares what is theoretically prohibited for use by the Nazir. The debate certainly is a late invention, in which the Hillelites as usual stress their own consistency and point up the Shammaites' inconsistency, much as Hillel asks Shammai why one vintages in a state of cleanness but does not pick olives in a similar state. All Shammai is allowed to say is that he can impose his view on Hillel by force. The allegation that Shammaite positions are self-contradictory and Hillelite ones internally harmonious and logical derives, if not from the House of Hillel, then from later Hillelite tradents.

The primary dispute may be authentic; it is a singleton, but is consistent in giving the Shammaites the stringent position, the Hillelites the lenient one; and the form is standard and balanced. Ḥananiah's saying is difficult to evaluate; we do not know whether he merely drew the consequences of an existing pericope, or whether he claimed to have an independent tradition on the matter.

II.i.42.A. On the night of the fourteenth [of Nisan] the *ḥameṣ* must be searched for by the light of a lamp. Any place into which *ḥameṣ* is never brought needs no searching. Then why have they said, "[They search] two rows in a wine-vault?" They are a place into which *ḥameṣ* might be brought.

B. The House of Shammai say, "[They must examine] the two rows *on the whole surface of* [the stack of jars in] the wine-vault."

And the House of Hillel say, "Only the two *outermost* rows that are uppermost."

[M. Pes. 1:1, trans. Danby, p. 136 (y. Pes. 1:1, b. Pes. 2a, 8b)]

Comment: Part B serves as a gloss on the foregoing, which presumably antedates the Houses. The Talmud explains the instructions of the Houses. What is of interest here is the further use of a Houses-clause as explanatory matter for a pre-existing law. As in other cases the implication is that the laws existed, in the very form in which we have them ("why have they said. . ."), before the Houses supplied their glosses, and that the law code therefore comes before the Houses. We have had no hint in the traditions of the named authorities that such a code existed, let alone in the precise form in which it comes down to us.

We should have expected some sort of superscription, e.g.:

Until where do they search?

House of Shammai: [Two rows] on the whole surface
House of Hillel: [Two] external [rows] which are the uppermost.

The sayings of the Houses are as balanced as one might have expected, since the changes in word-choice are necessary to convey the sense of the respective Houses. It is the absence of a superscription that is curious. The Houses' sayings merely repeat the gloss but do *not* answer the question, Why have they said ŠTY ŠWRWT BMRTP:

Shammaite: ŠTY ŠWRWT ʿL KL PNY HMRTP
Hillelite: ŠTY ŠWRWT HḤYṢWNWT

Then further glossed: ŠHN HʿLYWNWT. So the Houses differ on *outermost* vs. *on the whole surface*. See Epstein, *Mishnah*, p. 609.

II.i.43.A. Where the custom is to do work on the Ninth of Av, they may do so; where the custom is not to do work, they do not work. But everywhere the disciples of the sages cease from work.

Rabban Simeon b. Gamaliel says, "A man should always behave as a disciple of the sages."

B. Moreover the sages say, "In Judea they used to do work until midday on the eve of Passover, but in Galilee they used to do nothing at all."

C. And in [what concerns work on] the night [between the 13th and 14th of Nisan], the House of Shammai forbid [any work].

And the House of Hillel permit until sunrise.

[M. Pes. 4:5, trans. Danby, p. 140 (y. Pes. 4:6, b. Pes. 55a, b. Yev. 13b)]

Comment: Part B, while formally separate from part A, depends upon it for context and meaning. It is therefore much like the gloss in the foregoing. The materials in part A derive from Simeon b. Gamaliel and "the sages" and refer to Judah and Galilee, rather than regions such as those mentioned in the letter of Simeon b. Gamaliel and Yoḥanan b. Zakkai (Upper South, Lower South). The issue is the night between the thirteenth and fourteenth *in Galilee* (presumably in Judah they worked through the night). The House-dispute is conventional:

And the night before the fourteenth
House of Shammai prohibit
And House of Hillel permit.

The gloss *until dawn* clarifies the Hillelite definition of *night*; it is redundant.

II.i.44. If a man became a proselyte on the day before Passover—

The House of Shammai say, "He immerses himself and consumes his Passover-offering in the evening."

And the House of Hillel say, "He that separates himself from the foreskin is like one that separates himself from a grave."

[M. Pes. 8:8, trans. Danby, p. 148 (y. Pes. 8:8, b. Pes. 92a)]

Comment: The form is perfect—until we come to the saying of the Hillelites. It is a substantial development over what must have been originally stated, for otherwise, we have to assume that the Hillelites responded not according to the subject under discussion, but with an enigmatic, allusive phrase. The saying means that the one who has just been circumcized is like one who has just touched a grave: he requires sprinkling on the third and seventh day after the circumcision, just like someone who has been made unclean by a corpse (Num. 19:18-19). The Hillelites ought to have said, following the Shammaite pattern:

He requires sprinkling (HZ'H) etc.

or merely the negative:

He does *not* immerse [and consume his Passover-offering].

I do not understand the preference for a somewhat elliptical expression, which, while comprehensible, carries us far afield, unless the Hillelite lemma is a development over its original language.

The authority is R. Yosi, M. ʿEd. 5:2, so Epstein, *Mevo'ot*, p. 147; see also *Mishnah*, p. 516.

II.i.45. After they have mixed him his first cup—

The House of Shammai say, "He says the Benediction first over the day and then the Benediction over the wine."

And the House of Hillel say, "He says the Benediction first over the wine and then the Benediction over the day."

[M. Pes. 10:2, trans. Danby, p. 150 (y. Pes. 10:2, b. Pes. 114a)]

Comment: See M. Ber. 8:1, above, p. 43. *After-cup* is a redactional gloss to tie the dispute to the context: laws of the *Seder*. The Houses-lemmas are identical in both places.

II.i.46. How far does he recite [the *Hallel*]?

The House of Shammai say, "To '*A joyful mother of children.*' "

And the House of Hillel say, "To '*A flintstone into a springing well*' (Ps. 114:8)."

[M. Pes. 10:6, trans. Danby, p. 151 (y. Pes. 10:5, b. Pes. 116b-117a)]

Comment: The opinions of the Houses are followed by a dispute of R. Ṭarfon and R. ʿAqiba on the conclusion of the *Hallel* at the Passover

Seder, which takes for granted the existence of the Houses dispute and therefore supplies a *terminus ante quem*. The sages assume that one has referred to the Exodus from Egypt, that is, the opinion of the Hillelites: One already has said, "*When Israel went forth from Egypt*. The form is conventional. Citing Scripture was necessary, so the usual practice of using key-words has been dropped.

III.ii.11. How far does he recite it?

The House of Shammai say, "Until *When Israel came forth out of Egypt* (Ps. 114:1)."

And the House of Hillel say, "Until *Not unto us, O Lord, not unto us* (Ps. 115:1)."

(b. Pes. 117a)

Comment: This form *ought* to antedate the version of II.i.46, and it ought to be what the Yavneans would have had before them.

II.ii.36.A. The House of Shammai say, "They do not burn clean meat with unclean meat."

And the House of Hillel permit.

B. At first they would say, "They do not sell *ḥameṣ* to a gentile and do not give it to him as a gift, unless (ʾLʾ KDY Š) he eats it before the hour of Removal comes."

Until R. ʿAqiba came and taught that they sell and give as a gift even at the hour of Removal.

C. R. Yosah said, "These [= *at first*] are the words of the House of Shammai, and these [= ʿAqiba] are the words of the House of Hillel. R. ʿAqiba decided to support the words of the House of Hillel."

[Tos. Pisḥa 1:6, at the end, and 1:7, ed. Lieberman, p. 142, lines 29-34 (y. Pes. 1:6, 3:6 [*re Terumah*]; b. Pes. 15b; b. Pes. 21a, b. Shab. 18b)]

III.ii.12. As to *piggul*, *notar*, and unclean [sacrificial meat], the House of Shammai say, "They are not burned together."

The House of Hillel say, "They are burned together."

(b. Pes. 15b)

III.ii.13. TNW RBNN: "A man does not sell his leaven to a gentile, unless he knows that it will be consumed before Passover"—the words of the House of Shammai.

And the House of Hillel say, "As long as he [the Jew] may eat it, he may sell it."

(b. Shab. 18b)

Comment: II.ii.36: The dispute of part A comes at the end of a set of discussions on burning unclean and clean sanctities, e.g. Heave-offering of various categories of uncleanness, etc. R. Simeon reports, "R. Liezer and R. Joshua did not dispute concerning clean and unclean, that they burn this by itself and this by itself. Concerning what did they differ? Concerning suspended [unclean] with unclean, for R. Liezer says, 'This is burned by itself and this by itself,' and R. Joshua [says], 'The two of them together.' " The positions of the Houses are sufficiently parallel, though in reference to different matters, so that it looks as if Eliezer = House of Shammai and Joshua = House of Hillel. The dispute logically comes before the issue discussed in Sifra Ṣav = M. M.S. 3:9, above, p. 13, 100.

The pericope of the Houses (part A) is preceded by a saying of R. Yosah and may in fact be read as part of that saying; in any case he supplies the *terminus ante quem*.

Part B's opening ruling, that the gentile has to be able to consume the leaven before the hour of Removal, is similar to the ruling of the House of Shammai (M. Shab. 1:7), that the gentile must be able to reach his home before sunset. In b. Shab. 18b, the ruling on leaven is attributed to the House of Shammai. So *at first* the law followed the Shammaites. R. ʿAqiba then reversed matters. R. Yosah then makes the whole explicit: *At first*. . . is the ruling of the House of Shammai, and ʿAqiba's ruling is the House of Hillel, and ʿAqiba decided matters in favor of the House of Hillel. (See Lieberman, *Tosefta Kifshuṭah*, to Tos. Shab. Chap. 1, line 51, p. 21, for further comment.)

Ḥanina, Prefect of the Priests, M. Pes. 1:6, y. Pes. 1:6, is in accord with the Hillelite position, I, p. 402.

II.ii.37.A. "The *pesaḥ*—they return it whole and they do not return it in pieces.

"Concerning what did they dispute?

"Concerning the limbs, for

"The House of Shammai say, 'They return.'

"And the House of Hillel say, 'They do not return.' "

[Tos. Pisḥa 7:2, ed. Lieberman, p. 176, lines 6-10 (Sifré Deut. 134, y. Shab. 1:11)]

Comment: The dispute of the Houses pertains to the *pesaḥ*-sacrifice. The sacrifice was cut apart by the limbs. The House of Shammai say one does not return them to the oven, the House of Hillel that one does. Simeon builds the dispute on the basis of Yosi and Judah. For the parallel problem with reference to the Sabbath, see Tos. Shab. 2:13, ed. Lieberman, pp. 9-10, lines 42-45. Indeed the verbal formulae are so close that it again looks as if the same rulings have been assigned to different disputes:

Tos. Shab. 2:13	*Tos. Pisḥa 7:2*	*M. Shab. 3:1*
1. He removed	1. . . .concerning the limbs	1. —
2. House of Shammai say he does not put back	2. House of Shammai say, *They* put back	2. House of Shammai say, They *take but* do not put back
3. and House of Hillel say he puts back	3. House of Hillel say, *They* do not put back	3. House of Hillel say, They *also* put back

Clearly, a tradition involving the root ḤZR, causative, third person singular or plural, with or without the negative particle, has been everywhere developed into a Houses-dispute, with the various possible combinations of singular and plural, affirmative and negative, assigned to each of the Houses. All that changes is the legal setting and superscriptions, just as in M. Pes. 10:2 = M. Ber. 8:1.

See Epstein, *Mevo'ot*, p. 332.

II.ii.38.A. R. Leazar b. R. Ṣadoq said, "The House of Shammai and the House of Hillel agree concerning an uncircumcized male (Israelite), that he receives sprinkling and eats.

"Concerning what did they dispute?

"Concerning an uncircumcized gentile [convert, who was converted and circumcized on the eve of Passover], for (Š)

B. "The House of Shammai say, 'He immerses and eats his *pesaḥ* in the evening.'

"And the House of Hillel say, 'He who separates from the foreskin is like him who separates from the grave.' "

[Tos. Pisḥa 7:14, ed. Lieberman, p. 181, lines 63-66 (b. Pes. 92a)]

Comment: See M. Pes. 8:8, M. 'Ed. 5:2. Judah the Patriarch has followed Eleazar b. R. Ṣadoq's version, part B, adding the necessary superscription. But then as I suggested, the original dispute must have been as follows:

An uncircumcized Jew who circumcized on the eve of Passover before the sacrifice
House of Shammai: Immerses [= sprinkling] and eats
House of Hillel: Does not etc.

Eleazar now has the Hillelites go over to the Shammaite position in that case, but differ concerning the gentile.

II.ii.39.A. They mixed for him the first cup—

The House of Shammai say, "He blesses the day and afterward he blesses the wine, for the day causes that the wine should come, and the day is already sanctified, and still the wine has not come."

And the House of Hillel say, "He blesses the wine and afterward he blesses the day, for the wine causes that the Sanctification of the day should be said.

B. "Another matter, the blessing of the wine is perpetual, and the blessing of the day is not perpetual."

C. And the law is according to the words of the House of Hillel.

(Tos. Pisḥa 10:2-3, ed. Lieberman, p. 196, lines 4-8)

Comment: See M. Ber. 8:1:

M. Ber. 8:1	*Tos. Pisḥa 10:2-3 [M. Pes.* 10:2*]*
1. These are the things that are between the House of Shammai and the House of Hillel concerning the meal.	1. *They mixed for him the first cup*
2. The House of Shammai say, He blesses the day, and afterward he blesses the wine.	2. ,, ,, ,, *for the day causes* etc.
3. And the House of Hillel say, He blesses the wine, and afterward he blesses the day.	3. ,, ,, ,, *for the wine causes* etc.

The glosses explaining the positions of the Houses come after the simple formulae of those positions. The Shammaites hold that if it were not for the festival, there would be no wine. The day is sanctified as soon as it gets dark, and the wine still has not come. Therefore its blessing comes first. The Hillelites hold that if there is no wine, the Sanctification is not said—all just as in Tos Ber., above, p. 50.

The *other matter*, Part C, defends the foregoing argument against a possible criticism. Even if he did not yet say the Sanctification of the day in his prayer, and he does so without wine, the blessing of the wine comes first, since it is perpetual obligation. The contrary critique therefore would have been that he certainly does have to sanctify the day—in prayer—even though there is no wine. One therefore cannot say that the wine causes the Sanctification of the day to be said. While the Shammaite critique is not given, the answer to it thus lies before us.

We do not have to suppose the Shammaites said such a thing. The later masters were stern logical critics of their own positions and would have seen the difficulty and willingly responded to it, whether or not Shammaites were available to point out the difficulty. The *other matter* is therefore apt to be a gloss, justifying the Hillelite position against a theoretical critique. The Shammaites are (probably rightly) not credited with it.

II.ii.40. The House of Shammai said to the House of Hillel, "And have they already gone forth [from Egypt, in the evening] that they should make mention of the Exodus from Egypt?"

The House of Hillel said to them, "Even if he should wait until the cock crows, lo, if they did not go forth until the sixth hour of the day, how should he say [words concerning] redemption, for they still were not redeemed?"

[Tos. Pisḥa 10:9, ed. Lieberman, p. 198, lines 24-28 (y. Pes. 10:5)]

Comment: The debate explains the reasoning of each side in M. Pes. 10:6. The Shammaites are not given a reply. y. Pes. 10:5 gives a fuller version of the Hillelite lemma:

"If he waited until the cock crows, still they have not reached half the redemption. How are they to make mention of redemption, and still they have notbeen redeemed? And is it not so that they did not go forth until noon. . . But since he began with the *miṣvah*, he said 'Finish (MRQ)' [talking about it]."

Note House of Shammai in Mekh. de R. Simeon b. Yoḥai to Ex. 12:6, Epstein-Melamed p. 12, ls. 4-5, on *evening*, (Vol. I, p. 156).

II.i.47.A. [If a man] brings together (KNŚ) coins and said, "Lo, these are for my *sheqel*"—

The House of Shammai say, "The surplus falls as a free-will offering (NDBH) [to the Temple fund]."

And the House of Hillel say, "The surplus is free for common use (ḤLYN)."

B. [If he said that] I shall bring *from* them for my *sheqel*, they agree that their surplus is for common use (ḤLYN).

C. [But if he said], "These are for my sin-offering," they agree that the surplus falls as a free-will offering (NDBH) [to the Temple fund].

[But if he said], "I will bring my sin-offering from them," they agree that the surplus is free for common use (ḤLYN).

[M. Sheq. 2:3, ed. Danby, p. 153 (y. Sheq. 2:3, y. Naz. 5:1)]

Comment: The Houses-dispute is in conventional form:

He who gathers together coins and said, Lo, these are my sheqel
The House of Shammai say, [Their excess is] free-will offering (NDBH)
The House of Hillel say, [Their excess is] unconsecrated (ḤLYN).

Part B preserves the apodosis of the superscription, taking for granted the protasis, so the pericope is a unity.

The legal issue is the effect of the man's intention. The Hillelites hold that while he only intended to sanctify what was necessary, his language was imprecise. The Shammaites regard the actual language as decisive. The dispute of the Houses on whether what is erroneously consecrated is regarded as consecrated recurs elsewhere; the various specific disputes all turn on that principle and look like variations of that single fixed difference. In the second case the Houses obviously agree, since the language now conforms to the precise intention. As to the sin-offering, part C, here the Shammaites' position is accepted by the Hillelites. R. Simeon specifies the reason in M. Sheq. 2:4. The *sheqel* has a limit, while there is no limit on sin-offerings. So the Hillelites now have no reason to disagree. On this basis Epstein, *Mevo'ot*, p. 152, assigns 2:3-4 to Simeon.

II.i.48. If the flesh of the Most Holy Things (QDŠY QDŠYM) contracted uncleanness, whether from a primary uncleanness or from a derived uncleanness, whether inside [the Temple Court] or outside it—

The House of Shammai say, "All must be burnt inside, save when it has contracted uncleanness from a primary uncleanness—outside."

And the House of Hillel say, "All must be burnt outside, save when it has contracted uncleanness from a derived uncleanness—inside."

[M. Sheq. 8:6, trans. Danby, p. 161 (y. Sheq. 8:3)]

Comment: See M. M.S. 3:9, where the superscription pertains to *Second Tithe which entered Jerusalem:*

M.M.S. 3:9	*M. Sheq. 8:6*
1. Second Tithe that entered Jerusalem and became unclean	1. *Flesh of Holy of Holies that became unclean*
2. Whether unclean by a Father of Uncleanness or an Offspring of Uncleanness	2. whether by a Father ,, ,, ,, [Omits: *made unclean*]
3. Whether inside or outside	3. ,, ,, ,,
4. House of Shammai say, All is redeemed and eaten inside, except what is made unclean by a Father of Uncleanness [which is eaten] outside	4. All is *burned* inside ,, ,, ,,
5. House of Hillel say, All is redeemed and eaten outside, except what is made unclean by an Offspring of Uncleanness [which is eaten] inside	5. All is *burned* outside ,, ,, ,,

The opinions of the Houses are the same, except *is redeemed* of Second Tithe becomes *is burned* for the meat, a change required by the legal context, and the verb *made unclean* is not repeated in M. Sheq. no. 2, a stylistic change of no importance. Here again, it looks as though a standard Houses-opinion has been placed into several appropriate contexts by doctoring the superscriptions. This is Judah's version in Sifra Ṣav 8:6, so Epstein, *Mevo'ot*, pp. 73-4.

II.ii.41.A. Meat of the Most Holy Things which contracted uncleanness, whether from a Father of Uncleanness or an Offspring of Uncleanness, whether inside or outside—

The House of Shammai say, "All will be burned inside, except for that which was made unclean by a Father of Uncleanness, [which is burned] outside."

And the House of Hillel say, "All will be burned outside, except for that which was made unclean by an Offspring of Uncleanness, [which is burned] inside."

B. R. Liezer says, "What is made unclean by a Father of Uncleanness, whether inside or outside, is burned outside, and by an Offspring of Uncleanness, whether outside or inside, is burned inside."

C. R. Judah says, "R. Liezer speaks [says] according to the words of the House of Shammai. R. 'Aqiba speaks [says] according to the words of the House of Hillel."

[Tos. Sheq. 3:16, ed. Lieberman, pp. 216-7, lines 46-52 (Sifra Ṣav 8:6, M. M.S. 3:9, Tos. M.S. 2:16)]

Comment: See M. Sheq. 8:6, and above, pp. 100-105. Here R. Judah b. Ilai makes explicit what we surmised above. What is missing here is the opinion of 'Aqiba, which is in M. Sheq. 8:7. See also Sifra Ṣav 8:6.

III.ii.19. How much must one have drunk to become culpable [for drinking on the Day of Atonement]?

The House of Shammai say, "One fourth [of a *log*]."

The House of Hillel say, "One mouthful."

R. Judah in the name of R. Eliezer says, "As much as a mouthful."

(b. Yoma 80a)

Comment: The form is standard. The Houses-sayings consist of the following:

Shammai: RBY'YT
Hillel: ML' LWGMYW

The sayings consist of standard measures of liquid, therefore are as balanced as one could expect. Eliezer's difference from the House of Hillel is discussed in the accompanying *gemara*. The Hillelites are not exact as to the matter. Eliezer insists it must be exactly a mouthful. The Shammaite's minimum is greater than the Hillelites'; they therefore are in the more lenient position, and R. Hoshaiah observes, "If so, it would be a case in which the House of Shammai take the more lenient view, the House of Hillel the more stringent one."

This is a singleton. The difference between the Houses is not considerable, and it may be that, if the traditions are authentic, the real difference is in word-choice. That is, curiously, the sole Houses-tradition pertaining to the Day of Atonement.

II.i.49.A. An old *Sukkah*—

The House of Shammai declare invalid

And the House of Hillel declare valid.

B. And what is deemed an old *Sukkah*? Any that was made thirty days before the Feast.

But if it was made for the sake of the Feast, even at the beginning of the year, it is valid.

[M. Suk. 1:1, trans. Danby, p. 173 (y. Pes. 2:4 = old *maṣṣah*; y. Suk. 1:2, b. Suk. 9a)]

Comment: The form is standard. Part B serves as a neutral, later gloss to the Houses-dispute.

II.i.50. If there was a timber roofing that had no plastering—

R. Judah says, "The House of Shammai say, 'He loosens and removes one beam between each two.'

"And the House of Hillel say, 'He [either] loosens or removes one beam between each two.' "

R. Meir says, "He removes one beam between each two, but does not loosen the roofing."

[M. Suk. 1:7, trans. Danby, p. 173 (y. Suk. 1:8, b. Suk. 15a)]

Comment: Judah b. Ilai records a Houses-dispute on a *Sukkah* covered by a timbered roofing. To render the *Sukkah* valid, the Shammaites say, the man has both to loosen the timbers *and* to remove one of every two, and then to place *śekhakh* over the whole instead. The House of Hillel say it is sufficient either to loosen the whole *or* to remove one of every two beams, then to place the *śekhakh*, but one does not have to do both. Meir says, following the Hillelite view, that one must remove alternate beams but does not loosen; thus there is no choice as to the procedure.

Meir does not attribute his view to the House of Hillel. But in effect, the dispute is between Meir and Judah and concerns whether there is a choice as to the matter; Judah says there is, Meir, there is not. No one regards the Hillelite opinion as other than law. Both interpret it. One must therefore wonder, Why has Judah b. Ilai preserved the Houses-dispute? For the purposes of the law, it would have sufficed to give his opinion in the following setting:

If there was a timber roofing that had no plastering
Judah says, He [either] loosens or removes
Meir says, He removes and does not loosen.

Dropping the Houses-materials, Judah would have adequately stated his view of the legal issue before the second-century masters. Since I can see no purpose served by preserving the Houses-form, I suppose Judah may report an authentic Houses-pericope. To be sure, whether the Houses-pericope goes back to the actual Houses, or to earlier masters who made use of the Houses-form, we cannot say for sure. But as it stands, the pericope seems to me possibly to reflect an intention accurately to preserve the traditional materials.

See Epstein, *Mishnah*, p. 1064 on disputes as to ʾW.

II.i.51.A. If a man's head and the greater part of his body are within the *Sukkah*, but his table is within the house—

The House of Shammai declare it invalid (PŚL).

And the House of Hillel declare it valid (KŠR).

B. The House of Hillel said to the House of Shammai, "Was thus not the incident, that (WLʾ KK HYH MʿSH Š) the Elders of the House of Shammai and the Elders of the House of Hillel went to visit R. Yoḥanan b. HaḤorani and found him sitting with his head and the greater part of his body within the *Sukkah*, while his table was within the house, and they did not say a thing to him [MS Kaufmann omits *and-him*]?"

C. The House of Shammai said to them, "Is there proof from that? They *indeed* (ʾP) said to him, 'If such has been your custom you have never in your life fulfilled the law of the *Sukkah*.' "

[M. Suk. 2:7, trans. Danby, p. 175 (b. Ber. 11a, y. Suk. 2:8, b. Suk. 3a, 7b, 28a-b)]

Comment: Part A is standard. The legal issue is whether the *Sukkah* is sufficiently large. If the man cannot go into it, but leans into it while sitting in his own house, he has not fulfilled the obligation, so the Shammaites. But their language is *not* YṢ'!

The Hillelites accept so small a *Sukkah* as valid. YS'—also in part C, would be better.

The debate-form in part B is used not for an exchange of principles, but rather to trade stories. What we in fact have is two separate versions of the incident, joined by *they said to them* and revised to support the positions of the respective Houses.

The House of Hillel's version is that a Shammaite disciple followed the law according to the House of Hillel. Sages of both Houses knew about it and said nothing to him. Hence good Shammaites follow the Hillelite law, the evidently well-known Yoḥanan b. HaḤorani among them, and even the elders of the House knew about it and registered no complaint. The Hillelite House thus contend the Shammaite position is not what the House of Shammai now allege it to be! The Shammaite House does not even know the authentic Shammaite tradition.

The House of Shammai do not reject the story. They merely claim that the sages of *both* Houses say the man has never carried out the commandment. Their allegation, therefore, is the precise opposite of the Hillelites': The sages of the Hillelite House in fact concurred in the Shammaite ruling. So the little debate concerns the validity of part A, each party maintaining the other had agreed with its position—there ought to be no dispute at all.

It is not difficult to reconstruct an original for the story cited in the debate. It looks to me as if the Shammaite version would be as follows:

A. The Elders of the House of Shammai and the Elders of the House of Hillel went to visit R. Yoḥanan.
B. They found him sitting with his head and greater part of his body within the *Sukkah*, while his table was within the House.
C. They said to him, "If such has been your custom, you have never in your life fulfilled the law of the *Sukkah*."

This story has been revised for redactional purposes. The opening lines obviously do not need to be repeated. But the imposition of the debate-form has required the inclusion of *is there proof from that, but. . . indeed.* This now connects the operative statement, *If such. . .* to the dispute. The Hillelite version of the story is before us without alteration.

It serves no purpose to speculate on what "really" happened, if anything. The fact is that the Houses made use of incidents involving the elders as precedents. Presumably, the Shammaites told how Hillel had obeyed the law as the Shammaites taught it (Temple sacrifice), just as the Hillelites alleged all good Shammaites followed Hillelite law (Baba b. Buṭa). The involvement of Yoḥanan is the real problem before both Houses. The Hillelites allege that, while he is claimed by the Shammaites, he really followed the law of the House of Hillel. The Shammaite response is: If so, he *never* kept the law at all. This is a rather weak reply, since it implicitly accepts the allegation of the

Hillelites and merely repeats the Shammaite position without new testimony. We should have much preferred a Shammaite story about how Yoḥanan had never done any such thing at all, but had built his *Sukkah* in the proper dimensions to begin with. So it looks to me as if the Shammaite version of the story is just that—a version. They have revised the antecedent *Hillelite* story to serve their own purposes, but they have no other story to substitute in its place, or whatever other story they had has been suppressed.

If this is the case, it is striking that the Shammai-Hillel-Houses-form has prevailed. The Hillelites do not suppress the Shammaite answer. As usual, the Houses enjoy full formal parity with one another. If so, why could the Shammaites not have introduced their own version, which would not have had Yoḥanan's *Sukkah* improper to begin with? We cannot suppose concern for veracity prevented them, since they were prepared to revise the Hillelite story at its crucial point. It looks to me as if the Shammaites of this story come long after the fact (if any), and that they invent no new account because, coming sufficiently long after he died, they could only contradict Hillelite allegations about him, but not invent new facts. We have no further stories of visits of the Elders of both Houses to this particular master, so we cannot speculate on what the Shammaites would have preserved as a record of the occasion, instead of the issue of the size of his *Sukkah*. We shall see further versions of the Ḥoranite-problem, Tos. Suk. 2:3, below, p. 155.

Note Epstein, *Mevo'ot*, pp. 213, 353; *Mishnah*, pp. 630, 635.

III.ii.15. If the rays of the sun cannot be seen through it [the covering of the *Sukkah*]—

The House of Shammai declare invalid.

And the House of Hillel declare valid. (b. Suk. 22b)

Comment: This is a singleton, part of a *beraita* but unattested elsewhere. The form is entirely conventional. The problem pertains to the foregoing, II. i. 51.

II.i.52. [A citron] of *demai*-produce—

The House of Shammai declare invalid.

And the House of Hillel declare valid.

[M. Suk. 3:5, trans. Danby, p. 176 (y. ʿEruv. 3:2; y. Suk. 3:5, b. Suk. 35b)]

Comment: The form is standard. The issue is whether one may make use of citrons of various sorts: stolen, withered, from an *asherah*, from an apostate city, ʿ*orlah*-fruit, unclean Heave-offering, clean Heave-offering, then *demai*, finally, Second Tithe. The Houses rule only on one detail; all the rest of the laws are given anonymously and unanimously. The implication is that the other laws come earlier and form part of a a standard code, with the Houses' supplying a minor addition to the list.

If one is not sure whether the citron comes from tithed produce, he must not make use of it but may feed it to the poor, as in the case of *demai* in general. So the case of *demai* pertains to doubtful, not certain status, while the other items in the list are all certainly in the category of produce to which laws surely pertain (stolen, or Heave-offering, and so forth). The Houses-dispute pertains to the most ambiguous matter.

Compare M. Eruv. 3:2: They make an *'eruv* with *demai*.

II.i.53.A. And where do they shake the *Lulav*?

"At the beginning and the end of the Psalm, *O give thanks unto the Lord* (Ps. 118) and at *Save now, we beseech thee, O Lord*"—according to the words of the House of Hillel.

The House of Shammai say, "Also ('P) at *O Lord, we beseech thee, send now prosperity.*"

B. R. 'Aqiba said, "I once watched Rabban Gamaliel and R. Joshua, and while all the people were shaking their *Lulavs*, they shook them only at *Save now, we beseech thee, O Lord.*"

[M. Suk. 3:9, trans. Danby, p. 177 (y. Suk. 3:8, b. Suk. 38a)]

Comment: The form is egregious, for it places the House of Hillel before Shammai, and it is KDBRY, rather than 'MRYM. As it stands, part B supplies the information that the masters had apparently done things according to *neither* House. The pericope therefore breaks the normal form. The testimony of 'Aqiba tells us something we cannot relate to the antecedent dispute. We should have expected the following

Where do they shake?

The House of Shammai say, At *O Lord we beseech thee, send now prosperity*

The House of Hillel say, (1) At the beginning and (2) the end of the Psalm: *O give thanks unto the Lord* and (3) at *Save now*.

As it now stands, the difference is four (Shammai) vs. three (Hillel). In the revised form, we have simply rearranged the opinions of the Houses. But to do so, we must drop the *also*, which here serves only redactional purposes, from before the Shammaite opinion. The dispute then is one vs. three.

Let us now introduce 'Aqiba's story:

R. 'Aqiba said, I once watched Rabban Gamaliel and R. Joshua, and while all the people were shaking their *Lulavs*, they shook them only at *Save now, O Lord, we beseech thee*.

The Hillelites say one shakes at Ps. 118:1 and Ps. 118:25A. The Shammaites say one shakes at Ps. 118:25B only:

A. *Save us, we beseech thee, O Lord*
B. *O Lord, we beseech thee, send now prosperity.*

ʿAqiba's story therefore now tells us that Gamaliel and Joshua followed the Shammaite practice. So the issue between the Houses was whether one shakes at the start and at the end of Ps. 118 (Hillel) or only at the end (Shammai). The form is now standard, and the ʿAqiban report makes sense; we have several other stories of ʿAqiba's reporting Gamaliel's and Joshua's following Shammaite practice.

It seems to me that the pericope has been revised so as deliberately to obscure the meaning of ʿAqiba's point, and to do so, the Shammaite ruling has been phrased in terms of part B, rather than part A, of Ps. 118:25. Had normal reference to a Scripture been made, it would have been merely to the opening words, *Save us, we beseech thee*, and everyone would have understood the reference.

This theory depends on the supposition that shaking was done at a whole Scripture, and not in response to reading only a part of it. If that is *not* the case, then we have the following:

Ps. 118:1	House of Hillel, House of Shammai
Ps. 118:25A	Gamaliel and Joshua, House of Hillel and House of Shammai
Ps. 118:25B	House of Shammai

In that case, ʿAqiba's story serves to establish a third position on the question: One shakes only at Ps. 118:25A. Form-critical considerations cannot be decisive, merely suggestive.

For a summary of traditional views, See Epstein, *Mishnah*, p. 359.

II.ii.42.A. R. Leazar b. R. Ṣadoq said, "When I was studying with Yoḥanan b. HaḤoranit, I saw that he ate a dry piece of bread, for they were years of drought. I came and told father. And he said to me, 'Here are olives for him.'

"I brought olives to him. He took them and looked at them and saw that they were moist [and susceptible to uncleanness].

"He said to me, 'I do not eat olives [without mentioning possible uncleanness, as a respectful gesture].'

"I came and I told father.

"He said to me, 'Go, say to him, It was broached [therefore the liquid has *not* made them susceptible to uncleanness], according to the words of the House of Hillel; [according to the House of Shammai, even if it were *not* broached, the olives would *not* have been susceptible —thus the concern of Yoḥanan shows he followed the Hillelite view; see M. ʿEd. 4:6] but the lees had stopped it up.' "

B. [This is] to tell you that he ate his unconsecrated food in a state of ritual purity.

C. For (Š) even though he was of the disciples of the House of Shammai, he behaved only according to the words of the House of Hillel.

D. The law is always according to the House of Hillel.

E. He who wishes to be stringent on himself to behave according to the House of Shammai and according to the words of the House of Hillel—of such a one it is said, *And the fool walks in darkness* (Qoh. 2:14).

He who holds to the lenient rulings of the House of Shammai and the lenient rulings of the House of Hillel is evil.

But if according to the words of the House of Shammai, then according to their lenient and their strict rulings, or [if] according to the words of the House of Hillel, then according to their lenient and strict rulings [should he behave].

[Tos. Suk. 2:3, ed. Lieberman, pp. 261-2, lines 16-26 (y. Ber. 1:4, b. 'Eruv. 6b, b. R.H. 14b, y. Yev. 1:6; M. 'Ed. 2:2; y. Qid. 1:1, b. Ḥul. 43b-44a, y. Soṭ. 3:4, b. Yev. 15b)]

Comment: Compare M. Suk. 2:7. The story of part A is a unity. It is another version of the "Hillelization" of Yoḥanan, this time in connection with his observance of the purity laws. Part B is a gloss, explaining the point of Leazar's father's message. Then comes the usual subscription, part C, a stock-phrase attached to pretty much any story about a good Shammaite.

Part D introduces a new and separate pericope, formed of parts D and E. It is addressed to inconsistent people. It seems to me a curious tradition, for the message should be, as with Ishmael, Ṭarfon, and other early Yavneans, that one who follows the teachings of the Shammaites is worthy of supernatural retribution (death, in the case of Ṭarfon). One can suppose two possible times in which such a ruling could have been made, either long after anyone seriously threatened Hillelite predominance (*the law is always according. . .*), or at a time that the Houses were of equal strength or the Shammaites superior, so that the best the Hillelites could do was to say, "Be consistent one way or the other."

It is difficult to choose between these alternatives. Obviously, Yavneh does not present itself as a likely location. Before that time, when the Hillelites probably were subordinated within Pharisaism, the Shammaites presumably would have had a different logion, and the Hillelites would, as I said, have had to have satisfied themselves with this sort of counsel. Dating logia by the criterion of their content is surely a questionable procedure; one can only guess, and my guess is that the saying comes *after* the Shammaites represented a serious alternative within the Pharisaic-rabbinic movement, presumably at the time of the Bar Kokhba War, and, because of the date of Tos., certainly before ca. 250; this is consistent with my suggestion for the equally ironic saying of M. Yev. 1:4, below, p. 190.

As to part A, the story of Leazar seems to me quite credible. It is, to be sure, told from the Hillelite perspective, but that Leazar told it—perhaps, after the fact, justifying his father's choice of a master—seems to me reasonably certain. What is curious, if we discount the Hillelite glosses, is that Leazar did study with a Shammaite. As above, we should have preferred no story at all to a story raising significant doubt about Yoḥanan's true loyalty. "Yoḥanan would not eat more than minimal meals in years of drought" or some such theme would have been preferable from the Shammaite viewpoint.

III.ii.16.A. R. Abba stated in the name of Samuel, "For three years there was a dispute between the House of Shammai and the House of Hillel, the former asserting, 'The law is in agreement with our views' and the latter contending, 'The law is in agreement with our views.'

"Then an echo came forth and said, 'Both are the words of the living God, but the law is in agreement with the rulings of the House of Hillel.' "

Since, however, both are the words of the living God, what was it that entitled the House of Hillel to have the law fixed in agreement with their rulings?

Because they were kindly and modest, they studied their own rulings and those of the House of Shammai, and were even so [humble] as to mention the words of the House of Shammai before theirs, as may be seen from what we have learnt:

If a man had his head and the greater part of his body within the *Sukkah* but his table in the house, the House of Shammai say [that the booth was] invalid but the House of Hillel say that [it was] valid.

Said the House of Hillel to the House of Shammai, "Did it not so happen that the elders of the House of Shammai and the elders of the House of Hillel went on a visit to R. Yoḥanan b. HaḤoranit and found him sitting with his head and greater part of his body within the *Sukkah* while his table was in the house?"

The House of Shammai replied, "From there may proof be drawn? They indeed told him, 'If you have always acted in this manner you have never fulfilled the commandment of *Sukkah*.' "

This teaches you that him who humbles himself the Holy One, blessed be He, raises up, and him who exalts himself the Holy One, blessed be He, humbles; from him who seeks greatness, greatness flees; but him who flees from greatness, greatness follows; he who forces time is forced back by time, but he who yields to time finds time standing at his side.

B. Our rabbis taught: For two and a half years were the House of Shammai and the House of Hillel in dispute, the former asserting that it were better for man not to have been created than to have been created, and the latter maintaining that it is better for man to have been created than not to have been created.

They finally took a vote and decided that it were better for man not to have been created than to have been created, but now that he has been created, let him investigate his past deeds or, as others say, let him examine his future actions.

[b. ʿEruv. 13b, trans. I. W. Slotki, pp. 85-7 (y. Suk. 2:8)]

Comment: Samuel's story includes the citation of M. Suk. 2:7.

III.i.5. [This rule applies] before the echo went forth, but after the echo went forth, the law is always according to the words of the House of Hillel, and whoever transgresses the words of the House of Hillel is liable to death.

TNY: An echo went forth and said, "These and these are the words of the living God, but the law is according to the words of the House of Hillel."

Where did the echo go forth?

Rabbi Bibi said in the name of Rabbi Yoḥanan, "In Yavneh the echo went forth."

(y. Ber. 1:4, ed. Gilead, p. 17)

Comment: The foregoing is appended to the rule about consistently following the Houses. It corrects the false impression that one may *ever* follow the Shammaites. The Babylonian discussion on the same matter differs, b. Yev. 11a ff.

II.i.54.A. If an egg was laid on a Festival-day—

The House of Shammai say, "It may be eaten."

And the House of Hillel say, "It may not be eaten."

B. The House of Shammai say, "An olive's bulk of leaven and a date's bulk of what is leavened."

And the House of Hillel say, "An olive's bulk of either (ZH WZH KZYT)."

C. If a man slaughtered a wild animal or a bird on a Festival-day—

The House of Shammai say, "He digs with a mattock and covers up [the blood]."

And the House of Hillel say, "He should not slaughter unless he had earth set in readiness [to cover up] from the day before [MS Kaufmann omits *from-before*]."

But they agree that if he had slaughtered, he digs with a mattock and covers up [the blood].

[Moreover they agree] that the ashes of a stove may count as set in readiness [See b. Ḥul. 88b, below, pp. 167-168].

D. The House of Shammai say, "They do not remove a ladder from one dovecot to another, but only incline it from one opening (ḤLWN) to another [of the same dovecot]."

And the House of Hillel permit it.

E. The House of Shammai say, "A man may not take [pigeons for slaughtering on a Festival-day] unless he stirred them up the day before (MBʿWD YWM—while it is still day)."

And the House of Hillel say, "He stands and says, 'This one and this one shall I take.' "

F. The House of Shammai say, "They do not take off cupboard-doors (TRŚYN) on a Festival-day."

And the House of Hillel permit even to put back.

G. The House of Shammai say, "They do not lift up a pestle to hack meat on it."

And the House of Hillel permit.

H. The House of Shammai say, "They do not put a hide before the treading-place, and they may lift one up only if there is an olive's bulk of flesh on it."

And the House of Hillel permit.

I. The House of Shammai say, "They do not carry out a child or a *Lulav* or a scroll of the Torah into the public domain."

And the House of Hillel permit.

J. The House of Shammai say, "They do not take Dough-offering or [Priests'] Dues (MTNWT) to the priest on a Festival-day, whether they were set apart (HWRMW) on the day before (MBʿWD YWM) or on the same day."

And the House of Hillel permit.

K. The House of Shammai said to the House of Hillel, "It is a *gezerah shavah*: Dough-offering and [Priests'] Dues are a gift to the priest, and the Heave-offering is a gift to the priest. Just as they do not bring Heave-offering, so they do not bring [Priests'] Dues."

The House of Hillel said to them, "No! If you argue of Heave-offering, which [a man] has not the right (ZKYY) to set apart [on a Festival-day], would you also argue of [Priests'] Dues, which [a man] *has* the right to set apart [on a Festival-day]?"

L. The House of Shammai say, "Spices are pounded with a wooden pestle, and salt in a cruse and with a wooden pot-stirrer."

And the House of Hillel say, "Spices may be pounded, after their usual fashion, with a stone pestle, and salt with a wooden pestle."

M. If a man picked out pulse on a Festival-day, the House of Shammai say, "He [forthwith] eats the edible parts as he picks them out."

And the House of Hillel say, "He picks them out after his usual fashion—into his lap or into a basket or into a dish; but not on to a board or into a sifter or sieve."

Rabban Gamaliel says, "He even swills them and separates the husks."

N. The House of Shammai say, "They send only [prepared] portions (MNWT) [as gifts on a Festival-day]."[1]

And the House of Hillel say, "They send cattle, wild animal, or bird, whether alive or slaughtered."

O. They may send wine, oil, flour, or pulse, but not grain. But R. Simeon permits grain.

[M. Beṣ. 1:1, 2, 3, 5, 6, 7, 8, 9, trans. Danby, pp. 181-3 (y. Demai 4:3 = M. 1:6, b. Yoma 79b = M. 1:1; y. Pes. 5:4 = M. 1:1; y. Beṣ. 1:1, 2, 3, 4, 6, 7, 8, 9, 10, 11; y. Beṣ. 4:7 = part E; b. Shab. 124a-b = part I; b. Beṣ. 2a-b, 6b-7a, 7b, 9a, 9b, 10a, 10b, 11a, 11b, 12a, 12b, 14a, 14b, 37a; y. A.Z. 2:7)].

III.ii.17. If it [an egg] is laid on a Sabbath, it may be eaten on a Festival; [if it is laid] on a Festival it may be eaten on a Sabbath.

R. Judah says in the name of R. Eliezer, "The dispute still continues: for the House of Shammai say, 'It may be eaten;' and the House of Hillel say, 'It may not be eaten.' "

(b. Beṣ. 4a)

Comment: The pericope pertains to work that may be done on a festival in connection with the preparation of food, according to Ex. 12:16.

[1] On the interpretation of Num. 15:17-21 and Deut. 18:3, see Geza Vermes in *Cambridge History of the Bible* (Cambridge, 1970), I, p. 222.

The first part of the collection, parts A-I, M. Beṣ. 1:1-5, concerns *muqṣeh*, that is, something which has not been set aside for use on the festival. It is prohibited to make use of it on the festival, just as on the Sabbath.

Part A (M. Beṣ. 1:1) sets forth the principle under debate in terms of the particular instance of an egg born on the festival. The House of Shammai say it may be eaten on the festival; just as it is permitted to slaughter the hen on the festival for food, so it is permitted to eat its egg. The House of Hillel regard the egg as a 'new thing,' and it is not like the egg which the day earlier was in the hen. That which is born thus is not *ready* (MWKN) the day before the festival, but *muqṣeh* (Albeck, *Seder Mo'ed*, p. 287).

Part B (M. Beṣ. 1:1) pertains to Ex. 13:7, *No leavened bread* (ḤMṢ) *shall be seen with you, and no leaven* (S'WR) *shall be seen with you.* The House of Shammai understand the measurements to be different from one another. One does not transgress the taboo of appearance of leaven in a quantity less than those specified. But one may not consume any quantity at all. Part B does not belong here, having nothing to do with the other items on the list. It furthermore lacks a superscription, and no explanatory gloss is inserted into the Shammaite saying, as one would expect. The redactional purpose in including it is not evident to me.

Part C, M. Beṣ. 1:2, is superficially in conventional form:

[Statement of the legal problem] *He who slaughters a wild animal, etc.*
House of Shammai: He may dig with a mattock and cover
House of Hillel: [*Should be*: He may *not* dig with a mattock].

The Hillelite opinion, however, is that under the specified conditions, one may not *slaughter* at all! So the opinions are not evenly matched. That would not matter, except that the superscription ("He that slaughters") leads to the supposition that they *will* be balanced opposites, as usual. So the superscription is wrong.

The Hillelites hold one may not slaughter at all unless the dust for covering the blood has been made ready before the festival day. Now, that opinion in fact is *not* that one may not slaughter. One may slaughter. The Houses differ only on whether one may now prepare the dirt—a secondary consideration. So the superscription and consequent rulings should have been:

One who has not prepared the dirt the preceding day:
House of Shammai: He may slaughter (and dig and cover).
House of Hillel: He may not slaughter (at all).

What has been changed to reach the foregoing form? We have placed the operative element of the present superscription into the lemma of the Shammaites, and supplied a new superscription. If, therefore, the original tradition consisted only of the opinions of the Houses, then someone would merely have taken part of the Shammaite opinion and placed it as a superscription. The condition of the Hillelite rule, about preparing the dirt the day before, clearly belongs as the superscription; dropping the redactional formula *unless* (ʾLʾ ʾM KN), and adding the negative, we have

He did not have dirt ready the preceding day
House of Shammai: He may slaughter [and dig and cover]
House of Hillel: He may not slaughter.

So what may have happened is now fairly clear. The gloss on the Hillelite opinion has been taken from the superscription, and the first clause of the original Shammaite opinion has replaced it.

But why should this have been done? Neither the present pericope, nor the one I have reconstructed, differs from Part A, which supplies a superscription, then the Houses' opinions in brief matched pairs. To be sure, part B lacks a superscription; but it also does not belong here at all. The *meal*-collection (M. Ber. 8:1-8) may supply the key. There the Houses' rulings are not preceded by superscriptions, except for the general one at the outset: *concerning the meal*. Here, by contrast, the *collection*-form has been amplified by the inclusion of superscriptions at the outset, *egg born on festival*. But that superscription does not serve the whole list, merely the first item on it. So someone has apparently modified the *collection*-form by the inclusion of superscriptions, as is common in discrete Houses-pericopae. Part A has been given the wrong superscription, according to our theory of the original *collection*-form. Part B has been given none—it is the primary tradition, without modification.

Part C then has required the construction of an appropriate superscription—a general rule, parallel to *concerning the meal*. Rather than supplying a narrow and limited item, *he did not have dirt ready*, the editor has preferred the more general description, *he who slaughters*, intending it to serve as the beginning of an entirely new collection. He has botched the job, for reasons stated earlier, but not entirely. His superscription does serve the *next* items on the list: parts D-E concern slaughtering pigeons. The editor has succeeded in arranging things so that a common theme unites otherwise unrelated laws, thus linking parts C, D, and E, by announcing that common theme. This would account for his preference for the general, rather than the specific, superscription.

Parts D-E (M. Beṣ. 1:3) are in still another form already familiar everywhere except in collections: the superscription is inserted into the Shammaites' opinion. One may not carry a ladder, but may incline it toward different openings in the same dovecot. His purpose is to take the pigeons to slaughter them on the festival. The Hillelites permit carrying the ladder. A better-integrated form would be something like this:

The ladder
House of Shammai: Lean and *not* remove [carry]
House of Hillel: Lean *and* remove.

That simple form, using the same verbs for both opinions, and differentiating the opinions only with the negative (Shammai) and the conjunction (Hillel) would have been developed into the more polished form before us.

Part E is a still further form. The law pertains to taking pigeons. The House of Shammai hold that the day before the man must have signified his intention of using them by stirring them. The House of Hillel say he does not actually have to touch the pigeons, but may signify his intention merely by so stating. The two opinions are *not* matched; both represent secondary developments of whatever primary lemmas existed, for in each case we have full sentences, spelling out what actions need to be taken. The Shammaite lemma is elliptical, as in M. Shab.:

He should *not* take/unless he *stirred*/the day before.

The key word is therefore in the middle. The House of Hillel's lemma does not contain *the day before*, but it should, for the Hillelite opinion pertains to that same time. So *the day before* should either be dropped or placed in the superscription. The *unless*-construction clearly is to be rephrased as a simple, affirmative verb, presumably *stirs*, since *take* pertains to the situation addressed by both Houses. As to the Hillelite lemma, what the man says (*This and this I am going to take*) serves as a gloss on *says*. The two verbal participles seem to me essential: He [merely] *stands* [down below] *and says*. So the whole should begin something like the following:

[Unstated superscription:
He who wishes to slaughter pigeons on the festival must on the preceding day signify which pigeons he intends to slaughter.]

House of Shammai:	He stirs [N'N', as present participle].
House of Hillel:	He stands and says [Understood: *which one he wants*].

The *which-wants* phrase is then rephrased into direct discourse as a gloss. What we have in the end, therefore, is a brief set of lemmas, with the opinions of the Houses given as present participles. As to the rather complex superscription, a simple, if not entirely clear, form would have been *on the preceding day*. The developed and complete statement I have proposed is neither better nor worse than a brief one.

Much depends upon the purposes of the redactors, who were prepared to attach whatever superscriptions served their purposes. Clarity of intent was not a dominant consideration (as in part B, where the omission of a superscription leaves an enigma). So while we may reasonably speculate on the forms of the Houses-sayings, we cannot locate the principles guiding the development of superscriptions for those sayings.

Parts F-I (M. Beṣ. 1:5) follow a single, rigid form:

[No superscription]

House of Shammai:	Negative plus list of actions
House of Hillel:	Permit [either entirely, or in some detail of the foregoing list, in the latter instance joined by *also* ('P)].

The law of part F concerns removing cupboard doors. The House of Shammai prohibit it, because it looks like tearing down a building, which is not allowed. The House of Hillel say one may both remove and restore the doors so as to take out the food therein. Part G concerns a separate issue, the pestle. This on weekdays is used for things which may not be used on the festival, so it is *muqṣeh*, and may not be used even for the processes permitted on the festival. Part H concerns the hide of a beast slaughtered on the festival. One may not tread it unless some flesh adheres, for it is permitted to move the hide only on account of the meat. The House of Hillel permit it, for if not, the man will not slaughter the animal to begin with. Part I has the House of Shammai prohibit moving things which have nothing to do with the meal. The House of Hillel hold that, since it is permitted to remove objects for the meal, removing objects *not* connected with the meal may also be done. This position is consistent with part H, so much so that part I may simply represent a gloss serving to make explicit, with reference to common things (Scroll of the Torah, child, *Lulav*), what has already been said about something uncommon (the hide). See Simeon b. Gamaliel, above, p. 133.

Part J (M. Beṣ. 1:6) conforms to the foregoing pattern, but part K diverges from it by supplying a Houses-debate. Here, however, the House of Shammai come first, contrary to the usual debate-form. They hold that since one may not bring Heave-offering, one may also not bring other Priestly gifts. The House of Hillel come last and distinguish between the two sorts of gifts. Normally, we should have expected to see the Shammaites last, answering the Hillelite argument. The form of the argument is consistent with others already examined: the second party answers, *No, if you say concerning so-and-so, the reason is such and such, but will you say so concerning something to which that same reason does not pertain?* Part K presumably represents a Hillelite gloss on part J. It completely violates the integrity of the *collection*-form, even in the loose state of the form before us.

Part L constitutes still another, and quite different form from those in the earlier segments of the list. It has a full account of the opinions of both Houses. Clearly a superscription specifying the items under discussion would have allowed a very simple Houses-dispute:

Crushing Spices:

House of Shammai:	With a wooden pestle
House of Hillel:	After their usual fashion

Salt:

House of Shammai:	In a cruse, with wooden pot-stirrer
House of Hillel:	With a wooden pestle.

We do not gain much by such a rearrangement; in this case, the opinions, though phrased in a considerable number of words, are still evenly balanced, element by element, and the contrasts are clear as given. What is more interesting is the progression of the wooden pestle:

Spices may be pounded:

House of Shammai:	With a wooden pestle
House of Hillel:	As usual.

Salt:

House of Shammai:	In a cruse, with wooden pot-stirrer
House of Hillel:	In a wooden pestle.

In the salt-case, the Hillelites do require a change in the usual manner of preparing the salt. The wooden pestle occurs in the opinions of each House, though in reference to different items. One can hardly propose, however, that the whole matter from a formal viewpoint depends simply upon the placement of the wooden pestle.

Part M returns to what we have called 'conventional' form. The Shammaite opinion has been lightly glossed, with the addition of *edible parts*. Two verbs would have sufficed: *pick-eat*. The Hillelite opinion has been heavily glossed. It was sufficient to say, *he picks after his usual fashion*. The rest, moreover, not merely glosses, but changes the meaning! The issue is, Does he do it after the usual fashion or not? The original opinion of the Hillelites is that he does. Then the gloss adds, *but not quite*—for he may use his lap, a basket, or a dish, but *not* a board, a sifter, or a sieve, all of which were no less part of his "usual fashion" than the first three specified. So the gloss has the Hillelites requiring a slight change in the usual practice after all. Gamaliel stands within the Hillelite tradition in the unglossed form, for he adds further procedures which are *after his usual fashion*, and he would presumably have been surprised by the exclusions listed in the gloss. In this instance it seems sure that Gamaliel supplies a *terminus ante quem* for the Houses-dispute.

Part M thus represents the form without a superscription. The Houses-sayings are not balanced. The Shammaites say one may send only prepared portions. The House of Hillel say one may send whole animals, alive or prepared. The issue is divided into two parts, but concerns only one matter, namely, whether or not the gifts of meat have to be prepared. The balance is difficult to restore out of the words before us:

House of Shammai: [One may send only] *portions*
House of Hillel: [One may send] 1. cattle-animal-bird 2. whether alive or slaughtered

How can one reduce both elements of the Hillelite opinion to a single word or extremely brief phrase? It looks to me as if two disputes have been reduced to one, by the device of abbreviating the Shammaite ruling; or, alternatively, one dispute has been expanded to two, by augmenting the Hillelite one. But the single word *portions* cannot produce both Shammaite arguments on both of the issues specified in the Hillelite ruling.

It remains to observe that this "collection" is quite unlike more primitive exempla of the *collection*-form, and had best be regarded as a separate formal category, which we may call the *compilation*. By *collection* we have meant lists in which the Houses-materials are preserved in extremely brief and gnomic form, without superscriptions, and always in rigidly consistent form, with every element carefully matched. We are misled, therefore, to regard the complex of pericopae before us as comparable to the simple collection-form of M. Ber. 8:1-8. What characterizes the *compilation*-form seems to me to be the use of a single theme or principle to organize pre-existing, highly developed constituent pericopae.

Epstein, *Mevo'ot*, p. 102 assigns M. Beṣ. 1:1-2 to Meir, by analogy to M. Pes. 3:8. He observes (pp. 354ff.) that Mishnah-tractate Beṣah is based on sources of the disciples of ʿAqiba, though the laws in it are earlier than Usha. M. Beṣ. 1:1-2 derives from M. ʿEd. 4, the leniencies of the House of Shammai. The dispute about leaven etc., which does not belong here, proves that M. ʿEd. is the primary source.

See also Epstein, *Mishnah*, p. 125, M. Beṣ. 1:1 = Meir; pp. 255-6: in M. Beṣ. 1:1-2, the Hillelites take the stringent position, and afterward, the lenient one; also pp. 368, 393, 466, 652-3, 955, 967, 1003. 1012.

II.i.55.A. If a Festival-day fell on the eve of the Sabbath, [a man] may not cook on the Festival-day food [intended] from the outset for the Sabbath. But he *may* cook food [intended solely] for the festival-day, and if any is left over, it is left over for the Sabbath; or he may prepare a dish on the eve of the Festival-day and depend (ŚMK) on it for the Sabbath.

B. The House of Shammai say, "Two dishes."

And the House of Hillel say, "One dish."

But they agree that a fish covered with an egg counts as two dishes.

If the dish [intended for the Sabbath] was eaten or lost, a man may not cook another anew in its stead, but if aught soever of it remained, he may depend on that for the Sabbath.

C. If [a Festival-day] fell on the day after the Sabbath, the House of Shammai say, "They immerse all on the day before the Sabbath."

And the House of Hillel say, "Vessels [must be immersed] before the Sabbath, but men [may immerse themselves] on the Sabbath."

D. Howbeit they agree that [on a Festival-day] they may render [unclean] water clear by [surface] contact in a stone vessel, but they may not immerse it, and that they may immerse [vessels on a Festival-day] if they are to be changed from one use to another, or [at Passover] from one company to another.

E. The House of Shammai say, "They may bring Peace-offerings [on a Festival-day] and do *not* lay their hands thereon; but [they may] not [bring] Whole-offerings ('WLWT)."

And the House of Hillel say, "They may bring [both] Peace-offerings and Whole-offerings *and* do lay their hands thereon."

F. The House of Shammai say, "A man may not heat water for his feet unless it is also such as could be drunk."

And the House of Hillel permit.

A man may make a fire and warm himself before it.

G. In three things Rabban Gamaliel rules stringently, according to the opinion of the House of Shammai:

(1) Hot food may not be covered up on a Festival day for the Sabbath;

(2) nor may a candle stick be put together on a Festival-day;

(3) nor may bread be baked into large loaves (GRYṢWT) but only into thin cakes (RQYQYM)."

Rabban Gamaliel said, "Never did my father's household bake bread into large loaves but only into thin cakes."

They said to him, "What shall we infer from your father's household, which applied the stringent ruling to themselves but the lenient ruling to Israel, so that they might bake the bread both in large loaves and thick cakes!"

H. Moreover he gave three opinions applying the more lenient ruling:

(1) They may sweep up between couches, and

(2) put the spices on the fire on a Festival-day, and

(3) prepare a kid roasted whole on Passover night.

But these things the sages forbid.

M. Beṣ. 2:1, 2, 3, 4, 5, 6, 7, trans. Danby, pp. 183-4 (y. Beṣ. 2:1, 2, 4, 5, 6; b. Shab. 39b = Part F; b. Pes. 36b-37a, baking a thick loaf on Passover = Part G; b. Beṣ. 15b, 17b, 19a, 20a, 21b, 22a, 22b)]

III.ii.18. Our rabbis taught: "One may cover up [the blood] only with dust," the words of the House of Shammai.

But the House of Hillel say, "We find ashes referred to as dust, for it is written, *And for the unclean they shall take of the dust of the burning of the purification from sin* (Num. 19:17)."

The House of Shammai, however, say, "It [ashes] might be referred to as the 'dust of the burning' but it is never referred to as simply 'dust'."

[b. Ḥul. 88b (b. Soṭ. 16a)]

III.ii.19. Our rabbis taught: The House of Shammai say, "One may not bake thick bread on Passover."

And the House of Hillel permit.

It was taught likewise: The House of Shammai say, "One may not bake a large quantity of bread on a Festival."

And the House of Hillel permit.

(b. Beṣ. 22b)

III.ii.20. An objection was raised: R. Simeon b. Eleazar said, "The House of Shammai and the House of Hillel do not differ concerning a burnt-offering which is *not* for the Festival, [both agreeing] that it may not be offered on a Festival, and concerning peace-offerings of the Festival, that they *may* be offered on the Festival.

"They differ concerning a burned-offering which *is* for the Festival and concerning peace-offerings which are *not* for the Festival.

"The House of Shammai say, 'He may not bring [them].'

"And the House of Hillel say, 'He may bring [them].' "

Reconcile it by saying thus:

R. Simeon b. Eleazar said, "The House of Shammai and the House of Hillel do not differ concerning a burned-offering or peace-offering which are not connected with the Festival, that they may *not* be offered on the Festival; and concerning peace-offerings connected with the Festival, that they may be offered on the Festival; they differ only concerning a burnt-offering connected with the Festival.

"The House of Shammai say, 'He may not bring.' And the House of Hillel say, 'He may bring.' "

(b. Beṣ. 19a)

III. ii. 21. It was taught: The House of Hillel said to the House of Shammai, "If, when it is forbidden [to slaughter to provide food] for a layman, it is permitted [to slaughter] for the Most High, when it *is* permitted on behalf of a layman, it is surely logical that it is permitted for the Most High."

The House of Shammai said to them, "Let vows and freewill-offerings prove [the contrary], for they are permitted for a layman and yet forbidden for the Most High."

The House of Hillel said to them, "As for vows and freewill-offerings, that is because there is no fixed time for them. Will you say [the same] with respect to a pilgrimage burned-offering (ʿWLH), seeing that it has a fixed time?"

The House of Shammai said to them, "Even [for] this [sacrifice] there is no [strictly] fixed time, for we have learned: He who did not bring his Festival offering on the first day of the Festival may bring it during the whole of the remaining days of the Festival, even on the last day."

The House of Hillel replied to them, "Even [for] this there is indeed a time fixed, for we have learned: If the Festival passes and he has not brought his Festival offering, he is unable to bring it after the Festival."

The House of Shammai said to them, "Surely it is said, *[That only may be done] for you* (Ex. 12:16)—but not for the Most High God."

The House of Hillel said to them, "Surely it is said, *[And you shall keep it as a feast] unto the Lord* (Lev. 23:41)—whatever is for the Lord."

(b. Beṣ. 20b, trans. M. Ginsberg, pp. 105-6, = y. Beṣ. 2:4)

Comment: b. Beṣ. 19a shows how not only Houses-materials but also direct quotations of early masters might be fabricated in the context of much later discussions. Simeon b. Eleazar said either one thing or the other, but not both. The obvious fact is that the editors of the pericope have made him say what he logically ought to have said. b. Beṣ. 20b = y. Beṣ. 2:4 supplements the preceding Mishnah with a full repertoire of arguments for both sides.

b. Beṣ. 22b supplies a Houses-dispute in conformity with part E. Since Gamaliel follows the Shammaites, it was easy enough to create a dispute in the conventional model.

If the dispute of III.ii.18 goes back to the early period, then the Hillelite lemma has been developed over the primitive form, which should have been, "Also ashes." Instead we have an argument in favor of that position, complete with a Scripture. The antecedent Mishnah in Ḥullin (M. Ḥul. 8:1) mentions neither dust nor ashes; but it cannot accord with the position of the Shammaites, who say *only* dust, or with the Hillelites by inference, for they accept dust and ashes, but not the other items in the same list.

M. Beṣ. 2:1-5 adds further disputes to the list. I have included M.

Beṣ. 2:6-7 to supply the context for M. Beṣ. 2:6, discussed above, Vol. I, p. 380.

Parts A-B, M. Beṣ. 2:1, now deal with a complication of the foregoing pericope, namely the festival that coincides with the Sabbath. Part A has the festival on Friday. One may not cook on the festival for the Sabbath, though he *may* cook on the festival for the needs of that day. If food remained over, he may make use of it. Part A concludes with the rule that he may prepare a dish on Friday, and, depending on that, he may continue to cook on the festival for the Sabbath—thus at the outset he did not cook for the Sabbath, merely happened to continue. This dish (TBŠYL), called *ʿeruvē-tavshilin*, mitigates the effects of the foregoing rule. So part A is in two sections, an apparently old rule, followed by a quite contrary one, in which the foregoing is set aside.

The dispute of the Houses, part B, then concerns *how many* dishes he prepares so that he may make food for the Sabbath. The House of Shammai say *two*, the House of Hillel, *one*—a classic form for the dispute, originally consisting merely of the numbers *two/one*. The tradents would readily have assigned the stricter ruling (two) to the House of Shammai. Then comes an agreement, using the verb *shavin* (ŠWYN) rather than the more common *mōdin* (MWDYN). The agreement is curious, for it takes for granted that the Shammaite ruling is decisive. The Hillelites ought not to have bothered to specify a particular dish that constitutes two *tavshilin*, when in the first place they require merely one. So the clause should be Shammaite only, unless we suppose that the unlikely antecedent as the subject of *shavin* is the House of Shammai, accounting for the difference in word-choice.

Part C, M. Beṣ. 2:2, now places the festival on Sunday. The issue is when the ritual of purification from Levitical uncleanness takes place. The House of Shammai say everything, both men and vessels, must be immersed before the Sabbath. The House of Hillel say vessels must be done on Friday, but men may immerse on the Sabbath itself. The reason is that men may in any case immerse on the Sabbath for the pleasure of it, so they may also immerse to wash away ritual uncleanness. The form is conventional:

If after the Sabbath:
House of Shammai say, They immerse *all* before the Sabbath
House of Hillel say, *Vessels* before the Sabbath, *man* on the Sabbath.

The Hillelite lemma takes for granted, and depends upon, the Shammaite one. Standing independently it would have had to include the verb, *they immerse*. One might suppose the verb could have stood in the superscription, and placing it in the Shammaite lemma instead provides a more fluent text. But the difference is slight, one way or the other.

Part D, M. Beṣ. 2:3, supplies an agreement, with ŠWY, but does *not* pertain to the law discussed in part C at all! The agreement pertains either to a Sabbath or to a festival—therefore has nothing to do with a festival *on Sunday*. The details of the law are of no interest here. What is striking is that the redactor's *and they agree*, parallel to the same usage above, part B, leads us to suppose the foregoing dispute is now to be narrowed in scope or otherwise modified, while in fact there is no substantive connection whatever. Without *and they agree that*, the law would have stood as an independent, anonymous pericope, and the Houses would have no bearing on it at all. It looks as if a redactor has joined it to the foregoing, on the model of part B, but here without good reason. The only good reason for *and they agree* would be agreement *following* disagreement of the Houses.

Part E, M. Beṣ. 2:4, is familiar from M. Ḥag. 2:2 and from the story of Hillel in the Temple. The Houses' positions are as follows:

Shammai: (1) They bring peace-offerings and do not lay on hands. (2) They do not bring whole-offerings at all.
Hillel: (1) They bring peace-offerings *and* whole-offerings. (2) They lay hands on both.

I see no formal problems here. The opinions are as balanced as they could be, given the fact that *three* rulings, including *two* disagreements, have been compressed into one pericope:

Shammai: [They bring peace offerings and] do *not* lay on hands
Hillel: [They bring peace offerings and] do lay on hands.

Thus originally:

[They bring] peace-offerings on the festival
Shammai: Not lay on hands
Hillel: Lay on hands.

That is, M. Ḥag. 2:2! Then comes:

Whole-offerings
Shammai: Do *not* bring
Hillel: Bring.

The third ruling pertains only to the Hillelites: They *also* lay on hands. Obviously, it is superfluous for the Shammaites to rule on the issue. All this is compressed, as I said, and so deftly that the strict conventions of the simple dispute-form have not been greatly stretched, an example of a secondary development closely following the primary form. Note also the following:

III.ii.22 TNY': Peace-offerings which are offered on account of the festival:

The House of Shammai say, "He lays [hands] on them on the eve of the festival, and slaughters them on the festival."

And the House of Hillel say, "He lays [hands] on them *on* the festival and slaughters them on the festival."

But all agree that vows and freewill-offerings are not offered on a festival.

(b. Beṣ. 19a-b)

Now the dispute is reduced to the issue of laying on of hands, since the second clause in both lemmas is identical. This is a far simpler version than M. Beṣ.

Part F, M. Beṣ. 2:5, by contrast is not at all balanced:

House of Shammai: For his feet a man may heat only drinking water [since the work may be done only for preparation of food].
House of Hillel *permit* [making a fire for a purpose not connected with food].

Our earlier observations on this form apply here.

Part G adds three rulings of the House of Shammai:

1. Hot food may not be covered up on a festival for the Sabbath [and the House of Hillel permit]
2. They do not put together a candlestick on the festival [and the House of Hillel permit]
3. They bake only thin cakes on the festival [and the House of Hillel permit].

We have before us in fact a *collection* of the stringent Shammaite rulings followed by Gamaliel. What we do not have is the reformulation of the collection into generalized statements of law, or balanced disputes of the Houses in any of the several conventional forms. That comes, as I said, in b. Beṣ. 22b, for no. 3. Equally striking is the omission of the Hillelite ruling entirely. We then have Gamaliel's recollection of his father's House's following Shammaite practice, and as usual this is dismissed as private idiosyncracy, nothing more.

Part H resumes the pericope, which has been broken by the little colloquy. We shall return to this collection below, M. ʿEd. 3:3-12.

II.ii.43. The House of Shammai say, "An olive's bulk of leaven and a date's bulk of what is leavened."

And the House of Hillel say, "An olive's bulk of either."

[Tos. Yom Ṭov 1:4, ed. Lieberman, p. 280, lines 9-10 (M. ʿEd. 4:1, y. Beṣ. 1:2, y. Pes. 5:4, b. Beṣ. 7b)]

Comment: See M. Beṣ. 1:1b. Lieberman discusses the problem of the relevance of the pericope to M. Beṣ.-Tos. Yom Ṭov, *Tosefta Kifshuṭah ad loc.*, p. 911, s.v. *And in the novellae of the Meiri.* He makes it clear that the classical commentators observed most, if not all, of the literary phenomena before us. He cites the earlier discussions, and then adds, "And in the language of our time, the principle [appearance] of the whole Mishnah is in M. ʿEd., Chapter Four, and the Tanna repeated here (according to) the language of M. ʿEd."

II.ii.44.A. R. Simeon b. Leazar said, "The House of Hillel and the

House of Shammai agree that they may move the ladder from one dovecot to another.

"Concerning what did they differ? Concerning bringing it back—

"For (Š) the House of Shammai prohibit, and the House of Hillel permit."

[Tos. Yom Ṭov 1:8, ed. Lieberman, p. 281, lines 24-6 (b. Beṣ. 9b)]

II.ii.44.B. R. Simeon says, "The House of Shammai say, 'A man should not take a pigeon [which is ownerless, and which he has not yet acquired] until he ties (QŠR) it.'

"And the House of Hillel say, 'A man should not take [it] until he stirs [it].' "

(Tos. Yom Ṭov 1:8, ed. Lieberman, p. 281, lines 29-30)

II.ii.45. R. Simeon b. Leazar said, "The House of Shammai and the House of Hillel agree that if he set [them] aside in the nest and found [them] before the nest, they are prohibited."

[Tos. Yom Ṭov 1:10, ed. Lieberman, p. 282, lines 33-4 (b. Beṣ. 25a)]

II.ii.46.A. R. Simeon b. Leazar said, "The House of Shammai and the House of Hillel agree that they remove the doors [of the cupboard] on the festival day.

"Concerning what did they dispute?

"Concerning returning it—

"For the House of Shammai prohibit, and the House of Hillel permit."

B. "They agree that if he hacked on the pestle, it is prohibited to move it."

C. "They agree that they do not salt hides on the festival, but they salt *on* it a piece of meat for roasting."

D. Rabban Simeon b. Gamaliel said, "The House of Shammai and the House of Hillel agree that they may bring full vessels on account of the need [of preparing food], and empty ones for filling.

"Concerning what did they dispute?

"Concerning *empty ones* that were *not* on account of the need [of preparing food]—

"For (Š) the House of Shammai prohibit, and the House of Hillel permit."

[Tos. Yom Ṭov 1:10b, 11a, ed. Lieberman, pp. 282-3, lines 37-43 (y. Shab. 17:4 = part D; b. Beṣ. 11a, b. Shab. 123a, y. Beṣ. 1:5, y. Shab. 17:4)]

II.ii.47.A. R. Judah said, "The House of Shammai and the House of Hillel agree that they may take the gifts that were taken up [set aside] the day before the festival with the gifts which were taken up on the festival.

"Concerning what did they differ?

"Concerning gifts which were taken up by themselves the day before the Festival—

"For the House of Shammai prohibit, and the House of Hillel permit.

"The House of Shammai said, 'It is an analogy: Dough offering and gifts are a gift to the priest, and Heave-offering is a gift to the priest. Just as they do not bring the Heave-offering, so they should not bring the gifts.'

"The House of Hillel said to them, 'No, if you say so concerning Heave-offering, which a man has not the right to set apart, will you say so concerning the gifts, which a man *has* the right to set apart?' "

B. R. Yosah says, "The House of Shammai and the House of Hillel agree that they *may* take the gifts on the festival.

"Concerning what did they disagree?

"Concerning the Heave-offering—

"For the House of Shammai prohibit, and the House of Hillel permit.

"The House of Hillel said, 'It is an analogy. Dough offering and gifts are a gift to the priest, and Heave-offering is a gift to the priest. Just as they take the gifts, so they should take the Heave-offering.'

"The House of Shammai said to them, 'No, if you say so concerning gifts, which he *is* permitted to raise up, will you say so of Heave-offering, which he is *not* permitted to raise up?' "

Others say, "The House of Shammai and the House of Hillel agree that they do *not* take the Heave-offering on the festival day.

"Concerning what did they disagree?

"Concerning the gifts—

"For the House of Shammai prohibit, and the House of Hillel permit."

[Tos. Yom Ṭov 1:12-14, ed. Lieberman, pp. 283-4, lines 46-60 (y. Beṣ. 1:8, b. Beṣ. 12b)]

II.ii.48.A. R. Meir said, "The House of Shammai and the House of Hillel agree that the spices are pounded with a wooden pestle, and the salt with them.

"Concerning what did they disagree?

"Concerning the salt by itself, for—

"The House of Shammai say, 'In a cruse and with a wooden pot-stirrer for roasting.'

"And the House of Hillel say, 'With anything.' "

B. The House of Shammai say, "They take spices and the pestle to the crusher, and not the crusher to them."

And the House of Hillel say, "They take this to this, and this to this, and there is no reason to be wary."

C. The House of Shammai say, "They take the knife and the butcher to the beast, and not the beast to them."

And the House of Hillel say, "They take this to this and this to this, and there is no reason to be wary."

[Tos. Yom Ṭov 1:15-17, ed. Lieberman, p. 284, lines 62-9 (b. Beṣ. 14a)]

II.ii.49. If a man picked pulse on the festival—

R. Judah says, "The House of Shammai say, 'If the inedible (ṢRWRWT) parts are more numerous than the edible parts, he picks the edible parts and leaves the inedible parts.'

"The House of Hillel say, 'He picks whatever he likes.' "

[Tos. Yom Ṭov 1:21, ed. Lieberman, p. 284, lines 77-9 (b. Beṣ. 14b, b. Shab. 142b)]

Comment: The set of pericopae exhibits a single common theme: agreements of the Houses, leading to redefinition of their differences. Simeon b. Leazar in the Toseftan traditions alleges that the Mishnaic record is not accurate. What the Mishnah-traditions say is in dispute, the Toseftan ones say is unanimously agreed upon, and new distinctions need to be read into the Houses-lemmas. The pericopae derive principally from mid-second-century masters, who therefore supply a *terminus ante quem* for the whole set of M. Beṣ-pericopae.

One must ask, Which version is likely to have come first, that presented in the Mishnah, or that of the second-century masters? It seems to me obvious that the primary version is the one selected by Judah the Patriarch. The allegation that the Houses agreed upon a given point of law (now *verbatim* in the Mishnah) but differed upon a subset of that same law (now in the Tosefta) can mean only one thing. The second-century masters had before them the law now in the Mishnah, and *after* the fact proposed revisions in the traditions. *They did not differ concerning* thus comes to mind only when provoked by the contrary assertion, that the Houses *did* differ. Without it who would have invented the legal problem to begin with? But that does not prove the antiquity of the Mishnaic formulations, merely that they were revised by the authorities represented in the Tosefta.

The contrary possibility is that Judah the Patriarch has consistently revised the Toseftan allegations, and where the earlier masters say the Houses did not differ, he has said they did and has further dropped the differences alleged by the Toseftan traditions to have separated the Houses. His tendency would therefore have been to broaden the range of disagreement. This seems to me less likely than the foregoing, for the tendency normally was to find further refined distinctions in general principles, rather than to drop fine distinctions in favor of gross generalities.

II.ii.44.A, *Moving the ladder* = M. Beṣ. 1:3. Simeon uses the language now in the Mishnah: *they move the ladder from dovecot to dovecot*, but denies the Houses differed on the matter. The only issue is whether one may *bring it back*.

II.ii.44.B, *Taking the pigeon* = M. Beṣ. 1:3b. Lieberman explains (*Tosefta Kifshuṭah*, *ad loc.* p. 926) that the Mishnah pertains to tame pigeons, and the passage before us to wild ones. Here the House of Hillel require not merely a spoken word as sufficient specification, but the act of acquisition, and the House of Shammai require not merely stirring but tying up. So Simeon has supplemented the law of the Mishnah with a new case, in which the difference between the Houses is a fixed difference, but more stringent by a degree as the circumstances change. The Houses-dispute presumably has come before Simeon and been supplemented by him through the creation of a new situation.

II.ii.45. R. Simeon b. Leazar now adds a further agreement. The antecedent, anonymous tradition held that if he set the birds aside in the nest and found them before it, they were prohibited, but if at the door, they were permitted. Simeon says the Houses are unanimous on the first point. This pertains to M. Beṣ. 1:4, in which the Houses do not appear at all. He alleges that the Houses agree that pigeons of the dovecot require specification in advance of the festival, and are not regarded as house (tame) pigeons; and the disagreement in the Mishnah pertains only to how one makes a sign of specification.

II.ii.46.A. *Returning the cupboard doors* = M. Beṣ. 1:5. The Mishnah has the Houses differ on removing the doors. But it adds to the Hillelite lemma not only permission to do so, but *also to return*, an allusion to the dispute created by Simeon. Judah the Patriarch thus claims that the Houses differed on the removal, all the more so on the restoration of the doors. Including the latter detail makes sense only if Judah knew the contrary assertion of Simeon in the Tosefta concerning the nature of the dispute, for otherwise the Hillelite ruling is superfluous.

II.ii.46.B. *Using the pestle* = M. Beṣ. 1:5. The House of Shammai say that after work is done on the pestle, it may not be moved. In the Mishnah the Shammaites hold he may not make use of it to begin with. The Hillelite position is constant. The same difference between the Houses is therefore present in both versions. The real problem is the Shammaite position: May he use the pestle at all? Judah the Patriarch says they say he may not. Simeon says they say he may use it, but he may not move it thereafter.

II.ii.46.C. *Salting the hide* = M. Beṣ. 1:5 has the House of Shammai prohibit bringing the hide to the tanner. Here it may not be salted, a later stage in the process of preservation of the leather. But the Hillelites now agree that one may not salt the hides—a limitation of the foregoing Hillelite position. Only if some flesh adheres, so that preparation of food is involved, do the Houses permit salting the hide.

II.ii.46.D. *Moving vessels* = M. Beṣ. 1:5. The House of Hillel prohibit taking out the child, *Lulav*, and Torah to the public domain. The House of Hillel permit. Simeon b. Gamaliel introduces two distinctions not present in M. Beṣ. 1:5, namely, whether the vessels are used for need, and whether they are empty—irrelevant to the cases of M. Beṣ.!

II.ii.47. *Taking the priestly gifts* = M. Beṣ. 1:6. We have four versions of the dispute about bringing the priestly gifts:

M. Beṣ. 1:6	*Tos. Y.Ṭ. 1:12: Judah*	*Yosah*	*Others*
1. House of Shammai say, They do not bring dough-offering and gifts to the priest on the Festival	1. [Agree about gifts taken before the festival with gifts taken up on the festival. Differ:] *Gifts taken up before the festival by themselves.*	1. [Agree on *all* gifts on the festival. Differ on:] *Heave-offering.*	1. [They agree about Heave-offering, but differ concerning] the *gifts.*
2. whether taken up yesterday or today	2. —	2. —	2. —
3. House of Hillel permit	3. *House of Shammai prohibit and* ,, ,, ,,	3. [= Judah's version]	3. [= Judah's version]
4. House of Shammai said to them,	4. ,, ,, ,,	4. House of *Hillel*	4. —
5. Analogy	5. ,, ,, ,,	5. ,, ,, ,,	5. —

M. Beṣ. 1:6	*Tos. Y.Ṭ. 1:12 Judah*	*Yosah*	*Others*
6. Dough-offering and gifts are a gift to the priest, and Heave-offering is a gift to the priest.	6. „ „ „	6. „ „ „	6. —
7. Just as they do not bring the Heave-offering, so they do not bring the gifts.	7. „ „ „	7. *Just as they bring gifts, so they should* bring *Heave-offering*	7. —
8. The House of Hillel said to them,	8. „ „ „	8. *Shammai*	8. —
9. No, if you say so concerning Heave-offering, which a man has not the right to set apart, will you say so concerning gifts, which a man has the right to set apart?	9. „ „ „	9. *gifts. . . Heave-offering*	9. —

Judah the Patriarch has followed *others say* in defining the dispute, namely, concerning the gifts. But he has added *dough-offering.* He further alludes to Judah's version by specifying that it makes *no* difference when the gifts were taken up, before or on the festival. Judah's version itself refers to a disagreement about the same distinction and says that disagreement is not at issue. So before both Judah the Patriarch and Judah b. Ilai was a dispute not represented here, in which the distinction of *when* the gifts were taken up was important.

The positions of the Houses are fixed, and the editorial difference between M. Beṣ. no. 3 and the other versions is readily explained. Judah the Patriarch is working within a different redactional and formal framework:

House of Shammai say [in such-and-such a case]—prohibit
House of Hillel permit.

The more conventional form is used in the Tosefta:

Statement of Law
Houses: prohibit/permit.

Then comes the argument. This appears without alteration, except for Yosah's version, which places Hillel first and has the argument concern Heave-offering. It is curious that not infrequently the same arguments or opinions serve a number of different disputes. This suggests that the formation of the argument took place before anyone had settled the issue, To what disagreement did the debate actually pertain? The debate required little revision, since the main point is the validity of the analogy of Heave-offering. What is interesting is that Judah the Patriarch has added the debate-materials to *others say*, which lacks them.

Yosah's view of matters cannot be ignored. Two important facts should be observed. First, Yosah has preserved the proper order for a debate, Hillel then Shammai. Second, he has the only superscription which accounts for the inclusion of *Heave-offering* in the debate-form. The other superscriptions do not even allude to it; Yosah's does. Since the substance of the debate focuses upon Heave-offering and *its* distinctions from other gifts, it looks to me as though Yosah has drawn the most reasonable conclusion from pre-existing *debate*-materials and made Heave-offering the center of the dispute.

The *others* are aware of, therefore come after, Yosah's formulation, and Judah has accepted their view of matters and revised the debate to conform to it. So he stands in this instance at the end and has taken account of all the second-century versions. His tradition is not independent and presumably as old as, if not older than, the Toseftan ones, but refers to the Toseftan ones in the superscription. M. Beṣ. no. 2 mentions Judah b. Ilai no. 1; M. Beṣ. no. 1 depends upon *others* no. 1 and has added the detail about dough-offering (which ought to have been taken for granted) for reasons I cannot discern. One cannot, on the other hand, attribute to Yosah the oldest and therefore the supposedly most authentic account, merely because his follows the form we should have expected.

II.ii.48.A. *Spices and salt* = M. Beṣ. 1:7. The Mishnah has the House of Hillel's requiring no change in the normal preparation of spices, and small change in the normal preparation of salt. On the legal issues, see Lieberman, *Tosefta Kifshuṭah*, p. 933.

II.ii.48. B-C has no counterpart in M. Beṣ.

II.ii.49. *Picking pulse* = M. Beṣ. 1:8. The Mishnah's version of the House of Hillel's opinion is no different from the one before us, except in formulation. Here he picks whatever he likes, there he picks *in his usual way*. The Shammaite rule there concerns whether he must separate, and thereby implies the same, he picks *food*—and leaves the rest. So the differences are merely in the formulation of the argument. The superscriptions are identical. The glosses of M. Beṣ. 1:8 are of course absent. See Lieberman, *Tosefta Kifshuṭah*, pp. 937-8 for important clarifications of the legal issues. See also Epstein, *Mishnah*, p. 258.

II.ii.50. R. Simeon b. Leazar said, "The House of Shammai and the House of Hillel agree that they are two *tavshilin*.

"Concerning what did they disagree?

"Concerning the fish with the egg that is on it, for

"The House of Shammai say, '[They constitute] one *tavshil*.'

"And the House of Hillel say, 'Two *tavshilin*.' "

"They agree that if he cooked two different species in the same pot, or if he mashed an egg in the fish, or if he cut porret under the fish, that they are two *tavshilin*."

[Tos. Yom Ṭov 2:4, ed. Lieberman, p. 287, lines 10-14 (y. Beṣ. 2:1, b. Beṣ. 17b)]

Comment: The Tosefta now makes sense of the dispute of the Houses in M. Beṣ. 2:1, concerning the fish and egg dish. As we observed, in M. Beṣ. 2:1 that "agreement" is pointless, for the Hillelites need not rule on the question at all. Simeon now tells us the disagreement is the heart of the matter, since both Houses agree two *tavshilin are* required and need only to determine whether certain mixed dishes constitute one or two—a considerable limitation on the range of differences between the Houses.

For the difficulty in ascertaining the reading here, see Lieberman, *Tosefta Kifshuṭah*, pp. 946-7.

II.ii.51. R. Simeon b. Leazar said, "The House of Shammai [and the House of Hillel] did not differ concerning those which were gathered together in the enclosure, that they bring [them], and concerning those scattered in the field, that they do not bring [them].

"Concerning what did they disagree?

"Concerning those scattered in the enclosure and gathered together in the field—

"For the House of Shammai say, 'They do not bring [them].'

"And the House of Hillel say, 'They do bring.' "

R. Judah said, "The House of Shammai and the House of Hillel did not differ concerning what was scattered in the enclosure and gathered in the field, that they bring [them]. Concerning what did they dispute? Concerning what was scattered in the field—

"For the House of Shammai say, 'They do not bring.'

"And the House of Hillel say, 'They do bring.' "

[Tos. Yom Ṭov 3:10, ed. Lieberman, pp. 295-6, lines 34-41 (y. Beṣ. 4:1, 2; b. Beṣ. 31a)]

Comment: The passage has no conterpart in Houses-pericopae in M. Beṣ., but does have a parallel in M. Beṣ. 4:2:

> They bring wood from the field from that which is gathered together; and from the enclosure, even from what is scattered.

So Judah the Patriarch has settled matters. The Toseftan traditions are as follows:

Simeon	*Judah*
Gathered in field Scattered in enclosure	Scattered in the field

Shammai:	Not bring	Shammai:	Not bring
Hillel:	Bring	Hillel:	Bring

Judah the Patriarch has followed Simeon's version, but has dropped the tradition that the *Houses* disputed the matter, and given only the Hillelite position as the law.

II.i.56. [There are four New Year days: on the first of Nisan is the New Year for kings and feasts. On the first of Elul is the New Year for the Tithe of Cattle. R. Eleazar and R. Simeon say, "The first of Tishri." On the first of Tishri is the New Year for (the reckoning of) the year (of foreign kings), of the Years of Release and Jubilee years, for the planting (of trees) and for vegetables.] And—

"The first of Shevaṭ is the New Year for the [fruit-] trees"—the words of the House of Shammai.

And the House of Hillel say, "On the fifteenth thereof."

[M. R.H. 1:1, trans. Danby, p. 188 (y. R.H. 1:2, b. R.H. 8a, 14b)]

Comment: The form of the Houses-pericope is unconventional, for the Shammaite opinion is not quoted, merely cited: *On the first. . . for the tree [according to] the words of the House of Shammai.* Then the House of Hillel *say*.

The practical result concerns when the tithe of the produce of trees is to be given. One does not give tithe from produce that has ripened before the first of the year for produce that has ripened thereafter. The legal consequences therefore are important, but not specified. It looks as if someone has drawn the implication of antecedent lemmas and not cited the words *verbatim*; the ʿAqiba story (p. 80) may therefore come before the formulation of the Houses-dispute and may supply the earliest evidence of the existence—but not the language—of the dispute.

II.ii.52.A. If the festival of the New Year coincides with the Sabbath—

The House of Shammai say, "He prays ten."

And the House of Hillel say, "He prays nine."

If a festival coincided with the Sabbath—

The House of Shammai say, "He prays eight, and says that of the Sabbath by itself and that of the festival by itself, and begins with that of the Sabbath."

And the House of Hillel say, "He prays seven, and begins with that of the Sabbath and concludes with that of the Sabbath and says the Sanctification of the Day in the middle."

B. The House of Hillel said to the House of Shammai, "Is it not so that in the presence (MʿMD) of all of you, Elders of the House of Shammai, Ḥoni the Little went down [as leader of the prayers] and said seven, and all the people said to him, 'May it be a pleasure for you.'"

The House of Shammai said to them, "[It was] because it was a time appropriate for cutting short."

The House of Hillel said to them, "If the time was appropriate for cutting short, he should have cut short all of them [rather than omitting one]."

[Tos. R.H. 2:17, ed. Lieberman, pp. 320-1, lines 88-96 (Tos. Ber. 3:13, y. Shav. 1:5, b. ʿEruv. 40a, b. Beṣ. 17a)]

Comment: Part A of the dispute occurs in Tos. Ber. 3:13, ed. Lieberman, p. 15, line 58. Part A is not changed from Tos. Ber. Part B is new. Lieberman observes that the dispute of part A takes for granted that the subject is the Morning, not the Additional Prayer, therefore comes before the *Shofar*-sounding was moved to the Additional Prayer.

Part B pertains to a festival that coincided with the Sabbath. Ḥoni said seven blessings in their order, unabbreviated, but he began with the Sabbath, said the Sanctification of the Day in the middle, and ended with the Sabbath, following the House of Hillel. The people praised him for doing so. The Shammaites explain that he had had to make haste. The Hillelites reply that he has dropped the eighth blessing entirely and should have abbreviated each of them and not dropped one alone.

The form of the debate is exceptional, in that the Hillelites have two speeches, the Shammaites only the one in the middle. The pericope should have had an equal number for each House. Perhaps the closing Hillelite saying is a later gloss, and the whole should have ended with the Shammaite answer. But the Hillelite question would have had to have been raised, for the point of the story was that seven *were* said, as the Hillelites taught, and not eight. So the Shammaite answer is not to the point at all. It is therefore wholly a Hillelite story, not shaped like other *debate*-forms.

We have no further information on Ḥoni the Small.

II.ii.53.A. He who has carried out the rule of overturning the couch [as a sign of mourning] for three days before the festival does not overturn it after the festival.

R. Liezer b. Jacob says, "Even one day."

B. R. Leazar b. R. Simeon says "The House of Shammai say, 'Three days,' and the House of Hillel say, 'Even one hour.' "

[Tos. M.Q. 2:9, ed. Lieberman, p. 370, lines 20-24 (b. M.Q. 20a)]

Comment: The anonymous rule is the Shammaites'. No one gives the Hillelite opinion. What came before Leazar b. R. Simeon's saying? He does not supply a complete superscription, but rather depends upon the foregoing. What he contributes is the identification of the authority behind the anonymous rule.

b. M.Q. 20a gives the anonymous rule in the name of R. Eliezer b. Hyrcanus. The sages say, "A day or even an hour." Simeon b. Eleazar then says the House of Shammai and the House of Hillel are herein represented, and he gives for the House of Shammai *three days*, and for the Hillelites, *one day*. It looks as if the primitive pericope, if any, read *three/one*. Then Tos. M.Q. glossed with *hour* (rather than day) which was "improved" in some texts of the *beraita*, being changed to *day*, to match the Shammaite lemma.

II.i.57.A. Who is deemed a child? "Any that cannot ride on his father's shoulders and go up from Jerusalem to the Temple Mount," according to the words of the House of Shammai.

And the House of Hillel say, "Any that cannot hold his father's hand and go up [on his feet] from Jerusalem to the Temple Mount, as it is written, *Three regalim* (Ex. 23:14)."

B. The House of Shammai say, "The *Re'iyyah*-offering [must be not less in value than] two pieces of silver and the Festival-offering [not less than] one *ma'ah* of silver."

And the House of Hillel say, "The *Re'iyyah*-offering [must be not less in value than] one *ma'ah* of silver, and the Festal-offering [not less than] two pieces of silver."

C. Whole-offerings during mid-festival are brought from [beasts bought with] unconsecrated money, and Peace-offerings also from [what is bought with Second] Tithe [money].

D. On the first Festival-day of Passover, the House of Shammai say, "[They are brought from beasts bought with] unconsecrated money (ḤLYN)."

And the House of Hillel say, "[Also] from [what is bought with Second] Tithe (M'SR) [money]."

[M. Ḥag. 1:1, 2, 3, trans. Danby, pp. 211-2 (y. Ḥag. 1:1, 2, 3, b. Ḥag. 2a, 6a, 7b, 8a)]

III.i.6. The House of Hillel said to the House of Shammai, "Is it not better to learn [the law pertaining to] the sacrifice of an individual from [the law pertaining to] the sacrifice of an individual, and not to learn [the law pertaining to] the sacrifice of an individual from [that pertaining to] the sacrifice of the community?"

The House of Shammai said to them, "Is it not better to learn [the law pertaining to] a matter which is observed for all generations from [the law pertaining to] a matter which is observed through all generations, and do not bring to me [the law pertaining to] the sacrifice of princes, which is not observed through all generations."

(y. Ḥag. 1:2)

Comment: II.i.57.A glosses the foregoing Mishnah, which says that all are liable to the commandment to appear before the Lord (Ex. 23:14) except for a child (among others). The Houses' definitions therefore come to say what sorts of children are *not* obligated, hence phrased in the negative: Whoever cannot go up by foot is a child, therefore exempt. See above, Sifré Deut. 143, p. 35.

II.i.55.B preserves a House-dispute in which the operative words are placed in contrary order:

	Re'iyyah	*Ḥagigah*
House of Shammai	*T*wo silver	*Ma'ah* of silver
House of Hillel	*Ma'ah* of silver	*T*wo silver

So the problem is to assign the right opinion to the right House. It is a common difficulty for the later tradents working with primitive Houses-lemmas.

Part C-D has a Houses-dispute on the final clause of a general, anonymous ruling. The law concerns the funds to be used for the purchase of the festival offerings. The House are concerned with the peace-offerings to be brought on the first day of every festival, referred to in A-B. The House of Shammai say the funds must come from unconsecrated funds; the House of Hillel permit taking part from Tithes. That is, it is permitted to add the coins of Second Tithe to the two silver coins of the festal-offering-money, which come from unconsecrated funds, and to buy with them a better sacrifice, since the offering is to be eaten by the worshipper. But, Albeck observes, the *re'iyyah* mentioned above, which is wholly offered on the altar and not eaten, must be purchased only from unconsecrated funds, not from Second Tithe money.

The Houses-rulings are not part of a collection or compilation. While they appear in contiguous pericopae, they are in two instances merely glosses, and not separate rulings such as would have been brought together in a compilation.

y. Ḥag. 1:2 adds a debate for parts B-C. On *according to the words of* in the Mishnah, see the important discussion of Epstein, *Mishnah*, p. 403. Note also pp. 633-4.

II.i.58.A. The House of Shammai say, "They bring Peace-offerings [on a Festival-day] and do not lay the hands thereon; but [they do] not [bring] Whole-offerings."

And the House of Hillel say, "They bring [both] Peace-offerings and Whole-offerings and lay their hands thereon."

B. If the Feast of Pentecost fell on the eve of a Sabbath, the House of Shammai say, "The day for slaughtering is after the Sabbath."

And the House of Hillel say, "The day for slaughtering is *not* after the Sabbath."

But they agree that, if [the Feast] fell on a Sabbath, the day for slaughtering is after the Sabbath.

[M. Ḥag. 2:3-4, trans. Danby, p. 213 (y. Ḥag. 2:3, 4; b. Ḥag. 7b, 17a, 17b)]

III.i.7. The House of Shammai say, "Laying on of hands not in the ordinary manner has been permitted."

And the House of Hillel say, "Laying on of hands not in the ordinary manner has not been permitted."

What is 'laying on of hands not in the ordinary manner'? It is laying on of hands *on the preceding day*.

(y. Ḥag. 2:3)

Comment: II.i.59.A, see above, M. Beṣ. 2:4.

II.i.58.B, M. Ḥag, 2:4, concerns the slaughter of the *Re'iyyah*-sacrifices. The House of Shammai say they must be sacrificed on Sunday, since they do not override either the festival or the Sabbath. The House of Hillel say it may be done both on the Sabbath and on the festival itself, as above, II.i.87.A, one brings and lays on hands—therefore one slaughters on the festival day.

The form is fully articulated, but conventional:

If Pentecost fell on Friday
House of Shammai say, The day of slaughter is after the Sabbath
House of Hillel say, The day of slaughter is *not* after the Sabbath

The Hillelite opinion is not explicitly stated, merely implied through the negative of the Shammaite one. But the outcome is clear, having been specified in the immediately antecedent Mishnah.

Another reading (MS Kaufmann) for the Hillelite opinion is, "It has no day of slaughter," meaning no special day needs to be set aside, for the slaughter is done on the festival itself. The reading before us is preferable merely for form-critical reasons.

y. Ḥag. 2:3 gives us a consistent issue. The Shammaites say one may then lay on hands the preceding day, since on the day itself one may not do so; and the Hillelite position follows.

See Epstein, *Mevo'ot*, pp. 50-51, *Mishnah*, p. 634.

II.ii.54. The House of Shammai say, "The measure of the *re'iyyah* is greater than the measure of the festal sacrifice (*ḥagigah*)."

"The *re'iyyah* is entirely for the One Above, which is not so for the *ḥagigah*."

The House of Hillel say, "The measure of the *ḥagigah* is greater than the measure of the *re'iyyah*, for the *ḥagigah* was practiced both before the Word [= giving of the law at Sinai, being referred to in Ex. 5:1] and afterward, which is not so of the *re'iyyah*."

[Tos. Ḥag. 1:4, ed. Lieberman, p. 376, lines 22-25 (y. Ḥag. 1:2, b. Ḥag. 6a)]

Comment: This is an expansion of M. Ḥag. 1:2, in which the Shammaites say more money goes for the *re'iyyah* than for the *ḥagigah*, and the Hillelites say the opposite. It supplements M. Ḥag. 1:2, explaining the opinions of the Houses. This pericope would represent a third stage in the development of the single tradition. The first had the specifications of coins, the second created of these a dispute between the Houses, and third explained the dispute. Alternatively, the above saying, which would have been entirely theoretical, was translated into the dispute of stage two.

II.ii.55. R. Simeon b. Leazar said, "The House of Shammai and the House of Hillel did not disagree concerning offerings that come always, that he should bring [them] only from unconsecrated funds, or concerning peace offerings which come on the rest of the days of the year, that if he wants to depend on [supplement with] Tithe [money], he depends on it.

"Concerning what did they differ? Concerning the *ḥagigah* of the festival day itself—

"For the House of Shammai say, 'He brings all from unconsecrated funds.'

"And the House of Hillel say, 'He brings his obligation from unconsecrated funds, and if he wants to depend on Tithe-funds, he does so, and the rest of the days of the year he brings his obligation from unconsecrated funds.' "

[Tos. Ḥag. 1:4, ed. Lieberman, p. 377, lines 31-6 (b. Beṣ. 19a)]

Comment: Simeon's revision pertains to M. Ḥag. 1:3. Offerings on the festival come from unconsecrated funds, and peace-offerings from the Tithe. As to the first day of the festival, the House of Shammai say, "From unconsecrated funds," and the House of Hillel say that money may be added from Tithe-funds.

The reference is to sacrifices of *re'iyyah*, which, according to the House of Shammai, are offered continually through the festival. The House of Hillel agree with reference to the Sabbath, and affirm that one may not purchase from Tithe-money a sacrifice which a man does not eat. But as to sacrifices that come on the first day of the festival—meaning the festal peace-offerings—the Houses differ. So Simeon has clarified the dispute, rather than revising it altogether. Having defined the matter, Simeon allows the language of the House of Shammai in the Mishnah to stand without alteration. This is characteristic of his method, as we have seen. The opinions of the Houses generally are fixed, but the laws to which they pertain need to be specified. But here, the Hillelite opinion is considerably expanded. When the Hillelites say *from the Tithe*, the meaning is that he brings the measure of his obligation (two silver coins) from unconsecrated money, and the rest from the Tithe. But he cannot bring the whole from Second-Tithe funds, for whatever is an obligation may come only from unconsecrated funds, and this is specified in the following clause, *the rest of the days of the year.*

Note Epstein, *Mishnah*, p. 634, re 1:4.

II.ii.56.A. What is the laying on of hands concerning which they differed?

B. The House of Shammai say, "They do not lay on hands on the festival, and as to peace offerings, the one who celebrates through them lays hands on them the day before the festival."

The House of Hillel say, "They bring peace-offerings and whole-offerings and lay hands on them."

C. The House of Hillel said, "Now, if at a time that you are not permitted to work for an ordinary person, you are permitted to work for the Highest One, when you *are* permitted to work for an ordinary person, are you not permitted to work for the Highest One?"

The House of Shammai said to them, "Vows and free-will offerings will prove [the matter], for you *are* permitted to work [= make them] for an ordinary person, and you are not permitted to work for the Highest One."

D. The House of Hillel said to them, "No, if you say so concerning vows and free-will offerings, whose time is *not* set (QBW'), will you say so concerning the *ḥagigaḥ* [= *re'iyyah* sacrifice], whose time *is* set?"

The House of Shammai said to them, "So too with the *ḥagigah*, sometimes its time is *not* set, for he who did not celebrate (ḤG) [the *ḥagigah* = *re'iyyah*-sacrifice] on the first day of the festival offers [it] the whole festival and [even] the last day of the festival [according to your view]."

E. Abba Saul would say it in a different language in the name of the House of Hillel: "If when your stove is closed [you cannot cook = the Sabbath], the stove of your Lord is open, when your stove is open, will not the stove of your Lord [also] be open?"

[Tos. Ḥag. 2:10, ed. Lieberman, pp. 384-5, lines 68-81 (y. Ḥag. 2:3, y. Beṣ. 2:4, b. Beṣ. 19b-20a-b)]

Comment: The superscription refers to M. Ḥag. 2:3=M. Beṣ. 2:4 and distinguishes among the several disputes therein combined. The laying on of hands to which reference is made pertains to festival offerings. As to the *ḥagigah*, the person lays on hands the preceding day (= y. Ḥag. 2:3). The House of Hillel say one brings peace-offerings and sacrifices and lays on hands, just as in the Mishnah.

So the revisions pertain primarily to the Shammaite lemma:

M. Ḥag.:	A.	They bring peace-offerings and do not lay on hands.
	B.	They do not bring whole-offerings.
Tos. Ḥag.:	A.	They do not lay on hands on the festival [on any offerings].
	B.	As to the festival offering, they lay on hands the preceding day.

The clarification therefore serves M. Ḥag. clause A: When *do* they lay on hands? Tos. underlines the ruling and explains how to carry out the sacrifice. The Hillelite position is unchanged. The principle under discussion is whether or not one lays hands on the sacrifice on the festival, debated by the pairs (M. Ḥag. 2:2) as well as by the Houses. But no one debated *whether* to bring offerings on the festival.

Part C: The Hillelites argue that one may not work on the Sabbath, even in connection with preparation of food, yet one may offer the perpetual sacrifices and the supplementary sacrifices. On the festival, when one *is* permitted to work for an ordinary person, one should be permitted to lay on hands, and the consideration of Sabbath-rest does not enter. The Shammaites reply that even when one *is* permitted to work for the ordinary person (the festival), one still does not offer vow- and free-will sacrifices, with which the Hillelites agree.

Part D: The Hillelites distinguish between vow- and free-will offerings and the *ḥagigah*. The time for offering it is set. The Shammaites deny this invariably is the case. There the debate ends, with the Shammaites having the last word.

Part E: The revision of Abba Saul is of great importance, for the debate before us must thereby be dated back to Yavneh and cannot be regarded as a second-century expansion of first-century legal logia. This shows not only that the dispute existed, but also that the debate had already taken shape, therefore that the *debate*-form comes quite early in the formation of traditions. Afterward it was used in classical style. Abba Saul holds that the House of Hillel say vow- and free-will offerings are sacrificed on the festival, for if the man's oven is open, all the more so that the oven of the Master should be open for vow- and free-will offerings. So it is not merely a matter of a new image for pretty much the same argument.

The context for this pericope is interesting. Immediately following is the story of Hillel the Elder, who laid on hands on the sacrifice in the courtyard and then assured Shammaites that it was a female and needed merely for peace-offerings, above, I, p. 309. The Hillel-story comes after the legal dispute of the Houses, another instance in which a law or exegesis is turned into a narrative or "historical" account illustrating the same law or exegesis.

III.ii.23.A. TNW RBNN: The House of Shammai say, "Heaven was created first and afterwards the earth was created, for it is said, *In the beginning God created the heaven and the earth*" (Gen. 1:1).

The House of Hillel say, "Earth was created first and afterwards heaven, for it is said, *In the day that the Lord God made earth and heaven*" (Gen. 2:4).

B. The House of Hillel said to the House of Shammai, "According to your view, a man builds the upper story [first] and afterwards builds the house, for it is said, *It is he that buildeth His upper chambers in the heaven, and hath founded His vault upon the earth*" (Amos 9:6).

Said the House of Shammai to the House of Hillel, "According to your view, a man makes the footstool [first], and afterwards he makes the throne, for it is said, *Thus saith the Lord, The heaven is My throne and the earth is My footstool*" (Is. 66:1).

[b. Ḥag. 12a = y. Ḥag. 2:1 (Lev. R. 36:1, Gen. R. 1:1, Gen. R. 12:14)]

Comment: The pericope, part A, follows the classic form, heavily glossed with interpolated Scriptures; the debate is equally conventional. But the form cannot dictate the date or demonstrate authenticity, especially where the Houses are assigned the only positions for debate (assuming no one supposed heaven and earth were made at the same instant, in which case the Houses would have had no argument).

iii. Nashim

II.i.59.A. The House of Shammai permit [Levirate marriage between] the co-wives and the [surviving] brothers.

And the House of Hillel forbid.

B. [If] they had performed *ḥaliṣah*, the House of Shammai declare them ineligible (PŚL) to marry a priest.

And the House of Hillel declare them eligible (KŠR).

C. [If] they had been taken in Levirate marriage, the House of Shammai declare [them] eligible.

And the House of Hillel declare ineligible.

D. Notwithstanding that these forbid (ʾŚR) what the others permit (HTR), and these declare ineligible (PŚL) whom the others declare eligible (KŠR), yet the House of Shammai did not refrain from marrying women from the House of Hillel, nor the House of Hillel from marrying women from the House of Shammai.

E. [Despite] all [the disputes about what is] clean and unclean, wherein these declare clean what the others declare unclean, neither refrained from preparing cleannesses with one another.

[M. Yev. 1:4, trans. Danby, pp. 218-9 (y. Yev. 1:2, 6; b. Yev. 9a, 13a-b, 14a-b, 15a-b, 16a, 27a)]

Comment: While the wives themselves may not enter Levirate marriage with the surviving brothers, the co-wives may do so, according to the House of Shammai, contrary to M. Yev. 1:1, which conforms to the Hillelite opinion without attribution to the House of Hillel.

Parts B and C spell out the consequences of part A. If the co-wives carried out the *ḥaliṣah* ceremony, the House of Shammai prohibit them from marrying a priest, for the *ḥaliṣah* was necessary; she is completely in the status of a *ḥaluṣah*, and prohibited to marry priests (M. Yev. 2:4). The House of Hillel permit it, for the *ḥaliṣah* was not necessary. If the co-wives entered Levirate marriage and were widowed, the House of Shammai permit them to marry a priest. The House of Hillel prohibit it, for the Levirate marriage was in fact prohibited, and the woman is in the same category as a prostitute, prohibited to wed a priest (Lev. 21:7).

The form of part A is standard, with the Shammaite opinion somewhat articulated. With a superscription it would have been as follows:

As to the Levirate marriage of co-wives to the brothers

The House of Shammai:	Permit.
The House of Hillel:	Prohibit.

As usual, therefore, the operative words are the matched pairs: *prohibit/permit*, and these will be assigned to the Houses according to the demand of the superscription. Parts B and C, by contrast, follow the simpler form, with the Shammaites' lemma lightly glossed (in italics):

They carried out the ḥaliṣah-ceremony

House of Shammai:	Declare ineligible *from the priesthood*
House of Hillel:	Declare eligible.

Part C is simplest of all:

They entered Levirate marriage

House of Shammai:	Declare eligible
House of Hillel:	Declare ineligible.

The formation of disputes is therefore around diametrically opposite rulings on given questions, with positions assigned to the Houses according to whatever principles the tradents had available. The Houses' opinions here are phrased in contrasting verbs in active, participial form, with minimum adornment. Only the presence of a superscription or the (alternative) articulation of the dispute within the Shammaite lemma distinguishes developed from somewhat more primitive exempla. The latter possibly would have come after the former, though redactional considerations may sometimes have affected the choice of form.

Parts D and E present an interesting interpolation, tacked on to the foregoing and alleging a kind of compromise. Part D is artfully built on the verbs of parts A-B-C, *permit/prohibit, declare ineligible/declare eligible*. The order is correct. The predicate is neatly balanced as a legal condition: each side of the agreement is specified—these marry those, those marry these. We may take for granted that the women are not active participants in the Houses, but daughters of male members.

Part E then takes up the theme and carries the compromise position even further:

All the cleannesses and uncleannesses which

These declared clean and these declared unclean—
They did not refrain making [preparing] purities
These with these.

One should have expected *from* [M] plus the infinitive, parallel to the foregoing *refrain from (to) marry*. The *unclean* element is ignored, logically, since if one party regarded the other's uncleannesses as clean, it obviously would have made use of them. Hence the operative category is cleanness only.

So we are told the Houses intermarried, even though such marriages would have produced *mamzerim*, or illegitimate children, according to one or the other party. In this instance, for example, the children of the co-wives who entered Levirate marriage according to the House of Shammai would be *mamzerim* according to the House of Hillel. Likewise, they would lend one another cooking ports. The picture is incredible. If the disputes came to so little that the Houses ignored the practical consequences of violating their own rulings, then why should the disputes have been carried on at all? Why should the Houses have troubled to register their contrary views of law, if they did not intend to live by them? The subscription is not meant to denigrate the disputes—that much is clear—but rather to deny their results in social life. Since the Shammaites take or are given the more stringent side in the great number of disputes, the assertion seems on the face of it to be directed toward them. But the case before us has the Hillelites declaring Shammaite children to be *mamzerim*—yet supposedly allowing their progeny to marry such *mamzerim*! In a community so conscious of genealogical purity as Palestinian Jewry, that is, as I said, simply unbelievable. One recalls, with reference to part E, that when Gamaliel's daughter married a non-observant Jew (not specified as a Shammaite, to be sure), he had to agree that cleannesses would *not be* prepared in his house at all.

One therefore must ask, When would such an assertion have been made, by whom, and for what purpose? It is in the language of historical narrative, so we cannot suppose the intention was to settle the disputes by a legal compromise. Indeed, nothing is compromised at all. My guess is that it was important to say such a thing at a time that someone was attempting to unify the Houses, among other Jews, for action in a common purpose. The Houses by now could not have been so vigorous, or their disputes so vital, as in the past. It looks like an epitaph on a dying age: whatever the disputes may have been, the parties ignored their practical consequences and really loved one another.

Anyone who believed the stories about how the Shammaites mobbed Hillel in the Temple and used a sword in the school house would not have believed this allegation. Those Yavneans who held that following Shammaite rulings would be punishable by heaven likewise would have been surprised by it. If relations between the Houses were as characterized in those stories, they would not have yielded so benign a conclusion.

The assertion of parts D-E therefore needs to be placed at a time that the Houses' disputes no longer divided the Pharisaic-rabbinic movement, but still *were* vividly remembered, as remnants of the old Houses persisted into a new age. That time obviously must come before Judah the Patriarch. My guess is that it was toward the end of Yavneh's consistory, on the eve of the Bar Kokhba War. The historical

Houses were a dim memory. To be sure, disputes continued to be shaped within the literary-redactional framework of the Houses, but the Houses tended to serve as convenience-names to which to assign opposing viewpoints, and by which to ascertain the acceptable law (Hillel) without logical difficulty. It was now important to obliterate old disputes, in the face of the current one, about the messianic hopes associated with Bar Kokhba. The ʿAqibans who backed Bar Kokhba may well have asserted that the old Houses really loved one another, and remaining followers of the Shammaites in particular should be free to join as equals in the new cause. Since followers of the Hillelites would have regarded them as *mamzerim*, it was particularly important to assert the contrary; but the purity-laws had significant practical consequences as well. Now the Houses were able to eat with one another and trust the purity-laws were kept—or did not matter—for the first time in a century. The pericope would have entered the tradition and persisted long afterward, alongside contrary views of the practical consequences of the Houses-disputes. Having located an appropriate time, we may therefore suppose the assertion derives from an ʿAqiban authority and was issued in connection with efforts to unify the rabbinic movement behind the ʿAqiban-Bar Kokhban War. Ishmael's school's view is above, p. 48.

This theory is virtually certain, since Simeon b. Yoḥai refers to part E, Tos. Yev. 1:12 (p. 204), so the saying had reached final form by Ushan times. Since the vigorous disputes on Levirate rules are verified by several early Yavneans, the allegation must come between ca. 100 and ca. 150.

III.ii.24. In the days of R. Dosa b. Harkinas the rival [co-wife] of a daughter was permitted to marry the brothers. This ruling was very disturbing to the sages, because he was a great sage and his eyes were dim so that he was unable to come to the house of study. When a discussion took place as to who should go and communicate with him, R. Joshua said to them, "I will go."

They began to address to him (Dosa) all sorts of questions on legal practice until they reached that of the daughter's rival.

"What is the law," they asked him, "in the case of a daughter's rival?"

"This," he answered them, "is a question in dispute between the House of Shammai and the House of Hillel."

"In accordance with whose ruling is the law?"

"The law," he replied, "is in accordance with the ruling of the House of Hillel."

"But, indeed," they said to him, "it was stated in your name that the law is in accordance with the ruling of the House of Shammai!"

He said to them, "Did you hear, 'Dosa' or 'the *son* of Harkinas'? "

"By the life of our Master," they replied, "We heard no son's name mentioned."

"I have," he said to them, "a younger brother who is the first-born of Satan, and his name is Jonathan, and he is one of the disciples of Shammai. Take care that he does not overwhelm you on questions of established practice, because he has three hundred answers to prove that the daughter's rival is permitted. But I call heaven and earth to witness that upon this mortar sat the prophet Haggai and delivered the following three rulings: That a daughter's rival is forbidden, that in the lands of Ammon and Moab the tithe of the poor is to be given in the Seventh Year, and that proselytes may be accepted from the Cordyenians and the Tarmodites."

(b. Yev. 16a, trans. W. Slotki, pp. 85-87 = y. Yev. 1:6)

Comment: The story provides a valuable *terminus ante quem* for M. Yev. 1:4. On the tithe of Ammon and Moab in the Seventh Year, see *Development*, pp. 58-60, and above, pp. 106-108.

II.i.60.A. If two of four brothers married two sisters, and the two that married the two sisters died, the sisters must perform *ḥaliṣah* and may not contract Levirate marriage; and if the brothers had already married them, they must put them away.

R. Eliezer (Eleazar) says in the name of the House of Shammai, "They may continue [the marriage]."

And the House of Hillel say, "They must put [them] away."

B. If there were three brothers, two married to two sisters and one unmarried, and one of the married brothers died, and the unmarried one bespoke [performed a *ma'amar*] the widow, and then his second brother died—

The House of Shammai say, "His [bespoken] wife [abides] with him, and the other goes forth as being the wife's sister."

And the House of Hillel say, "He must put away his [bespoken] wife [both] by bill of divorce (GṬ) and by *ḥaliṣah*, and his brother's wife by *ḥaliṣah*."

C. This is the case whereof they have said, "Woe to him because of [the loss of] his wife! and woe to him because of [the loss of] his brother's wife!"

[M. Yev. 3:1, 5, trans. Danby, pp. 221-2 (y. Yev. 3:1, 4, b. Yev. 28a, 29a-b, b. Ned. 74b, b. Yev. 51b, M. 'Ed. 4:9, 5:5)]

Comment: The form of the Houses opinions in part A uses single, matched verbs in the future tense:

If they had already married them as Levirate wives
House of Shammai say, They will continue (QYM).
House of Hillel say, They will divorce (YṢ').

The antecedent Mishnah (A) follows the Hillelite opinion (B). Then Eliezer's view of the history of the tradition must come first, that is, in the form of a Houses-dispute. Later on someone dropped the Shammaite position entirely and rephrased the whole following the Hillelite view, bypassing reference to the Hillelite *origin* of the law. This indicates that Houses-disputes later on could be suppressed, as the law was settled in favor of the Hillelites. But it also shows once again that conservative tradents preserved early as well as late formulations of the same law, as M. Yev. 1:1,4.

In part B, M. Yev. 3:5, the House of Shammai say that the *word* (M'MR) has effected marriage, and when her sister comes for Levirate marriage, she is free both from the marriage and even from the *ḥaliṣah*-ceremony because she is the sister of his wife. The House of Hillel hold that the *word* did not effect marriage, and when the sister comes to him as a Levirate wife, *both* are subject to him and prohibited, since one of them is subject to him. Therefore he can marry neither. He has to undertake the *ḥaliṣah*-ceremony with both, and in addition gives a *geṭ* to his bespoken wife, to free her from the tie imposed by the *word*.

The concluding remark, part C, then applies to such a situation a popular proverb: he lost both women.

The form is extremely complex:

[*Elaborate superscription, stating* not *a problem of law but a case*]
Three brothers:
Two married to two sisters, one free
One of the husbands of the sisters died, and the free one bespoke the widow
Then the second brother died.

This is not a superscription—it is a whole story! The Houses address themselves not to a problem of law, but to the position of the characters in the story:

House of Shammai:
His wife is with him
That one goes forth because of *sister of the wife*
House of Hillel:
He divorces his wife with a *geṭ* and with *ḥaliṣah*
And the wife of his brother with *ḥaliṣah*.

We can by no means reduce the whole to a simple dispute about the effect of the *word*, even though the case is a conflict about that principle. Nor can we take upon ourselves to reconstruct a simple dispute concerning *words*, in which the complications of the laws of Levirate marriage would not enter. That by definition is impossible, since the issue of *word* would not be before us without those very complications.

To be sure, we might suppose that in some early form the whole would have come down to this:

*Word (*Ma'*amar)*

House of Shammai: Does sanctify (MQDŠ)
House of Hillel: Does not sanctify

Then the requirements of the form are met. But the dispute before us plays no role. Such a debate would have had to occur in the tractate on betrothals, and it does not. This means that an alleged Houses-dispute has been preserved only in a highly complex state—hardly evidence of origin early in the formation of the tradition.

See Epstein, *Mevo'ot*, p. 437; on Eliezer/Eleazar *Mishnah*, pp. 1162-3.

II.i.61.A. If a woman awaiting Levirate marriage inherited property, the House of Shammai and the House of Hillel agree that she sells it or gives it away, and [the act] is valid (MWKRT WNWTNT WQYYM).

B. If she died, what should be done with her *Ketuvah* and property that comes in and goes out with her?

The House of Shammai say, "The heirs of her [deceased] husband share with the heirs of her father (YḤLWQW etc.)."

And the House of Hillel say, "The property falls to them [both] (NKŚYM BḤZQTN): the *Ketuvah* falls to (BḤZQT) the [deceased] husband's heirs, and the property that comes in and goes out with her falls to (BḤZQT) her father's heirs."

[M. Yev. 4:3, trans. Danby, p. 223 (y. Yev. 4:3, b. Yev. 38a-b; b. Soṭ. 24a, b. Ket. 81a)]

Comment: Part A could as well have omitted reference to the Houses, since no dispute concerns that situation, and we have at the outset no reason to believe the Houses would have differed. Furthermore, part A's agreement ought formally to follow part B. But because logic requires the case of the woman who is still alive to come before that of the woman who dies, the traditions have been reversed. Actually it should look something like this:

One who was awaiting Levirate marriage who inherited property
[before that time, the husband would have controlled it]
She may sell and give, and [the act] is valid.

Part B depends upon the superscription of part A, One who was awaiting. . . *and died.*

Had the woman lived, her new husband by Levirate marriage would have inherited the whole. What now are his rights, and what are the rights of her estate (= inheritors of the father)? The Shammaites say the Levirate husband inherits, because she died in the status of a "doubtful marriage." She was not free to marry, therefore is like any already-married woman. But she was not yet married to her Levir. So the Levir acquires as one of the heirs of the husband, on account of that ambiguous situation. And half the estate returns to her father, as if she were unmarried. The House of Hillel divide the estate. The marriage-settlement goes to the husband's estate. The property that remained entirely hers ("that comes in and goes out with her") goes to her father (or his heirs). So there is no division according to the equal claim of each party, rather according to the rightful claim *as if* no doubt of the marriage existed, according to the Hillelites. Both Houses agree that until she has entered Levirate marriage, she is free to dispose of her property as if she were not married. This position can have been taken by each House without compromising its view of the division of her estate.

The form superficially is standard, with the superscription and the Houses' opinions in proper order. But the lemmas of the Houses are not evenly balanced. They however would be conventional if left unglossed:

House of Shammai: They divide—(*the heirs of the husband with the heirs of the father*)
House of Hillel: *(The property (NKŚYM) [is])* in their possession (BḤZQTN)—(*the Ketuvah in possession of the heirs of the husband; the property that comes in and goes out with her in the possession of the heirs of the father*).

Accordingly, the Houses use different words, rather than the same word plus negative, or the usual syzygies. But that is necessitated by the nature of the dispute. Hence we do not have to regard the pericope before us as much developed; it is simply heavily glossed, and the conventional form, with superscription, may well have come down from earlier times. The respective roots are

ḤLQ vs. ḤZQ

That is, a difference of a single letter in the root; each side has the same number of syllables:

Shammaite: yaḤaLoQu
Hillelite: beḤeZQaTan

So the different word-choices still produce contrasting lemmas for mnemonic purposes.

Note Epstein, *Mishnah*, p. 1099.

II.i.62.A. No man may abstain from keeping the law *Be fruitful and multiply*, unless he already has children.

B. The House of Shammai say, "Two males."

The House of Hillel say, "A male and a female, for it is written, *Male and female created he them* (Gen. 1:27)."

[M. Yev. 6:6, trans. Danby, p. 227 (y. Yev. 6:6, b. Yev. 61b-62a)]

Comment: The Houses-dispute glosses the foregoing general rule. The form is standard. The rule (A) serves as the necessary superscription; nothing more is needed.

Here the content of the pericope is remarkable, for it tells us that Pharisees wished to abstain from sexual relations and had to be required to continue to procreate until they had fulfilled their obligation to maintain the population. So within Pharisaism were ascetics who preferred the solitary life.

II.i.63.A. The House of Shammai say, "Only they that are betrothed ('RWŚWT) exercise the right of Refusal."

And the House of Hillel say, "[Both] they that are betrothed, *and* they that are married."

B. The House of Shammai say, "[They may exercise the right] against a husband [only], and not against a brother-in-law (YBM)."

And the House of Hillel say, "Against a husband *and* against a brother-in-law."

C. The House of Shammai say, "[It must be exercised] in his presence."

And the House of Hillel say, "In his presence and not in his presence."

D. The House of Shammai say, "[It must be] before the court."

And the House of Hillel say, "Before the court and not before the court."

E. The House of Hillel said to the House of Shammai, "While she is yet under age, she may exercise right of Refusal even four or five times."

The House of Shammai answered, "The daughters of Israel are not ownerless property (HPQR). But ('L') she exercises right of Refusal and waits until she is come of age, and [then] she exercises right of Refusal and [forthwith] marries [some other]."

[M. Yev. 13:1, trans. Danby, p. 237 (y. Yev. 13:1, b. Yev. 101b, 107a-b)]

Comment: Parts A-D constitute a perfect model of the collection-form, lacking merely a one-word superscription (parallel to *concerning the meal*, M. Ber. 8:1), such as *concerning refusal*, perhaps with the further gloss, *These are the differences between the House of*. . . The opinions are matched, so far as possible:

1. House of Shammai say, [They do not allow the right of refusal except to] betrothed	
House of Hillel:	Betrothed *and* married.
2. House of Shammai:	Against the husband, and *not* the Levir.
House of Hillel:	Against the husband *and* Levir.
3. House of Shammai:	Before him.
House of Hillel:	Before him and *not* before him.
4. House of Shammai:	In court.
House of Hillel:	In court and *not* in court.

It would be difficult to invent a better model of the collection-form, indeed of the most primitive sort of Houses-pericopae. The only explanatory matter has been inserted in the opening clause of the Shammaite opinion, then understood throughout: *they do not allow the right of refusal except*—the double negative already familiar in the collection of M. Shab. 1:4-8.

The Houses take extreme positions, with the Hillelites consistently given the more lenient one as usual. The differences are compressed into affirmative or negative statements of the same proposition (B, C), or in inclusion or exclusion of the same detail (D). The Shammaite saying in part A ought to have had *betrothed, and not married*, but the explanatory matter prevented it, since *not*. . . *except*. . . leaves no room for a further exclusion. This shows the explanatory matter here is not a gloss, but is entirely integral to the collection. To be sure, the collection may have been consistent even in part A, and may have been revised to the form before us, but in this instance too close adherence to the subsequent form may not, even at the outset, have been required.

Part E of course is anomalous. It has the House of Hillel debate with the House of Shammai, without an antecedent statement of their two disagreements. We may readily construct:

1. House of Shammai:	Adolescent and *not* child
House of Hillel:	Adolescent *and* child
2. House of Shammai:	Three times
House of Hillel:	Even four [or five] times.

The elements of part E in this form could readily have been attached to the foregoing list. I see no reason to suppose they have been removed and revised. Rather, someone else has a different version of the Houses' disputes on the right of refusal, with different legal issues, and a quite different form. Part E standing by itself follows the usual debate-model, with the House of Hillel first, the House of Shammai second, and decisive. The opinions are not matched, but in the debate-form they not infrequently are whole sentences, even unrelated to one another in diction. The closing Shammaite clause is extremely compressed and should have had a Hillelite counterpart along the same lines.

III.ii.25. The House of Hillel said to the House of Shammai, "(M'SH B) Pishon the camel driver's wife made her declaration of refusal in his absence."

The House of Shammai said to them, "Pishon the camel driver used a reversible measure (MDD BKPYŠH). They therefore used against him a reversible measure."

(b. Yev. 107b = y. Yev. 13:1)

Comment: This clause of the debate pertains to part C. The Hillelites have a precedent, which is taken as fact, then explained away by the Shammaites. It looks to me like an artificial construction, showing what each House theoretically might make of a known case. Pishon looks like a name formed of KPYŠH, and the story seems a play on words.

II.i.64.A. The House of Hillel say, "We have heard no such tradition [that a woman is believed to testify that her husband has died] save of a woman that returned from the harvest and within the same country, and according to a case that happened in fact."

The House of Shammai answered, "It is all one whether she returned from the harvest or from the olive-picking or from the vintage, or whether she came from one country to another. The sages spoke of the harvest only as of a thing that happened in fact."

The House of Hillel reverted to teach according to [the opinion of] the House of Shammai.

B. The House of Shammai say, "She marries again and takes her *Ketuvah*."

The House of Hillel say, "She marries again and does not take her *Ketuvah*."

The House of Shammai said to them, "You have declared permissible the graver matter of forbidden intercourse, and should you not also declare permissible the less important matter of property?"

The House of Hillel answered, "We find that brothers may not enter into an inheritance on her testimony."

The House of Shammai answered, "Do we not learn from her *Ketuvah*-scroll that he thus writes for her: 'If thou be married to another, thou shalt take what is prescribed for thee?' "

The House of Hillel reverted to teach according to the opinion of the House of Shammai.

[M. Yev. 15:2-3, trans. Danby, pp. 241-2 (y. Yev. 15:2, 3; b. Yev. 116b, 117a, 122a [woman may remarry on the evidence of an echo], y. Ket. 4:8, b. Ket. 81a)]

Comment: The chapter opens with the case of a woman who went abroad with her husband, returned alone, and announced that her husband has died. If their marital relation was good and times of peace prevailed, she may remarry or enter Levirate marriage; if the relation was good, but it was a time of war, or if their relation was poor, but it was peacetime, she is not believed.

The saying of the House of Hillel then serves as a commentary on the problem of whether a woman is believed when she is the sole witness to her husband's death. They report a case in which a woman came from the harvest in that same province. The specification of the details of the case leads to two general rules. She was working with her husband in a situation that might readily produce the husband's death (sunstroke). And it was nearby, so that others might clarify the matter. The House of Shammai say it does not matter whether it was a harvest (of wheat) or a cutting of olives, whether it was in the same area or a distant place. The details specified relate merely to the case at hand and were not meant to serve as precedent. The House of Hillel accept this opinion.

y. Ket. 15:2 adds another Shammaite argument: the entire year is a harvest time for something or other, so the Hillelites grant the Shammaite viewpoint. The Shammaite argument here is built on their lemma in the Mishnah.

Part B is attached both because it concerns the woman in the same situation (she has testified of her husband's death), and because to it is assigned the same amiable superscription: The Hillelites changed their minds. Now, however, the dispute is phrased first as a legal pericope:

House of Shammai say, She marries and receives her *Ketuvah*
House of Hillel say, She marries and does *not* receive her *Ketuvah*.

The usual balanced form is then supplemented with a debate. The House of Shammai begin—which is unusual. But the subscription explains why. The Shammaite argument will be accepted, therefore may come first, since the Hillelite argument will be balanced by another Shammaite argument and a conclusive decision. The Shammaites ask how one can distinguish: Is she believed to remarry but regarded as a liar in regard to her marriage-contract? The House of Hillel point out that as regards property, her word is not everywhere taken as law. The brothers do not inherit. The House of Shammai recognize that distinction, but point out that the language of the *Ketuvah* is decisive. If she can remarry, she can also collect her *Ketuvah* from her first marriage. And the House of Hillel agree.

Since the Mishnah is a document produced by the descendants of Hillelite masters (ʿAqiba and his disciples, then Judah their disciple), we do not have to attribute the pericope before us to Shammaite tradents, and indeed, probably cannot. It seems to me unlikely that such a Shammaite pericope would have survived, had not the Hillelites wanted it to. The pericope cannot be compared to those in which both parties enjoy parity, but rather to those in which good Shammaites are represented as following the Hillelite law. Since no "good Hillelites" here are represented as following Shammaite law ("for they know that the law always follows the House of Shammai. . ."), we may take it for granted that this story has survived because the Hillelites preserved it. They preserved it because they either wrote it or did not object to its contents. Of the former we cannot be sure, though it seems to me unlikely that this is how the Hillelite tradents at the outset would have represented matters. But they need not have objected to it, since what the Shammaites provide is *not* testimony derived from their own, partisan tradition, but rather, testimony from evidence unanimously believed to be accurate. In the latter case, the language of the *Ketuvah* settled matters—and everyone knew that Hillel had interpreted for legal purposes the language of the *Ketuvah*, as in the case/story of the Alexandrians. So the procedure of the Shammaites conformed to the Hillelite law to begin with, and part B shows that the Shammaites, *like Hillel*, expounded the language of legal documents of ordinary folk. And that fact is made explicit in y. Yev. 15:3, b. Ket. 81a, etc. Presumably others alleged the contrary. We have no Shammaite saying that one does *not* do so, but that does not much matter. The strong assertions about Hillel and the story before us together suggest that someone—if not Shammaites—thought it an important matter.

As to the story in part A, all the Hillelites had to accept was the Shammaite assertion that the Hillelite tradition was accurate, *but* was meant merely as an example, not as a statement of the sole condition in which the law would pertain. It does not seem to me that the Hillelites had to concede a great deal. Their story was accepted as valid. The House of Shammai merely offered an interpretation for what the Hillelites alleged as fact. This is consistent with the way Hillelites represent the Shammaite response to precedents cited by Hillelites: The Shammaites always accept the story (MʿSH) as fact, merely offer an alternative interpretation of the precedent. So the Hillelites' precedents are conceded by Shammaites, who therefore are made to attest to the veracity of Hillelite records!

Note Halivni, *Meqorot*, p. 120.

II.ii.57.A. "Just as they [the co-wives] free [the others] from marriage, so they free [them] from betrothal.

"Under what circumstances? In the case of a woman whom he may not ordinarily marry [Lit.: in whom he does not have *qiddushin*]. But in the case of a woman whom he may ordinarily marry [in whom he does have *qiddushin*], their co-wives undergo the *ḥaliṣah* ceremony and do not enter Levirate marriage"—the words of the House of Hillel.

The House of Shammai permit the co-wives to the brothers.

B. The six forbidden connections are more stringent than these, because [if] they are married to others, their co-wives are permitted, for the co-wife is only from the brother.

If they married brothers not in transgression [of the law], their co-wives are free.

C. These co-wives went and married—

The House of Shammai say, "They are unfit, and the progeny is unfit [for the priesthood]."

And the House of Hillel say, "They are fit, and the progeny is fit."

[If] they entered Levirate marriage—

The House of Shammai say, "They are fit, and the progeny is fit."

And the House of Hillel say, "They are unfiit, and the progeny is a *mamzer*."

D. R. Yoḥanan b. Nuri said, "Come and see how this law is widespread in Israel: [If we] carry out the law according to the words of the House of Shammai, the progeny is a *mamzer* according to the House of Hillel. [If we] carry out the law according to the House of Hillel, the progeny is impaired (PGWM) according to the words of the House of Shammai.

"But come and let us ordain that the co-wives carry out the *ḥaliṣah* ceremony and do not enter Levirate marriage."

They did not suffice to complete the matter before the hour was unfit (NṬRPH).

E. R. Simeon b. Gamaliel said, "What shall we do for the first cowives?"

F. They asked R. Joshua, "The children of the co-wives—what is their status?"

He said to them, "Why do you put my head between two great mountains, between the House of Shammai and the House of Hillel, who will cut off my head?

"But I testify concerning the family of the House of ʿAlubaʾi (ʿLWBʾY) from the house of soldiers (BYT ṢBʾYM), and concerning the family of the House of Qipaʾi (QYPʾY) from the house of [the] gatherer (BYT MQŠŠ), that they are the children of co-wives (ṢRWT), and from them were high priests, and they were offering [sacrifices] at the altar."

R. Ṭarfon said, "Would that (T'YB) the rival of the daughter would fall to me so that I could marry her to the priesthood."

G. R. Eleazar said, "Even though the House of Shammai differed from the House of Hillel concerning co-wives, they agree that the progeny is not a *mamzer*, for a *mamzer* comes only from a woman, [for violation of] the prohibition [of whose marriage] they [she and the husband] are liable for *cutting off*."

H. Even though the House of Shammai disagreed with the House of Hillel concerning co-wives, sisters, a woman whose marriage-tie was dubious, an old divorce-document, in reference to one who betrothes a woman with something worth a *peruṭah*, concerning him who divorces his wife and spends the night with her in the same inn—

The House of Shammai did not hold back from marriage with women from the House of Hillel, nor the House of Hillel from the House of Shammai, but they behaved in truth and peace among themselves, as it is said, *They loved truth and peace* (Zech. 8:19).

I. Even though these prohibit and these permit, they did not hold back [from] preparing clean things with one another, to carry out that which is said (Prov. 21:2), *Every way of a man is right in his own eyes, but the Lord weighs the heart.*

J. R. Simeon says, "From doubtful matters they did not hold back, but they did hold back from those which were certain."

K. The law always follows the words of the House of Hillel.

L. He who wants to be stringent on himself to behave according to the words of the Houses of Shammai and Hillel, concerning this one is said, *The fool walks in darkness* (Qoh. 2:14).

He who holds to the leniencies of the House of Shammai and the leniencies of the House of Hillel is evil. But if according to the words of the House of Shammai, then according to their leniencies and stringencies, and if according to the words of the House of Hillel, then according to [both] their leniencies and their stringencies.

[Tos. Yev. 1:7-13, ed. Lieberman, pp. 2-4, lines 18-44 (M. ʿEd. 4:8; R. Yoḥanan: y. Yev. 1:6, 3:1, b. Yev. 13b, 14b, 27a; R. Simeon: y. Yev. 1:6, y. Qid. 1:1, b. Yev. 14b; He who holds: Tos. Suk. 2:3, Tos. ʿEd. 2:3, b. ʿEruv. 66b, R. H. 14b, b. Ḥul. 43b, y. Ber. 1:7, y. Soṭ. 3:4; y. Qid. 1:1)]

Comment: Part A is a supplement to M. Yev. 1:4: the House of Hillel forbid Levirate marriage between the co-wives and the surviving brothers. The Houses differ not only on the fifteen categories of women listed in M. Yev. 1:1, but also on other categories of women. The House of Hillel prohibit the co-wives from entering Levirate marriage with the brothers of the deceased, and the House of Shammai permit. Lieberman however observes (*Tosefta Kifshuṭah*, p. 5), that the positions of the Houses may well be reversed in the correct reading of the Tosefta, and the reading before us may have been corrected to conform to the Mishnah. He observes that the vast majority of dispute-pericopae have Shammai first, then Hillel.

The clause beginning *under what circumstances* pertains to M. Yev. 1:4, the House of Hillel permit the co-wives to marry the Levirate brothers. This permission pertains to those normally forbidden to marry the deceased brother.

Part B pertains to M. Yev. 1:3, and Part C to M. Yev. 1:4.

Parts D-E relate to the co-wives who, relying on the ruling of the House of Shammai, married brothers-in-law who were priests, prior to the ordinance of Yoḥanan b. Nuri. The children would be regarded as *mamzerim*.

Part F: Joshua testifies concerning certain families, that they were children of co-wives and from them had come forth high priests. R. Ṭarfon agrees with Joshua's position. For a full explanation, see Lieberman, *Tosefta Kifshuṭah* to *Nashim*, p. 6: Joshua affirms the Hillelite position.

Part H supplies a whole list of Houses-disputes in marital law, rendering the conclusion all the more impressive. Parts K-L appear above, Tos. Sukkah 2:3.

For our purposes, it suffices to observe that the Houses-dispute comes no later than early Yavneh (Joshua, Ṭarfon). Since Joshua refers to the Houses' dispute on the same question, in this instance it stands to reason that the dispute may derive from Temple times, a supposition supported by Joshua's testimony concerning families of the priesthood of that day.

It is noteworthy that Gamaliel supposedly married his daughter's co-wife:

> It happened that (M'SH B) R. Gamaliel's daughter was married to his brother Abba, who died childless. Gamaliel married her rival.
>
> How do you understand this? Was R. Gamaliel one of the disciples of the House of Shammai?
>
> But R. Gamaliel's daughter was different because she was barren. . .
>
> (b. Yev. 15a)

The story standing by itself clearly supposes Gamaliel followed the view of the Shammaites, and this is consistent with other such stories.

II.ii.58.A. Four brothers, two of them married to two sisters, and those who had married the sisters died—lo, these [women] undergo the *ḥaliṣah* ceremony and do not enter Levirate marriage.

And if they [the other brothers] had earlier married, they must divorce.

R. Leazar says, "The House of Shammai say, 'They remain married.'

"The House of Hillel say, 'They divorce.' "

B. R. Simeon says, "They remain married."

C. Abba Saul says, "The lenient position is the House of Hillel's in this matter."

[Tos. Yev. 5:1, ed. Lieberman, p. 13, lines 1-4 (y. Yev. 3:1; M. 'Ed. 5:5, Tos. 'Ed. 2:9)]

Comment: Part A = M. Yev. 3:1, M. 'Ed. 5:3. In part B, R. Simeon holds the Houses do not differ at all. Abba Saul agrees with Simeon on the Hillelite opinion. Alternatively, he corrects it by assigning the lenient ruling (remain married) to the Hillelites. See Lieberman, *Tosefta Kifshuṭah*, p. 35.

y. Yev. 3:1 gives Abba Saul's lemma as QWL HWWY BYT HLL BDBR HZH.

II.ii.59. R. Nathan says, "The House of Shammai say, 'Two sons, like the sons of Moses, as it is said, *The sons of Moses, Gershom and Eliezer* (I. Chron. 23:15).'

"And the House of Hillel say, 'Male and female, as it is said, *Male and female he created them* (Gen. 1:27, 5:2).' "

R. Jonathan says, "The House of Shammai say, 'Male *and* female.'

"And the House of Hillel say, 'Male *or* female.' "

[Tos. Yev. 8:4, ed. Lieberman, p. 25, lines 18-21 (y. Yev. 6:6, b. Yev. 62a)]

Comment: See M. Yev. 6:6. Judah the Patriarch ignores Jonathan's tradition and copies Nathan's, dropping the proof-texts as usual.

II.ii.60. The House of Hillel say, "In a court and not in a court—and on condition that [*not* in a court] there are three."

[Tos. Yev. 13:1, ed. Lieberman, p. 45, lines 2-3 (b. Yev. 107b)]

Comment: See M. Yev. 13:1. The condition is a gloss, making the Hillelite position into the Shammaite one!

III.ii.26. R. Judah stated, "The House of Shammai and the House of Hillel agree that a man who cohabited with his mother-in-law renders his wife unfit [to live with him]; they differ only where a man cohabited with his wife's sister, in which case the House of Shammai maintain that he thereby causes [his wife] to be unfit for him, while the House of Hillel maintain that he does not thereby cause her to be unfit for him."

R. Yosi stated, "The House of Shammai and the House of Hillel agree that a man who cohabits with his wife's sister does not thereby render his wife unfit for him; they differ only where a man cohabited with his mother-in-law, in which case the House of Shammai maintain that he thereby causes [his wife] to be unfit for him, while the House of Hillel maintain that he does not cause her to be unfit for him."

[b. Yev. 95a (y. Yev. 10:6)]

II.i.65. If a man vowed to have no intercourse with his wife, the House of Shammai say, "Two weeks."

And the House of Hillel say, "One week."

B. "Disciples [of the sages] may continue absent for thirty days against the will [of their wives] while they occupy themselves in the study of Torah; and laborers for one week. The *duty of marriage* (ʿWNH) enjoined in the Torah is: every day for them that are unoccupied, twice a week for laborers, once a week for ass-drivers, once every thirty days for camel-drivers, and once every six months for sailors," so R. Eliezer.

[M. Ket. 5:6, trans. Danby, p. 252 (y. Ket. 5:6, 7, b. Ket. 61b, 71a-b)]

III.ii.27.A. Was it not taught: If a woman vowed not to suckle her child—

The House of Shammai say, "They pull the breast out of its mouth."

And the House of Hillel say, "They compel her to suckle it."

(b. Ket. 59b = y. Ket. 5:7)

III.ii.27.B. TNW RBNN: "A nursing mother whose husband died within twenty-four months [of the birth of their child] shall neither be betrothed nor married again until the [completion of the] twenty-four months," the words of R. Meir.

R. Judah permits [remarriage] after eighteen months.

R. Jonathan b. Joseph said, "These are the words of the House of Shammai and the House of Hillel, for—

"The House of Shammai say, 'Twenty-four months.'

"And the House of Hillel say, 'Eighteen months.' "

[b. Ket. 60a-b (y. Soṭ. 4:3, below p. 227)]

II.ii.61. He who keeps his wife by vow from having sexual relations The House of Shammai say, "Two weeks, *like the birth of a female.*" The House of Hillel say, "One week, *like the birth of a male, and like the days of her menstrual period.*"

[Tos. Ket. 5:6, ed. Lieberman, p. 73, lines 32-3 = y. Ket. 5:7]

Comment: The italicized words of II.ii.61 are glosses, dropped by Judah the Patriarch.

II.i.65 is standard, with the Houses' opinions merely numbers *one/two* perhaps glossed with *weeks* (ŠBT). The wife waits for a week or two, then may demand a writ of divorce and collect her marriage-contract.

Part B has nothing to do with part A. The superscription of A pertains to a vow, and the contents of part B relate to other circumstances preventing the couple from maintaining a normal sexual relationship.

III.ii.27.A, a singleton, is in unconventional form. The positions of course are diametrically opposed, but the word-choices are unbalanced.

III.ii.25B is the usual *twenty-four vs. eighteen* dispute. See below, p. 227.

On b. Ket. 60a, see Halivni, *Meqorot*, p. 205.

II.i.66.A. [If] a woman inherited goods before she was betrothed, the House of Shammai and the House of Hillel agree that she sells [them] or gives them away and [that her act is] valid.

B. [If] she inherited them after she was betrothed, the House of Shammai say, "She sells [them]."

And the House of Hillel say, "She does not sell [them]."

C. But they agree that if she sold them or gave them away, her act is valid.

D. R. Judah said, "They said before Rabban Gamaliel, 'Since [the betrothed husband] gets possession of the woman, does he not get possession of [her] property?'

"He said to them, 'We are at a loss (BWŠYM) [to find reason for giving him right] over her new [possessions], and ('L' Š) would you even burden us with (MGLGLYN 'LYNW) the old!' "

E. [If] she inherited [goods] after she married, both agree that if she sold them or gave them away, the husband may take them out of the hands of the buyers.

F. If [she inherited them] before she married, and she then married, Rabban Gamaliel says, "If she sold them or gave them away her act is valid."

G. R. Ḥananiah b. 'Aqaviah said, "They said before Rabban

Gamaliel, 'Since he gets possession of the woman, does he not get possession of her goods also?'

"He said to them, 'We are at a loss [to find reason for giving him right] over her new [possessions], and would you even burden us with the old also!' "

II.i.67. If a woman awaiting Levirate marriage inherited property, the House of Shammai and the House of Hillel agree that she may sell it or give it away, and the act will be valid.

If she died, what should be done with her *Ketuvah* and property that comes in and goes out with her?

The House of Shammai say, "The heirs of her [deceased] husband share with the heirs of her father."

And the House of Hillel say, "Her property falls to them [both]; the *Ketuvah* falls to the [deceased] husband's heirs, and the property that comes in and goes out with her falls into the possession of her father's heirs."

[M. Ket. 8:1, 6, trans. Danby, p. 256-7 (y. Ket. 8:1, 9, 9:1; b. Ket. 78a-b, 80b, 81a-b, y. Pe'ah 6:2; b. Soṭ. 25a, b. Yev. 38b)]

Comment: II.i.66, M. Ket. 8:1, follows the same pattern as II.i.67, M. Ket. 8:6 = M. Yev. 4:3. Part A begins with an agreement, therefore in the wrong order, but logic requires the present arrangement, for the sequence is *before* she is betrothed, *after* she is betrothed, *then* (part C), after she is married. The opinion of the Houses in part A is in the same language as M. Ket. 8:6 = M. Yev. 4:3, hence a stock-phrase equally useful to settle different questions. Part B is in the expected form. The superscription depends on that of part A, dropping the words to be understood: *the woman who. . . property. . .* The several pericopae therefore seem to have been put together by a single hand. The opinions of the Houses are as expected, the same verb, in the same form, with or without the negative. Then comes an agreement in proper sequence, *these and these agree*. Part C has the Hillelites go over to the Shammaite view. Part D relates to the same problem as the foregoing ruling. Judah b. Ilai therefore supplies a *terminus ante quem* for the Houses, but Gamaliel does not. Why do the Houses agree that she may dispose of her property after she is betrothed? The answer is that we are concerned with the property she receives after marriage (part E): how to justify the husband's control over it?

Part F goes back over the ruling of part B: property that comes to the woman after betrothal. Now the superscription is, If she inherited before she married and then she married—the same situation as before, namely, while she is betrothed, for, were she *not* betrothed, the question would not be raised. Gamaliel disagrees with the Houses' agreement. He employs the language of part A:

Part B

She may sell them

Part F

If she *sold*, or *gave*, [her act is] *valid*

Part A

She *sells* and *gives* — [the act is] *valid.*

Gamaliel's language uses the same verbs, but in the past tense. It looks as if the lemma of Gamaliel has shaped that of the Houses, or vice versa, or that all use a fixed formula.

The pericope now is to be separated into its constituent elements, which are Houses-disputes and Gamaliel-rulings:

Houses	*Gamaliel*
1. [If property came to her] *Before betrothed* Houses agree she sells and gives and valid	—
2. *After betrothed* Shammai: She may sell Hillel: She may not sell	[*After betrothed*] R. Judah said, They said before R. Gamaliel, Since he has acquired the woman, should he not acquire the property? [= Hillelite position is accepted *but* questioned.]
3. Both agree that if *after* betrothal she sold or gave, [the act is] valid.	—
4. *After married* =	[Property came] before she was married, *and she was married.*
Houses agree husband can retrieve the property [act thus is *invalid*].	R. Gamaliel said, If she sold or gave, [the act is] *valid* [= contrary to the Houses].

The Houses' agreement concerning her actions (no. 3) after the betrothal is astonishing. The Hillelites have ruled she may *not* sell the property. Yet immediately following, we are told the Houses agree that if she *did* sell or give it away, her action *is* valid. This is strange, since it has the Hillelites reversing themselves after the fact. Gamaliel is represented by Judah as recognizing the difficulty of the Hillelite position.

The rulings after the marriage thus are diametrically opposed. The Houses agree that the husband controls the property, and Gamaliel says *she* may dispose of it.

Clearly, the pericope consists of two quite separate traditions, the first concerning the Houses, the second concerning Gamaliel, with the latter also in two separate forms. The first Gamaliel-lemma is simply the report of R. Judah. But the second is in conventional form, with a superscription *before she was married and she was married*, then the opinion, *R. Gamaliel says*—thus an independent, finished lemma.

Since the second Gamaliel-lemma shows no knowledge of the Houses-dispute, we may suppose that the Houses-dispute was shaped after his time. As to the first, we can be less certain, for the tradent is Judah b. Ilai—*prima facie* evidence of a second-century redaction—but the content of the pericope is not different from the Hillelite position: by implication, she *may* dispose of the property. By the looks of it, therefore, the Houses-materials probably do come after Gamaliel, who is then "Hillelized." Matters now are organized more lucidly and present the whole in a simple and symmetrical scheme. Perhaps the model of M. Ket. 8:6 has served for the highly complex materials of M. Ket. 8:1.

See Epstein, *Mishnah*, pp. 1099-1101.

III.ii.28. It was taught: At what period of her age is a husband entitled to be the heir of his wife [if she dies while still] a minor?

The House of Shammai say, "When she attains to womanhood."

And the House of Hillel say, "When she enters into the bridal chamber."

R. Eliezer said, "When connubial intercourse has taken place."

Then he is entitled to be her heir, he may defile himself for her, and she may eat *Terumah* by virtue of his rights. (b. Yev. 89b)

Comment: The *beraita*, a singleton, introduces a separate issue from M. Ket. 8:6, M. Yev. 4:3, supplying factual information pertinent to those disputes.

III.ii.29.A. TNW RBNN: How does one dance before the bride?

The House of Shammai say, "The bride as she is."

And the House of Hillel say, "Beautiful and graceful bride!"

The House of Shammai said to the House of Hillel, "If she was lame or blind, does one say of her: 'Beautiful and graceful bride'? Whereas the Torah said, *Keep thee far from a false matter* (Ex. 23:7)."

Said the House of Hillel to the House of Shammai, "According to your words, if one has made a bad purchase in the market, should one praise it in his eyes or deprecate it? Surely, one should praise it in his eyes."

Therefore, the sages said: Always should the disposition of a man be pleasant with people. (b. Ket. 17a)

Comment: The original "dispute" is presumably as spurious as the debate, which has the Houses in reverse order and ends with an appropriate homily of "the sages"—in the tradition of kindly Hillel and petulant Shammai.

II.i.68. If a man saw others eating [his] figs and said, "May they be *Qorban* to you!" and they were found to be his father and brothers and others with them—

The House of Shammai say, "They are permitted, but the others with them are prohibited."

And the House of Hillel say, "Both are permitted." [The vow is binding for neither of them.]

II.i.69.A. They vow to murderers, robbers, or tax-gatherers that [what they have] is Heave-offering even though it is not Heave-offering; or that they belong to the king's household even though they do not belong to the king's household.

B. The House of Shammai say, "They vow in all [forms of words] save in [the form of an] oath."

And the House of Hillel say, "Even in [the form of] an oath."

C. The House of Shammai say, "He should not be first with a vow, [but he should vow only under constraint]."

And the House of Hillel say, "He may even be first [with a vow]."

D. The House of Shammai say, "[Only] in a matter in which a vow is imposed."

And the House of Hillel say, "Even ('P) in a matter over which no vow is imposed."

E. How so?

If they had said to him, "Say, '*Qonam* be any benefit my wife has of me'," and he said, "*Qonam* be any benefit my wife and sons have of me"—

The House of Shammai say, "His wife is permitted to him and his children are forbidden."

And the House of Hillel say, "Both are permitted."

[M. Ned. 3:2, 4, trans. Danby, pp. 266-7 (y. Ned. 3:2, 4, b. Ned. 25b-26a, 28a)]

III.ii.30. R. Ashi answered, "This is what is taught: The House of Shammai say, 'There is no absolution for an oath.'

"And the House of Hillel say, 'There is absolution for an oath.' "

(b. Ned. 28a)

Comment: II.i.68, M. Ned. 3:2, like M. Yev. 3:1,5, is superficially in the conventional form, but has a superscription that is a story, not the statement of a legal problem. The case is as follows: A man saw people eating his figs. He assumed they were not relatives. He prevented them from eating figs by a vow, saying that the figs are to them as a Temple sacrifice (*Qorban*). Then he found out his father and brothers were together with the others. Is the vow valid, having been made under a false supposition? The House of Shammai say, "They [the relatives] are permitted, and those with them are prohibited," and the House of Hillel say, "These and these are permitted." The lemmas of the Houses are as balanced as they could have been under the circumstances. We cannot reduce the whole story to the sort of brief superscription more common in Houses-materials. Nor can we read into the brief sayings of the Houses a simpler superscription. So the protasis is exceptional, but the apodosis normal.

II.i.69, M. Ned. 3:4, has the Houses serve as commentators to an antecedent general law. The rule is, One may swear falsely under specified circumstances. The issue is, What sort of oath or vow is permitted? The House of Shammai say, One may use any sort of vow, except for the oath (ŠBW‘H). The House of Hillel permit even that.

The form is standard and the pericope constitutes a brief *collection*:

B.	Shammai:	[With all vows], *except* the oath
	Hillel:	*Even* the oath.
C.	Shammai:	[He may] not open for him [with a vow]
	Hillel:	*Also* ('P) he may open for him.
D.	Shammai:	In that which he makes him vow
	Hillel:	*Even* ('P) in that which he does *not* make him vow.

Part E glosses the foregoing with an example, but the Houses-rulings are in standard form, much as in II.i.68.

M. Ned. 3:2	*M. Ned. 3:4*
They are permitted	*His wife is* permitted
Those with them prohibited	*And his sons are* prohibited.
These and these are permitted	*These and these are* permitted.

The opinions match, so far as possible, with the Shammaites listing the permitted category before the prohibited ones; and the Hillelite opinion is given word for word. Leaving out the glosses, we have the Shammaite opinion as *prohibited/prohibited* and the Hillelite opinion—closely corresponding—as *these and these are permitted*, the more lenient judgment. Obviously, one may drop *these and these*, added for the same purpose as the other glosses, to tie the opinions to the foregoing cases. Part E is an addition to the foregoing collection, closely related in theme, but quite different in form. The list would have been complete without it; there was hardly need to add a specific example to clarify what was already clear.

III.ii.30 makes explicit the general principle underlying the several disputes, similar to the principle concerning erroneous consecrations below, p. 218.

See Epstein, *Mevo'ot*, pp. 378-9: M. Ned. 9:6 has ʿAqiba in the position of the Hillelites. Note also *Mishnah*, pp. 1016 (*re* ʾP), 1109.

II.ii.62.A. [With reference to the father's and husband's annulling a girl's vows], if the father heard [the oath] and annulled it, but the husband did not yet hear [it] before he died, the father goes and annuls the share of her husband.

B. R. Nathan said, "These are the very words of the House of Shammai.

"The House of Hillel say, 'He cannot annul [the oath] (ʾYNW YKWL LHPR).' "

[Tos. Ned. 6:3, ed. Lieberman, p. 117, lines 13-15 (y. Ned. 10:1, b. Ned. 69a, 71a-b)]

II.ii.63.A. The father and last husband annul the vows of a betrothed girl (NʿRH HMʾWRŚH). If the father heard [the vow] and did annul it, and the husband had not yet heard [the vow] before he died, and she was betrothed even to ten, this is that which they said, "Her father and her last husband annul her vows."

If her father heard and annulled it, and the husband had not yet *heard* [it] before he died, and she was betrothed to another, her second husband goes and annuls the portion of the first.

B. R. Nathan said, "These are the very words of the House of Shammai.

"The House of Hillel say, 'He cannot annul.' "

[Tos. Ned. 6:4, ed. Lieberman, pp. 117-18, lines 16-21 (b. Ned. 69a, 71a, y. Ned. 10:1)]

Comment: The issue between the Houses is the right of the husband to annul the girl's vow. The Shammaites say the father can take over the husband's responsibility in the matter, and the House of Hillel say he cannot. In the second case the situation is complicated by successive betrothals, but in the end the disagreement is the same as before. The Hillelites hold that the father has already annuled his share and cannot annul that of the husband. See Lieberman, *Tosefta Kifshuṭah*, *ad loc.*, pp. 481-4.

Nathan has not bothered to follow the usual Houses' form, but has allowed the operative superscription to stand as a separate lemma, which he has then assigned to the Shammaites. But the Hillelite lemma is standard and brief. A more commonplace form would have had the long superscription, followed by *he may/may not annul.*

II.i.70.A. [If he said,] "I will be an abstainer [= Nazir] from dried figs and fig-cake"—

The House of Shammai say, "He becomes a Nazirite."

And the House of Hillel say, "He does not become a Nazirite."

R. Judah said, "Howbeit when the House of Shammai said this, they spoke only of one that meant, 'May they be to me as *Qorban.*' "

B. If he said, "This cow thinks it will be a Nazirite if it stands up," or "This door thinks it will be a Nazirite if it opens!"—

The House of Shammai say, "He becomes a Nazirite."

And the House of Hillel say, "He does not become a Nazirite."

R. Judah said, "Howbeit when the House of Shammai said this, they spoke only of one that meant, 'May this cow be *Qorban* to me if it stands up.' "

[M. Naz. 2:1-2, trans. Danby, pp. 281-2 (y. Naz. 2:1, 2, b. Naz. 9a-b, 10a-b, b. Men. 81b, 103a)]

III.ii.31. Our Mishnah is not in agreement with the following Tanna. For it has been taught:

R. Nathan said, "The House of Shammai declare him both to have vowed [to abstain from figs] *and* to have become a Nazirite.

"And the House of Hillel declare him to have vowed [to abstain from figs], *but not* to have become a Nazirite."

According to another report, R. Nathan said, "The House of Shammai declare him to have vowed [to abstain from figs], but not to have become a Nazirite.

"And the House of Hillel declare him neither to have vowed, nor to have become a Nazirite."

(b. Naz. 9b)

Comment: The Houses' opinions are conveyed by the single word *Nazir*, with the Hillelites' adding *not* ('YNW). All the rest is an extended, narrative superscription.

The first case (Part A, M. Naz. 2:1) concerns a man's declaring himself a Nazir with respect to things not normally prohibited to a Nazir. The House of Shammai hold that as soon as he has said, "Lo, I am a Nazir," he has become one, and the rest of the sentence means nothing. The House of Hillel says that Naziriteship does not pertain to these things. Judah b. Ilai supplies a *terminus ante quem*. He also glosses the the Shammaite opinion to make it conform to the Hillelite one! When the man says, "They are like a *Qorban* to me," he has prohibited figs as if by vow, but he has *not* become a Nazir at all. So according to Judah, there was no dispute on the specified case at all, which is incredible. The whole thing now involves nothing more than a vow with respect to the produce. Nathan's revisions conform to Judah's.

Part B introduces a new superscription for the Houses' lemmas. The man's cow does not want to arise. He furiously remarks that she does not want to stand up because she will be a Nazir if the stands. Likewise the door is stuck, etc. As above, once the man has said, "Lo, I am a Nazir," *he*, not the cow, becomes one. Judah again revises the Shammaite opinion to conform to the Hillelite view. He has taken a vow not to make use of the cow. Judah does not help us with the door, but presumably he would say the Shammaites regard the door as no longer permissible for the man's use. But the man is no Nazir.

The pericopae are identical in the Houses' apodosis. The protasis given by the superscriptions consists of two quite separate cases, but in effect they set up the same conditions and lead to the same ruling. Therefore the pericopae duplicate one another. The superscriptions are long and involved, quite unlike the simple conventional superscriptions. In the end, to be sure, all we have is the Houses' rulings, consisting of single words—*Nazir*+/—*not*—assigned according to the principle of leniency vs. strictness.

On b. Naz. 9a, see Halivni, *Meqorot*, p. 364.

II.i.71.A. If a man vowed to be a Nazirite for a longer spell, and he fulfilled his Nazirite-vow and afterward came to the Land [of Israel]—

The House of Shammai say, "[He need continue] a Nazirite [only for] thirty days [more]."

And the House of Hillel say, "[He must again fulfill his] Nazirite-vow as from the beginning."

B. It once happened that (M'SH B) the son of Queen Helena went to war, and she said, "If my son returns in safety from the war, I will be a Nazirite for seven years." At the end of the seven years she came up to the Land [of Israel], and the House of Hillel taught her that she must be a Nazirite for yet another seven years. And at the end of this seven years she contracted uncleanness. Thus she continued a Nazirite for twenty-one years.

R. Judah said, "She needed to remain a Nazirite for fourteen years." [She was not unclean.]

C. If two pairs of witnesses testified of a man, and the one testified that he had vowed two Nazirite-vows and the other, that he had vowed five—

The House of Shammai say, "The testimony is at variance (NḤLQH HʿYDWT), and there is no Nazirite-vow here."

And the House of Hillel say, "The two are included within the five, so that he must remain a Nazirite for two [spells]."

[M. Naz. 3:6-7, trans. Danby, p. 283 (b. Ket. 7a, y. Naz. 3:6, 7, b. Naz. 19b-20a-b, b. Sanh. 31a, y. Sanh. 5:2; Sifré Zuṭṭa, Naso 6:5, ed. Horowitz, p. 241; note also Sifré Zuṭṭa 6:17, ed. Horowitz, p. 244)]

Comment: Part A (M. Naz. 3:6) sets forth a complex case, but the Houses' opinions again are phrased very briefly and, dropping the gloss, which is in this instance self-evident, we find single words:

Shammai: *Nazir* thirty *day[s]*
Hillel: *Nazir* at the outset (BTḤYLH; MS Kaufmann: *K*TḤYLH)

The man's original Naziriteship was for more than thirty days. The House of Shammai say that the man must fulfill a Naziriteship, that is, the usual thirty days, for all the time he was abroad he was in an unclean land and could not keep the vow. The House of Hillel take the more stringent position. The man must start all over again, since his Naziriteship abroad counted as nothing.

Part B repeats the Hillelite opinion, now in the form of a story, attached to the foregoing but independent of it. It begins with the usual superscription, MʿSH B. Helene of Adiabene took a vow that if her son came back from war, she would be a Nazirite for seven years. She then came to Palestine at the end of the seven years. The House of Hillel required her to remain in that status another seven years. She *then* became unclean, and so was a Nazirite twenty-one years. The story is incredible. Helene, Queen of Adiabene, achieved an excellent reputation with the Pharisees (among others), and, since she lived abroad, she was a good choice to be heroine of the story. But the likelihood that she did any such thing is remote. Judah treats the story appropriately: he simply changes it, in order to revise the law contained therein, ignoring the "historicity" of both his, and the former, narrative. The commentaries supply two explanations for his emendation. Some say she was *never* unclean at all, further emending the story. Some say he followed the Shammaite view. So she was a Nazirite in Palestine only thirty days, but was unclean and started the original seven years all over again, thus was a Nazirite fourteen years and thirty days. The fact that Judah (as usual) makes the Shammaites follow the opinion of the Hillelites as given in the earlier pericope renders the second explanation unlikely. The first is contrary to the original account. While Judah represents a useful *terminus ante quem* for the story, he had no independent information on what actually had happened.

Part C (M. Naz. 3:7) is a highly developed pericope; it is impossible to recover a simple mnemonic tradition underlying it. The Houses' opinions are not matched and contain quite different words. The diction is not balanced. The case concerns a man about whom one group of witnesses testified to a two-term Naziriteship, and the other to a five-term Naziriteship. The House of Shammai rule that the testimony of each group cancels that of the other, and no Naziriteship is involved. The Hillelites say the groups agree on two Nazirite-terms, to which the man is sentenced. The Houses' opinions compare as follows:

Shammai: The testimony is divided, and there is not here Naziriteship
Hillel: In five, two are contained, so he should be a Nazir two [terms].

The complex superscription is matched by highly developed lemmas.

See Epstein, *Mevo'ot*, pp. 384-5.

II.i.72.A. The House of Shammai say, "If a thing is dedicated in error, its dedication is binding (HQDŠ Ṭ'WT HQDŠ)."

And the House of Hillel say, "It is not binding ('YNW HQDŠ)."

B. How so?

If a man said, "The black ox that first comes out of my house shall be dedicated," and a white one came out—

The House of Shammai say, "Its dedication is binding (HQDŠ)."

And the House of Hillel say, "It is not binding."

C. [If he said,] "The golden *denar* that first comes to my hand shall be dedicated," and a silver *denar* came to his hand—

The House of Shammai say, "Its dedication is binding."

And the House of Hillel say, "It is not binding."

D. [If he said,] "The jar of wine that first comes to my hand shall be dedicated," and a jar of oil came to his hand—

The House of Shammai say, "Its dedication is binding."

And the House of Hillel say, "It is not binding."

E. If a man vowed to be a Nazirite, and he inquired of a sage, and he declared the vow binding, he must count [the thirty days] from the time that he vowed. If he inquired of a sage, and he declared it not binding, and he had cattle already assigned [for the three offerings], they may go forth and pasture with the flock.

F. The House of Hillel said to the House of Shammai, "Do you not agree that there, although it is a thing dedicated in error, it should go forth and pasture with the flock?"

The House of Shammai answered, "Do you not agree that if a man erred and called the ninth [of the herd] the tenth, or the tenth the ninth, or the eleventh the tenth, that its dedication is binding?"

The House of Hillel said to them, "It is not the rod that has dedicated them. What if he erred and laid the rod on the eighth or the twelfth—would he have done aught to all? But ('L') the Scripture which declared the tenth holy, has declared the ninth and the eleventh holy also."

H. If [six] persons were on a journey and another came towards them, and one of them said, "May I be a Nazirite if this is such-a-one!"

And another said, "May I be a Nazirite if one of you is a Nazirite!'

[And a fourth said,] "May I be a Nazirite if one of you is not a Nazirite!"

[And a fifth said,] ". . .if you both are Nazirites!"

[And a sixth said,] ". . .if all of you are Nazirites!"—

The House of Shammai say, "They are all Nazirites."

And the House of Hillel say, "None of them is a Nazirite excepting him whose words are not confirmed."

And R. Ṭarfon says, "None of them is a Nazirite."

[M. Naz. 5:1, 2, 3, 5, trans. Danby, pp. 286-7 (y. Naz. 2:2, 5:1, 2, 4; b. Naz. 31a-b, 32a-b; b. ʿArak. 23a, b. B.B. 120b, y. Ter. 3:4)]

Comment: Parts A-D: The Houses' opinions are carefully balanced and simply repeated from one superscription to the next:

Shammai: Sanctified (HQDŠ) [Danby: binding]
Hillel: Not sanctified.

The principle is then spelled out in parts B, C, and D, each of which supplies a new example for the rule that something sanctified in error is/is not sanctified:

B: Ox — black, white
C: *Denar* — golden, silver
D: Jar — wine, oil.

Parts B, C, and D are glosses on part A, and not very good ones. Any-one of them standing by itself would have sufficed for the reconstruction of part A. All of them together contribute nothing new. It is a little collection, in which part A should serve as the superscription:

A thing dedicated in error
House of Shammai: Binding
House of Hillel: Not binding.

Then the rest follow, each beginning with a much more substantial, articulated superscription than the first. If it is a collection, it is hardly a primitive one, but rather, the development of a single law into several illustrations, with each illustration accompanied by an elaborate superscription, followed by the repetition of the same ruling in primary form. The Shammaites hold that the man referred to the ox that would first come out and erred merely in specifying which one that would be (and so in the other cases). The House of Hillel deny it in each case. The Shammaites are consistent with their position in M. Naz. 2:1.

Part E intervenes and has nothing to do with the Houses' rulings. But part F explains the connection. If a man set aside a sacrifice for his Nazirite vow, and a sage freed him from the vow, the beast cannot be used by the man but is sent to pasture. The House of Hillel then point out to the House of Shammai that this apparently supports the Hillelite position. It is a thing dedicated in error, yet it is treated as an unconsecrated animal. The anonymous ruling thus backs up the Hillelite view that erroneous dedication is not binding. The House of Shammai bring up another case entirely, ignoring the one before them. All three of the misnumbered beasts are sanctified. The Hillelites give a good reply. The counting did not sanctify the animal. Scripture sanctified the tenth. He himself has sanctified the other two. But this more or less ignores the eighth and the twelfth animals specified by the Hillelites, for they too would have been sanctified by the man for the same reason as the ninth and eleventh.

The debate does not follow the usual primary form, with Shammaites last and winning the argument. It looks as if the anonymous ruling, which conforms to the Hillelite view and supports it, was shaped for just that purpose. Then the debate was artificially constructed by Hillelites alone. The Shammaites cannot respond to the case at hand, since by definition it supports the Hillelite position. So they bring up an irrelevant matter—and there too are bested. If it is a Hillelite pericope, pure and simple, that does not tell us when it would have been shaped. I take it for granted that the anonymous law of part E could have come anytime, and the debate of part F, drawing the consequences of that law for the antecedent collection, would have followed.

Part H has the Hillelites adhere to the foregoing rule: a thing dedicated in error is not binding. Here too, the ones whose words are proved false are Nazirites, and the others are not. The Shammaites are equally consistent. Once someone has said, "I am a Nazir," that completes the matter and he is now a Nazir. The position is consistent both with Parts A-D, and with M. Naz. 2:1. The presence of Ṭarfon supplies a useful *terminus ante quem* for the case, and, I think, for the Houses-opinions as well. Ṭarfon has moved beyond the Hillelite position. He holds that Naziriteship applies only if someone explicitly stated that he wishes to take upon himself the Naziriteship, while in this case the people merely wanted to 'strengthen their words' so the others would believe them.

The Houses-disputes on Naziriteship come down to a single issue, namely, the effect of stating, "I am a Nazir," whether intentionally or otherwise, whether accurately or in error. Any one of the specific cases could have produced a ruling on all the others, without further specification of the Houses' views. That does not mean that the whole began in some generalized account of the contrary positions. I think the opposite more likely. Generalized principles were rarely formulated before the *beraita*-stratum of Houses-materials. Rather, we find very brief statements of a case, law, or problem, followed by equally abbreviated positions for the Houses. It was only later that forms were available for better articulated and less casuistic statements of laws.

On b. Naz. 30b, see Halivni, *Meqorot*, p. 369, *re* erroneous consecrations. Note Epstein, *Mevo'ot*, pp. 106, 151, 390: Judah b. Ilai is the authority behind 5:1-3; *Mishnah*, pp. 332, *re* M. Naz. 5:5: whose words were +/—*not* confirmed.

II.ii.64.A. The House of Shammai say, "Substitutes for substitutes [for the form of words used to utter a Nazirite-vow] are prohibited. [The oath is binding]."

And the House of Hillel say, "Substitutes for substitutes are permitted. [The oath is not binding]."

B. The House of Shammai say, "They do not testify [concerning a woman that her husband has died] by means of an echo [from heaven]."

And the House of Hillel say, "They testify by means of an echo."

[Tos. Nez. 1:1, ed. Lieberman, p. 124, lines 1-3 (y. Naz. 1:1, b. Ned. 10b, b. Yev. 122a, M. Yev. 14:7, 16:6)]

Comment: The parallel rulings, M. Naz. 1:1 etc., use *Nazir* rather than *prohibited/permitted*. The meaning must be that the man is or is not made a Nazir by means of the substitute for the original euphemism. So the significant stylistic difference is in word-choice. Judah the Patriarch has improved matters by selecting for the apodosis more precise and appropriate language than *prohibited/permitted*, which makes no sense there, substituting the substantive *Nazir*, concerning which the ruling actually is made. Part A concerns a stage beyond the anonymous rule of M. Naz. 1:1, "Any substitute for [the form of words used to utter] a Nazirite-vow is as binding as the Nazirite-vow itself." Now the issue is secondary. We cannot on that basis suppose M. Naz. 1:1 is the Shammaite ruling.

Part B concerns whether one permits the woman to remarry on the testimony of an echo that her husband has died. The Shammaites rule negatively. M. Yev. 16:6 accords with the Hillelite rule, "They permit a woman to marry again [on the evidence given] by an echo." One recalls the several stories of the echo's message about Hillel's failure to receive the holy spirit and the echo's testimony that the law follows the Hillelites. Hillelite circles clearly were prone to believe in such matters. Shammaite ones were not. Joshua b. Hananiah's famous rejection of heavenly testimony (b. B.M. 59b) would place him in the Shammaite camp, Eliezer b. Hyrcanus in the Hillelite one.

II.ii.65. R. Simeon b. Leazar said, "The House of Shammai and the House of Hillel did not dispute concerning one who vowed to be a Nazir for thirty days, that if he shaved on the thirtieth day, he has not fulfilled [his obligation].

"Concerning what did they differ?

"Concerning one who vowed without specifying the term—

"For the House of Shammai say, 'If he shaved on the thirtieth day, he has not fulfilled his obligation.'

"And the House of Hillel say, 'If he shaved on the thirtieth day, he has fulfilled his obligation.' "

[Tos. Nez. 2:10, ed. Lieberman, p. 128, lines 23-26 (M. Naz. 3:1, Tos. Meg. 1:9, Sifré Num. 25; b. Naz. 5b)]

Comment: M. Naz. 3:1 makes no mention of the Houses:

A. If a man said, "I will be a Nazirite," he should cut off his hair on the thirty-first day. But if he cut it off on the thirtieth day, he has fulfilled his obligation.

B. If he said, "I will be a Nazirite for thirty days," and he cut off his hair on the thirtieth day, he has not fulfilled his obligation.

Part B corresponds to the agreement specified by Simeon. Part A accords with the Hillelite rule, that if he did not specify a term and ended the term on the thirtieth day, it is sufficient. The Mishnah ignores the allegation that a Houses-dispute was at hand. Simeon b. Eleazar persistently refines Houses-disputes, and we may suppose that before him was a tradition that a dispute on the first point did exist. The Shammaites would have held that one should wait until the day after the completion of the specified period, all the more so the day itself; or the Hillelites would have held that one may shave on the very day. If there were no such antecedent disagreement, it is difficult to understand Simeon's claim that there was no disagreement, for the pattern is well established that he claims no disagreement existed where the Mishnah preserves one. As to the disagreement, unspecified terms of Naziriteship permit shaving only on the thirty-first day. Therefore the House of Shammai rule as they do. The Hillelites say that he should cut off the hair on the thirty-first day (M. Naz. 3:1), but if he did so a day early, it is acceptable.

The underlying issue is whether *part* of a day counts as a whole day. The Shammaites take the negative, the Hillelites the affirmative.

Lieberman points out (*Tosefta Kifshuṭah*, p. 520) that some texts give the Hillelites the more stringent position.

II.ii.66. R. Ishmael b. R. Yoḥanan b. Beroqah said, "The House of Shammai and the House of Hillel did not differ concerning two *groups* of witnesses testifying concerning him [that he took an oath to be a Nazirite], that he is a Nazir for the smallest period therein. Concerning what did they differ?

"Concerning two *witnesses* testifying about him, for—

"The House of Shammai say, 'The testimony is divided, and no Naziriteship is here.'

"And the House of Hillel say, 'There is in the sum of five [at least] two, so let him be a Nazir for two [terms].' "

[Tos. Nezirot 3:1, ed. Lieberman, p. 131, lines 1-4 (Tos. ʿEd. 2:4, b. Naz. 20a, M. ʿEd. 4:11, b. B.B. 41b, y. Sanh. 5:2)]

Comment: Ishmael refines the dispute recorded in M. Naz. 3:7, above, p. 216. He says it does not concern *groups* of witnesses, concerning which all parties agree with the Hillelite position, but rather two *individual* witnesses. The opinions of the Houses are precisely as given in the Mishnah; the refinement is effected, as usual, through altering the superscription.

III.ii.32. It has been taught: R. Simeon b. Eleazar said, "The House of Shammai and the House of Hillel do not differ with respect to two sets of witnesses, [of which] one attests a debt of two hundred [*zuz*] and the other of one hundred [a *maneh*], since one hundred is included in two hundred. They differ only where there is but one set.

"The House of Shammai say, 'Their testimony is divided.'

"And the House of Hillel say, 'Two hundred include one hundred.' "

(b. Sanh. 31a = b. B.B. 41b)

Comment: The debate shifts to other problems, but the substance is the same.

III.ii.33. A bald Nazirite—

The House of Shammai say, "He needs to pass a razor over his head."

And the House of Hillel say, "He must not pass a razor over his head."

(b. Naz. 46b = b. Yoma 61b, y. Naz. 6:11)

Comment: The form is standard:

ṢRYK LHʿBYR TʾR ʿL RʾŠW +/— ʾYN

The substance of the debate is not reflected in other pericopae. I have followed the text of y. Naz. 6:11. b. Naz. 46b reverses the opinions, then explains them away, so as to conform to the outcome of y. Naz.!

See Halivni, *Meqorot*, p. 414.

II.ii.67. The House of Shammai say, "A man does not impose on his son the vow of Naziriteship."

And the House of Hillel say, "He imposes the vow."

[Tos. Nezirot 3:17, ed. Lieberman, p. 134, lines 51-2 (y. Naz. 4:6, Tos. ʿEd. 2:2, M. Naz. 4:6, y. Soṭ. 3:8)]

Comment: The form is standard, with the Shammaite lemma bearing the usual explanatory matter. The rulings of the Houses are *impose vow/not impose vow* (MDYR/Lʾ MDYR). The Mishnah (4:6) preserves the Hillelite ruling, without saying so, in the precise language of this pericope, "A man imposes the vow of Naziriteship on his son." The Mishnaic tradition derives from the one before us; Judah the Patriarch has borrowed the explanatory matter from the Shammaite lemma. I see no way of predicting which of the Houses disputes will be preserved as such in the Mishnah, and which will be dropped in favor of the Hillelite law, given anonymously. See also M. ʿEd. 2:2; Epstein, *Mishnah*, p. 1037.

II.ii.68.A. He who vowed as a Nazir and inquired of a sage and he declared the vow binding—

The House of Shammai say, "He counts from the hour that he inquired."

And the House of Hillel say, "He counts from the hour that he vowed [Lieberman: *that he permitted*, meaning, according to the days that he *transgressed* his vow]."

(y. Naz. 5:2: House of Hillel: From the hour that he made the Nazirite vow [NZR]).

B. If he inquired of a sage and he permitted him, these and these agree that [in the event his vow is lifted], if he had a cow set aside [for his Nazirite sacrifice], it may go forth and pasture with the flock.

C. This is the error which Nahum the Mede made when he unloosed the vow.

D. If they were going on the way, and one was coming toward them—

One of them said, "Lo, I am a Nazir if this is so-and-so."

And one says, "Lo, I am a Nazir if this is not so-and-so."

"Lo, I am a Nazir if one of you is a Nazir."

And one says, "Lo, I am a Nazir if none of you is a Nazir."

"Lo, I am a Nazir if two of you are Nazirites."

And one says, "Lo, I am a Nazir if all of them are Nazirites."

The House of Shammai say, "They are all Nazirites."

The House of Hillel say, "The only one who is Nazirite is he whose words were not verified. And they bring a sacrifice in partnership."

R. Judah says in the name of R. Ṭarfon, "None of them [is a Nazir], for Naziriteship applies only through uttering a distinct vow (LHP-L'H)."

E. R. Yosi said, "The House of Shammai used to say concerning him who says, 'Lo, I am a Nazir that [if] this is Joseph' and it turns out to be Joseph, 'that this is Simeon' and it turns out to be Simeon, that he is a Nazir.

"If he saw an androgynous creature, and said, 'Lo, I am a Nazir that this is a man,' and one says, 'Lo, I am a Nazir that this is not a man;' 'Lo, I am a Nazir that this is a woman,' and one says, 'Lo, I am a Nazir that this is not a woman;' 'Lo, I am a Nazir that this is a man and a woman,' and one says, 'Lo, I am a Nazir that this is not a man and a woman;' 'Lo, I am a Nazir that one of you is a Nazir,' 'Lo, I am a Nazir that none of you is a Nazir;' 'that two of you are Nazirites;' 'that all of you are Nazirites'—they are all Nazirites. And they all count for nine Naziriteships [of thirty days]."

[Tos. Nez. 3:19, ed. Lieberman, pp. 135-6, lines 58-73 (b. Naz. 34a; y. Naz. 5:2, M. Naz. 5:5)]

Comment: The Hillelite opinion in part A occurs in M. Naz. 5:3. Both parties agree about the cow, which explains why in M. Naz. 5:3 the Hillelites can address the Shammaites as they do.

Part C refers to M. Naz. 5:4.

Part D is M. Naz. 5:5, in augmented form. The Houses' opinions are given in the same language as in the Mishnah. The Hillelites' lemma is glossed by the sacrifice. Judah now becomes the authority for Ṭarfon's opinion, which makes him the *terminus ante quem* for the whole pericope.

Yosi then develops the Shammaite opinion, but ignores the foregoing materials. Obviously the Shammaites agree that if a person vows on a condition and the condition is valid, he is a Nazir; they would have held that even in the contrary situation, the vow would have applied. In the case of the androgynous creature, we have a more pertinent record of the Shammaite position. As to the facts, all are right. But merely saying, "Lo, I am a Nazir" makes a Nazir out of the one who says "that none of you is a Nazir." It looks as if we have several versions of the Houses' opinions, shaped toward the middle of the second century, and Judah the Patriarch has selected the first, leaving out Yosi's, though it would have served. One could easily supply the Hillelite and Ṭarfon opinions there as well.

As to the disposition of the sacrifice, part B, although the House of Shammai hold that what is erroneously sanctified is nonetheless sanctified, the vow had never been properly made, therefore the cow had never been sanctified at all, erroneously or otherwise.

II.i.73.A. These do not drink and do not receive their *Ketuvah*: She that says, "I am unclean," and she against whom witnesses have testified that she was unclean, and she that says, "I will not drink."

But she whose husband is not minded to make her drink, or she whose husband has connection with her while on the way, she receives her *Ketuvah* and does not drink.

B. If their husbands died before their wives drank [the bitter water]—

The House of Shammai say, "They receive their *Ketuvah* and do not drink."

And the House of Hillel say, "They do not drink, and they do not receive their *Ketuvah*."

[M. Soṭ. 4:2, trans. Danby, p. 297 (y. Soṭ. 4:1, 2, b. Soṭ 24a-b, 25b, y. Sanh. 8:6, y. Ket. 9:7)]

III.ii.34. On what point [do the two Houses] differ? The House of Shammai are of opinion that a bond which is due for redemption is considered as having been redeemed; whereas the House of Hillel are of opinion that a bond which is due for redemption is not considered as having been redeemed.

[b. Soṭ. 25a-b (b. Shev. 48b)]

Comment: The essentials are:

Shammai: [They] *take* [*Ketuvah*] and do not *drink*
Hillel: They do not *drink* and do not *take* [*Ketuvah*].

I cannot understand the reversal of the order of the participles. Obviously, *drink* could be dropped, since the dispute concerns only the *Ketuvah*. But once the *not-drink's* have been supplied, presumably by a glossator, why should the Hillelite opinion follow the order of the superscription, while the Shammaite one does not?

III.ii.34 explains the underlying legal principle in dispute.

Epstein, *Mevo'ot*, pp. 409-410, sees Simeon b. Eleazar as the authority for part A. His comments on this pericope, p. 410, are important for the lower criticism of the Mishnaic text. See also *Mishnah*, pp. 428, 524.

II.ii.69. A woman that commits lewdness with her little son and he committed the first stage of cohabitation with her—

The House of Shammai declare [her] ineligible [to the priesthood] (Lev. 21:7).

And the House of Hillel declare eligible.

[Tos. Soṭ. 4:7, ed. Zuckermandel, p. 301, lines 27-8 (b. Sanh. 69b, y. Giṭ. 8:8)]

Comment: The Houses-opinions here are not quotations, e.g., *say*, *is eligible*, but syzygous, present participles. The antecedent ruling is that a woman may be made unclean by any man except a child and one who is not a man. Yosi says that the woman must undergo the ordeal, "perhaps. . . the child will grow up" and persist in adultery. So she *is* made unclean by a child. The rulings of the Houses pertain to *Yosi's* saying, with the Shammaites agreeing with Yosi.

III.i.8. [M. Soṭ. 3:3: If the writing on the scroll was blotted out, and she then said, 'I am unclean,' the water is poured away and her meal-offering is scattered on the ash-heap. If the writing on the scroll was blotted out, and she said, 'I will not drink,' they urge her and give her to drink against her will.]

How much is blotted out?

TNY: R. Ḥanin: "The House of Shammai say, 'One.'

"And the House of Hillel say, 'Two.' "

(y. Soṭ. 3:3 = y. Soṭ. 2:4)

Comment: The reference is to blotting out the name of the Lord written in the scroll referred to in the Mishnah. The Houses opinions are the usual *one/two*. In this instance, however, we know who made up the Houses-pericope in the conventional form, namely, Ḥanin, not an early Tannaitic authority. This shows how in later times it was commonplace to follow the Houses-form in fabricating data. The name of the authority frequently was dropped, leaving the impression that the whole derives from "very ancient times."

III.i.9. TNY: "A nursing mother whose husband dies should not be married for twenty-four months," the words of R. Meir.

R. Judah [b. Ilai] says, "Eighteen months."

R. Jonathan b. Yosi says, "The House of Shammai say, 'Twenty-four months.'

"And the House of Hillel say, 'Eighteen months.' "

[y. Soṭ. 4:3 (b. Ket. 60a-b, above, p. 207)]

Comment: Here what Meir and Judah give as their own opinions recurs in Jonathan's version as a Houses-dispute. The operative opinions are identical in both versions, so in this instance one cannot reasonably suppose separate and independent traditions on the same subject were handed on in the names of Ushan masters, on the one side, and the Houses, on the other. Simeon b. Gamaliel comments on the dispute, but does not name the antecedent masters; he supplies what we already have, namely, a *terminus ante quem* for the dispute. The *twenty-four/eighteen* sequence is familiar in other Houses-materials, but that proves nothing about the origin of the apodosis. What is furthermore interesting is that Jonathan has not even troubled to supply an appropriate superscription for the argument; it in fact depends upon "the words of R. Meir." It looks as if all he has done is to assign the opinions to the Houses instead of to the Ushans, *prima facie* evidence that the Ushans originated the whole. Since Meir and Judah supply numerous disputes in the names of the Houses, we may suppose they here do otherwise because the traditions are their own. Jonathan's revision of the attribution then is difficult to explain; later Palestinians follow the rule of twenty-four months, without commenting that it is Shammaite.

II.i.74.A. "If a man was half-bondman and half-freedman he should labor one day for his master and one day for himself"—the words of the House of Hillel.

B. The House of Shammai said to them, "You have ordered [it well] for his master, but for him you have not ordered [it well.] He cannot marry a bondwoman, since he is half freedman; and he cannot marry a freedwoman since he is half bondman.

"May he never marry? And was not the world only created for fruition and increase, as it is written, *He created it not a waste; he formed it to be inhabited* (Is. 45:10)?

"But for the order of the world they compel his master and he sets him free; and [the bondman] writes him a bond for indebtedness for half his value."

C. The House of Hillel reverted to teach according to the words of the House of Shammai.

[M. Giṭ. 4:5, trans. Danby, p. 311 (y. Giṭ. 4:5, b. Giṭ. 40b, 41a-b, b. ʿArakh. 26b, b. B.B. 13a, b. Ḥag. 2a, b. Pes. 88a-b)]

Comment: This curious pericope starts out like a normal Houses-dispute, with a superscription, *He who was half a slave and half a free man.* The Hillelite opinion, coming out of turn, then pertains to arranging the man's working hours. We should have expected a Shammaite opinion first. Theoretically, the House of Shammai would have divided the man's working time within a given day, rather than by alternating days. Instead, part B changes the form, which now becomes a debate. But this too is truncated, since the debate contains no Hillelite lemma at the outset. Furthermore, the debate also changes the subject! It now pertains not to the man's working hours, but to whether he may *marry*. The Shammaite lemma is highly developed through several clauses, and I cannot propose a brief version. Then comes a subscription consisting of a stock-phrase found in same form elsewhere in the chapter; and the phrase itself is a conglomerate of stock-phrases, *on account of the order of the world*, *they force the master and he makes him a free man*, etc., as in M. Giṭ. 4:5. Finally, part C adds that the Hillelites were persuaded by the category of half-slave/half-free. Clearly, one might invent some sort of Hillelite counterpart to the Shammaite argument, but this serves no purpose. We do not know what the Hillelites originally thought about the half-slave's marriage.

This collection of forms and stock-phrases—"conventional" dispute, then debate, then *order of the world*, then *the House of Hillel changed their opinion*—makes it difficult, as I said, to suggest what might have constituted the primary version (if any) of the pericope. Even if we drop glosses, e.g., the Scriptural proof-text, the rhetorical introduction ("*You have ordered it well...*"), we are still left with a pericope quite unlike any we have seen. It looks as if two separate arguments have been joined because of their thematic connection: the status of the half-slave, with the first part pertaining to the work-arrangements, the second to the marriage. But the position of the House of Shammai is that such a status cannot be allowed to exist at all, therefore no arrangements need be made.

The content is puzzling. Were there no precedents for the half-slave? Did such a status come into being "just at this time"? It seems to me unlikely. What is more likely is that the status is a legal fabrication, created to explore the ambiguous personal status of someone who may not have existed outside the lawyers' imagination. The discussion supposes the Houses legislate in such a case for the first time. All the preceding centuries, such people were left in a double limbo: They did not know either how to arrange their working hours or whom to marry.

The appearance of the root TQN ("*ordered well*," "*order of the world*") may provide a key. Perhaps the pericope represents another theoretical ordinance, but the usual ordinance-form, *at first... they ordained...*, has been confused with two different Houses-forms. I cannot envision what the ordinance-form would have done with the Shammaite position and assume it omitted the Shammaites. The Hillelite ordinance would have been simple enough:

> At first the half-slave [would have] worked for the master one day, himself one day. [It turned out that] he could not marry. So they ordained that he should work entirely for himself [therefore abandoning the earlier status] and should pay back the master—on account of the order of the world.

The Shammaites could have produced no equivalent *taqqanah*, for to begin with they denied such a status was within the law.

Part C poses no problem. The Hillelites do not give up their view that the man must work both for himself and his master. They simply accept an arrangement different from the one they originally proposed but producing the same result. The man is still in bondage, but his personal status has been clarified. The Shammaite view, that the status to begin with is inconceivable, plays no role in the Hillelite reversion.

On *according to the words of*, Epstein, *Mishnah*, p. 403.

II.i.75.A. The House of Shammai say, "A man may dismiss (PṬR) his wife with an old bill over divorce."

And the House of Hillel forbid (ʾŚR) [it].

B. What is an old bill of divorce? If he continued alone with her after he had written it for it, [it becomes an old bill of divorce].

[M. Giṭ. 8:4, trans. Danby, p. 317 (b. Giṭ. 79b, y. Giṭ. 8:9)]

Comment: The form is somewhat developed, with the superscription inserted into the Shammaite lemma:

The House of Shammai say, A man frees his wife with an old *Geṭ*	
The House of Hillel:	Prohibit.

In a simpler version we should have had:

An old Geṭ

House of Shammai:	Permit
House of Hillel:	Prohibit.

The Shammaite lemma has been revised, not merely glossed, and the syzygous *permit* has been changed to a declarative sentence, *a man frees his wife*; thus YṢʾ changes to PṬR.

Part B glosses the dispute. Clearly, the tradition of a Houses' dispute about an old *Geṭ* circulated in many forms and produced references such as we have already observed (above, p. 204). This version is the most serviceable for the purposes of Judah the Patriarch, but not the most primitive.

See Epstein, *Mishnah*, p. 86.

II.i.76. If a wrote [a bill of divorce] to divorce his wife and changed his mind—

The House of Shammai say, "He has rendered her ineligible (PŚL) [for marriage with] a priest."

And the House of Hillel say, "Even if he gave it to her on a condition, and the condition was not fulfilled, he has not rendered ineligible (PŚL) for marriage with a priest."

II.i.77.A. If a man divorced his wife and she then lodged with him in an inn—

The House of Shammai say, "She does not need from him a second bill of divorce."

And the House of Hillel say, "She needs from him a second bill of divorce."

B. This applies when she was divorced after wedlock.

C. But they agree that if she was divorced after betrothal [only], she does not need a second bill of divorce from him, since he is not yet shameless before her.

[M. Giṭ. 8:8-9, trans. Danby, p. 318-9 (b. Giṭ. 81a-b, b. Qid. 65a-b)]

Comment: II.i.76, M. Giṭ. 8:8, like the foregoing pericopae, begins as if it were standard, but, curiously, fails to balance the Houses lemmas:

> *He who wrote [a Geṭ] to divorce his wife and changed his mind:*
> House of Shammai say, He has rendered her unfit from the priesthood.

The House of Hillel *should* say:

> He has *not* rendered her unfit. . .

That in fact is the Hillelite opinion, but before the opinion is given, we have an intervening phrase:

> Even though he gave it to her on a condition and the condition was not fulfilled

Then comes:

> He has *not* rendered her unfit. . .

The intervening phrase glosses the Hillelite saying by extending the Hillelite opinion to a more extreme case than is described in the superscription. In the new case the man has actually given the *Geṭ*, but it turns out to be impaired. Even here the woman is not regarded as having been subjected to divorce, therefore remains fit to marry a priest, according to the Hillelites. The glossator apparently regarded the original opinion as not representing the full extent of the Hillelite leniency.

II.i.77, M. Giṭ. 8:9, is standard; the lemmas of the Houses pertain to, and complete, the superscription, and are matched, the difference being the use of the negative in the Shammaite opinion.

The agreement of part C clarifies the foregoing, therefore is merely a gloss, not a revision, such as is often supplied by Simeon b. Leazar in Toseftan pericopae. The meaning of the Houses-dispute is unchanged.

See Epstein, *Mishnah*, p. 86, 266.

II.i.78. The House of Shammai say, "A man may not divorce his wife unless he has found unchastity in her, for it is written, *Because he hath found in her indecency in anything.*"

And the House of Hillel say, "[He may divorce her] even if she spoiled a dish for him, for it is written, *Because he has found in her indecency in anything.*"

R. ʿAqiba says, "Even if he found another fairer than she, for it is written, *And it shall be if she find no favor in his eyes. . .*"

[M. Giṭ. 9:10, trans. Danby, p. 321 (y. Giṭ. 9:11, b. Giṭ. 90a, y. Soṭ. 1:1)]

Comment: See above, Sifré Deut. 269, p. 37.

II.ii.70. The House of Shammai say, "A man does not free his wife with an old *Geṭ, so that her Geṭ may not be older than her son.*"

(Tos. Giṭ. 8:3, ed. Zuckermandel, p. 332, 1. 20)

Comment: The italicized words gloss M. 8:4—but for the opinion of the House of Hillel! The Shammaites say one *may* do so. Other MSS properly correct to *Hillel.*

II.ii.71. He who gives a *Geṭ* to his wife, and they did not bear witness [to it]—

The House of Shammai say, "He rendered her ineligible from the priesthood."

II.ii.72. R. Simeon b. Eleazar said, "The House of Shammai and the House of Hillel did not differ concerning him who divorces his wife, and [then] she spends the night with him in an inn, that she does not require from him a second *Geṭ.*

"Concerning what did they disagree?

"Concerning a situation in which he [actually] had intercourse [with her]."

[Tos. Giṭ. 8:8, ed. Zuckermandel, p. 333, lines 4-5, 7-9 (b. Giṭ. 8a-b, b. Qid. 65a-b)]

Comment: II.ii.71 corresponds to M. Giṭ. 8:8, if a man gave a *Geṭ* and changed his mind. The House of Shammai say that he has rendered her ineligible, and the House of Hillel say that he has not rendered her ineligible. It looks like a separate superscription for the same argument. The apodosis is defective.

II.ii.72 conforms to the general tendency of Simeon b. Eleazar. Now the dispute concerns not a married couple, for all agree no further *Get* is necessary. The issue is now, What is necessitated by actual intercourse? The opinions of the Houses are not given. We may assume that the House of Shammai would say no new *Get* is needed, and the House of Hillel would require a new one.

In this instance the Shammaite position is made more extreme. Obviously, the Hillelites will require a new *Get*, just as before. But the Shammaites now treat the act of intercourse as having no legal consequence. The old *Get* remains valid, even though the couple has engaged in marital relations; therefore the act of intercourse, having no legal implications, is treated as prostitution.

b. Giṭ. 81a has it that witnesses testify the couple actually had intercourse, or the witnesses saw them alone, thus solving the problem of who is to testify against the validity of the *Get*.

II.i.79.A. By three means is the woman acquired and by two means she acquires her freedom. She is acquired by money or by writ or by intercourse.

B. By money—the House of Shammai say, "By a *denar* or a *denar's* worth."

And the House of Hillel say, "By a *peruṭah* or a *peruṭah's* worth."

C. And how much is a *peruṭah*? The eighth part of an Italian issar.

[M. Qid. 1:1, trans. Danby, p. 321 (y. Qid. 1:1, b. Qid. 11a-b, 12a, b. Bekh. 50b, y. Shav. 6:1)]

Comment: The Houses-lemma, part B, glosses part A, and then part C glosses the Hillelite clause of part B. Part C certainly comes after the Hillelite view of law became normative. We may presume part B comes after part A as well, but we do not know when part A was redacted. The form of the Houses-dispute is conventional, and the Houses' opinions are presented in brief and balanced form: *denar/peruṭah*, with the additional gloss that *the equivalent thereof* is acceptable.

II.ii.73. He who gives permission to three men to betrothe for him the woman—

R. Nathan says, "The House of Shammai say, 'Two may serve as witnesses and one as agent.'

"And the House of Hillel say, 'All three of them are agents and cannot serve as witnesses.' "

[Tos. Qid. 4:1, ed. Zuckermandel, p. 340, lines 3-4 (y. Qid. 2:1, b. Qid. 43a)]

Comment: The issue is whether an agent can become a witness or not. The pericope recurs *verbatim* in b. Qid. 43a. *without* attribution to Nathan. Then a separate *beraita* occurs:

> R. Nathan said, "The House of Shammai say, 'An agent and a witness [serve as attestation.]'
> "And the House of Hillel say, 'An agent and *two* witnesses.' "

The Tosefta is cited, but Nathan dropped; then a parallel pericope is created for Nathan, in which the same principle is discussed, *but* with reference to different circumstances.

Shammai the Elder rules on the same issue, I, p. 201.

On b. Qid. 42b-43a, Halivni, *Meqorot*, p. 663.

IV. Neziqin

We shall review the 'Eduyyot collections below, section vii.

II.ii.74. He who steals the beam and builds it into the group of buildings (BYRH) —

The House of Shammai say, "He must tear down (Q'Q') the [entire] group of buildings and take out the beam."

And the House of Hillel say, "He estimates how much it was worth and pays the owner, on account of the [good] order of penitents."

[Tos. B.Q. 9:5, ed. Zuckermandel, p. 367, lines 3:5 (y. B.Q. 9:1, y. Giṭ. 5:6, b. Giṭ. 55a, b. B.M. 101a)]

II.ii.74*. He who goes down into the ruin of his fellow and builds it without permission. When he goes forth, he says, "Give me my wood and stones." They do not listen to him.

Rabban Simeon b. Gamaliel says, "The House of Shammai say, 'The right is in his hand.'

"And the House of Hillel say, 'They do not listen to him.' "

[Tos. Ket. 8:9, ed. Zuckermandel, p. 271, lines 1-3 (ed. Lieberman, pp. 85-6 *omits* the saying of Simeon b. Gamaliel)]

Comment: The form is conventional, but the lemmas of the Houses are not obviously balanced; they choose quite different words, but are metrically matched, four to each lemma. The lemmas of the Houses could have stood quite independent of one another. It looks to me as if the language of M. B.Q. 9:1 etc. has influenced the revision of the

Hillelite lemma. The Shammaite ruling would have been suitably balanced by a simple negative for the Hillelites: *He does not take down. . .* The Hillelites do not merely rule on the first question, but they go on to explain what the man must do instead. They thus take for granted the ruling we should have expected. So the Hillelite lemma develops what would have been the primary form; the Shammaite one is the model for that form. The same pattern recurs in II.ii.74*.

II.i.80.A. If a man put to his own use what had been left in his keeping, the House of Shammai say, "He is at a disadvantage whether its value rises or falls."

And the House of Hillel say, "[He must restore the deposit] at the same value as when he put it to his own use."

R. ʿAqiba says, "At its value when claimed."

B. If a man had expressed his intention of putting the deposit to his own use, the House of Shammai say, "He is liable."

And the House of Hillel say, "He is not liable until he puts it to his use, for it is written, *If he have not put his hand unto his neighbor's goods.*"

C. Thus if he tilted the jar and took from it a quarter-*log* [of wine] and the jar was then broken, he need only repay [the value of the] quarter-*log* [of wine]; but if he lifted it up and took from it a quarter-*log* and the jar was then broken, he must repay the value of the whole.

[M. B.M. 3:12 (y. B.M. 3:9, b. B.M. 43a-b, 44a, y. Shev. 8:1, b. Qid. 42b, Sifra Vayiqra 13:13b)]

Comment: Part A, see Sifra Vayiqra 13:13, p. 11. Part B pertains to the man's intention. The Shammaite opinion is ḤYYB, liable, and the Hillelite one should have been either *not* ḤYYB, or, preferably, PṬWR, with the gloss being understood. The gloss required by *not liable* adds *until*, then carefully spells out the point at which liability is incurred, finally supplies a proof-text. Afterward comes a new and separate gloss, part C, in which a case is given to illustrate the Hillelite position, ignoring the Shammaite one.

In this instance, if the original Hillelite lemma consisted merely of the negative, it invited a gloss, lest someone suppose the man would never be liable. But the gloss is in a measure redundant, since everyone knew that misappropriation of the bailment certainly would incur liability. So my guess is that the glossator felt uncomfortable with the Hillelite lemma before him, not only for reasons of clarity, but also for the sake of diction (ʿD Š).

See Epstein, *Mevo'ot*, p. 77; *Mishnah*, pp. 310, 507, 1034.

III.ii.35.A. Our Rabbis taught: [*Then the master of the house shall be brought unto the judges. . .*] *For all (KL) manner of trespass* (Ex. 22:8).

The House of Shammai say, "This teaches that he is liable on account of [unlawful] intention just as for an [unlawful] act."

And the House of Hillel say, "He is not liable until he actually puts it to use, for it is said, [To see] *whether he have put his hand unto his neighbor's goods.*"

B. Said the House of Shammai to the House of Hillel, "But it is already stated, *For any word of trespass*!"

The House of Hillel said to the House of Shammai, "But it is already stated, [to see] *Whether he have put his hand unto his neighbor's goods!* If so, what is the teaching of, *For any word of trespass*? For I might have thought: I know it only of himself; whence do I know [that he is liable if] he instructed his servant or his agent [to use it]? From the teaching, *For any word of trespass.*"

[b. B.M. 44a (Mekh. deR. Ishmael, Nez. 15:49-55; b. Qid. 42b)]

Comment: The several versions compare as follows:

M. B.M. 3:12	*Mekh. Nez̧. 15:49-55*	*b. B.M. 44a*
1. He who thinks of putting forth a hand on a bailment	1. —	1. DTNW RBNN: For every word of trespass
2. The House of Shammai say, Liable (ḤYYB)	2. For the House of Shammai declare liable (MḤYYBYN) for the thought of the heart in sending forth the hand, as it is said Ex. 22:7, *For every word (DBR) of trespass*	2. The House of Shammai say, It teaches that he is liable (ḤYYB) for thought as deed (‘L MḤŠBH KM‘SH)
3. And the House of Hillel say, He is *not* liable until he will put forth on it a hand, as it is said Ex. 22:7 *If he has not sent his hand*	3. And the House of Hillel do not declare liable (MḤYYBYN) except from the time that he put on it a hand, therefore it is said Ex. 22:7	3. And the House of Hillel say, He is not liable until he sends forth a hand, as it is said Ex. 22:7
4. —	4. —	4. The House of Shammai said etc. [Debate]

M. B.M. 3:12 is the briefest version of the dispute. It drops the Shammaite exegesis or does not bother to invent it, and the Hillelite opinion in context is perfect. Mekh. follows, and *reports* the foregoing rather than citing the opinions in direct address ("say, liable" becomes "declare liable"), furthermore adding a Shammaite exegesis to balance the Hillelite one. b. B.M. 44a then takes both exegeses and turns them into a debate, but not in standard form, for it gives the decisive place and argument to the Hillelites. This seems to me to be evidence that the *beraita*-debate follows and depends upon Mekh. Nez. I do not see how the former could be seen as summarized and abbreviated in the latter. It also looks as if M. B.M. 3:12 is the simplest and earliest version of the pericope, and that Mekh. has expanded it by supplying balanced exegeses, rather than leaving the Shammaites without one.

II.ii.75.A. If a man put to his own use what had been left in his keeping, the House of Shammai say, "He is at a disadvantage whether its value rises or falls."

How so?. . .

(Tos. B.M. 3:12, ed. Zuckermandel, p. 377, 1. 3)

Comment: The language occurring in the Mishnah is cited, then glossed.

II.i.81.A. If the house fell down on a man and his father, or upon a man and any from whom he inherits, and he was liable for his wife's *Ketuvah* or to a creditor, the father's heirs may say, "The son died first and the father died afterward," and the creditors may say, "The father died first and the son died afterward."

The House of Shammai say, "They divide."

And the House of Hillel say, "The property is in its presumptive [possessors' hands]."

II.i.81.B. If the house fell down on a man and his wife, the husband's heirs may say, "The wife died first and the husband died afterward," and the wife's heirs may say, "The husband died first and the wife died afterward."

The House of Shammai say, "They divide."

And the House of Hillel say, "The property is in its presumptive [possessors' hands]—the *Ketuvah* to the husband's heirs and the property that comes in and goes out with her to her fathers' heirs."

[M. B.B. 9:8-9 (b. B.B. 157a, y. B.B. 9:9)]

Comment: See M. Yev. 4:3, M. Ket. 8:6. Here the superscription changes twice, but the opinions of the Houses are in all respects identical, except for the glosses of M. Yev. = M. Ket., which, naturally, are dropped in II.i.81.A. but left in II.i.81.B. Once again we observe that the Houses-materials can be attached to a wide range of superscriptions. The legal principle and language of the Houses do not change, therefore antedate the various superscriptions and accompanying glosses.

II.ii.76. If the house fell on him and on his mother, since both [forms of property] come to him as an inheritance, these and these agree that they divide.

R. ʿAqiba said, "I agree in this instance with the words of the House of Hillel that the property remains in the presumption [of the possessors' hands] (BḤZQTN)."

(Tos. B.B. 10:13, ed. Zuckermandel, p. 412, lines 34-5)

Comment: See M. B.B. 9:8-9. ʿAqiba supplies important evidence that the original debate took place at Yavneh or earlier. The language of the Houses must have been fixed by then, for ʿAqiba cites the Hillelite ruling *verbatim*.

II.ii.77.A. The House of Shammai say, "There are three groups. One is for eternal life. One is for eternal shame and perdition. These are the completely evil people. That (Š) the least of them (QWLYHN) descend to Gehanna and squeal and rise again and are healed."

"As it is said, *And I will bring the third part through fire and will refine them as silver is refined and will try them as gold is tried. And they shall call on my name and I will answer them*" (Zech. 13:9).

Concerning them Ḥannah said, "*The Lord kills and resurrects, brings down to Sheol and raises up*" (I Sam. 2:6).

B. The House of Hillel say, "He that abounds in grace inclines [the scales] towards grace [and they do not go to Gehenna at all]."

And concerning them, David said, "*I love that the Lord should hear my voice and my supplication*" (Ps. 116:1).

And concerning them the entire passage [of David] was said.

[Tos. Sanh. 13:3, ed. Zuckermandel, p. 434, lines 11:17 (ARN, trans. Goldin, pp. 173-4)]

Comment: The requirements of the Houses-form are utterly ignored in this *aggadic* passage. The opinions are in no way balanced; they are heavily glossed with Scriptures and references to biblical heroes. The Shammaite saying is obviously defective. We hear only about two groups, and the third ("the least of them") is not introduced properly, but tied to the foregoing with *that* (Š), so at first glance it looks as though the completely wicked are under discussion. Only as we proceed do we see that still a third group is meant, namely, the ones who are neither wholly righteous nor wholly wicked. These go down but come up again.

The Hillelite ruling then pertains to this same group: They do not go down at all. A simple version of the pericope presumably would have the Houses as usual debate that ambiguous group, with both sides agreeing on the wholly righteous, who go straight up, and the wholly wicked, who go straight down and stay there:

The intermediates:
The House of Shammai: They go down [and come up again]
The House of Hillel: They do not go down [at all]

Presumably in a legal pericope, something like this simple form would have underlain the complex and highly developed pericope. But in *aggadic* materials we have yet to see such an unadorned version of a House-dispute. See S. Lieberman, *Tosefet Rishonim* (Jerusalem, 1938), II, p. 161.

b. R.H. 16b-17a corrects the pericope, *but* loses the point of the Houses' dispute:

III.ii.36. It has been taught: The House of Shammai say, "There will be three groups at the Day of Judgment—one of thoroughly righteous, one of thoroughly wicked, and one of intermediate. The thoroughly righteous will forthwith be inscribed definitively as entitled to everlasting life; the thoroughly wicked will forthwith be inscribed definitively as doomed to Gehinnom, as it says, *And many of them that sleep in the dust of the earth shall awake, some to everlasting life and some to reproaches and everlasting abhorrence* (Dan. 12:2).

"The intermediate will go down to Gehinnom and squeal and rise again, as it says, *And I will bring the third part through the fire, and will refine them as silver is refined, and will try them as gold is tried. They shall call on my name and I will answer them* (Zech. 13:9). Of them, too, Hannah said, *The Lord killeth and maketh alive, he bringeth down to the grave and bringeth up* (I Sam. 2:6)."

The House of Hillel say, "He that abounds in grace inclines [the scales] towards grace, and of them David said, I love that the *Lord should hear my voice and my supplication* (Ps. 116-1), and on their behalf David composed the whole of the passage, *I was brought low and he saved me* (Ps. 116:6)."

(b. R.H. 16b-17a)

v. Qodashim

II.i.82.A. The House of Shammai say, "Any offering whose blood must be sprinkled on the outer altar makes atonement, even if it is sprinkled with but one act of sprinkling: or, [if it is] a sin-offering, [with] two acts of sprinkling."

And the House of Hillel say, "Even ('P) if it is a sin-offering, it makes atonement if it is sprinkled with but one act of sprinkling."

B. Therefore if the first act of sprinkling was done in the manner ordained, but the second outside the proper time, it [still] makes atonement. But if the first act of sprinkling was done outside its proper time, and the second outside its proper place, the offering is rendered Refuse (PYGWL) and punishment by Extirpation (KRT) is thereby incurred.

[M. Zev. 4:1, trans. Danby, p. 472 (b. Zev. 36b, 37b, b. Sanh. 4a)]

Comment: The dispute concerns the number of times blood must be sprinkled for a sin-offering. The House of Shammai say *two*, the House of Hillel *one*. According to our earlier observations, we should have expected the dispute to be phrased in terms of numbers, with a brief explanation inserted into the Shammaite lemma or set as a superscription. The end of the Shammaite lemma would have served:

In a sin-offering
House of Shammai: Two placings [sprinklings]
House of Hillel: One.

The whole of part C as usual depends upon the Hillelite opinion.

As it stands, the opening part of the Shammaite lemma is complex:

1. All the sprinklings on the outer alter,
2. that (Š) if ('M) he sprinkled them one sprinkling, he atoned
3. And in a sin-offering, two sprinklings.

The House of Hillel's opinion is glossed, primarily for redactional reasons, as indicated in italics:

Also the sin-offering, *that* [should be, *if*] he sprinkled one sprinkling, he atoned.

The glosses have been inserted to tie the primary Hillelite lemma to the foregoing Shammaite one. What has complicated matters is the introduction of the topical sentence, actually serving as a superscription *not* for the Houses but for the first two pericopae of the chapter, into the Shammaite lemma:

All the sprinklings [on the outer altar].

This is tied to the next clause with *that* (Š). Dropping these redactional materials, we have

If he sprinkled them one sprinkling, he atoned, and in a sin-offering, two sprinklings.

Now the Hillelite lemma closely corresponds, though it still is somewhat glossed,

Also as to a sin-offering (that =) if he sprinkled one sprinkling, he atoned.

The primary pericope, as I said, would therefore have been *two/one* attached to sin-offering. Everything else is added either to gloss that dispute, or to serve the redactional needs of the context into which the dispute has been placed.

II.ii.78.A. R. Eliezer b. Jacob says, "One thing of the lenient rulings of the House of Shammai and the strict rulings of the House of Hillel [is as follows]:

"The House of Shammai say, 'Two sprinklings make fit and render *piggul* [abhorred—the flesh of the sacrifice which the officiating priest has formed the intention of eating at an improper time, Lev. 7:18] in a sin-offering, and one sprinkling in all [other] sacrifices.'

"And the House of Hillel say, 'It is all the same for a sin-offering and for all sacrifices—one sprinkling makes fit and renders [the sacrifice susceptible to] *piggul*.' "

B. How so? If he sprinkled once in silence and the blood was poured out—

The House of Shammai declares [*sic*] unfit (PWŚL).

And the House of Hillel declare fit (MKŠYRYN).

If he sprinkled twice in silence and the blood was poured out, all agree that it is fit.

C. If he sprinkled once outside of the proper time and the blood was poured out—

The House of Shammai say, "It is unfit, but the punishment of *cutting off* does not pertain to it."

And the House of Hillel say, "It is *piggul*, and they are liable on its account for the punishment of *cutting off*."

D. [If he sprinkled] twice outside of the proper time and the blood was poured out, all agree that it is *piggul*.

E. [If he sprinkled] once outside of the proper time and once outside of the proper place, the House of Shammai say, "It is unfit, but the punishment of *cutting off* does not apply."

And the House of Hillel say, "It is *piggul*, and they are liable on its account for the punishment of *cutting off*."

F. In what circumstances? The sin-offering. But as to all the rest of the sacrifices, if he sprinkled once in silence and the blood was poured out, all agree that it is fit.

If he sprinkled once outside of the proper time, and the blood was poured out, all agree that it is *piggul*.

If he sprinkled once outside of the proper time and outside of the proper place, it is unfit, and the punishment of *cutting off* does not apply.

[Tos. Zev. 4:9, ed. Zuckermandel, p. 486, lines 2-15 (b. Zev. 38b)]

Comment: M. Zev. 4:1 now stands out as a highly abbreviated summary of Tos. Zev. 4:9. Eliezer b. Jacob observes that the Shammaites take the more lenient position. The Hillelites are more strict because a *piggul*-intention in merely one application suffices to render the sin-offering *piggul*.

Judah the Patriarch has selected the essentials of Eliezer's long catalogue of possibilities. Here it seems clear that the Mishnaic version depends upon and summarizes the Tosefta's.

II.i.83.A. If he slaughtered with a hand-sickle or with a flint or with a reed, what he slaughters is valid.

All slaughter, and they slaughter at any time, and they slaughter with any implement excepting a reaping-sickle or a saw or teeth or the finger-nails, since these [do not cut but tear the windpipe and] choke [the beast].

B. If a man slaughtered with a reaping-sickle, drawing the blade backwards (KDRK HWLKTH)—

The House of Shammai declare it invalid.

And the House of Hillel declare it valid.

C. But if its teeth are filed down, then it is like a knife.

[M. Ḥul. 1:2, trans. Danby, p. 513 (b. Ḥul. 18a)]

Comment: The Houses-dispute glosses the foregoing general rule. It is in conventional form, with the opinions a matched syzygy: unfit (PŚL), fit (KŠR). The Shammaites prohibit drawing the blade backwards, lest he draw it in the other direction. The Hillelites do not prohibit the one on account of the other—a principle commonly debated by the Houses.

b. Ḥul. 18a observes that *declare valid/invalid* and *permit/forbid* are synonymous.

II.i.84.A. No flesh may be cooked in milk, excepting the flesh of fish and locusts. It is forbidden to serve it up on the table together with cheese excepting the flesh of fish and locusts.

If a man vowed to abstain from flesh, he is permitted the flesh of fish and locusts.

B. "A fowl comes up on the table [= is served] together with cheese, but it is not eaten [with it]"—the words of the House of Shammai.

And the House of Hillel say, "It does not come up [with it], and it is not eaten [with it]."

C. R. Yosi said, "This is one of the cases where the House of Shammai followed the more lenient, and the House of Hillel the more stringent, ruling."

D. Of what manner of table did they speak? Of a table whereat men eat; but on a table whereon the food is arrayed, a man may put the one beside the other without scruple.

[M. Ḥul. 8:1, trans. Danby, p. 524 (b. Ḥul. 104b, b. Shab. 13a)]

Comment: The Shammaite lemma has been slightly rearranged for redactional reasons. Two other versions would have been possible:

Fowl with cheese on the table
House of Shammai: Served up [and not eaten]
House of Hillel: *Not* served up [and not eaten].

Alternatively, the superscription could have been assigned to the Shammaite lemma, as often happens; if so, it would have appeared in precisely the present form. The Hillelite lemma depends upon the Shammaite one, dropping *fowl*, *with the cheese*, *on the table*, as one would expect. So the whole revision for redactional purposes consists of replacing *House of Shammai say* with *words of. . .*, and placing the attribution at the end.

Normally, the Shammaites prohibit one thing on account of another —that is, extend the range of prohibitions beyond what the law strictly requires—while the Hillelites prohibit only that which may not be done. The disputes in details of law often come down to that single fundamental difference ("building a fence around the law") in which the Hillelites take the lenient position throughout; if they do not, as here, it is noteworthy.

See Epstein, *Mevo'ot*, p. 142. The Mishnah is Yosi's, *Mishnah*, p. 671. This would suggest the pericope comes after, and is shaped in accord with, his opinion on the respective positions of the Houses, but the theme of the dispute of the Houses on the matter comes before his time. The same judgment applies to the rest of M. ʿEd's attributions of Houses-pericopae.

III.ii.37. It was taught: The House of Shammai say, "One must clean [the mouth]."

The House of Hillel say, "One must rinse it."

(b. Ḥul. 104b-105a)

Comment: The issue is, What must one do between eating cheese and meat? The Houses-lemmas are in perfect form:

House of Shammai: MQNḤ
House of Hillel: MDYḤ

We have no superscription. The singleton would mean nothing outside of the context of Amoraic discussion in which it appears. The discussion makes it clear that the House of Shammai hold one must clean the mouth *and* also rinse it; the House of Hillel say one needs *only* to rinse. This is made explicit in what is presented as a theoretical Amoraic formulation:

The House of Shammai say, MQNḤ and that is the law as to LMDYḤ
The House of Hillel say, MDYḤ and that is the law as to LMQNḤ

And a further follows, substituting for the gloss, *and that is the law*, an Aramaic lemma, WL' B'Y. The primary lemma, unglossed and without an interpretive superscription, obviously consisted of varying word-choices, nothing more, and these are then given significance in later discussions. But that does not mean the original lemma goes back to pre-70 times. The pericope before us depends upon M. Ḥul. 8:1b. Without knowledge of that rule we should not have expected any discussion of further separation of cheese and meat. And we do not know when that issue first provoked study.

II.i.85. And how many [must they be] [to be liable for the fleece-gift to the priest]?

The House of Shammai say, "Two sheep, for it is written, *A man shall nourish a young cow and two sheep* (Is. 7:21)."

And the House of Hillel say, "Five, for it is written, *And five sheep ready dressed* (I Sam. 25:18)."

R. Dosa b. Harkinas says, "Five sheep that have fleeces each of a *mina* and a half are subject to the law of *the first of the fleece*."

But the sages say, "Five sheep, however much may be their fleeces."

[M. Ḥul. 11:2, trans. Danby, p. 528 (b. Ḥul. 135a, Sifré Deut. 166)]

Comment: See Sifré Deut. 166, above, p. 36. ʿAqiba has been dropped, and Dosa takes his place. Granting that one must have five sheep—following the Hillelites—how *much* fleece do they have to produce to be subject to the law. This rule places Dosa in the Hillelite camp, *after* its original opinion has been shaped; that opinion presumably derives from Yavneh, if not earlier.

Note Epstein, *Mevo'ot*, p. 433; *Mishnah*, pp. 569, 1160. On Dosa's relationship to Yavnean Hillelites, see above, p. 193.

II.ii.79. A reaping sickle, etc.

(Tos. Ḥul. 1:6, ed. Zuckermandel, p. 500, 1. 29)

Comment: No change from M. Ḥul. 1:2.

II.ii.80.A. The fowl does not come up and is not eaten.

B. R. Yosi said, "This is one of the leniencies of the House of Shammai and the stringencies of the House of Hillel:

"The House of Shammai say, 'It comes up and is not eaten.'

"And the House of Hillel say, 'It does not come up and is not eaten.' "

C. R. Eleazar b. R. Ṣadoq says, "The fowl comes up with the cheese on the table."

(Tos. Ḥul. 8:2-3, ed. Zuckermandel, p. 509, lines 19-21)

Comment: Part A is the Hillelite ruling, but without attribution to that House, unlike M. Ḥul. 8:1. Part B contains Yosi's observation, and then presents the Houses' sayings, without the explanatory glosses of M. Ḥul. 8:1. This proves that the simple version proposed above (p. 243) in fact circulated, and the version of the Mishnah is a revision by Judah the Patriarch.

Part C indicates that the issue was faced before the time of Yosi. Eleazar now presents the opinion later on attributed to the Shammaites. On Eleazar's affinity for Shammaite opinion, see above, p. 155. But he does not attribute his opinion to the Shammaites, so the attribution to that House must come between ca. 80 and ca. 150, but not earlier.

See Lieberman, *Tosefet Rishonim*, II, p. 239.

II.i.86. The House of Shammai say, "An Israelite may not be numbered [in the same company] with a priest for [the consumption of] a Firstling."

And the House of Hillel permit even a gentile.

[M. Bekh. 5:2, trans. Danby, p. 535 (b. Bekh. 32b-33a, b. Tem. 24a)]

Comment: The firstling is blemished. The foregoing rule, given anonymously, states that ineligible offerings may be sold in the market, except for the firstling and tithe, which are enjoyed by their owners. The House of Shammai hold that an Israelite may not share with a priest in the firstling. The House of Hillel permit even a gentile to do so. The form is not standard:

House of Shammai:	An Israelite may not be numbered with the priest for a firstling
House of Hillel:	Permit *even a gentile.*

The Hillelite ruling extends the dispute; *even*. . . looks like an ʿAqiban gloss. No theoretical superscription obviously presents itself.

See Epstein, *Mevo'ot*, pp. 78-9, 454-5.

II.ii.81.A. The House of Shammai say, "They number on firstlings only priests alone."

And the House of Hillel say, "Even an Israelite."

R. ʿAqiba permits even a gentile, as it is said, *Like a deer and like a locust* (Deut. 12:15).

B. The flesh of the firstling—

The House of Shammai, "They do not feed it to menstruating women (NDWT)."

And the House of Hillel say, "They do feed it to menstruating women."

[Tos. Bekhorot 3:15-16, ed. Zuckermandel, p. 538, lines 2-4 (b. Bekh. 33a)]

Comment: Now we see the source of the difficult form of M. Bekh. The House of Hillel's lemma there has been glossed to include ʿAqiba's opinion, so ʿAqiba supplies the *terminus ante quem* for the original dispute. A more primitive superscription for part A may now be proposed:

Numbering Israelites with priests on firstlings:

House of Shammai:	Prohibit
House of Hillel:	Permit.

The dispute concerning gentiles would not readily be phrased as a separate dispute, for neither House went that far.

Part B is standard in form. It could have been given *permit/prohibit* form, or *verb +/— negative* form, by adding *to a menstruating woman* to the superscription. The Shammaite reason is that Num. 18:18 says priests may eat but lay-Israelites may not, and the same rule applies here. The Hillelites say that that rule applies only to an unblemished firstling, but Deut. 15:22 pertains to a blemished one: *The unclean and clean shall eat it* —all the more so a layman (b. Bekh. 33a).

III.ii.38.A. Our rabbis taught: How long is the period before we receive him [as a *ḥaver*]?

The House of Shammai say, "As regards [the purity of] liquids (LMŠQYN), [the period is] thirty days, but as [regards the purity of his] garment, [the period is] twelve months."

And the House of Hillel say, "Both in the one case as well as in the other, the period is twelve months."

B. If this be so, then have you here a ruling where the House of Shammai is more lenient and the House of Hillel is the stricter? Rather [read]:

The House of Hillel say, "Both in the one case as well as in the other, the period is thirty days."

[b. Bekh. 30b (Tos. Dem. 2:12)]

Comment: The issue concerns accepting a neophyte into the *ḥavurah*. The pericope is the only one attributed to the Houses which pertains to that society for meticulous tithing and ritual purities. The pericope follows the standard form, with the superscription, then the Houses sayings:

House of Shammai:	For liquids, thirty day(s) For garment, twelve month(es)
House of Hillel:	For both ('ḤD ZH W'ḤD ZH) twelve month(es).

We could have expected no other form but the one before us. But the Amoraic discussion of part B then provides definitive evidence that Amoraim were quite well prepared completely to revise Houses-materials, following the standard form, for reasons of logic. In this case, they have assigned to the Hillelites an entirely new opinion:

'ḤD ZH W'ḤD ZH *LŠLŠYM*

They have thus dropped twelve months and substituted the more "credible" opinion. Without the discussion we should have assumed the pericope was classic, therefore "early." This means that merely conforming to the standard form by itself supplies no evidence whatever as to the antiquity of a pericope.

Tos. Dem. 2:12 gives the Hillelite lemma as "This and this for thirty days (ZH WZH LŠLŠYM YWM)," so evidently has been corrected to conform to the Amoraic discussion. Lieberman observes, "And in all readings of the Tosefta [the passage follows] the correction of the Babylonian Talmud." So the Tosefta's tradition was preserved only in the b. Bekh. *beraita*, but the Tosefta itself was revised in later times.

III.ii.39. Our rabbis taught: The House of Shammai say, "If a man said, 'I take upon myself [to offer] a *marḥeshet*,' [the vow] must stand over until Elijah comes."

(They are in doubt as to whether [these terms] refer to the vessel or to the pastry prepared therein.)

But the House of Hillel say, "There was a vessel in the Temple called *marḥeshet*, resembling a deep mold, which gave the dough that was put into it the shape of Cretan apples and Grecian nuts." (b. Men. 63a)

Comment: In this *beraita*, by contrast, the form is so obviously defective that an early attribution seems on the face of it unlikely. In this instance archaeological data about whether such a vessel actually existed in the Temple would be helpful, but not decisive; the Hillelites might know what they were talking about, not from direct observation, but from the testimony of people unconnected with the Houses.

II.ii.82.A. He who sanctifies his property and intended to divorce his wife—

R. Eliezer says, "He prohibits her by vow not to enjoy benefit, and she collects her *Ketuvah* from the sanctified property."

[Lieberman, *Tosefet Rishonim*, II, p. 279: R. Eleazar b. R. Simeon says, "The House of Shammai say,] 'If he wants to bring her back, he may bring her back.' "

R. Joshua says, "If he wants to bring her back, he may not bring her back."

B. And the House of Hillel say, "If he wants to bring her back, he may not bring her back."

C. R. Eliezer says according to the words of the House of Shammai, and R. Joshua says according to the words of the House of Hillel.

[Tos. ʿArakh. 4:5, ed. Zuckermandel, p. 547, lines 9-13 (b. ʿArakh. 23a)]

III.ii.40. TNY': If a man dedicates his possessions to the sanctuary while still liable for his wife's *Ketuvah*,

R. Eliezer says, "When he divorces her, he must vow that he will not derive further benefit from her."

And R. Joshua says, "He need not do so."

And R. Eleazar b. Simeon said, "These are the very views of the House of Shammai and the House of Hillel, for—

"The House of Shammai say, 'A consecration made in error is a consecration.'

"And the House of Hillel say, 'It is not a valid consecration.' "

(b. ʿArakh. 23a)

Comment: Tosefta corresponds to M. ʿArakh. 6:1:

> If a man sanctifies his property to the Temple while he was liable for the payment of his wife's *Ketuvah*—
> R. Eliezer says, "When he divorces her, he must vow to derive no further benefit from her."
> R. Joshua says, "He need not."

The issue in Tos. ʿArakh. however is *not* whether he may make such a vow, but whether he may later *remarry* the woman.

The dispute of the Houses in relation to M. ʿArakh. concerns whether a man erroneously consecrates something to the sanctuary. The House of Hillel hold one cannot do so, and the House of Shammai hold it is a valid consecration. R. Eliezer rules that even though the possessions included his wife's property (*Ketuvah*), they are still sanctified, so he must vow not to make use of them. By extension to the Tosefta case before us, the couple may then remarry since the sacred property is protected by the vow. The Hillelites hold the property was not sanctified.

The pericope provides a good example of the effort to standardize a few Eliezer-Joshua disputes in Houses-forms. The presumption is that Eliezer follows the opinion of the Shammaites, Joshua, the Hillelites, but that they did not *constitute* the Houses. On the one hand, the anonymous subscription introduces the Houses. On the other, part B repeats the opinion of Joshua, now as an attribution to the House of Hillel—as if the two lemmas circulated separately and were not related to one another. A corresponding opinion of the Shammaites has not been supplied. It should have been identical to Eliezer's.

If we had had such a matched pair of pericopae, containing the same words attributed both to the Houses and to the Yavnean masters, respectively, a literary, not a historical difficulty, would have to be faced first of all. Did the named masters shape their opinions in reference to the Houses' dispute? If so, why did they not say so: *The House of Shammai say. . .*—just as do the Ushans later on (e.g. Simeon b. Eleazar, Yosi, Judah b. Ilai). Perhaps they shaped their opinions independently of the Houses, about whom they would have known nothing. Then, later on, someone has removed *their* names and replaced them with the Houses'. But the original tradition circulated alongside as well. Alternatively, the Houses' dispute on fundamental principles comes before the time of the Yavneans, who take up positions in matters of detail consistent with what the Houses had earlier said in general on those fundamental principles. Then, later authorities observed the consistencies and remarked on them, hence part C.

The historical consequence of each of these theories is obvious. On the one hand, the Houses and the Yavneans are one and the same. For some reason someone has chosen to drop the names of the masters and replace them with those of the Houses. There can have been no significant mnemonic gain. It may have had something to do with the relations of the second generation Yavneans to the early masters, or perhaps with Eliezer's excommunication. No Houses actually existed, according to this theory, but they were merely mnemonic conventions.

Alternatively, the Houses did flourish as historical institutions before 70. At Yavneh, the major disciples of Yoḥanan b. Zakkai, Joshua and Eliezer, having mastered the principles about which the Houses debated, proceeded to apply those principles, in a manner preserving a consistent pattern, to numerous concrete cases, both actual and theoretical. They proved so consistent in their own decisions that they were associated with the respective Houses, and it became difficult to distinguish Eliezer from the House of Shammai, Joshua from the House of Hillel.

See Lieberman, *Tosefet Rishonim*, II, p. 279.

II.ii.83. The House of Shammai say, "There is an Added Fifth to the Additional Payment."

And the House of Hillel say, "There is no Added Fifth to the Additional Payment."

[Tos. 'Arakh. 4:22, ed. Zuckermandel, p. 548, lines 26-7 (b. 'Arakh. 27b)]

Comment: The form is standard. The dispute pertains to M. 'Arakh. 8:1-2.

II.ii.84. Olive-presses whose doors open inward [to Jerusalem] and whose empty space outward, or vice versa—

The House of Shammai say, "They do not redeem in them Second Tithe, as if they were inside, and they do not eat in them the light sanctities, as if they were outside."

The House of Hillel say, "The part directly above the wall and inwards is deemed within, and the part directly above the wall and outwards is deemed outside."

R. Yosi said, "This is the Mishnah of R. 'Aqiba. The first Mishnah [is as follows]:

"The House of Shammai say, 'They do not redeem in them Second Tithe as if they were outside, and they do not eat in them light sanctities, as if they were inside.'

"The House of Hillel say, 'Lo, they are like the chambers: where the door opens inward it is deemed inward, and contrarywise.' "

(Tos. 'Arakh. 5:15, ed. Zuckermandel, p. 550, lines 26-33)

Comment: See M. M.S. 3:7, p. 101.

III.ii.41.A. Our rabbis have taught: If he gave her [a harlot] wheat [as hire] and she made it into flour, olives, and she made them into oil, grapes, and she made into wine—

One [*beraita*] taught: They are forbidden [for the altar].

And another [beraita] taught: They are permitted [for the altar].

B. Said R. Joseph, "Gurion who came from Asporak recited: 'The House of Shammai forbid, and the House of Hillel permit.'

"The House of Hillel say, '[Scripture says (Deut. 23:19)]: *Them*, implying but not their issue; '*them*', but not their products.'

"The House of Shammai say, '*Them*' implying but not their issue; and the word *even* includes their products.' "

[b. Tem. 30b (b. B.Q. 65b, b. B.Q. 93b-94a)]

Comment: R. Joseph's (4th c. Babylonian) tradition accounts for the contradictory *beraitot*, assigning each to a House. Gurion indicates how pericopae were memorized. In this instance we know only the apodosis; Joseph assigns the standard Houses-rulings to the usual authorities. The exegesis of 'P is ʿAqiban, and the Houses' attribution is spurious.

II.i.87.A. If she miscarried in the night of the eighty-first day, the House of Shammai declare her exempt from an offering.

And the House of Hillel declare her liable.

B. The House of Hillel said to the House of Shammai, "How does the night of the eighty-first day differ from the eighty-first day? If they are alike in what concerns uncleanness, are they not also alike in what concerns the offering?"

The House of Shammai answered, "No! as you argue of her that miscarries on the eighty-first day (who was thus delivered at a time when it was fitting to bring an offering), would you likewise argue of her that miscarries on the night of the eighty-first day (who was thus delivered not at a time when it was fitting to bring an offering)?"

C. The House of Hillel answered, "She that miscarries on an eighty-first day that falls on a Sabbath affords proof, for she was delivered not at a time when it was fitting to bring an offering, yet she is liable to bring an offering."

D. The House of Shammai answered, "No! as you argue of her that miscarries on an eighty-first day that falls on a Sabbath (when even if it is not fitting to bring the offering of the individual, it is nevertheless fitting to bring the offering of the congregation), would you likewise argue of her that miscarries on the night of the eighty-first day (when it is not fitting to bring the offering either of the individual or of the congregation)?"

E. Her blood [-uncleanness] affords no proof, for if she miscarried before her days of uncleanness were fulfilled, her blood is still unclean and she is not liable to bring an offering."

(M. Ker. 1:6, trans. Danby, p. 564)

II.ii.85.A. The House of Shammai and the House of Hillel agree concerning the night before the eighty-first that she should be liable for a sacrifice.

B. The House of Hillel said to the House of Shammai, "Do you not agree concerning the night before the eighty-first that her blood is unclean, and that she who aborts on the eighty-first should be liable for a sacrifice? What is the difference between day and night, and between blood and giving birth?"

The House of Shammai said to them, "No, If you say so concerning the day, which is fit for bringing a sacrifice, will you say so concerning the night, which is not fit for bringing a sacrifice?"

"As to the blood that you mentioned, [Scripture] distinguished between blood and giving birth, for she who sees [it] during the period [after giving birth]—her blood is unclean, but she who aborts during the period, her blood is unclean. She who aborts during the period is free of all obligation."

C. The House of Hillel said to them, "Lo, she who aborts on the day of the eighty-first which coincides with the Sabbath will prove it. For it did not come forth in an appropriate time in which to bring a sacrifice. And this proves that the one who aborts on the night before the eighty-first of any day of the year, when it did go forth at a time appropriate for bringing a sacrifice, is liable for a sacrifice."

The House of Shammai said to them, "No, if you say so concerning the one who aborts on the eighty-first day on any other day of the year [but the Sabbath], that it is joined with the following day, that even though it is not appropriate for a private sacrifice, it is appropriate for a public sacrifice, will you say so concerning her who aborts on the night of the eighty-first of any day of the year, for the night is not appropriate either for a private sacrifice or for a public sacrifice?"

D. The House of Hillel said to them, "Lo, you have said that the night is joined with the following day. Just as she is liable on the eighty-first day, so she should be liable on the night of the eighty-first day. And let not the eighty-second day prove the matter, for [then] it went forth at a time appropriate for bringing the sacrifice."

[Tos. Keritot 1:9, ed. Zuckermandel, p. 561, lines 16-32 (b. Ker. 7b-8a)]

Comment: See Sifra Tazri'a 3:6, and synopses, above, pp. 16-22. See also Lieberman, *Tosefet Rishonim*, II, p. 293; Epstein, *Mishnah*, p. 340.

VI. ṬOHAROT

II.i.88.A. If there was a jar full of clean liquids with a siphon inside it, and the jar had a tightly stopped-up cover, and it was put in a "Tent" wherein was a corpse—

The House of Shammai say, "The jar and the liquids remain clean, but the siphon is unclean."

The House of Hillel say, "The siphon also is clean."

B. The House of Hillel reverted to teach according to the opinion of the House of Shammai.

[M. Kel. 9:2, trans. Danby, p. 617 (M. Kel. 10:1, M. Oh. 5:3, 15:9, M.'Ed. 1:4)]

Comment: The form is developed, but nearly conventional. Since the sole point of disagreement is the siphon, the antecedent superscription could have made place for both the jar and the liquids:

If there was a jar. . . wherein was a corpse, the jar and the liquids remain clean—and the siphon:

House of Shammai: Declare unclean.
House of Hillel: Declare clean.

So the original pericope would have consisted of *siphon* + *the Houses*, and the rest would have been supplied by the editor.

M. Kel. 10:1 states explicitly that an earthenware vessel with a tightly stopped-up cover affords protection only to foodstuffs, liquids, and other earthenware vessels, but not to metal. That teaching clearly contradicts the House of Hillel's here. Rather than permit an anonymous Mishnah to follow the Shammaite view, the glossator has added part B, to account for the fact that the law was decided against the Hillelite view before us.

We may generalize that where we are told the Hillelites agreed with the Shammaites, and we cannot account for that fact in some other way, we may suppose that the later legal decision has required the tradents to revise the position attributed to the Hillelites. It is therefore striking that they did not change matters around, but preserved what they had, and then, through a new subscription or story, accounted for the changed circumstances, leaving the Hillelites in control of the law. This again underlines the conservatism of the tradents in preserving what they had received.

See Epstein, *Mevo'ot*, p. 466; *re* 'P, *Mishnah*, p. 1024.

II.i.89.A. Articles made from iron ore, or a piece of (unshaped) smelted iron, or the iron hoop of a wheel, or of sheetmetal, or metal plating, or the bases or rims or handles of other vessels, or metal chippings or filings, are not susceptible to uncleanness.

R. Yoḥanan b. Nuri says, "Also (such as are made) from broken up (metal) articles. If they were made from the fragments of (other) articles or from the refuse, or from nails known to have been made from other articles, they are unclean."

B. If [they were made] from [common] nails—

The House of Shammai declare unclean.

And the House of Hillel declare clean.

(M. Kel. 11:3, trans. Danby, p. 620)

Comment: The form is standard. The Houses' lemmas are balanced syzygies, set against the superscription. The Houses here refine a general rule, which presumably comes before their time. The usual sequence will be *Shammai + unclean/Hillel + clean*, with the presumption that making things susceptible to uncleanness is the more stringent ruling. The issue is that one is not sure whether the nails have been made from other articles, therefore B depends upon Yoḥanan b. Nuri in A.

Part B is assigned to Eleazar b. R. Yosi by Epstein, *Mevo'ot*, p. 179. See Tos. Kel. B.M. 1:2, as follows:

R. Eleazar b. R. Yosi said, "The House of Shammai and the House of Hillel did not differ concerning nails of which it is known that they are made from articles, that they are unclean, and concerning nails of which it is known that they are not made of articles, that they are clean.

Concerning what did they differ?

Concerning the common ('L HŚTM), for

"The House of Shammai declare unclean.

"And the House of Hillel declare clean."

II.i.90.A. A staff that has a club-headed nail fashioned on its end is susceptible to uncleanness. One that is studded with nails is susceptible.

R. Simeon says, "Only if three rows [of nails] are put in it."

But whensoever they are put in only for adornment, [the staff] remains insusceptible. If a tube was put on the end (so, too, in the case of a door) it remains insusceptible.

But if [the tube] had already served as some utensil and was fastened to it, it remains susceptible.

B. When does it become insusceptible (ṬHRTH)?

The House of Shammai say, "So soon as it has suffered damage."

And the House of Hillel say, "So soon as it is fastened on."

(M. Kel. 14:2, trans. Danby, p. 624)

Comment: Here, the difference between the Houses rests on a single letter. When does it become susceptible to receive uncleanness:

House of Shammai: MŠYḤB*L*
House of Hillel: MŠYḤB*R*.

Perhaps a confused mnemonic tradition has come down, with verbs different from one another only in the third radical.

The House of Shammai say that once the object can no longer be used, it no longer is susceptible. The House of Hillel say once it is clean when properly affixed for its new function. See M. Kel. 20:6 for a similar sequence. See Albeck, *Seder Ṭoharot*, p. 522.

It looks as if the Shammaites assign an earlier time for the purification, just as happens in other such disputes, and therefore are in the lenient position.

II.i.91.A. A chest—

The House of Shammai say, "It is measured on the inside [to determine its capacity]."

And the House of Hillel say, "It is measured on the outside."

But they agree that the thickness of the legs and the thickness of the rim [should not be included in the] measurement.

B. R. Yosi says, "They agree that the thickness of the legs and of the rim should be included, but that the space between them should not be included."

C. R. Simeon of Shezur says, "If the legs were a handbreadth high the space between them should not be included in the measurement; but if less than this, the space between them should be included."

[M. Kel. 18:1, trans. Danby, p. 631 (b. Men. 31a)]

Comment: The purpose of measuring is given in M. Kel. 15:1:

"A chest. . .that has a flat bottom and holds not less than forty *se'ahs* of liquid, or two *kors* of dry wares, is not susceptible to uncleanness."

The Shammaites measure from within, the Hillelites, from without, and the language is perfectly balanced:

The chest
House of Shammai: [Measured from] within
House of Hillel: [Measured from] without.

One of the standard syzygies for Houses-opinions is *within/without*, as in connection with the olive press on the wall of Jerusalem, the uncleanness *inside/outside* the walls of Jerusalem, and so forth.

If the vacuum space itself holds forty *se'ahs*, it is clean. The Hillelites include in the measurement even the thickness of the sides to reach the measure of forty *se'ahs*; they therefore take the more lenient position, since one wants to reach forty *se'ahs* and therefore render the chest incapable of receiving uncleanness.

II.i.92.A. Bagpipes are not susceptible to *midraś*-uncleanness.

B. A trough for mixing mortar—

The House of Shammai say, "[Susceptible to] *midraś*-[uncleanness]."

And the House of Hillel say, "[Susceptible to] corpse-uncleanness [alone]."

(M. Kel. 20:2, trans. Danby, p. 635)

Comment: The issue is the degree of uncleanness to which the mixing mortar is susceptible; all parties agree that it may be made unclean. The Houses-sayings are simply the words signifying the degree of uncleanness:

House of Shammai: *Midraś*
House of Hillel: *Corpse-uncleanness.*

The Hillelite lemma is not unbalanced; the idiom is ṬM'-MT, not merely ṬM', which would have been ambiguous. The difference cocerns whether one sits on the object. Since the Shammaites hold one does, it *is* susceptible to *midraś*. The Hillelites exclude *midraś*, but, by saying *corpse-uncleanness*, they mean to include *all* other forms of uncleanness (Albeck, *Seder Ṭoharot*, p. 89). In that case, one might suppose the opinions could have been more nearly balanced with a mere negative added to the Hillelite lemma. But this too would have been ambiguous, for the Hillelite opinion might have been understood to mean the trough could not be made unclean at all. Therefore the only accurate and precise language is as given, and the pericope is as brief and balanced as it could have been. *MDRŚ/ṬM'-MT* are balanced elsewhere.

See Epstein, *Mevo'ot*, p. 112, 130-1, 462.

II.i.93.A. If a sheet that was susceptible to *midraś*-uncelanness was used as a curtain it becomes insusceptible to *midraś*-uncleanness, but it is still susceptible to corpse-uncleanness.

When does it cease to be susceptible [to *midraś*-uncleanness] (ṬHRTH)?

The House of Shammai say, "After it has been sewn up."

And the House of Hillel say, "After it has been tied up."

R. ʿAqiba says, "After it has been fixed up [in its new place]."

(M. Kel. 20:6, trans. Danby, p. 636)

Comment: As above, M. Kel. 14:2, the Houses-opinions consist of verbs differing in the first two radicals:

Shammai:	MŠY*TB*R
Hillel:	MŠY*QŠ*R
ʿAqiba:	MŠYQB

The issue is, When does the sheet cease to be used for its ordinary purpose and so become susceptible not to severe *midraś*-uncleanness, but only to corpse-uncleanness? It is interesting that the question is, When is its *purification* [from *midraś*-uncleanness]? even though it remains susceptible to other uncleannesses.

The Shammaites say, "When the sheet is ready for hanging." The Hillelites say, "Only when it has been hung up." ʿAqiba says, "When it is *nailed* up," that is permanently. The positions are thus in logical order. But it looks as if the point at which the sheet enters the diminished, therefore more lenient, status, *begins* with the Shammaite saying. If we had *gemara*, it presumably would note that fact and perhaps reverse matters. Note Tos. Kel. B.M. 11:7.

Epstein, *Mevo'ot*, pp. 23-4, says that the Houses here comment on a pre-existing tradition; also pp. 77, 112; p. 128: the tradition is Yosi's, in M. Kel. 27:9. Note Epstein, *Mishnah*, p. 549.

II.i.94.A. If a bride's stool lost its seat-boards—

The House of Shammai declare it still susceptible to uncleanness.

And the House of Hillel declare it not susceptible.

B. Shammai says, "Even ('P) the frame of the stool remains susceptible to uncleanness."

C. If a stool is fixed to a baking-trough—

The House of Shammai declare it susceptible to uncleanness.

And the House of Hillel declare it not susceptible.

D. Shammai says, "Even one that was made [to be used] inside it [is susceptible]."

(M. Kel. 22:4, trans. Danby, p. 637)

Comment: See above, I, p. 194. In both parts, the Houses-opinions are here in the intensive of ṬM'/ṬHR. Shammai's saying breaks the pattern. The issue is whether the chair may continue to be used. In part A the Shammaites say the stool may still be used by ordinary folk; in part C, it may still be used, if inconveniently. The "cleanness" is from *midraś*-uncleanness, see Albeck, *Seder Ṭoharot*, p. 95. On 'P, Epstein, *Mishnah*, p. 1026.

II.i.95. A leather bag or wrapper for garments is susceptible to *midraś*-uncleanness.

A leather bag or wrapper for purple wool—

The House of Shammai say, "*Midraś*[-uncleanness]."

And the House of Hillel say, "Corpse-uncleanness."

(M. Kel. 26:6, trans. Danby, p. 643)

Comment: The considerations mentioned above, M. Kel. 20:2, apply here. The words *midraś/temē-met* therefore form a syzygy no different from ṬM'/ṬHR.

See Epstein, *Mevo'ot*, pp. 113, 133.

II.i.96.A. "Scroll-wrappers, whether figures are portrayed on them or not, are susceptible to uncleanness," according to the words of the House of Shammai.

And the House of Hillel say, "If figures are portrayed on them, they are not susceptible to uncleanness. If figures are not portrayed on them, they are susceptible."

B. Rabban Gamaliel says, "In either case they are not susceptible to uncleanness."

(M. Kel. 28:4, trans. Danby, p. 646)

Comment: The lemmas are not balanced, because two different situations have been reduced to a single pericope. The Houses agree on the uncleanness of scroll-wrappers without figures. They differ on those with figures. The Shammaite saying is not properly attached to the attribution; *according to the words of* is inappropriate here, where the intent obviously is to cite the Houses directly. A simpler form would have been:

Scroll-covers with figures
House of Shammai: Declare unclean
House of Hillel: Declare clean.
And they agree that those with figures are unclean.

Why has that conventional form been upset? A glance at the foregoing pericope provides the answer:

28:2: "If a piece of cloth less than three handbreaths square was used to block up [a hole in] the bath-house... *whether it was kept in readiness or whether it was not kept in readiness*, it is susceptible," according to the words of R. Eliezer.

R. Joshua says, "*Whether it was kept in readiness or whether it was not kept in readiness*, it is not susceptible."

R. ʿAqiba says, "*If it was kept in readiness*, it is susceptible, *if it was not*, it is not..."

M. Kel. 28:4 now follows the form of M. Kel. 28:2, using the *BYN... BYN...* form, with distinctions being introduced on that basis. ʿAqiba's lemma of 28:2 corresponds to the Hillelites' in 28:4; Eliezer's, to the Shammaite one in every detail. It therefore looks as if whatever primary lemma existed has been revised to follow the forms of later materials in the same setting; alternatively, the primary lemma is before us and has been shaped by reference to the same form as Eliezer-Joshua-ʿAqiba.

See Epstein, *Mevo'ot*, pp. 114, 131-2; *Mishnah*, p. 133.

II.i.97.A. The length of the remnants [of the shaft] below the broad blade of the ox-goad [that serves as a connective] is seven handbreadths.

B. Of the shaft of a householder's trowel—

The House of Shammai say seven.

And the House of Hillel say eight [handbreadths].

C. Of the shaft of a plasterer's trowel—

The House of Shammai say nine.

And the House of Hillel say ten [handbreadths].

(M. Kel. 29:8, trans. Danby, pp. 648-9)

Comment: The Houses-sayings are numbers attached to superscriptions:

	B	C
Shammai:	seven	nine
Hillel:	eight	ten

The existence of a dispute presumably led the tradent to assign appropriate numbers to Houses, then to compose the whole as we have it. Since the foregoing numbers, on which all parties agree, begin with seven, it was natural to start with seven, then to proceed upward, as the materials required.

II.ii.86.A. Vessels of alum-crystal—

The House of Shammai say, "They render unclean from their midst and from their air space like vessels of clay (KLY ḤRŚ), and from their outer surfaces like (KLY ŠṬP) vessels which require rinsing in order to be restored to Levitical cleanness [Jastrow, II, p. 1555, s.v. ŠṬP]."

And the House of Hillel say, "Vessels of alum-crystal are like clay vessels in every respect."

B. R. Simeon b. Eleazar says in other language:

"The House of Shammai say, 'They render unclean like a half-vessel and render unclean like a whole vessel.'

"And the House of Hillel say, 'Vessels of alum crystal are like clay vessels in every respect.' "

(Tos. Kel. Bava Qamma, 2:1, ed. Zuckermandel, p. 570, lines 22-5)

Comment: The Hillelite lemma of part A could have stood by itself. The Shammaite one is not balanced, and even though the superscription is standard, one could not easily revise the whole to form a conventional pericope. Still, the disagreement pertains only to the difference from a clay vessel, and an agreement clause would produce a semblance of balance:

The outer surfaces of an alum-vessel:
House of Shammai: Declare unclean
House of Hillel: Declare clean.

Perhaps the superscription is the problem. It has been inadequately articulated, therefore the bulk of the problem is intruded into the Shammaite lemma. Simeon's version would be similarly revised. The materials before us therefore look as if they have been considerably developed over the simpler forms we should have expected.

The corresponding Mishnah, M. Kel. 2:1, follows the Hillelite view: Vessels of alum-crystal and earthenware vessels are alike in what concerns uncleanness, but the details, unlike the Hillelite lemma here, are spelled out. See Lieberman, *Tosefet Rishonim* III, p. 5: They receive uncleanness like a half-vessel, for they follow the law of an earthenware vessel as to their air, and of the KLY ŠTP as to their externals. But as to imparting uncleanness, their law is identical to that of the earthenware vessels, which render unclean from their midst *and* from their outer surfaces.

II.ii.87. A. Peat. . . which was prepared under conditions of cleanness and became unclean and fell into the air-space of an oven when it was heated (BŠʿT HŚYQH), it [the oven] is unclean. When not heated, (ŠLʾ BŠʿT HŚYQH), it is clean. . .

B. And R. Eleazar b. R. Simeon says, "The House of Shammai

declare [the oven] unclean, and the House of Hillel declare [it] clean."

C. In what circumstances? In the case of new [peat], but in the case of old, all agree that it is clean.

(Tos. Kel. Bava Qamma 6:18, ed. Zuckermandel, p. 576, lines 24-27)

Comment: Eleazar b. R. Simeon has adopted the simplest mode of forming the Houses' opinions. This is attached to part A, making A into a long superscription. Without the tradition of Eleazar b. R. Simeon, we should have assumed the law followed the House of Hillel. M. Kel. 9:5 gives the case when the oven was heated, but makes no mention of a cold oven. See Lieberman, *Tosefet Rishonim* III, p. 23.

II.ii.88. [If a shovel has lost its entire blade]—

R. Nathan [Jonathan] b. Yosef said, "In this, the House of Shammai declare unclean, and the House of Hillel declare clean."

(Tos. Kelim Bava Meṣi'a' 3:8, ed. Zuckermandel, p. 581, lines 26-7)

Comment: Like Simeon, Nathan follows the simplest form. The standard idiom is clearly, *House of Shammai declare unclean*, *House of Hillel declare clean*; this can be attached to pretty much any disputed situation. As noted, the simplicity of the Houses-lemma establishes no claim on authenticity. Anyone could have made use of such a stock-phrase for any purpose.

See Lieberman, *Tosefet Rishonim* III, p. 43.

II.ii.89.A. A tube which he fixed under the door, even though he makes use of it, is clean.

B. If it was unclean and he fixed it under the door, it is unclean until it is made clean.

When does it become clean?

"The House of Shammai say, 'So soon as he damages [it] (YḤBWL).'

"The House of Hillel say, 'So soon as it is fastened on (YḤBR)' "—the words of R. Meir.

C. R. Judah says, "The House of Shammai say, "So soon as it is damaged (YḤBL) *and* it is fixed (YḤBR)."

"The House of Hillel say, 'So soon as it is damaged (YḤBL) *or* it is fixed (YḤBR).' "

(Tos. Kel. Bava Meṣi'a' 4:5, ed. Zuckermandel, p. 582, lines 24-28)

Comment: Judah the Patriarch has selected Meir's version, but has given both verbs the same form. Judah gives another picture of the tradition, which assigned *both* verb-roots to both Houses, but represented the difference as whether each stage had to be passed, or merely one.

II.ii.90. R. Eleazar b. R. Ṣadoq said, "The House of Shammai and the House of Hillel did not dispute concerning a mustard strainer in which *three* holes in the bottom merged into one another, that it is clean.

"Concerning what did they dispute?

"Concerning *two*:

"The House of Shammai declare unclean.

"And the House of Hillel declare clean."

(Tos. Kel. Bava Meṣi'a' 4:16, ed. Zuckermandel, p. 583, lines 16-19)

Comment: M. Kel. 14:8 contains the agreement of the Houses without mentioning them. The issue is whether the strainer can still be used and therefore constitutes a vessel. When a smaller hole has been made, the Shammaites say it can, the Hillelites, that it cannot be used. The pericope presumably derives from Yavneh.

II.ii.91. R. Simeon b. Shezuri said, "The House of Shammai and the House of Hillel did not disagree concerning the thickness of the legs and the thickness of rim, that they *are* measured with it [the chest, for determining its capacity; if it contains forty *se'ahs* or more, it is insusceptible to uncleanness].

"Concerning what did they disagree? Concerning [the empty spaces] between them ('L HBYNYM), for

"The House of Shammai say, 'They are not measured.'

"And the House of Hillel say, 'They are measured.' "

(Tos. Kel. Bava Meṣi'a' 8:1, ed. Zuckermandel, p. 587, lines 5-7)

Comment: M. Kel. 18:1 has the agreement referred to by Simeon, in the same words, but omits Simeon's name. The difference there concerns measuring the inside of the chest or the outside. R. Yosi then says the space between the legs and rims should *not* be included, according to all parties. Simeon Shezuri says whether one measures the space between the legs depends on the height of the legs. The disagreement reported here therefore is missing in M. Kel. The form for Simeon's report is standard in Tosefta. See Lieberman, *Tosefet Rishonim*, III, p. 59.

II.ii.92.A. A trough for mixing mortar which holds from two *logs* to nine *qabs*—

The House of Shammai say, "*Midraś*."

And the House of Hillel say, "Corpse-uncleanness."

B. And the bag—

The House of Shammai, "It is filled and stands."

And the House of Hillel say, "It is filled and tied up (ṢRWRH)."

C. R. Yosi b. R. Judah says, "The matters are reversed."

[Tos. Kel. Bava Meṣi'a' 11:3, ed. Zuckermandel, p. 589, lines 17-20 (M.'Ed. 5:1)]

Comment: Part A corresponds to M. Kel. 20:2 (M. 'Ed. 5:1):

A trough for mixing mortar
Shammai: *Midraś*
Hillel: Corpse-uncleanness.

The qualification of the size follows:

If a trough that holds from two *logs* to nine *qabs* is split, it becomes susceptible to *midraś*-uncleanness. If it was left out in the rain and it swelled, only to corpse-uncleanness.

That clause in the Mishnah depends upon the Hillelite one, since the Shammaites hold that whether or not it is split, it *is* susceptible to *midraś*-uncleanness. Judah the Patriarch has dropped the qualification of the size and kept the rest without revision.

Part B does not specify what kind of bag. M. Kel. 20:2 refers to a bagpipe, and holds they are not susceptible of *midraś*-uncleanness. The issue is whether one may sit upon it, and the Mishnah concludes one may not. Here the rulings are phrased in other language. The House of Shammai say it is not used for sitting, therefore is not susceptible to *midraś*-uncleanness. The House of Hillel say if one ties it up, it can be sat upon, therefore it is subject to *midraś*-uncleanness (compare M. Kel. 20:3 at the end). The Mishnah follows the Shammaite opinion. Yosi b. R. Judah has reversed the opinions presumably to accommodate the actual law.

See Lieberman, *Tosefet Rishonim* III, p. 67; Epstein, *Mevo'ot*, pp. 94, 172, 436, and compare M. Kel. 26:2, Meir and Yosi. See also Epstein, *Mishnah*, p. 1188.

II.ii.93. "When does it become clean (ṬHRTH) [insusceptible to uncleanness]?

"The House of Shammai say, 'When it has suffered damage (YḤBL).'

"The House of Hillel say, 'When it is fixed (YḤBR)' "—the words of R. Meir.

R. Judah says, "When it has suffered damage *and* has been fixed on. And the House of Hillel say, 'When it has suffered damage *or* been fixed on.' "

(Tos. Kel. Bava Meṣi'a' 11:7, ed. Zuckermandel, p. 589, lines 33-5)

Comment: Judah's lemma is defective, for it has lost *the House of Shammai say*. Otherwise it is identical to II.ii.89. But the whole has been attached to a completely different problem, here concerning matting spread over roof beams. The following passage concerns the same matter as M. Kel. 20:6, a sheet made into a veil, but does not refer to the Houses' opinions on when the sheet becomes insusceptible to uncleanness. But Lieberman assigns the pericope to the *sheet*, *Tosefet Rishonim* III, p. 68. See Epstein, *Mevo'ot*, p. 77, *Mishnah*, p. 1064.

II.ii.94.A. [If a stool is fixed to a baking trough as one sits on it, it is unclean; if not as one sits on it, it is clean.]

B. "As to one that was made [to be used] inside it, the House of Shammai declare unclean, and the House of Hillel declare clean" — the words of R. Meir.

C. R. Judah says, "The House of Shammai and the House of Hillel did not differ concerning one that was made [to be used] inside it, that it is clean, and Shammai was [the one who] declared it unclean.

"Concerning what did they differ? Concerning one which he brought from another place and attached to it, for—

"The House of Shammai declare unclean.

"And the House of Hillel declare clean."

D. R. Yosi said, "I see [prefer] the words of the House of Shammai, which does not say a frame even from the workshop is unclean."

(Tos. Kel. Bava Batra 1:12, ed. Zuckermandel, p. 591, lines 18-22)

Comment: The corresponding passage is M. Kel. 22:4. Judah the Patriarch says the dispute concerns a stool fixed to a baking trough, hence *not* according to Meir. For Judah the Patriarch, *Shammai* alone rules on one made to be used inside it, holding it *is* susceptible—that is, Meir's *House of* Shammai. In this detail, therefore Judah the Patriarch follows Judah b. Ilai. Our interest is in the *terminus ante quem* of the Houses-dispute. It cannot come later than ca. 150. But it does not look as though it is much earlier.

See Lieberman, *Tosefet Rishonim* III, p. 73; Epstein, *Mevo'ot*, pp. 118-119.

II.ii.95. R. Eleazar b. R. Yosi said, "The House of Shammai and the House of Hillel did not differ concerning a bag for purple wool or wrapper for purple wool, that they are unclean.

"Concerning what did they differ?

"Concerning a wrapper for garments and a bag for garments, for—

"The House of Shammai declare unclean.

"And the House of Hillel declare clean."

(Tos. Kel. Bava Batra 4:9, ed. Zuckermandel, p. 594, lines 17-19)

Comment: In M. Kel. 26:6, Judah the Patriarch has the Houses differ on the purple-wool containers, with the House of Shammai ruling *midraś*, the House of Hillel, corpse-uncleanness. As to the garment-containers, the law is unanimous that they *are* subject to *midraś*-uncleanness. So Eleazar b. R. Yosi has the reverse tradition. Judah the Patriarch has given the Shammaites' opinion on the wrapper for garments as the unanimous one, and then has the Houses debate the purple-wool bags. Appropriately, Judah has chosen *midraś*/corpse uncleanness, rather than ṬM'/ṬHR, for his predicate. See Epstein, *Mevo'ot*, p. 113.

II.ii.96.A. If one makes a girdle from one side of a garment and from one side of a sheet—

The House of Shammai declare unclean.

And the House of Hillel declare clean, until he hems [the girdle] (ŠYMWL).

B. From the middle of the garment and from the middle of the sheet he makes a hem on one side [of the piece which he cut out of the middle of a piece of cloth]—

The House of Shammai declare unclean.

And the House of Hillel declare clean, until he makes a hem from the second side (MṢDW HŠNY).

C. R. Simeon b. Judah says in the name of R. Simeon, "The House of Shammai and the House of Hillel did not differ concerning him who makes a girdle from the middle of a garment and from the middle of a sheet from one side, that it is clean until he hems it from the second side.

"Concerning what did they differ?

"Concerning him who makes a girdle from the side of the garment and from the side of the sheet, for the House of Shammai declare unclean and the House of Hillel declare clean, until he hems it."

(Tos. Kel. Bava Batra 5:7-8, ed. Zuckermandel, p. 595, lines 15-21)

Comment: See Lieberman, *Tosefet Rishonim* III, p. 86. Compare M. Kel. 28:7.

II.ii.97.A. The shaft of a trowel of the householders—
The House of Shammai say, "Seven,"
And the House of Hillel say, "Eight."
B. And of plasterers:
The House of Shammai say, "Nine,"
And the House of Hillel say, "Ten."

(Tos. Kel. Bava Batra 7:4, ed. Zuckermandel, p. 597, lines 8-10)

Comment: The passage appears verbatim in M. Kel. 29:8.

II.i.98.A. These convey uncleanness by contact and carrying, but do not convey uncleanness by overshadowing: a barleycorn's bulk of bone, earth from a foreign country, [earth from] a grave-area, a member from a corpse or a member from a living man that no longer bears its proper flesh, a backbone or a skull in which aught is lacking (ḤŚRW).

B. How much must be lacking in the backbone? The House of Shammai say, "Two links (ḤLYWT)."

And the House of Hillel say, "Even ('PYLW) one link."

C. And in the skull? The House of Shammai say, "As much as [a hole made by] a drill (KML' MQDḤ)."

And the House of Hillel say, "So much that, if it was taken from a living man, he would die (KDY ŠYNṬL MN HḤY WYMWT)."

D. Of what kind of drill did they speak?

"A physician's small drill," the words of R. Meir.

But the sages say, "The large drill that lay in a chamber in the Temple."

[M. Oh. 2:3, trans. Danby, p. 652 (b. Bekh. 37b-38a, b. Ḥul. 42b, 52b; b. 'Eruv. 7a)]

Comment: The chapter opens with a list of those things which convey uncleanness by overshadowing, that is, by being under the same "tent", or roof, with another object susceptible of receiving uncleanness. These include a corpse or part of a corpse, the backbone or skull or larger bones. The pericope before us now excludes things which do not convey uncleanness by overshadowing by a tent. The Houses-sayings of parts B and C gloss the foregoing law, then R. Meir and the sages gloss the Shammaite ruling about a drill (but see Abraham Goldberg, *Maśśekhet Ohalot* [Jerusalem, 1956], p. 18).

Part B poses no formal problem. It opens with a superscription, tying the Houses-rulings to the foregoing law. The Houses-rulings are *two/one*, glossed with *link* and, for the Hillelites, *even*. Such explanatory matter clarifies matters which were already obvious.

Part C opens with the same sort of superscription, but the Houses-lemmas are quite unrelated to one another:

Shammai:	As much as a drill (KML' MQDḤ)
Hillel:	So that it may be taken from the living man and he will die.

In this instance, it is impossible to reformulate the rulings so that they will use much the same words and present a balance. No one glosses by saying the opinions are near one another. But part D is a gloss of the House of Shammai in C.

See Epstein, *Mevo'ot*, pp. 23, 139.

II.i.99.A. If a baking-oven stood within the House and it had an arched outlet (QMWRH) that projected outside [the house], and corpse-bearers overshadowed it [with the corpse]—

The House of Shammai say, "All becomes unclean."

And the House of Hillel say, "The oven becomes unclean, but the house remains clean."

R. ʿAqiba says, "Even ('P) the oven remains clean."

B. If over a hatchway ('RWBH) between a house and the upper room there was set a cooking-pot which had a hole such that liquid could filter into it (BKWNŚ MŠQH)—

The House of Shammai say, "All becomes unclean."

And the House of Hillel say, "The cooking-pot becomes unclean, but the upper room remains clean."

R. ʿAqiba says, "Even the cooking-pot remains clean."

C. If the cooking-pot was sound—

The House of Hillel say, "It protects (MṢLT) all [from uncleanness]."

The House of Shammai say, "It protects only food, liquids, and earthenware vessels."

The House of Hillel changed their opinion and taught according to the opinion of the House of Shammai.

D. If there was a flagon full of clean liquid [in the upper room], the flagon contracts seven-day uncleanness, and the liquid remains clean.

But if the liquid was emptied out into another vessel, it becomes unclean.

If a woman [in the upper room] was kneading in a trough, the woman and the trough contract seven-day uncleanness, and the dough remains clean.

But if she emptied it into another vessel, it becomes unclean.

The House of Hillel changed their opinion and taught according to the opinion of the House of Shammai.

[M. Oh. 5:1-4, trans. Danby, pp. 655-6 (b. Ḥag. 22a)]

Comment: Part A: M. Oh. 5:1 presents a secondary development of the Houses-dispute. A simpler version would have had *oven* in the superscription, so that the Houses-rulings would have referred only to the house, and the lemmas would have been:

Shammai: Unclean
Hillel: Clean.

R. ʿAqiba provides important evidence for the *terminus ante quem*.

Part B, M. Oh. 5:2 exhibits precisely the same pattern, this time with the *cooking pot* in the superscription.

Part C, M. Oh. 5:3: The difference between the Houses concerns things which may be rendered clean in a ritual bath. The pot protects those things—food, liquids, and earthen-ware vessels—which *cannot* be rendered clean in a ritual bath. The opinions of the Houses have been reversed. The reversal has nothing to do with the content. On the contrary, in part A, the Hillelite lemma is longer and makes distinctions, the Shammaites refer to *all*; and in part B, it is just the opposite. So the arrangement does not depend upon formal or literary considerations.

While we therefore cannot change the places of the Houses and leave the opinions as they are, we can account for the reversal of order. The pericope ends with the Hillelites agreeing with the Shammaites, so rearranging the Houses is meant to leave the impression that, having heard the Shammaite opinion in second place, the Hillelites "then" changed their minds. In fact, M. ʿEd. 1:14 presents matters in just this way (below, pp. 281-284). The rules are given as above, then comes a debate, beginning with the Hillelites asking the Shammaites "Why?" The Shammaites reply, then the Hillelites answer. Finally, the Shammaites give a definitive answer, and the Hillelites change their opinion. The version before us omits the debate but preserves the operative legal rulings. The whole thus is shaped within the *debate*-form, leaving the Shammaites last, and victorious.

Part D, M. Oh. 1:4, refers to the same situation. It ends with the superscription, implying that we have had a Houses-dispute, but the dispute is missing. The subscription is tacked on because the final rule follows the Shammaite view, that the liquid and the dough are clean. But the vessel, the trough, and the woman are unclean, since they can be rendered clean in a ritual bath. The law was framed without reference to Shammaites at all. A tradition containing a contrary Hillelite ruling persisted, so it was important both to assign the anonymous law to the Shammaites and to explain that the Hillelites had accepted the Shammaite view. Then the debate was created to explain the reversion of the Hillelites. Alternatively, the opinions were to begin with attributed to the respective Houses, but when the Shammaite principle was accepted, the "debate" had to explain why.

From a critical viewpoint, the single important result is unchanged: the tradents did *not* drop the inconvenient Hillelite tradition, nor did they assign an opinion which turned out to be the accepted law to the Hillelites, the rejected opinion to the Shammaites. The Hillelite reversion comes after the fact, excellent evidence that the fact has not been doctored.

While the pericopae before us do not constitute a collection, they cannot be called a compilation either, for we are dealing in effect with a single *situation*, spelled out in one detail after another, rather than with a set of laws shaped around a single *principle*. The situation concerns the oven with an arched outlet projecting outside the house, which was overshadowed by corpse-bearers. The Shammaites say everything is unclean. The Hillelites say only the oven becomes unclean. Then the house is given a hatchway and an upper room, and the hatchway is covered by a pot with a hole. The same problem recurs. Then the pot is analyzed. It has no hole at all. What does it then protect through intervening over the hatchway? Finally comes a related situation: a flagon in that same upper room. All of these situations pose problems only within the theory of the Shammaites, that something other than the oven becomes unclean (in the first instance), or that the cooking pot does not protect all from uncleanness, in the third. So the whole collection of pericopae depends upon Shammaite rulings throughout. No wonder, then, that it was necessary to specify that the law follows the Shammaites and that the Hillelites concede. Otherwise, the considerable amplification of cases depending on the Shammaite opinion makes no sense at all.

See Epstein, *Mevo'ot*, pp. 60, 77, 139, 466. He says (p. 60) that reports of the reversion of the Hillelites derive from Joshua, by comparison of M. Oh. 5:3-4, Tos. Ah. 5:10-12, and b. Ḥag. 22b, where it is *Joshua* who reverts. But this would seem to me to indicate that here Joshua is the House of Hillel.

II.i.100.A. [If] a corpse [lay] in a house to which were many entrances, they are all unclean. If one entrance was opened, it [alone] is unclean and the rest are clean.

B. [If there was] intention (ḤŠB) to take out [the corpse] through one of them, or through a window which measured four hand breadths square, it afforded protection (HṢYL) to all other entrances.

The House of Shammai say, "The intention must have been formed (YḤŠWB) before the corpse was dead."

And the House of Hillel say, "[It suffices] even ('P) after it was dead."

C. If an entrance had been blocked up and it was determined (NMLK) to open it—

The House of Shammai say, "[It affords protection to all other entrances only] when he has opened as much as four handbreadths square."

And the House of Hillel say, "So soon as he begins [to open it]."

D. But they agree that if he opens for a first time, he should open four handbreadths [before it can afford protection].

(M. Oh. 7:3, trans. Danby, p. 659)

Comment: The Houses again gloss earlier traditions. In part B the issue is, When does intention (= thought, HŠB) effect protection for the other doors? The House of Shammai say it must come before the man has died; the Hillelites say it may be even afterward. The pericope has the explanatory matter in the Shammaite lemma:

Shammai: [*He must think*] before *he has died.*
Hillel: [Even] after *he has died.*

The italicized words serve both lemmas, and those in brackets constitute an internalized superscription for the Shammaites, redactional matter for the Hillelites.

Part C is a parallel, but different disagreement. If the man plans to open a window, when does the window effect protection for the other entrances? The Shammaites say it must have been completely opened to the requisite space; the House of Hillel say when he begins the work. They agree that it must eventually be opened to four *tefaḥs.*

The formal problem of part C is clear: the lemmas are by no means balanced. But if we recognize that *four tefaḥs* is a gloss, being the opinion of both Houses, the dispute comes down to two words: *when he opens/when he begins* (*KŠYPTḤ, KŠYTḤYL*), a satisfactory balance: √PTḤ vs. √TḤL, P vs. L.

The agreement at the end (D) then appropriately makes use of both verb-roots: when he opens *at first* (KTḤYLH) *he will open* (YPTḤ) four *tefaḥs*, thus built on the roots common to the antecedent dispute, effecting a mnemonic fusion of the two. The agreement moves the Hillelites to the Shammaite position that mere intention is insufficient.

II.i.101.A. If [the whole roof of] a house was split and uncleanness lay [in the house] in the outer side, the vessels [in the house] on the inner side remain clean.

If the uncleanness was within, the vessels outside remain clean if, according to the House of Shammai, the split is four handbreadths wide.

But the House of Hillel say, "[They remain clean] however wide it is."

R. Yosi says in the name of the House of Hillel, "[If it is one] handbreadth."

B. [If he set there] a thick cloak or a thick wooden block, they do not give passage to the uncleanness unless they are raised one handbreadth above the ground. If garments lay folded one above the other, they give passage to the uncleanness so soon as the upper one is raised one handbreadth above the ground.

C. If a man was put there [below the split]—

The House of Shammai say, "He does not give passage (MBY') to the uncleanness."

And the House of Hillel say, "*A man is hollow, and his upper side* does give passage (MBY') to the uncleanness."

D. If a man looked out of the window and overshadowed the corpse-bearers—

The House of Shammai say, "He does not give passage to the uncleanness."

And the House of Hillel say, "He gives passage to the uncleanness."

E. But they agree that if he was wearing his clothes, or if there were two men one above the other, that these give passage to the uncleanness.

F. If a man lay over the threshold and the corpse-bearers overshadowed him—

The House of Shammai say, "He does not give passage to the uncleanness."

And the House of Hillel say, "He gives passage to the uncleanness."

G. If there was uncleanness within the house and they that over shadowed him were clean—

The House of Shammai declare them clean.

And the House of Hillel declare them unclean.

H. If a candlestick stood in the cistern of a house, and its cup projected, and over it was an olive-basket [so placed] that, if the candlestick was taken away, the olive-basket would still stay over the mouth of the cistern—

The House of Shammai say, "The cistern remains clean, but the candlestick is unclean."

The House of Hillel say, "The candlestick also ('P) [remains] clean."

I. But they agree that if the olive-basket would fall in if the candlestick was taken away, all is unclean.

(M. Oh. 11:1, 3, 4, 5, 6, 8, trans. Danby, pp. 665-6)

Comment: Danby's translation of part A, M. Oh. 11:1, obscures the form:

The [roof of the] house which was split:
Uncleanness outside—the vessels inside are clean.
Uncleanness inside, the vessels outside—
House of Shammai say, "*Until there should be in the split* four *tefaḥs*."
House of Hillel say, "Any amount."

That is to say, the vessels outside are not clean, unless the split which divided the house is four *tefaḥs* wide; if less than that, the uncleanness *is* emitted (but not diffused). Excluding the italicized glosses, the opinions are balanced expressions of measurement. Yosi's version of course improves matters, since it yields *four/one*. The Tosefta explains the Hillelite opinion: If the split is as wide as a thread, the vessels outside are clean, since the uncleanness *is* diffused.

The problem is that the roof of the house has been split and divided in two. If the uncleanness is outside—that is, under the part of the roof near the door—the vessels inside are clean, since uncleanness does not enter a house, only exudes from it. The Houses debate the contrary situation.

Part B, M. Oh. 11:3, develops the problem set forth in M. Oh. 11:2:

> If the whole roof of a portico was split and uncleanness lay in it on one side, vessels on the other side remain clean. But if someone set his foot or a reed above the split, he has combined the uncleanness [making the two 'tents' into one, so the uncleanness passes from one side to the other].
>
> If he set the reed on the ground [below the split], it does not allow the uncleanness to pass, unless it is raised a handbreadth above the ground.

Part C, M. Oh. 11:3b, then introduces the problem of a man standing below the split. The House of Shammai hold that between the man and the ground there is not the necessary space of one handbreadth, so the uncleanness does not pass beneath him from one side of the portico to the other. The House of Hillel even "explains" its opinion. The form is perfect, excluding the obvious preliminary gloss of the Hillelite ruling:

If a man was placed there:
House of Shammai say, [He] does not bring the uncleanness.
House of Hillel say, *A man is empty and the upper part* brings the uncleanness.

Without the italicized gloss the Hillelite opinion is simply, *[He] does bring. . .*

Part D, M. Oh. 11:4, contains precisely the same ruling, in the same words, but now with a new superscription. The Hillelite gloss is dropped, but still serves to explain this ruling, as much as the foregoing one. In fact, parts C and D look like duplicates, in which the same principle is discussed through different examples. The clothing is above the earth by a handbreadth, so serves to conduct the uncleanness.

Part F, M. Oh. 11:5, is identical, with a new superscription. The problem is no different.

Part G introduces a new Houses-form: *declare clean, declare unclean.* The problem now is whether the by-passers have been rendered unclean by a man. The Shammaites hold that he cannot convey uncleanness (since he is not hollow), the Hillelites say the contrary, for a consistent reason. So part G in principle is no different from the foregoing.

Part H is a separate item. The Houses agree that the cistern remains clean, so the cistern could have been included in the superscription, leaving a balanced set of lemmas. It would then be:

The candlestick:
House of Shammai declare unclean.
House of Hillel declare clean.

The superscription, to be sure, is rather complex, not a problem of law but a *description* of an unusual situation. But at issue is a point of law, whether the candlestick is protected by the olive-basket. The cup projects but is covered by a basket. The Hillelites hold the basket protects the candlestick and the cup. But if the basket depends on the candlestick, then all agree it does not serve as protection.

We have now seen two composite pericopae in which the Houses dispute a single point of law through a series of examples of ascending complexity or difficulty, M. Oh. 5:1-4 and M. Oh. 11:1-6. These *composites* are different from both the *collections* and the *compilations* isolated above. What the previous forms have in common is that they list a number of rulings, on different legal principles, questions, or problems, and do *not* constitute elaborations of the same principle through different problems. The materials before us, by contrast, do not exhibit a tight and brief, apocopated form, like the collections; and they do not contain appropriate superscriptions, serving more than a single item in the list, like the compilations. The composites have in common the tendency to present an extended superscription, which tells a story or presents a detailed case.

Note Epstein, *Mevo'ot*, pp. 23, 139.

II.i.102.A. If a light-hole is newly made, its measure [that suffices to give passage to uncleanness] is that of a hole made by the drill that lay in the chamber [in the Temple]. The measure of the [unblocked] residue of a light-hole is two fingerbreadths high and one thumb-breadth wide.

By the residue of a light-hole is meant [also] any window which a man blocked up but was not able to finish.

If water had bored the hole, or creeping things, or if it had been eaten through by saltpetre, its measure must be the size of a fist; if a man had intended to make use of it, its measure must be one hand-breadth square; and if to make use of it as a light-hole, its measure must be that of a hole made by the drill.

B. If it is a light-hole covered with grating or latticework—

"The several holes are included together to make up the measure of the hole made by the drill," according to the words of the House of Shammai.

And the House of Hillel say, "There must be one hole having the measure of a hole made by the drill."

C. [If a man] makes a place for a rod or a [weaver's] stave or for a lamp—

"Its measure may be whatsoever [is needful]," according to the words of the House of Shammai.

And the House of Hillel say, "One handbreadth square."

[M. Oh. 13:1, 4, trans. Danby, p. 668 (Sifré Zuṭṭa, Ḥuqat 19:15 ed. Horovitz, p. 311)]

Comment: The Houses dispute whether the several holes are included together or not. The House of Shammai say they are included together to make up the measure of the hole made by the drill. The House of Hillel say one hole must be that large. The language is somewhat difficult:

> The grating and the lattice-work *are joined together as* the hole of the drill (*K*ML' MQDḤ)—according to the words of the House of Shammai.
>
> The House of Hillel say, Until there should be *in one place* the hole of the drill (ML' MQDḤ).

The Houses differ therefore at the italicized words. The *grating—work* and *the measure—drill* serve both Houses. It would have been better for the Hillelite opinion to be a simple negative: *do not join together*. We are not helped by the exceptional form of the attribution to the Shammaites. It looks as though the pericope has been somewhat revised for inclusion in the present pericope. In any event it is clear that the Houses gloss an antecedent legal tradition held in common by all parties.

M. Oh. 2:3 has the same Shammaite opinion, *as much as the hole of the drill* (*K*ML' MQDḤ), and the *K* has been attached here, where it does not belong, by analogy. The Houses here do not disagree on whether the measurement must be approximate (*K*ML') or exact (ML'), so the *K* presents the misleading impression that two disputes are before us.

Part C, M. Oh. 13:4, is a separate matter. It follows the preceding form, presenting the Shammaite attribution at the end of its opinion, rather than at the outset, where it normally comes. The opinions are as balanced as they could be, given the idioms for the differing measurements. *Its measure* serves both Houses. They differ only on *whatsoever* (KL ŠHW') vs. *handbreadth*. Uncleanness will pass through one or another of these spaces in the wall, made for the specified objects.

II.i.103. The forecourt of a tomb-vault—

He who stands in its midst [is] clean, if the space was not less than four cubits (*amot*), according to the words of the House of Shammai.

And the House of Hillel say, "[He remains clean if it measures only] four handbreadths (*tefaḥim*)."

[M. Oh. 15:8, trans. Danby, pp. 671-2 (b. Soṭ. 44a)]

Comment: The Houses-dispute is simply about measurements. It consists of *amot/tefaḥs*, nothing more. The superscription has been assigned *in toto* to the Shammaites, as before. Actually if we stop at the first *four*, and there introduce the Houses-sayings: *amot/tefaḥs*, we have the primary form of the dispute. But no editor could have been satisfied with such an irregular construction, therefore the revision in favor of the form before us.

Note Epstein, *Mevo'ot*, pp. 134, 139, 210; *Mishnah*, p. 1069.)

II.i.104.A. How do they gather the grapes in a Grave-area?

"Men and vessels must be sprinkled the first and the second time; they then gather the grapes and take them out of the Grave-area; others receive the grapes from them and take them to the winepress. If these others touched the grape-gatherers they become unclean"—according to the words of the House of Hillel.

The House of Shammai say, "They hold the sickle with a wrapping of bast, or cut the grapes with a sharp flint, and put them into a large olive-basket and bring them to the winepress."

B. A field of mourners may neither be planted nor sown; but its soil is clean and may be used for making ovens suitable for the Hallowed Things.

And the House of Shammai and the House of Hillel agree that one examines on [behalf of him that would]bring [his] Passover-offering, but not [on behalf of him that would eat] Heave-offering.

D. And for a Nazirite—

The House of Shammai say, "They examine."

And the House of Hillel say, "They do not examine."

E. How is the field examined?

Earth that is easily shifted is taken and put in a sieve that has narrow meshes, and rubbed. If a barleycorn's bulk of bone is found there, [he that has been there] is accounted unclean.

F. What do they examine?

The deep drains and the foul water.

The House of Shammai say, "Also the dunghill and loose earth."

The House of Hillel say, "Wheresoever a pig or weasel can penetrate does not require examination."

[M. Oh. 18:1, 4, 8, trans. Danby, pp. 674-5 (b. Ḥag. 25b; note also Sifré Zuṭṭa, Ḥuqat 19:16, ed. Horovitz, p. 313)]

Comment: The problem of part A, M. Oh. 18:1, is to keep the grapes clean. The reversal of the order of the Houses is a minor problem. The real difficulty is that the opinions of the Houses have nothing whatever to do with one another. Each could have stood apart from the other and would have been completely comprehensible.

The Hillelites provide the following scenario: One sprinkles the men and vessels used for the harvest twice, as if they were unclean by reason of corpse uncleanness. That is, Albeck explains, (*Seder Ṭoharot*, p. 183), to show that they do not lightly treat matters of uncleanness. Then they take the grapes out of the area. The grapes have not been made unclean by the men and vessels which were made unclean in the graveyard. Since there is no choice, the sages did not decree on them the uncleanness of the graveyard. Then others, who are clean and who have not entered the area, take the grapes and bring them to the wine-press, but those who actually gather the grapes do not do so, since it now *is* possible to let others do the work. If the people touched, the grapes are rendered unclean.

The Shammaites tell a different story. One merely interposes wrapping between the sickle and the man, or uses a flint, which does not receive uncleanness, and the man himself, who has not touched the grapes directly, may then bring them to the press.

Yosi then qualifies the foregoing: If a vineyard has been turned into a cemetery, one may make use of the grapes for wine, but otherwise, one may not.

In no way can the opinions of the Houses be matched. They agree that one may take the grapes, but differ on all else. What it comes down to, though, is whether one achieves satisfactory protection by wrapping up the tools or using tools that do not receive uncleanness, as the Shammaites say—and this seems to me the easier way—or whether one must use two sets of workers, with the actual workers clean when they enter the grave-area (even though as soon as they enter, they become unclean). The Houses want to make it clear that an unusual procedure is at hand. This pericope is completely outside the forms we have encountered.

Parts B, C, D, and E, M. Oh. 18:4, are in the wrong order. The agreement of the Houses on the one who makes the *Pesaḥ* and with reference to *Terumah* should have followed the disagreement on the Nazir, thus part D then part C. Part E serves as a gloss for the whole. The Houses lemmas are simply, *they examine/they do not examine*, just as one would expect.

The problem is this: The field was ploughed and a grave has been turned up. A man preparing to offer his *Pesaḥ* has ventured into it. On his account they search the field, as explained in part E, to find out whether or not he has touched a bone and been made unclean, in which case he may not offer his *Pesaḥ*. One does not take that trouble for a priest who eats Heave-offering. As to the Nazir, the House of Shammai say one makes a similar examination, and the House of Hillel take the more stringent position. Even if one finds no bone, the Nazir is unclean and has to be sprinkled. He loses the days of his uncleanness from the number needed to fulfill his Nazirite vow. This is consistent with Hillelite strictness in M. Naz., above, p. 216.

Part F, M. Oh. 18:8, returns to the problem of part E. The Houses' opinions are in the right order. But they again do not relate to one another at all. The Shammaites comment on the foregoing list. The Hillelite saying does not relate to that problem. They simply say what one does *not* have to search, which is irrelevant to the foregoing list, but is relevant to the opening question: What do they examine? The pattern is as follows:

A. What do they examine?
B. Drains and water
  + Shammai: Also dunghill loose earth.
A′. What do they *not* examine?
B′. Hillel: They do not examine places pigs and weasels can get at.

Thus the Houses are not paired in terms either of the form or of the substance of the law.

II.ii.98. A quarter (RWBʿ) [*qab*] of bones from the greater part of the corpse in size, and bones, even though they are less than a quarter [*qab*], are unclean.

R. Judah said [the tradition in] another language:

"The House of Shammai [say], 'A quarter [*qab*] of the bones of the body, from the greater part of the body or from the greater part of the number [of bones], [and] the majority of members and the greater part of the number [of bones] of the corpse, even though they are less than a quarter [*qab*], are unclean. . .' "

R. Joshua said, "I can make the words of the House of Shammai and the words of the House of Hillel [as] one.

"If from the joints and from the thighs there are found the greater part of the larger bones in quantity, and half the greater part of the larger in bones and half the greater part of the number, they do not join together [to form the requisite quantity to convey uncleanness.]"

[Tos. Ahilot 3:4, ed. Zuckermandel, pp. 599 600, lines 37-40, 1-4 (b. Naz. 52b, Sifré Zuṭṭa, Ḥuqat 11)]

Comment: M. Oh. 2:1 says that a quarter-*qab* from the larger bones or the greater number of the bones even if less than that quantity convey uncleanness by overshadowing. We have no hint of a Houses-dispute. M. Oh. 2:3 contains no debate on whether things join together or not. It concerns the lacking links in the backbone, or the hole in a skull. Judah apparently had a tradition of Houses-sayings about M. Oh. 2:1, but he preserved only the Shammaite part.

Compare M. 'Ed. 1:7, and Lieberman, *Tosefet Rishonim*, III, p. 100; Epstein, *Mevo'ot*, p. 118. The version of b. Naz. 52b is as follows (trans. B. D. Klien, p. 196):

II.ii.42. It has been taught:

The House of Shammai say, "A quarter [*qab*] of bones, whether from two [limbs] or from three [is sufficient to cause defilement by overshadowing]."

And the House of Hillel say, "A quarter [*qab* of bones] from a [single] corpse [is required], and [these bones must be derived] from [those bones which form] the greater part [of a skeleton], either in frame or in number."

R. Joshua said, "I can make the statements of the House of Shammai and the House of Hillel one.

"For the House of Shammai say, 'From two or from three, [meaning] either from two shoulders and one thigh, or from two thighs and one shoulder, since this is the major part of a man's structure in height.'

"And the House of Hillel say, '[The quarter *qab* must be taken] from the corpse, from the greater part either in structure or in number, for this [numerical majority] is to be found in the joints of the hands and feet.'

"Shammai says, 'Even a single bone from the backbone or from the skull [defiles by overshadowing]'."

Let us now compare the several versions:

M. 'Ed. 1:7	*M. Oh. 2:1*	*Tos. Ah. 3:4*	*b. Naz. 52b*
1. House of Shammai say	1. —	1. R. Judah says another language: House of Shammai say	1. TNY': House of Shammai say
2. RB' 'ṢMWT MN H'ṢMYM, BYN MŠNYM BYN MŠLŠH Quarter-*qab* of bones, whether of the bones of from two or from three (corpses) [conveys uncleanness by overshadowing.]	2. —	2. RWB' 'ṢMWT MN HGWYH MRWB HBNYN '*W* MRWB HMNYN = 2′, RWB BNYYNW WRWB MNYNW ŠL MT 'P 'L PY Š'YN BHN RWB'	2. RWB' 'ṢMWT MN H'ṢMYM 'W MŠHNYM 'W MŠLŠH
3. And the House of Hillel say, RB' 'ṢMWT MN HGWYH, MRB HBNYN WMRB HMNYN Quarter qab of bones from a [single] corpse, [from bones] which are the greater part in bulk and in number.	3. RB' 'ṢMWT MRB HBYN 'W MRB HMNYN		3. And the House of Hillel say, RWB' MN HGWYH, MRWB HBNYN 'W MRWB HMNYN
4. Shammai says, 'PYLW M'ṢM 'ḤD. Even [a quarter-qab] from one bone	4. —	4. —	4. See below, no. 9.

M. Oh. follows the Hillelite view, but with significant changes. There, *From the corpse* (MN HGWYH) is dropped—the context supplies it. Of greater significance, now it is a matter of choice: it may be *either* bulk *or* ('W) number. M. 'Ed. has *and* (W). Tos. Ah. has Judah assign to the Shammaites the exact words of the Hillelites in M. 'Ed. no. 3, except for the inclusion of *or* ('W) in place of *and*. 2′ looks like a development of the foregoing ruling; now we are told that even less than a *qab* will be sufficient *if* it is from a single corpse, which extends the antecedent rule by dropping quarter-*qab*. No. 2 of b. Naz. is nearly exact; 'W/'W replaces BYN/BYN, not an important change. b. Naz. no. 4 follows M. 'Ed. in specifying *from the corpse*, which M. Oh. leaves out, but it preserves *or* ('W) of M. Oh. Since that difference is substantive, b. Naz. no. 4 seems closer to M. Oh. than to M. 'Ed. As to the sayings of Joshua:

Tos. Ah.	*b. Naz.*
5. R. Joshua said,	5. „ „ „
6. I can make the words of the House of Shammai and the words of the House of Hillel one.	6. „ „ „ *as* one
7. MŠWQYM WMYRKYM NMṢ' RWB BNYNW BGWDL WḤṢY RWB BNYNW WḤṢY RWB MNYNW 'YNN MṢTRPYN (If from the shoulders and from the thighs there are found the greater part of the larger bones in quantity and half the greater part of the larger bones and half the greater part of the number, they do not join together).	7. For the House of Shammai say, MŠNYM 'W MŠLŠH 'W MŠNY ŠWQYM WYRK 'ḤD 'W MŠNY YRKYYM WŠWQ 'ḤD, HW'YL WRWB GWBHW ŠL 'DM MGWBH (From two or three—either from two shoulders and from one thigh or from two thighs and one shoulder since this is the major part of a man's structure in height).
8. —	8. And the House of Hillel say MN HGWYH 'W MRWB BNYN 'W MRWB MNYN HW'YL WYŠNN BMRPQY YDYM WRGLYM (From the corpse, from the greater part either in structure or in number, for this is to be found in the joints of the hands and feet).
9. —	9. Shammai says, Even a bone from the back bone or from the skull.

The Hillelite lemma of no. 4 has no counterpart in Tos. The b. Naz. no. 3 version of Shammai is scarcely related to Tos. Ah. no. 3, except that both make reference to shoulders and thighs. It is difficult to figure out what has happened. Obviously, Tos. Ah. is a defective text, since it ignores the Hillelites and in no way solves the problem of making the Houses say the same thing. b. Naz. is so slightly related to Tos. Ah. that it looks as though the editor of the *beraita* has simply worked things out on his own.

II.ii.99.A. If a woman [in the upper room, referred to in M. Oh. 5:4] was kneading in one trough, and her hands were busy in the dough, so long as she is raising this and putting down this, raising this and putting down this, the woman and the trough are unclean a seven-day uncleanness, but the dough is clean. If she removed her hand from it and returned it [the hand], it is unclean and makes the dough unclean.

B. R. Joshua said, "I am ashamed by your words, House of Shammai. Is it possible that the woman and the trough are unclean for seven days and the dough is clean? And that the flagon [M. Oh. 5:4] should contract seven-days uncleanness and the liquid should remain clean?"

C. After he stood up, a certain disciple from the disciples of the House of Shammai said before him, "Rabbi, May I say before you a reason (Ṭ'M) that the House of Shammai say concerning it?"

He said to him, "Speak."

"The vessel of an *'am ha'areṣ*, what is it, unclean or clean?"

He said to him, "Unclean."

"And does something unclean protect? If so, let this thing protect the vessels of a *ḥaver*.

D. "Another matter: And if an *'am ha'areṣ* says to you concerning his vessel that it is unclean, when we purified the food and liquid in it, we have purified [the thing] for himself, but when we have purified the vessel, we have purified for you and for him."

E. R. Joshua reverted to teach according to the words of the disciple.

F. R. Joshua said, "I bow (NM) to you, bones of the House of Shammai."

[Tos. Ah. 5:11, ed. Zuckermandel, pp. 602-3, lines 39, 1-9 (b. Ḥag. 22a)]

Comment: See M. Oh. 5:4, (II.i.99.D), in which the law of part A appears in somewhat different form. The Mishnah is not attributed to the House of Shammai, but by implication, as we saw above, it is a Shammaite saying. Now Joshua treats it as such and points out the anomaly.

Part D appears in M. 'Ed. 1:14 = b. Ḥag. 22b, as a Houses-dispute, and concerns the Shammaite rule that an earthenware vessel can protect only foodstuffs, liquids, and other earthenware vessels (M. Kel. 3:10). The case before us does not occur there. Joshua points out the (usual) Shammaite inconsistency.

For our present purpose, it suffices to note that the House of Hillel in M. 'Ed. 1:14, and, by implication, the unstated Hillelite opinion of M. Oh. 5:4 in fact are to be attributed to Joshua. Eliezer plays no part, presumably because he was dead, and the reference to the "bones of the House of Shammai" of part F might be to the deceased Eliezer. This pericope apparently derives not from the pre-70 Houses but from Joshua and Eliezer. See Epstein, *Mevo'ot*, p. 60.

III.ii.43.A. For we have learned: "An earthenware vessel protects everything [therein from contracting uncleanness from a corpse that is under the same roof]," so the House of Hillel.

The House of Shammai say, "It protects only foodstuffs and liquids and [other] earthenware vessels."

B. Said the House of Hillel to the House of Shammai, "Wherefore?"

The House of Shammai answered, "Because it is unclean on account of the *ʿam haʾareṣ*, and an unclean vessel cannot interpose."

C. Said the House of Hillel to them, "But have you not declared the foodstuffs and liquids therein clean?"

The House of Shammai answered, "When we declared the foodstuffs and liquids therein clean, we declared them clean [only] for [the *ʿam haʾareṣ*] himself; but should we [therefore] declare [also] the vessel clean, which would make it clean for you as well as for him?"

D. It is taught:

R. Joshua said, "I am ashamed of your words, O House of Shammai! Is it possible that if a woman [in the upper chamber] kneads [dough] in a trough, the woman and the trough become unclean for seven days, but the dough remains clean; that if there is [in the upper room] a flask full of liquid, the flask contracts seven-day uncleanness, but the liquid remains clean!"

E. [Thereupon] one of the disciples of the House of Shammai joined him [in debate] and said to him, "I will tell you the reason of the House of Shammai."

He replied, "Tell!"

So he said to him, "Does an unclean vessel bar [the penetration of uncleanness] or not?"

He replied, "It does not bar it."

"Are the vessels of an *ʿam haʾareṣ* clean or unclean?"

He replied, "Unclean."

"And if you say to him [that they are] unclean, will he pay any heed to you? Nay, more, if you say to him [that they are] unclean, he will reply, Mine are clean and yours are unclean. Now this is the reason of the House of Shammai."

Forthwith, R. Joshua went and prostrated himself upon the graves of the House of Shammai. He said, "I crave your pardon, O bones of the House of Shammai. If your unexplained teachings are so [excellent], how much more so the explained teachings!"

It is said that all his days his teeth were black by reason of his fasts.

(b. Ḥag. 22a-b, trans. Israel Abrahams, pp. 140-142)

Comment: The author of the *beraita* has greatly improved the version of Mishnah-Tosefta. The various versions compare as follows:

M. Oh. 5:4	*M. 'Ed. 1:14*	*Tos. Ah. 5:11*
1. A woman who was kneading in the trough	1. —	1. The woman who was kneading in a trough and her hands were busy with the dough, so long as she is raising up this and putting down this [duplicated]
2. The woman and the trough are unclean a seven day uncleanness	2. —	2. „ „ „
3. and the dough is clean	3. —	3. „ „ „
4. And if she emptied it into another vessel, unclean.	4. —	4. She removed her hands from it and put it back, she is unclean and renders unclean the dough.
5. The House of Hillel reverted to teach according to the words of the House of Shammai.	5. [Below, no. 10]	5. [Below]
6. —	6. An earthenware vessel protects all, according to the words of the House of Hillel. And the House of Shammai say, It protects only food, liquid, and an earthenware vessel.	6. —
7. —	7. The House of Hillel said to them, Why?	7. R. Joshua said, I am ashamed by your words, House of Shammai. Is it possible that the woman and the trough are unclean for seven days [similarly vessels]? After he arose, one disciple of the House of Shammai said to him, Rabbi, May I say before you the reason that the House of Shammai say concerning it? He said to him, Speak.
8. —	8. The House of Shammai said to them, Because it is unclean with ('L GB) an *'am ha'areṣ*, and an un-	8. He said to him, The vessel of *'am ha'areṣ*, what is it, unclean or clean? I shall say to him,

M. Oh. 5:4	*M. 'Ed. 1:14*	*Tos. Ah. 5:11*
	clean vessel does not protect (ḤṢṢ)	Unclean. And does unclean protect (MṢYL)? If so, let this one protect the vessels of a *ḥaver*.
9. —	9. The House of Hillel said to them, Have you not declared clean the food and liquids which are in it? The House of Shammai said to them, When we declared clean the food and liquids which are in it, for himself we declared unclean; but when you declared clean the vessel, you declared clean for you and for him.	9. Another matter: If an *'am ha'areṣ* says to you concerning his vessel that it is unclean, when we declare clean the food and liquids in it, himself have we declared clean, but when we declare the vessel clean, we declare it clean for you and for him.
10. —	10. „ „ „ [= M. Oh. no. 5]	10. R. Joshua reverted to teach (ŠNH) according to the words of the disciple. R. Joshua said, I bow to you, bones of the House of Shammai.

We see that M. 'Ed. presents the colloquy of Joshua and the "disciple" as a Houses' dispute, and reduces the whole to a few simple propositions. There can be no doubt that the M. 'Ed. version of the debate summarizes Tos. Ah. and makes it conform to the usual style. Thus M. 'Ed. hides the name of Joshua in "House of Hillel." b. Ḥag. cites M. 'Ed. without significant change, then adds, under the superscription TNY', the Toseftan story—now giving *both* versions and greatly expanding the latter. In general, the *beraita* closely follows Tos., but improves the diction of the conversation between Joshua and the disciple. The concluding passage is, as usual, substantially improved. Joshua now says N'NYTY instead of the apparently less clear NMTY (reminiscent of the changes of the Simeon the Righteous-use of the same verb NM, N'M, etc. See vol, I, pp. 44-47.)

II.ii.100.A R. Judah says, "He who opens at the outset [an entrance to remove a corpse, so effecting protection for the other entrances of the room in which the corpse is lying, as in M. Oh. 7:3]—

"The House of Shammai say, 'When he opens four *tefaḥs*.'

"And the House of Hillel say, 'When he begins.'

B. "He who opens a blocked-up passage—

"The House of Shammai say, 'When he begins.'

"And the House of Hillel say, 'When he thinks [of doing it, it affords protection]'."

(Tos. Ah. 8:7, ed. Zuckermandel, p. 605, 1. 40, p. 606, lines 1:2)

Comment: M. Oh. 7:3 is somewhat different. There the first argument concerns *when* he must have given thought to opening the door or window to remove the corpse. The Shammaites say it must be before the man has died; the House of Hillel, even afterward.

The second argument, concerning a blocked window or door, is accurately represented here. The Houses agree that when he opens at the outset, he must open four *tefaḥs*. But now Judah has that unanimous opinion in the name of the House of Shammai only. The opinion of the House of Hillel duplicates the first Shammaite opinion, but makes sense as a separate argument on the first point: he does not have to open completely at the outset, merely to begin the project. Judah the Patriarch has compressed the two arguments into the second argument of M. Oh. 7:3. For our purpose Judah b. Ilai supplies a *terminus ante quem* to M. Oh. 7:3: middle second-century.

II.ii.101. [M. Oh. 11:1: If the uncleanness was within, the vessels outside remain clean until there should be in the split four *tefaḥs*, according to the House of Shammai. The House of Hillel say, "(They remain clean) however wide it is."]

And how much must this split (ŚDQ) be?

The House of Hillel say, "However wide it is (KL ŠHW')—*the thickness of a plummet-string.*"

And R. Yosi says in the name of the House of Hillel, "An opening of a *tefaḥ*."

[Tos. Ah. 12:1, ed. Zuckermandel, p. 609, lines 29-30 (Compare Sifré Zuṭṭa, Ḥuqat 19:15, ed. Horovitz, p. 311)]

Comment: Judah the Patriarch has taken the anonymous version and has ignored both the gloss (in italics) and Yosi. Again we have a mid-second-century *terminus*. See Lieberman, *Tosefet Rishonim* III, p. 129-130.

II.ii.102. [He who makes a place for a rod or a stave, as M. Oh. 13:4]—

The House of Shammai say, "Its thickness."

And the House of Hillel say, "One handbreadth [*tefaḥ*] square."

(Tos. Ah. 14:4, ed. Zuckermandel, p. 611, lines 29-30)

Comment: See M. Oh. 13:4. The lamp of M. Oh. 13:4 is given anonymously; its measure is the same as the Hillelites', a *tefaḥ*. The Tos. tradition therefore limits the dispute to the first two items on the list. See Lieberman, *Tosefet Rishonim* III, pp. 137-8.

II.ii.103.A. If he made a bottle filled with [clean] liquid and tightly stoppered as a plug for a grave—

R. Eliezer b. R. Simeon said, "In this the House of Shammai declare unclean, and the House of Hillel declare clean.

B. "The House of Shammai said to the House of Hillel, 'And which is likely to receive uncleanness, a man or the liquid?'

"They said to them, 'Liquid [for man is made unclean only by a Father of Uncleanness].'

"They said to them, 'Now since if man, who is not likely to receive uncleanness, touched it [= the bottle], he is made unclean, the liquid which is in it [the bottle], ought it not become unclean?'

"The House of Hillel said to them, 'Do you not agree concerning a clean man who swallowed a clean ring and entered the tent of a corpse, even though he is unclean for seven days, the ring is [still] clean?'

"The House of Shammai said to them, 'No, if you say concerning the ring, which does not become unclean by the carrying of a *Zab*, will you say so of liquid, which does become unclean by the carrying of a *Zab*?'

"The House of Hillel said to them, 'We reason the seven day uncleanness from the seven-day uncleanness, and you reason the seven day uncleanness from an evening's uncleanness. It is better to reason a seven day uncleanness from a seven day uncleanness than to reason a seven day uncleanness from an evening's uncleanness. . .' "

(Tos. Ah. 15:9, ed. Zuckermandel, p. 613, lines 5-15)

Comment: See M. Oh. 15:9, which omits the Houses. The debate form is not closely followed. The whole may be attributed to Eliezer and represents a later fabrication of a Houses-dispute.

II.ii.104. He who searches—

"The House of Shammai say, 'He searches two ['*amahs*] and leaves an '*amah*.'

"And the House of Hillel say, 'He searches an '*amah* and leaves an '*amah*' "—the words of R. 'Aqiba.

And the sages say, "The House of Shammai say, 'He searches an *'amah* and leaves an *'amah*,' and the House of Hillel say, 'He searches an *'amah* and leaves two *'amahs*.' "

(Tos. Ah. 16:6, ed. Zuckermandel, p. 614, lines 14-17)

Comment: 'Aqiba supplies the *terminus ante quem* for the debate, which has no counterpart in M. Oh. 18:4 or 18:8. The dispute of 'Aqiba and the sages, however, may well concern an antecedent mnemonic tradition. 'Aqiba has *two/one*, the sages *one/two*, and the whole can be reconstructed from that simple disagreement about the bare bones of the tradition. The passage occurs in M. Oh. 16:4, as 'Aqiba's version of the Hillelite opinion, with no contrary opinions.

II.ii.105. If one cut grapes in this grave-area, he should not cut grapes in another grave-area, and if he cut grapes, he is unclean—these are the words of the House of Hillel.

(Tos. Ah. 17:9, ed. Zuckermandel, p. 616, lines 1-3)

Comment: See M. Oh. 18:1.

II.ii.106. The House of Shammai agree with the House of Hillel: "They do not search [a field on account of] *Terumah*, but it is burned."

(Tos. Ah. 17:13, ed. Zuckermandel, p. 616, lines 14-15)

Comment: II.ii.106 corresponds to the unanimous opinion given in M. Oh. 18:4, that one does not search on behalf of him that would eat Heave-offering. Here the disposition of the Heave-offering is explained.

II.i.105. The lid of a kettle which is joined to the chain—

The House of Shammai say, '[It counts as a] connective for [contracting] uncleanness, but not [as] a connective for sprinkling (ḤBWR LHZYH)."

The House of Hillel say, "[If a man] sprinkled on the kettle, he has sprinkled on the lid. [If he] sprinkled on the lid, he has not sprinkled on the kettle."

(M. Par. 12:10, trans. Danby, p. 713)

Comment: The Shammaites hold that the chain produces uncleanness for the kettle, but for sprinkling to effect purification, one must sprinkle the lid as well as the kettle. The House of Hillel say sprinkling the kettle affects the lid, but not contrarywise. The Hillelite position is therefore not completely contrary to the Shammaite one, for the chain can serve to connect the kettle to the lid when the *kettle* is sprinkled for cleanness, but not when the *lid* is sprinkled. The position completely contrary to the Shammaite one would have had the chain serving as a connector for sprinkling, no matter what is sprinkled (lid, kettle). Perhaps that accounts for the absence of a balanced pericope, which would have been,

It is a connector for uncleanness *and* it is a connector for sprinkling.

Given the complexity of the Hillelite position, one could probably not have produced a more succinct statement than the one before us.

II.ii.107. [M. Par. 5:1: He that brings the earthenware vessel for (the water or the ashes of) the sin-offering must immerse himself and spend the night by the furnace. . . .For a jar that is to contain Heave-offering the potter may open the furnace and take out (any jar). R. Simeon says, "Only from the second row." R. Yosi says, "Only from the third row."]

R. Simeon b. Judah says in the name of R. Simeon, "The House of Shammai say, 'From the third row,' and the House of Hillel say, 'From the second row.' "

(Tos. Par. 5:1, ed. Zuckermandel, p. 634, lines 19-20)

Comment: R. Simeon b. Judah's tradition has placed the second-century master's opinions in the mouth of the Houses.

II.ii.108.A. The lid of a kettle attached by a chain—

The House of Shammai say, "They are all one connection."

And the House of Hillel say, "If he sprinkled the pot, he has sprinkled the lid. If he has sprinkled the lid, he has not sprinkled the pot."

B. R. Yosi said, "These are the words of the House of Shammai. The House of Hillel say, 'The vessel (KLY) is one connection.' "

(Tos. Par. 12:18, ed. Zuckermandel, p. 641, lines 9-12)

Comment: Part A corresponds to M. Par. 12:10, and the House of Hillel's lemma is given verbatim. The House of Shammai's saying is not accurately represented, for here no distinction is made between contracting uncleanness and sprinkling—the connection serves both equally. Yosi's version of the Hillelite opinion would have nicely served for M. Par. 12:10, as I pointed out above, for there the Hillelites would more conveniently take a position diametrically opposite the Shammaite one. Yosi sets the *terminus ante quem*.

II.i.106.A. From what time do olives receive uncleanness?

"After they exude the moisture that comes out of them when they are in the vat (Z'T M'TN), but not the moisture that comes out of them when they are yet in the store-basket (Z'T HQPH)," according to the words of the House of Shammai.

R. Simeon says, "The prescribed time for the moisture [before it renders the olives susceptible to uncleanness] is three days."

The House of Hillel say, "After there is moisture enough for three olives to stick together (MŠYTḤBRW ŠLŠH ZH LZH)."

Rabban Gamaliel says, "After the preparation is finished."

And the sages say according to his words.

B. If a man left his olives in the basket to grow soft so that they may be easy to press, they [then] become susceptible to uncleanness.

But if to grow soft so that they may be salted, the House of Shammai say, "They become susceptible (MWKŠRYM)."

And the House of Hillel say, "They do not become susceptible ('YNN MWKŠRYM)."

C. If he wanted to take from them [only enough for] one pressing or for two pressings—

The House of Shammai say, "He may set apart (QWṢH) [what he needs] in [a condition of] uncleanness, but he must cover up (MḤPH) [what he takes] in [a condition of] cleanness."

The House of Hillel say, "He may also ('P) cover it up in a condition of uncleanness."

R. Yosi says, "He may [even] dig out [what he needs] with a metal axe and take the olives to the press in [a condition of] uncleanness."

(M. Ṭoh. 9:1, 5, 7, trans. Danby, pp. 729-30)

Comment: In *Part A*, M. Ṭoh. 9:1, the Houses' opinions in no way match. The issue is, When does the moisture render the olives capable of receiving uncleanness? The Shammaites say that the moisture that comes out of the olives in the vat renders them unclean, but not that which comes when they still are in the basket during the harvest. Simeon says the moisture that comes out in the vat before they have been there three days does not render them unclean. This seems to revise the Shammaite rule. The House of Hillel say that the olives are unclean only when the moisture has caused them to stick together in a mass—later than the time specified by the Shammaites, who hold the mere presence of moisture suffices. Gamaliel assigns a still later time, namely, when all the work is done, and the olives are ready to be taken to the crusher.

In this pericope, no effort has been made to frame the Houses' opinions in syzygies or in the normal forms. Presumably it would have been possible to specify a particular time, e.g., a number of days (as Simeon), rather than a particular condition. In any event the dispute comes from the time of Gamaliel, hence is a Yavnean pericope which, strikingly, in no way follows the Houses-forms used for other Yavnean materials. This suggests that in the earliest period the standard form was not carefully followed, while later on it was perfected.

Part B, M. Ṭoh. 9:5, is a more routine pericope, in which the Houses gloss the foregoing rule, and their superscription depends upon that rule:

That they may stand so he may salt them
House of Shammai: They are prepared [to receive uncleanness, MWKŠRYM]
House of Hillel: They are not prepared.

The issue is the same as in M. Ṭoh. 9:1: Is the liquid going to prepare the olives to receive uncleanness? The man intends to eat the olives after they are salted, but not to produce oil from them. Since the man does not *want* the moisture, it is not regarded as a liquid-food and therefore cannot receive uncleanness, so the Hillelites. The Shammaites do not pay attention to the man's intention, just as they ignore intention in the vow of the Nazir, and the consecration—even in error—of objects to the sanctuary.

Part C, M. Ṭoh. 9:7, concerns olives *not* ready to receive uncleanness. In case the farmer wants only part of the olives, the House of Shammai say he may set apart what he needs in a condition of uncleanness for a pressing or two, since the olives are not thereby made ready to receive uncleanness. But he must cover up the olives in cleanness to bring them to the press, for their work has been completed, and they are now ready to receive uncleanness. The Hillelites do not require him to cover in cleanness, for they hold the olives have not yet been made ready to receive uncleanness, though if he plans to take the whole mass to the press, he must do so in a condition of cleanness. Yosi takes a more extreme position than either House, and supplies a *terminus ante quem* for the rest.

The form is not quite balanced. All parties agree that he may set apart in uncleanness, so the issue concerns covering up only. If *cut off* and *cover up* were in the superscription, we should have the following:

If he wants to take from them enough for a pressing or two, he sets apart in uncleanness, and he covers
House of Shammai: In cleanness
House of Hillel: In uncleanness.

The difference between such a simple form and the more complex one resulting from the inclusion of part of the superscription in the Shammaite lemma is not consequential.

II.i.107.A. If a man put [grapes into the wine-press] from what was [stored] in baskets or from what was spread out on the ground—

The House of Shammai say, "He must put them in with clean hands. And if he put them in with unclean hands, he renders them unclean."

And the House of Hillel say, "He puts them in with unclean hands. And he must set apart his Heave-offering in cleanness."

B. All agree that [whether he takes them] from the grape-basket or from what are spread out on leaves, he must put them into the wine-press with clean hands. If he put them in with unclean hands, he renders them unclean.

(M. Ṭoh. 10:4, trans. Danby, p. 731)

Comment: The law concerns taking grapes from baskets and putting them in the press. The House of Shammai say it must be done with clean hands, lest the farmer touch the liquid coming out of the grapes and render them unclean. The House of Hillel rule, as above, that that moisture is not regarded as liquid capable of receiving uncleanness, since the man has no intention of using the moisture for food. The form is heavily glossed:

He who places from baskets, etc.

House of Shammai say, He places with clean hands *and if he placed with unclean hands, he has rendered them unclean.*

House of Hillel say, He places with unclean hands *and he separates his Heave-offering in cleanness.*

The italicized words in the Shammaite lemma are a gloss, making obvious what is already clear. The Hillelite gloss supplies a separate law, something we should not have known on the basis of a simple disagreement with the Shammaite lemma. The Shammaites obviously would agree. Hence while the Hillelite lemma contains two rules, the latter could have been set into a superscription, or, more aptly, as a subscription, *And they agree that he separates.*

Part B would have been the logical place for the foregoing agreement. It says *all agree* (HKL ŠWYN) rather than the more common, *And they agree* (WMWDYN). This limits the Hillelite position once again, so the form was ideal for the inclusion of the foregoing detail.

The pericope evidently is highly developed and diverges from the normal forms used for the purpose of recording both disputes and agreements.

II.ii.109.A. If one left his vessels before an *ʿam haʾareṣ* and said to him, "Guard these for me," they are unclean *midraś*- and corpse-uncleanness. If he left them on his shoulder, they are unclean *midraś* [and] corpse-uncleanness.

B. R. Dosetai b. R. Yannai said, "The House of Shammai and the House of Hillel did not differ concerning one who gives (MŚR) [them] to an individual, that they are unclean, and concerning one who leaves (MNYḤ) them in public, that they are clean.

"Concerning what did they disagree?

"Concerning one who gives them in public and leaves them with an individual, for—

"The House of Shammai declare unclean.

"And the House of Hillel declare clean."

(Tos. Ṭoh. 8:9b-10, ed. Zuckermandel p. 669, lines 19-22)

Comment: Dosetai, who comes at the beginning of the second century, reports a Houses-dispute for which we have no other attestation. The Houses dispute an ambiguous situation, and they take or are assigned the usual positions. A sage coming in the second century could readily refer to, e.g., Joshua and Eliezer as the House of Hillel and Shammai, and we have no reason to believe Dosetai held an independent tradition from Temple times. See Lieberman, *Tosefet Rishonim* IV, p. 86.

II.ii.110. R. Simeon b. Gamaliel says, "When their work is done [they receive uncleanness]," and the law is according to his words.

He who completes his olives in the same day [they are picked]—we have returned to the words of the House of Shammai and the House of Hillel.

(Tos. Ṭoh. 10:1-2, ed. Zuckermandel, p. 671, lines 8-9)

Comment: In M. Ṭoh. 9:1, it is Gamaliel. The clause pertaining to the Houses alleges that their difference pertains only to completing the whole process in a single day, but otherwise they are in agreement. See Lieberman, *Tosefet Rishonim* IV, pp. 93-4.

II.i.108. When are they again deemed clean (M'YMTY ṬHRTN)?

The House of Shammai say, "After they have been increased [by more than the like quantity of rain] *and* overflowed."

The House of Hillel say, "After they have been increased [by more than the like quantity of rain], even though they have not overflowed."

R. Simeon b. Gamaliel says, "After they have overflowed, even though they have not increased."

(M. Miq. 1:5, trans. Danby, p. 733)

Comment: The question pertains to a pool which has been made unclean by a man, or into which a corpse has fallen (M. Miq. 1:4). The pool may be deemed clean when sufficient rain has fallen into it. The House of Shammai hold that when most of the water in the pool is rain-water *and* it has overflowed, it is regarded as clean. The House of Hillel say it need not overflow to be deemed clean.

The question, When are they again deemed clean? (M'YMTY ṬHRTN) appears above, p. 257. Here the opinions of the Houses are clearly balanced, but the Hillelite one is slightly apocopated:

House of Shammai: MŠYRBW WYŠṬPW
House of Hillel: RBW, 'P 'L PY ŠL' ŠṬPW.

The Hillelites' first verb ought to have the same form as the Shammaites'; dropping the MŠ makes the Hillelite lemma depend on the foregoing. R. Simeon b. Gamaliel takes the third position, that if it *overflows* even though it has not been so *increased*, it is sufficiently clean for *Ḥallah* and for washing hands. So the Hillelite position is given with precision and could not have been made simpler in any detail, e.g., by dropping the *even though* clause.

II.i.109.A. If a man put vessels under the water-spout [that feeds the Immersion-pool],—it is all one whether they are large vessels or small vessels or even vessels of cattle-dung, vessels of stone or vessels of [unburnt] clay—they render the Immersion-pool invalid.

B. It is all one whether they were set there or left in forgetfulness, according to the words of the House of Shammai.

And the House of Hillel declare it clean (MṬHRYN) [if they were left] in forgetfulness.

C. R. Meir said, "They voted, and the House of Shammai outnumbered the House of Hillel.

"And they agree that if they were left in forgetfulness in the courtyard [and not under the water-spout], it is clean."

D. R. Yosi said, "The dispute still stands where is was—[= as in A]."

(M. Miq. 4:1, trans. Danby, p. 736)

Comment: Since drawn water spoils the ritual pool, the intervening vessels spoil the water, hence the pool. The Houses-dispute glosses the foregoing, raising the issue of whether intent changes matters. The House of Shammai say that intent does not matter, just as they said erroneously consecrating objects to the sanctuary is a valid consecration. The form is not standard:

It is all the same for one who leaves and for one who forgets ('ḤD HMNYḤ W'ḤD HŠWKḤ)—according to the words of the House of Shammai.

The House of Hillel declare clean (ṬHR) in the case of one who forgets (BŠWKḤ).

In fact, the Hillelite lemma uses the wrong verb, for the problem is not whether it is clean (ṬHR), but whether it is fit (KŠR). Further, an obvious balance would have been:

As to one who forgets,
House of Shammai declare unfit (PWŚLYN)
House of Hillel declare fit (MKŚYRYN).

Then all agree that *he who intentionally leaves* etc. The syzygy *KŠR/PŚL* recurs through the tractate. Its absence here is therefore remarkable, especially since it would have been natural to include it.

Meir then glosses the Houses' dispute, quoting the stock-phrase about the vote. The agreement now is attributed to Meir. If the man forgot the vessels in the courtyard but not under the water-spout, and the vessels are filled with water, the water does not spoil the bath, since he certainly did not intend to draw the water. But when the man forgot the vessels under the water spout, the House of Shammai suppose that, when he left them there, he intended to receive in them rainwater, *then* he forgot them, so it is as if he intended to draw the water. The water that has spilled into the pool is drawn water (Albeck, *Seder Ṭoharot*, p. 350). Yosi then differs with his contemporary, and says that even here the Houses differ. The Shammaites regard the water that has spilled into the pool as sufficient to render it unfit.

How much earlier than Meir and Yosi is the Houses-dispute to be dated? The second-century sages had differing versions of the dispute, so we may assume their traditions go back for a while. Meir's use of the stock-phrase indicates only that by his time it was routine to refer to it, especially when one wanted to assign the correct law to the Shammaites. If so, by Meir's time the decided law conformed to the Shammaite position. Yosi does not differ, merely extends the Shammaite position—therefore the decided law—to the case of the courtyard as well.

See Epstein, *Mevo'ot*, pp. 24, 147.

II.i.110.A. A trough hewn in the rock—they may not gather the water into it, or mix [the ashes] therein, or sprinkle from it; it does not need a tightly stopped-up cover, nor does it render an immersion-pool invalid.

If it was a movable vessel, although it had been joined [to the ground] with lime, they may gather water into it or mix the ashes therein or sprinkle from it; and it needs a tightly stopped-up cover; and it renders an immersion-pool invalid.

If there was a hole in it below or at the side such that it can hold no water at all, the water is valid. How large need the hole be? As large as the spout of a water-skin.

B. R. Judah b. Bathyra said, "It once happened that (M'SH B) the Trough of Jehu which was in Jerusalem had in it a hole as big as the spout of a water-skin, and all the acts in Jerusalem requiring cleanness were done [after immersing the vessels] therein ('L GBH).

"And the House of Shammai sent and broke it down (PḤT) for—

"The House of Shammai say, '[It is still to be accounted a vessel] until the greater part of it is broken down (YPḤT)'."

[M. Miq. 4:5, trans. Danby, p. 737 (b. Yev. 15a)]

Comment: There were two Judah b. Bathyras, one of whom lived in Temple times and was a Temple agent in Nisibis (see my *History*, Vol. I^2, pp. 46-52 and 130-134). If this is the same man, then he presumably knew what he was talking about, and the story is genuine.

Since only the Pharisees required cleanness outside of the Temple cult in connection with the preparation of ordinary, unconsecrated food, we may assume that the Trough here referred to served primarily the Pharisaic party in Jerusalem, which therefore could not have been very numerous. The Shammaites, who probably predominated, had the power to do just what Judah said they had done. We do not have the contrary, Hillelite lemma, but it obviously is represented in part A. The story raises the question of what was the state of objects immersed before the Shammaites imposed their will. Can we imagine that for decades, even centuries, matters did not conform to the law as the Shammaites taught it, until "one day" the Shammaites sent and broke the trough into sufficiently small parts? Or is it possible that the Shammaites did not approve of matters, but were able to change matters only when they came to power? If the latter, then they presumably came to power some decades before the destruction, but we do not know the state of affairs, or of the law, before that time. Judah does not refer to Hillelite opposition. His little story may well describe something that actually happened, and I think it does, but if so, it raises more problems than it settles.

II.i.111.A. The House of Shammai say, "They immerse vessels in a rain-stream."

The House of Hillel say, "They do not immerse."

B. But they agree that [a man] dams it with vessels and immerses therein, but the vessels by which he dammed it are not thereby immersed.

(M. Miq. 5:6b, trans. Danby, p. 738)

Comment: The form is perfect. Beforehand comes a list of places where one may immerse: trenches, ditches, donkey-tracks. A slight alteration would have taken the *rain-stream* from the Shammaite lemma and set it as a superscription. The Shammaites require forty *se'ahs* of water in the whole stream. The Hillelites say one must have forty *se'ahs* standing in one place. The agreement of the Hillelites is that a dam will establish such a collection of water in the rain-stream. But the vessels themselves, the Hillelites say, have not been cleansed, since the backs of the vessels, in the stream, are outside of the dam. The agreement thus is phrased entirely from the Hillelite viewpoint. The authority is Yosi, M. ʿEd. 5:2; Epstein, *Mevo'ot*, p. 147.

II.i.112. The House of Shammai say, "They do not immerse hot water in cold, or cold water in hot, or fresh water in foul, or foul water in fresh."

And the House of Hillel say, "They do immerse."

(M. Miq. 10:6, trans. Danby, p. 744)

Comment: The different kinds of water must be alike so that they are fully merged. The superscription is inserted into the Shammaite lemma. Originally the Houses-sayings would have been *immerse/not immerse*, just as above, M. Miq. 5:6.

II.ii.111. [When are they deemed clean, as M. Miq. 1:5]

Rains came down—

"They were increased [by more than the like quantity of rain] *and* overflowed"—according to the words of the House of Shammai.

And according to the words of the House of Hillel say [sic], "They were increased [by more than the like quantity of rain] *even though* they did *not* overflow."

And according to the words of R. Ṣimeon, "They overflowed even though they were not increased [by more than the like quantity of rain]."

—they are fit for *Ḥallah* and for *Terumah* and to wash the hands therein.

(Tos. Miq. 1:7, 1:10, ed. Zuckermandel, p. 652, line 37, 653, lines 1-2, and p. 653, lines 10-12)

Comment: See M. Miq. 1:5. Here the same verb, RWB, is assigned to all three lemmas.

II.ii.112. A kneading trough which is filled with pots, and he dipped it into the ritual pool, requires a hole the size of the spout of a water-skin and a fountain of any size.

R. Judah says in the name of the House of Shammai, "For a large vessel, [the whole should be equal to] four *tefaḥs* according to the greater part of it."

(Tos. Miq. 5:2, ed. Zuckermandel, p. 657, lines 1-3)

Comment: Judah's saying appears in M. Miq. 6:5, as follows:

Vessels may not be immersed in a box or a chest that is in the sea unless there was in them a hole the size of the spout of a water skin.

R. Judah says, "If it was a large vessel [the hole] must be four handbreadths; if a small vessel, the hole should be equal to the greater part of it."

Judah's saying is given defectively. Clearly, the concluding clause *according to the greater part* should be assigned to small vessels, just as the four *tefaḥs* is assigned to a large vessel. (See Lieberman, *Tosefet Rishonim* IV p. 21.)

II.i.113.A. Women may always be assumed clean in readiness for their husbands. When men have come in from a journey their wives may be assumed clean in readiness for them.

B. The House of Shammai say, "She needs two test-rags for every act; or [on every occasion] she should perform it [intercourse] by the light of a lamp (TŠMŠ L'WR HNR)."

And the House of Hillel say, "Two test-rags suffice her throughout the night (DYYH BŠNY 'DYM KL HLYLH)."

C. Five [kinds of] bloods are unclean in a woman: red, and black, and bright crocus color, and a color like earthy water, and like mixed [water and wine].

The House of Shammai say, "Also a color like water in which fenugreek had been soaked and a color like the juice that comes out of roast flesh."

And the House of Hillel declare clean.

[M. Nid. 2:4, 6, trans. Danby, pp. 746-7 (y. Ned. 2:4, 6, b. Nid. 11b, 16a-b, 19a)]

Comment: Part A, M. Ned. 2:4: M. Nid. 2:1 states, "It is the way of the daughters of Israel when they have sexual relations to use two test rags, one for him and one for her." The Houses' dispute, part B, here is out of place, for it pertains to, and glosses, that law (2:1), *not* the foregoing element (A) of its own pericope. The Shammaites hold that the examination must follow each act of intercourse, or she should make use of a lamp. The Hillelites say the examination may take place in the morning. The form is not balanced:

House of Shammai: [She needs] *two test-rags* for each act of intercourse (or she makes use of the light of the candle).

House of Hillel: [It is sufficient for her with] *two test rags* all the night.

The operative phrases are *for each act of intercourse* vs. *all the night*. The italicized words serve both, therefore would have been used in a superscription, and the bracketed words are glosses, which could have been made uniform for both sayings, preferably *she needs*. *It is sufficient* depends upon the antecedent Shammaite lemma. If the Hillelite lemma had stood separately, it therefore could not have used *it is sufficient*, for no contrary, more stringent rule would have existed against which to measure sufficiency. Hence the primary lemma, because of the content, could not have been stated in balanced opposites, but the Houses' opinions could have been conventionally brief.

If, however, the rule had followed M. Nid. 2:1, it would have read as follows:

The daughters of Israel use two test-rags:
House of Shammai: For each act of intercourse (ʿL KL TŠMYŠ WTŠMYŠ)
House of Hillel: All the night (KL HLYLH).

So originally the mnemonic fundament of the Houses apodosis could have been TŠMYŠ/LYLH. Everything else could have been constructed out of that brief set. The Hillel-lemma could have added *it is sufficient* (DYYH). Only after the Houses-dispute was separated from the antecedent law was it necessary to supply glosses, both *two test rags* and the verbs.

The second Shammaite rule, concerning the light of the candle, looks like a gloss.

Part C, M. Nid. 2:6: The Houses' dispute is nothing more than *unclean/clean*. The Shammaite lemma has been expanded and attached to the antecedent rule with *also*. Without it, one would have expected the two colors to be in a superscription, followed by House of Shammai *declare unclean*. Redactional considerations of Hillelite editors have produced the obvious developments. See above, p. 22.

Note Epstein, *Mevo'ot*, p. 439; *Mishnah*, p. 485.

III.ii.44.A. Our rabbis taught: Although [the Sages] have said, "He who has intercourse in the light of a lamp is contemptible," the House of Shammai say, "A woman needs two test-rags for every intercourse, or she must perform it in the light of a lamp."

And the House of Hillel say, "Two testing-rags suffice for her the whole night."

B. It was taught: The House of Shammai said to the House of Hillel, "According to your view, is there no need to provide against the possibility that she might emit a drop of blood of the size of a mustard seed in the course of the first act, and this would be covered up with semen during the second act?"

"But," replied the House of Hillel, "even according to your view, is there no need to provide against the possibility that the spittle, while still in the mouth, was crushed out of existence?"

["We maintain our view,"] they said, "because what is crushed once is not the same as that which is crushed twice."

C. It was taught:

R. Joshua stated, "I approve [see] of the view of the House of Shammai."

"Master, said his disciples to him, "what an extension [of the restrictions] you have imposed upon us!"

"It is a good thing," he replied, "that I should impose extensive restrictions upon you in this world in order that your days may be prolonged in the world to come."

(b. Nid. 16b, trans. I. W. Slotki, pp. 109-110)

Comment: The *beraita* supplies a debate in standard form. Part C is valuable evidence for an early date for M. Nid. 1:4, and would be still more valuable if it had Joshua actually quote the Shammaite lemma. As it stands, we merely assume it pertains to the pericope to which the editor has assigned it.

The *although*-clause in A follows the Houses-dispute, and adds a Hillelite commentary on the Shammaite position: the Shammaites counsel a contemptible course. In later times the Babylonian rabbis warned that using a lamp attracts demons and therefore endangers the couple and its progeny, a further "reason" for following the Hillelites.

II.i.114.A. The blood of a gentile woman and the blood of the purifying woman that is a leper—

The House of Shammai declare clean.

And the House of Hillel say, "It is like her spittle or her urine."

B. The blood of a woman after childbirth who has not [yet] immersed herself—

The House of Shammai say, "It is like her spittle or her urine."

But the House of Hillel say, "It conveys uncleanness whether [it is] wet or dried up."

[M. Nid. 4:3, trans. Danby, p. 748 (y. Nid. 4:3, b. Nid. 34a-b, 35b)]

Comment: Part A: The Hillelite lemma should be simply, *declare unclean*. As it stands, the lemma explains the (unstated) Hillelite ruling, therefore develops *declare unclean*. The Shammaite opinion is that Scripture (Lev. 15:2) concerning the *Zab* and the menstrual woman speaks only of the children of Israel; likewise, the leprous woman after childbirth is like other women after childbirth (Albeck, *Seder Ṭoharot*, p. 387, citing b. Nid. 34a-b). The Hillelites declare unclean: Since the sages decreed uncleanness on the spittle and urine of gentiles, who are regarded as *Zabim*, so they decreed uncleanness for the blood of gentile women; it also should be unclean, just like the spittle of a *Zab*, which renders unclean when moist, but not when dry. As to the blood of the leprous woman, it is unclean like spittle. Part A therefore would originally have been conventional, but the Hillelite lemma has been revised and turned into a gloss on the antecedent opinion.

In part B both lemmas have been developed. The Shammaites compare the blood to that of the purifying woman. It renders unclean like spittle, that is, when moist, but not when dry. The Hillelites compare it to the blood of a menstrual woman; the foregoing distinction does not apply. Here the Hillelite lemma is briefer. The Shammaite one should have been *it renders unclean when moist, but not dry*—that is, the opposite of the Hillelite one, rendered by the negative. Neither party could have *declared clean*. The second Shammaite opinion is identical with the first Hillelite one, and the second Hillelite opinion, plus the negative, could have served as the first Hillelite opinion.

The superscriptions require an ascending order of stringency:

Blood of gentile woman, etc.
House of Shammai: Declare clean
House of Hillel: When wet, unclean.

The superscription could have permitted the usual balance had it specified *moist*. At that point, *declare unclean* would have precisely rendered the Hillelite opinion. Perhaps the redactor preferred a less complicated superscription, but this then required a highly elliptical Hillelite lemma. The second superscription has imposed no such necessity, for the Hillelite lemma, as I said, shows what the Shammaite one should have been. The Toseftan equivalent in fact uses the simple language I have proposed here. Evidently the *beraita*-editors and Tosefta-compilers often preferred to "develop" Houses-lemmas by restating them in the simplest possible form. So what conforms to our theoretical model of the classic form is not necessarily the earliest version and may sometimes come late in the history of a pericope. Form-critical considerations cannot be decisive in solving historical problems.

II.i.115. "If a woman twenty years old has not grown two hairs, she must bring proof that she is twenty years old; she is reckoned sterile, and she may not perform *ḥalisah* nor may she contract Levirate marriage.

"If a man twenty years old has not grown two hairs he must bring proof that he is twenty years old; he is reckoned a eunuch, and he may neither submit to *ḥaliṣah* nor may he contract Levirate marriage"—these are the words of the House of Hillel.

The House of Shammai say, "In either case [this applies] when they are eighteen years old."

R. Eliezer says, "For a male the rule is according to the House of Hillel, and for a female it is according to the House of Shammai, since the growth of a woman is more speedy than that of a man."

[M. Nid. 5:9, trans. Danby, p. 751 (b. Yev. 80a, b. Nid. 47b)]

Comment: The order of the Houses is reversed, and their dispute is embedded in a fully-articulated lemma about the rules of maturation. The Houses-dispute could not have been other than:

Superscription
House of Shammai: Eighteen
House of Hillel: Twenty

The dispute certainly is an old one, since Eliezer b. Hyrcanus refers to it. It is pointless to revise the superscription so as to make place for a Houses-dispute in conventional form. The assertion that *these are the words of the House of Hillel* assigns the whole to the Hillelites, while what is theirs is only the first part of each clause, *a woman or man twenty years old.* The details are not subject to dispute. Further, the Shammaite lemma seems to presuppose Eliezer's opinion, for it alludes to *and* denies the distinction between male and female! But that distinction is *not* made in the Hillelite lemma. This points toward the post-Eliezer redaction of the pericope as we now have it. If we did not know of a distinction between male and female, we should not have expected the Shammaite lemma to refer to it, So we are left with the numbers *eighteen* and *twenty*, all that could have stood in the primary Houses-lemmas, *if* there was a dispute before Eliezer.

It is difficult to account for the reversal of order. We have seen numerous examples in which long superscriptions are assigned to the Shammaites, with the Hillelites' given a simple, brief word of disagreement. Obviously, it is convenient to have the language *this and this* together with Eliezer's saying, so that his distinction seems to depend on the foregoing. But it would have been just as convenient to have the Hillelites say *this and this at twenty years*. Nor do I see any mnemonic advantage in placing the lower number second. So the order is puzzling.

II.i.116.A. If a girl (TYNWQT) who had not yet suffered a flow was married—

The House of Shammai say, "They give her four nights."

And the House of Hillel say, "Until the wound heals."

If her time was come to suffer a flow, and she was married—

The House of Shammai say, "They give her the first night."

And the House of Hillel say, "Until the outgoing of the Sabbath—four nights."

If she suffered a flow while yet in her father's house—

The House of Shammai say, "They give her the coition of obligation."

And the House of Hillel say, "The whole night is hers."

B. [If a man or a woman that had a flux, or a menstruant, or a woman after childbirth, or a leper have died, they convey uncleanness by carrying, until the flesh has decayed. A gentile that has died does not convey uncleanness by carrying.]

The House of Shammai say, "All women that die are deemed [to have died while they were] menstruants (KL HNŠYM MTWT NDWT)."

And the House of Hillel say, "Only she who dies while a menstruant is deemed a menstruant ('YN NDH 'L' ŠMTH NDH)."

C. At first they used to say, "She that continues in *the blood of her purifying* would pour out water for [washing] the Passover-offering."

But they changed [their opinion] to say, "For the Hallowed Things she is as one that has had contact with one that suffered corpse-uncleanness (KMG' ṬM' MT)," according to the words of the House of Hillel.

The House of Shammai say, "Even as one that suffered uncleanness from a corpse ('P KṬM' MT)."

D. But they agree that she eats [Second] Tithe and sets apart Dough-offering, and brings near [to the other dough the vessel wherein she has put the portion set apart as Dough-offering] to designate it as Dough-offering, and that if any of her spittle or if the blood of her purifying fell on a loaf of Heave-offering, it remains clean [= M. Ṭ.Y. 4:2].

The House of Shammai say, "She needs immersion at the end [of the days of her purifying]."

And the House of Hillel say, "She does not need immersion at the end."

E. If she suffered a flux on the eleventh day and immersed herself at nightfall and then had a connection—

The House of Shammai say, "They convey uncleanness to what they lie upon or sit upon, and they are liable to an offering."

And the House of Hillel say, "They are not liable to an offering."

F. If she immersed herself the next day, and she had connection and afterward suffered a flux—

The House of Shammai say, "They convey uncleanness to what they lie upon or sit upon, but they are not liable to an offering."

And the House of Hillel say, "Such a one is gluttonous (GRGRN) [yet is not culpable]."

G. But they agree that if she suffered a flux during the eleventh day and immersed herself at evening and then had connection, they convey uncleanness to what they lie upon or sit upon, and they *are* liable to an offering.

[M. Nid. 10:1, 4, 6, 7, 8, trans. Danby, pp. 756-7 (b. Ket. 6a, b. Nid. 116, 64b-65a-b, 69b, 71a-b, 72a-b)]

III.ii.45.A. Our rabbis taught: And both agree that if a woman performs immersion at night after a *zibah*, the immersion is invalid, for both agree that if a woman who observed a discharge during the eleven days and performed immersion in the evening and then had intercourse, she conveys uncleanness to couch and seat, and both are liable to a sacrifice.

They only differ where a discharge occurred on the eleventh day, in which case the House of Shammai rule, "They convey uncleanness to couch and seat and are liable to a sacrifice."

And the House of Hillel exempt them from the sacrifice.

B. Said the House of Shammai to the House of Hillel, "Why should in this respect the eleventh day differ from one of the intermediate of the eleven days; seeing that the former is like the latter in regard to uncleanness, why should it not also be like it in regard to the sacrifice?"

The House of Hillel answered the House of Shammai, "No! If you rule that a sacrifice is due after a discharge in the intermediate of the eleven days, because the following day combines with it in regard to *zibah*, would you also maintain the same ruling in regard to the eleventh day, which is not followed by one that we could combine with it in regard to *zibah*?"

Said the House of Shammai to them: "You must be consistent: if one is like the other in regard to uncleanness, it should also be like it in regard to the sacrifice; and if it is not like it in regard to the sacrifice, it should not be like it in regard to uncleanness either."

Said the House of Hillel to them: "If we impose upon a man uncleanness in order to restrict the law, we cannot on that ground impose upon him the obligation of a sacrifice which might lead to a relaxation of the law.

"And, furthermore, you stand refuted out of your own rulings. For, since you rule that if she performed immersion on the next day and, having had intercourse, she observed a discharge, uncleanness is conveyed to couch and seat, and she is exempt from a sacrifice, you also must be consistent.

"If the one is like the other in regard to uncleanness, it should also be like it in regard to the sacrifice; and if it is not like it in regard to the sacrifice, it should not be like it in regard to uncleanness either.

"The fact, however, is that they are like one another only where the law is thereby restricted, but not where it would thereby be relaxed; here also, they are like one another where the law is thereby restricted, but not where it is thereby relaxed."

(b. Nid. 72a, trans. I.W. Slotki, pp. 500-501)

Comment: Part A, M. Nid. 10:1, presents three cases, in logical order. If a girl who has not yet begun her menstrual cycle is married, she is presumed clean for the first four nights of marriage. Whatever blood she sees is regarded as hymeneal blood, therefore clean. But if she sees blood after the four nights, it is presumed to be menstrual flow. The Hillelites regard the permitted period as the time needed to heal the original hymeneal injury. It is not clear to me that these periods greatly differ from one another.

The next situation pertains to a girl who has reached puberty but has not yet had a flow. The House of Shammai give a single night, and the Hillelites, four nights. The Hillelite lemma is glossed with *four nights*; the virgin is married on Wednesday, so *until the end of the Sabbath* duplicates *four nights*.

The third case pertains to a girl past puberty. The House of Shammai give a single act of intercourse. Any blood thereafter is presumed to be menstrual. The House of Hillel give her the whole night.

The presumption is that the Hillelites are lenient throughout. The Shammaites lemma carries the superscription, *they give her*. Without it, the Houses lemmas are as balanced as possible:

Shammai	*Hillel*
1. Four nights	Until the wound is healed
2. First night	Until end of Sabbath (four nights)
3. Coition of obligation	All her night.

I do not see how these disagreements could have been phrased so that the Houses rulings might be balanced opposites. The choices here are not fixed expressions, such as we saw with *midraś/temē-met*.

Part B, M. Nid. 10:4, preserves a Houses-dispute without a superscription, but in proximate balance:

House of Shammai say, All women die menstruous—KL HNŠYM MTWT NDWT

House of Hillel say, No menstruant, but she that dies menstruous 'YN NDH 'L' ŠMTH NDH

Obviously, a mere negative would have served for formal purposes. The Hillelite lemma has been phrased in the singular; the *not—but* form has replaced the simple negative; and while the last two words correspond to the Shammaites', the protasis has dropped *all* and used *menstruant* (NDH) in place of *women*, then joined the whole to the apodosis with 'L' Š. The Houses-opinions look like fixed stock-phrases which have been set against one another, rather than like a single opinion phrased affirmatively and negatively, or syzygies such as we have come to expect. Perhaps the stock-phrases should be regarded as equivalent to ṬM'/ṬHR or KŠR/PŚL and the like.

This suggestion presupposes that the Houses actually differ. But if we reconsider the difference between the lemmas before us *not* in the setting of a dispute, we find that the Houses are saying much the same thing. We shall phrase the whole in the singular, and restate the Hillelite lemma without *not. . . but. . .*, the double-negative:

House of Shammai:	Woman dies menstruous	'ŠH MTH NDH
House of Hillel:	Menstruous [—woman] dies menstruous	NDH MTH NDH

The substantive difference is in the protasis, *woman* vs. *menstruous* [*-woman*]—'ŠH vs. NDH! If we did not know that a Houses-dispute was at hand, we should have supposed that both Houses were saying that women who die are considered to be in a menstruous condition. The original Hillelite lemma, standing independently, repeats NDH fore and aft. This either is a tautology, or must have some "meaning." The redactor of the pericope obviously assumed that meaning would derive from a dispute with the Shammaites, and added 'YN. . . 'L' Š. . .—standard redactional particles. No one could have supposed it was merely a garbled tradition.

Part C, M. Nid. 10:6, has the Houses in reverse order again, just as in M. Nid. 5:9. Once more the dispute pertains not to the whole of the Hillelite lemma, but only to a clause in it. The Hillelites say that for hallowed things, the woman is like one who has touched a person who has suffered corpse-uncleanness. The Shammaites drop *touch*, leaving *like one who is unclean corpse-uncleanness*. Their lemma is introduced with the joining word 'P, *even*. The Hillelites say that she is like one who has touched a primary source of uncleanness, thus is prohibited from pouring out water for washing the Passover-offering, lest she touch the waters and make them unclean, and they make the Passover-offering unclean. The Shammaites make it even worse. It is as if she is a *Father* of Uncleanness, and *she* makes the vessel unclean, all the more so the water and the Passover-sacrifice. The practical difference is hardly significant. She is certainly prohibited by both Houses from doing the same action. The Houses' difference therefore pertains to the recollection of the accurate tradition (*touch*). I cannot account for the reversal of the Houses' order.

Part D, M. Nid. 10:7, continues the same discussion. The Shammaites adopt the Hillelite position. Her status is the same as one who has bathed on the day and awaits the sunset to complete purification. Then comes a standard balanced dispute. The difference of the Houses-lemmas is merely in the negative. The form obviously is perfect, if somewhat developed through the insertion of explanatory matter into the lemmas of both Houses. This makes it all the more curious that the foregoing pericope drops the conventional form.

The problem of M. Nid. 10:8 = III.ii.45 is this: Scripture distinguishes between a woman who has a flow of menstrual blood (Lev. 15:19: *When a woman has a discharge of blood which is her regular discharge... she shall be in her impurity for seven days*), and a woman who suffers a more extended flow (Lev. 15:25: *If a woman has a discharge of blood for many days, not at the time of her impurity, or if she has a discharge beyond the time of her impurity, all the days of the discharge she shall continue in uncleanness*). The former speaks of a menstrual woman, the latter of a woman suffering flow (ZBH). The difference is that when the woman sees blood at the outset, she is supposed to be in her menstrual period for seven days. If she sees a flow once during the period or throughout it, she immerses at the end, on the night of the eighth day and is clean. After the seven days of the menstrual period, the days of the flow (ZYBH) begin. If a woman has a flux during the eighth day, she waits a day and immerses. and if there is no further flow, she is regarded as clean. If she sees blood also on the ninth day, she immerses on the tenth, waits out the next day in cleanness, and is regarded as clean. But if she sees a flow also on the tenth day, that is, three days in succession after the end of the menstrual period, she is the ZBH of which Scripture speaks, and has to count seven clean days, immerse, and bring a sacrifice on the eighth day (Albeck, *Seder Ṭoharot*, p. 375). See Tos. Nid. 9:19 = M. Nid. 10:8, and compare M. Zab. 1:1-2.

Parts E-F-G, M. Nid. 10:8, revert to superscription-style:

> *If a woman saw [a flow] on the eleventh day and immersed at nightfall and had intercourse*
>
> House of Shammai: *They render unclean by lying or sitting* and are liable for a sacrifice
>
> House of Hillel: They are free of the sacrifice (= III.ii.45).

In this instance, the Hillelites accept the first clause of the Shammaite ruling, which could have been added to the superscription, leaving a perfect syzygy: ḤYYBYN/PṬWRYN. The issue on the eleventh day may be a case of flux (Lev. 15:25), and the beginning of the seven days when it may be a menstrual flow (Lev. 15:10). The law is that the woman was supposed to wait a day. She is in the ritual status of a *Zab*. The Hillelites do not differ on the uncleanness, but only on the sacrifice, for they hold that the requirement to wait a day is not in the Torah. But they agree that the couple renders objects unclean on account of a decree of the scribes.

The second dispute is in descending order of stringency. The woman now has waited a day, then had intercourse, then saw a flux. The House of Shammai say the same uncleanness pertains, but there is no sacrifice, and the House of Hillel say there is no punishment whatever.

The agreement at the end specifies the conditions in which the uncleanness and the sacrifice will pertain according to both parties. See Epstein, *Mevo'ot*, pp. 23, 63; *Mishnah*, p. 1030 ('P).

II.ii.114. "A nursing mother whose husband dies—lo, such a one should not become betrothed or married until twenty-four months have passed for her," the words of R. Meir.

R. Judah says, "Eighteen months."

R. Jonathan b. Joseph says, "The House of Shammai say, 'Twenty-four months.'

"And the House of Hillel say, 'Eighteen months.' "

[Tos. Nid. 2:2, ed. Zuckermandel, p. 642, lines 22-25 (b. Ket. 60a-b, y. Soṭ. 4:4)]

Comment: Jonathan phrases the dispute of the second-century masters in terms of the Houses, with Meir in the Shammaite position, Judah in the Hillelite. Since the named masters presumably would have stated their views in the names of the Houses had they derived them from the Houses, we may assume Judah and Meir have come to their conclusions independent of any Houses-traditions, and that Jonathan is responsible for translating the whole into the Houses-form. See above, p. 207.

II.ii.115.A. The blood of a gentile woman and the blood of the purifying of a woman that is a leper—

The House of Shammai say, "Lo, they are like the blood from her wound (MGPTH)."

B. "The blood of a woman who has given birth and not immersed renders unclean [when] moist, but does not render unclean [when] dry,"—the words of R. Meir.

And R. Judah declares unclean [when both] moist and dry.

C. R. Eliezer says [quotes] from the lenient rulings of the House of Shammai and from the stringent rulings of the House of Hillel:

"The blood of a woman who has given birth and who has not immersed—

"The House of Shammai say, 'It renders unclean when moist and does not render unclean when dry.'

"And the House of Hillel say, 'It renders unclean when both moist and dry.' "

D. The House of Hillel [following b. Nid. 35b] said to the House of Shammai, "Do you not agree concerning a menstrual woman, that, if her time to immerse has come and she has not immersed, she is unclean?"

The House of Shammai said to the House of Hillel, "No, if you say so concerning a menstrual woman, who, if she immerses today and sees [a flux] tomorrow, is unclean, will you say concerning a woman who has given birth, who, if she immerses today and sees a flux tomorrow, is clean?"

E. The House of Hillel said to them, "A woman who gives birth while in the status of a *Zab* will prove it."

The House of Shammai said to them, "If it is a woman who gives birth while in the status of a *Zab*, that is the law, and that is the reply: A woman who gives birth while in the status of a *Zab*, the days of her being in the status of a *Zab* count for her from the days of her cleanness but do not count for her from the days of her giving birth."

II.ii.116. She who has difficulty [in giving birth]—how much should she be relieved from pain so as to be in the status of a *Zab*?

R. Eliezer says, "From time to time," and the law is according to his words.

R. Simeon b. Judah says in the name of R. Simeon, "The House of Shammai say, 'Three days,' and the House of Hillel say, 'From time to time.' "

[Tos. Nid. 5:5-7, ed. Zuckermandel, pp. 645, lines 31-36, 646, lines 1-6 (b. Nid. 11b, 35b, 36a)]

Comment: Parts A-B correspond to M. Nid. 4:3. The first thing we notice is that Judah and Meir have phrased the dispute in the simpler language we should have expected above: *render unclean when moist/dry*. M. Nid. 4:3 looks like a development of Tos. Nid. 5:5. Therefore the dispute begins with Meir and Judah, and not earlier.

Meir is responsible for the whole (Lieberman, *Tosefet Rishonim* III, p. 269). It is his view that the Houses did *not* differ concerning the blood of a gentile woman. Even the House of Shammai agree that it renders unclean when moist, but not when dry. Meir is consistent with his view in M. Nid. 2:6: The blood conveys uncleanness as a liquid. Likewise, Meir holds, the Houses did not differ concerning the blood of one who gives birth; both hold it conveys uncleanness when moist, but not when dry. Meir has used the simplest language, *renders unclean when moist, not dry*. So Meir differs from the picture of M. Nid. 4:3 concerning the Houses-dispute. Judah then differs concerning the second clause of Meir's saying, and holds that the Shammaites regard the blood of one who gives birth as capable of rendering unclean, whether moist or dry; compare M. ʿEd. 5:5. Eliezer is therefore the authority of M. Nid. 4:3, since he has accurately portrayed the positions assigned to the two Houses.

Part E again pertains to M. Nid. 4:3: The Houses agree that if a woman gave birth while a *Zab*, the liquid (blood) conveys uncleanness whether moist or dry. The Tosefta here adds (Lieberman, *Tosefet Rishonim* III, p. 270) that it is precisely if she has *not* yet counted seven clean days. But if she has counted seven days of the days of her purification, the House of Shammai rule that they do count for her (as in b. Nid. 35b; Sifra Tazriʿa 1:13).

II.ii.116 appears in b. Nid. 7b. In M. Nid. 4:4, the pericope occurs without reference to the Houses. Here Eliezer is represented in the Hillelite position. So we cannot assume that Eliezer invariably is identical with the Shammaites.

See also M. Zab. 2:3.

II.ii.117.A. If a girl was married that had not yet suffered a flow—

The House of Shammai say, "They give her four nights not continuously (MŚWRGYN), even [spread over] four months."

And the House of Hillel say, "All the time that [the wound] is discharging (NYGPT)."

In what circumstances?

When she has not ceased [to discharge].

But if she has ceased [to discharge] and then she saw [blood] not on account of sexual relations, lo, this one is unclean as a menstruant.

B. And they give her until the wound is healed.

C. If the color of [her] blood changed and she saw [blood], lo, this one is unclean as a menstruant.

Concerning this one, the House of Hillel say, "All the night is hers."

R. Simeon b. Gamaliel says, "They give her a full period (ʿWNT ŠLMH)—half a day and its night."

D. . . .And in reference to all of them, R. Meir would say [rule] according to the words of the House of Shammai. . .

[Tos. Nid. 9:7-9, ed. Zuckermandel, p. 651, lines 2-5, 7-12 (b. Nid. 64b, 65a)]

Comment: The corresponding Mishnah is M. Nid. 10:1. Part B is borrowed from M. Nid. 10:1, the Hillelite opinion, and does not belong here. See Lieberman, *Tosefet Rishonim* III, p. 287.

II.ii.118.A. That one which the House of Hillel would call gluttonous, R. Judah would call, "One who has intercourse with a menstruant."

B. The House of Shammai said to the House of Hillel, "Do you not agree that one who sees [blood] during the eleven [days] and immersed at the evening and had intercourse is unclean for lying and sitting, and obligated for a sacrifice? Also the one who sees on the eleventh day should be liable for a sacrifice."

The House of Hillel said to them, "No, if you say so concerning one who sees [blood] during the eleven days, it is because the day which comes afterward joins with it for her [to remain in the status of] a *Zab*. Will you say so concerning one who sees [blood] on the eleventh day, for the day which follows does not join with it [for her to remain in the status of] a *Zab*?"

The House of Shammai said to them, "If so, she [also] should not be unclean for [uncleanness of] lying and sitting?"

The House of Hillel said to them, "If we have added the [uncleanness of] sitting and lying, which is severe, shall we diminish from bringing the sacrifice, which is lenient?"

(Tos. Nid. 9:19, ed. Zuckermandel, p. 652, lines 6-13)

Comment: The corresponding Mishnah is M. Nid. 10:8. In part A Judah b. Ilai adopts the Shammaite position.

Lieberman, *Tosefet Rishonim* III, p. 290, observes that Judah's father, Ilaʿi was a disciple of Eliezer b. Hyrcanus, a Shammaite, so here follows the Shammaite view. The debate here in the name of the Houses is in b. Nid. 72a given in the name of *Judah* and the House of Hillel. This proves that the debate-form was used for later materials, long after the Houses presumably had ceased to exist.

II.i.117.A. If a man shook a tree to bring down fruit or some uncleanness [and he brought down also drops of rain and these fell upon the fruit], the law *If water be put on* (Lev. 11:38) does not apply.

But if [he shook it] to bring down the drops of rain—

The House of Shammai say, "The law *If water be put on* applies to the drops that fell and to them that remained (HYWṢ'YN W'T ŠBW) [and that fell later]."

And the House of Hillel say, "The law *If water be put on* applies to the drops that fell but not to them that remained [since his purpose was that all should fall off together]."

B. If he shook a tree and the drops of rain fell on another tree; or a bush, and the drops of rain fell on another bush, and beneath them were seeds or unplucked vegetables—

The House of Shammai say, "The law *If water be put on* applies."

And the House of Hillel say, "It does not apply."

R. Joshua said in the name of Abba Yosi Ḥoliqofri of Tibeon, "Marvel at yourself, if anywhere the Torah prescribes that a liquid can render aught susceptible to uncleanness unless it was [intentionally] applied for a set purpose, for it is written, *But if water be put upon the seed* (Lev. 11:38)."

C. If man shook a bunch of herbs and [the drops of rain thereon] fell from the top side to the bottom—

The House of Shammai say, "The law *If water be put on* applies."

And the House of Hillel say, "The law *If water be put on* does not apply."

D. The House of Hillel said to the House of Shammai, "If a man shakes the stalk [of a plant], do we take thought lest the drops fall from one leaf to another?"

The House of Shammai said to them, "A stalk is but a single [thing], but a bunch is many stalks."

The House of Hillel said to them, "If a man pulled out a sack full of fruit [that had fallen into the river] and put it on the river bank, do we take thought lest water falls from the top to the bottom? Yet if he had pulled out two sacks and put them one above the other, the law *If water be put on* applies to the lower sack."

R. Yosi says, "Here also the lower one is not rendered susceptible."

(M. Maksh. 1:2-4, trans. Danby, p. 758)

Comment: Food is susceptible to uncleanness if liquid has moistened it. Liquid does so only if it is *intended* for drinking or other use not in connection with watering something attached to the soil. The liquid may, however, be spilled [put] by some accidental means, not merely by the man himself, according to Lev. 11:38, *When water* is placed *on the seed*, as in M. Maksh. 1:1:

> If any liquid was acceptable in the beginning, even though it was not acceptable in the end, or vice versa, the law *If water be put on* applies. Liquids that are unclean convey uncleanness whether acceptable or not.

The stock-phrase for the Houses' rulings is *If water be put on*, referring to liquid which renders food capable of receiving uncleanness; the meaning is that the liquid enters the category of Lev. 11:38. MKŠYR

= BKY YTN is therefore the equivalent of ṬM', unclean, and 'YNW MKŠYR = 'YNW BKY YTN is the equivalent to ṬHR, clean.

The form of *part A*, M. Maksh. 1:2, is standard. The Houses' sayings are perfectly balanced, within the limitations stated above:

To bring down the drops of rain

House of Shammai: Those that come forth (HYWṢ'YN) *and* that are on it (W'T ŠBW) [are] under (B) *If water be put on*

House of Hillel: Those that come forth [are] under *If water*... But those that are on it [are] not under *If water*, etc.

While the Houses agree on the first matter, it is just as simple to remember the opinions by stating them in full as to set the agreed item into the superscription.

The rest of the Hillelite saying is a gloss, explaining that the man shaking the tree did not give thought to the water that would remain on it, therefore those drops that fall later are not capable of rendering food ready to receive uncleanness.

Part B, M. Maksh. 1:3, extends the dispute to a neighboring bush. The Houses' lemmas are more perfectly balanced than Danby's translation suggests; they are simply: Under *If water be put*/Not under *If water be put*. The food was still attached to the ground. The Shammaites hold that the water comes under the category of *If water be put* and makes susceptible to uncleanness whatever fruits should fall on it. The Hillelites rule that the liquid fell on produce attached to the ground, therefore is not in the category of *If water be put*. But if afterwards the water remained on another tree, the House of Hillel agree that the water is in the category of *If water be put*, since they fell from tree to tree.

Abba Yosi Ḥoliqofri is cited by Joshua (b. Ḥananiah), that Scripture requires the man to intend *and* actually to place the water himself; hence he stands outside of the position of either House; but Epstein, *Mevo'ot*, p. 61, says Joshua gives the Hillelite *reason*.

Part C, M. Maksh. 1:4, concerns shaking a bunch of vegetables to rid them of water. The House of Shammai hold that the rule applies because the man has paid attention to the water.

The dispute, *part D*, is not in the normal form, for while the Hillelites begin it, the Shammaites do not end it. The Hillelites' question is in astonishment: Do we take thought of shaking a stalk, that the drops may fall from one leaf to another! The Shammaites reply that the bunch is different from a single stalk. The Hillelites raise the same question, now concerning a man with a sack of fruit taken out of the water. They agree that if there were two sacks, the lower would be subject to the rule—which looks like a gloss. So the Hillelites are made to accept the Shammaite rule of M. Maksh. 1:3!

The Hillelite "arguments" consist of a series of questions in which the astonishment of the Hillelites replaces any effort at reasoning. Yosi's saying ignores the gloss, therefore comes before it. The lower sack indeed is *not* subject to the rule. Since the second Hillelite lemma merely repeats the argument of the first, we may imagine that the primary form of the debate had only the first two elements, and the second Hillelite saying is a new version of the first. But see below (p. 314) for other versions and an alternative explanation.

Note Epstein, *Mevo'ot*, p. 78.

II.i.118.A. If water leaking from the roof dripped into a jar—
The House of Shammai say, "It must be broken."
And the House of Hillel say, "It must be emptied out."
But they agree that a man may put forth his hand inside and take out produce, and that this is not susceptible to uncleanness.

B. If water leaking from the roof dripped into a trough, the law *If water be put on* does not apply to [the water that] splashed out or overflowed (HNTZYN WHṢPYN).
If the trough was taken away to pour out [the water elsewhere]—
The House of Shammai say, "The law *If water be put on* applies to it."
And the House of Hillel says, "It does not apply."

C. If he had so set it that the water leaking from the roof should fall into it, as to what splashed out or overflowed—
The House of Shammai say, "The law *If water be put on* applies."
And the House of Hillel say, "The law *If water be put on* does not apply."

D. If it was taken away to pour out [the water elsewhere], these and these agree that the law *If water be put on* applies to them.

(M. Maksh. 4:4-5, trans. Danby, pp. 762-3)

Comment: Part A, M. Maksh. 4:4, has water dripping into the jar *not* at the man's desire. But the jar is full of fruit. How to get the fruit out? The Shammaites say the jar must be broken, but the man should not pour out the water, for, if he pours it out, he will willingly move the water from side to side, and it will then render the fruit susceptible. The Hillelites say he *may* pour out the water, for, until it has left the jar, it does not render the fruit susceptible. The Houses however agree that if he puts in his hand, the fruit remains clean. That would seem the best solution. The Houses' opinions are in the form of matched verbs: YŠBR/Y'RH. No other explanatory matter is supplied; all depends on the superscription.

Part B, M. Maksh. 4:5, contains three successive disputes. The first concerns taking the trough to pour out the water—hence willingly. The House of Shammai hold that the water that splashed out or overflowed is subject to the rule of *If water be put on*, because the man has paid attention to the water, as above. The House of Hillel take the same position as earlier. In the second case, he left the trough—again willingly. What overflows is in the same category as before. But the Hillelites here would hold that the water in the trough is subject to the rule of *If water be put*, for the man *has* intended to collect the water. In the third instance, the Houses agree that if he took the trough to pour it out elsewhere, he certainly intended to make use of the whole, even though he now disposes of it, and therefore his original, purposeful intention has not been annulled, as above, M. Maksh. 1:1.

See Epstein, *Mishnah*, pp. 783, 1176.

II.i.119. Any unbroken stream of liquid [that is poured from a clean to an unclean vessel] remains clean, save only a stream of thick honey or batter.

The House of Shammai say, "Also one of porridge made from grits or beans, since [at the end of its flow] it shrinks backwards."

[M. Maksh. 5:9, trans. Danby, pp. 764-5 (b. Naz. 50b)]

Comment: The Shammaites gloss the foregoing rule, and their saying is itself glossed ("since it shrinks backwards"). If what the bottom vessel contains is unclean, it does not render unclean what is poured out, for what is poured out does not render susceptible to uncleanness. See Epstein, *Mishnah*, p. 1088.

II.ii.119.A. [If a man] shook a tree to bring down from it the drops of rain, and they fell on those [fruits] that were unattached to it and on those that were attached [to the ground] below it—

The House of Shammai say, "Under *If water be put*."

And the House of Hillel say, "Those [that were] unattached are under *If water be put*, and those [that were] attached are not under *If water be put*."

B. R. Yosi b. R. Judah said, "The House of Shammai and the House of Hillel did not dispute concerning one who shook the tree to bring down from it liquid, and it [the liquid] fell on those [fruits] that were unattached which were in it, and on those that were unattached under it, that they are not under *If water be put;* and concerning the roots [Lieberman: Š'QRN], once they are dry, that they are not under *If water be put*.

"Concerning what did they disagree?

"Concerning him who shakes the tree to bring down from it fruits ('WKLYN = food), and they fell from basket to basket and from bush [of leaves] to bush in the same tree, that the House of Shammai say, 'Under *If water be put,*' and the House of Hillel say, 'They are not under *If water be put.*' " [Lieberman: Since the man does not intend to bring down the water, no *intent* is present, so the Hillelites. The Shammaites hold one cannot bring down fruit without water, so the intent *is* there.]

C. The House of Hillel said to the House of Shammai, "All agree concerning one who brings up a tied-up sack and places it on the side of the river, that, even though the water drips from the upper to the lower, they are not under *If water be put.*"

The House of Shammai said to them, "Do you not agree concerning him who brings up two tied-up sacks and places them one above the other so the water flows from the upper to the lower, that the lower is under the rule of *If water be put*?"

D. R. Yosi says, "It is all the same with one or two sacks:

"The House of Shammai say, 'It is under *If water be put.*'

"And the House of Hillel say, 'It is not under *If water be put.*' "

R. Judah says R. Eliezer says, "Both are under *If water be put.*"

R. Joshua says, "Both are *not* under *If water be put.*"

R. ʿAqiba says, "The lower one is under *If water be put*, and the upper is not under *If water be put.*"

(Tos. Maksh. 1:1-4, ed. Zuckermandel, p. 673, lines 16-13)

Comment: Parts A and B correspond to M. Maksh. 1:2-3, but only in a general way. The Houses' lemmas remain fixed, but the cases to which they are attached are different from the Mishnaic ones.

While the rule of M. Maksh. 1:4 is not given, we have four versions of the little debate of M. Maksh. 1:4 in parts C-D, which accounts for the strange form of the Mishnaic version of the debate. The real problem of M. Maksh. 1:4 is the presupposition of the second Hillelite argument, that the Shammaites agree that there *is* a difference between the upper sack and the lower one, but that the Hillelites *also* agree that the lower sack has been rendered unclean.

M. Maksh. 1:4	*Yosi b. R. Judah*	*Eliezer*	*Joshua*
Do we worry in the case of a single sack lest the water from the upper fruit render susceptible the lower fruit? [No!]	All agree concerning one tied up sack, that the lower is *not* under *If water be put.*	—	—
But if he brought up two sacks, the lower is under *If water be put*	Shammai: Do you not agree concerning two sacks, that etc.	*Both are* under the rule	Both are *not* under the rule

Finally, *'Aqiba* says the lower one is under *If water be put*, but not the upper one, which the Mishnaic version of the argument places in the Hillelites' mouth. Yosi b. R. Judah is consistent in this element, and Judah the Patriarch has used his version for the Hillelite opening, so the Mishnah in fact follows him—but with this difference: The Shammaites of Yosi are dropped in the Mishnah, leaving the Hillelites with the last answer—bad form. In their final clause, the Hillelites concede the Shammaites' view (as given here) about two sacks. So the Mishnah probably should have concluded, "The *House of Shammai* said to them, 'Do you not agree [or, is it not the case, HL'] that if he brought up two, and placed them'. . ." That would permit the restoration of the normal debate form. It now looks as if the *single-stalk* argument, with which the Hillelites open, is out of place. (See Lieberman, *Tosefet Rishonim* IV, pp. 106-7, Epstein, *Mevo'ot*, p. 78).

II.ii.120.A. [If water leaking from the roof dripped into the trough, the water that splashed out or overflowed *is* (contrary to M. Maksh. 4:5) under the rule of *If water be set.*]

If he took them to pour them out—

The House of Shammai say, "They are under *If water be set.*"

And the House of Hillel say, "They are not under *If water be set.*"

B. "Under what circumstances? In the case of purity (BṬHWRH). But in the case of impurity (BṬM'H), all agree that it is under the law of *If water be set,*" the words of R. Meir.

R. Yosi says, "It is all the same whether it is clean or unclean, the House of Shammai say, 'Lo, they are under *If water be set.*'

"And the House of Hillel say, 'They are not under *If water be set.*' "

[Tos. Maksh. 2:6, ed. Zuckermandel, p. 674, lines 18-23 (b. Shab. 17a)]

Comment: The Tosefta is equivalent to M. Maksh. 4:5. The Houses' opinions here correspond to the ones given in the Mishnah. What is different is the dispute of R. Meir and R. Yosi on whether a distinction is made between pure and impure water. The Mishnah follows the view of R. Yosi and omits such a distinction. Meir is consistent with M. Maksh. 1:1, above, p. 311. On the conflict of the anonymous. rule in part A with the Mishnah, see Lieberman, *Tosefet Rishonim* IV, pp. 111-112.

II.i.120.A. If a man has suffered one issue of flux (HRW'H R'YH 'ḤT ŠLZWB)—

The House of Shammai say, "He is like one that awaits day against day."

And the House of Hillel say, "Like one that has suffered a pollution (KBʿL KRY)."

B. If he suffered one issue, and on the second day it ceased, and on the third day he suffered two issues, or one as profuse as if it were two—

The House of Shammai say, "He is wholly a *Zab*."

And the House of Hillel say, "He conveys uncleaness to what he lies upon or sits upon, and he must bathe in running water, but he is exempt from the offering."

C. R. Eleazar b. Judah said, "The House of Shammai agree that such a one is not wholly a *Zab*.

"And about what did they dispute?

"About him that suffered two issues, or one as profuse as two, but suffered none on the second day, and on the third day again suffered one issue, [of such a one]—

"The House of Shammai say, 'He is wholly a *Zab*.'

"And the House of Hillel say, 'He conveys uncleanness to what he lies upon or sits upon, and he must bathe in running water, but he is exempt from the offering.' "

D. If he suffered an issue of semen (KRY) on his third day of reckoning after his flux—

The House of Shammai say, "It makes void (ŚWTR) the two clean days that went before."

And the House of Hillel say, "It made void (ŚTR) only that day."

E. R. Ishmael says, "If he suffered it on the second day it makes void the [clean] day that went before."

R. ʿAqiba says, "It is all one whether he suffered it on the second or on the third day."

F. For the House of Shammai say, "It has made void the two days that went before."

And the House of Hillel say, "It has made void that day only."

G. But they agree that if he suffered it on the fourth day, it makes void that day only if it was an issue of semen; but if he suffered a flux, even on the seventh day, it makes void [all] the days that went before.

[M. Zab. 1:1-2, trans. Danby, p. 767 (b. Nid. 72b)]

Comment: Lev. 15:1-15 pertains to bodily discharges, which are unclean. Whether a man's body runs with his discharge or is stopped from discharge, it is unclean. The bed on which he lies and places on which he sits are unclean; one who touches the bed shall wash and bathe and is unclean until evening. Whoever touches his body likewise must bathe and is unclean until evening. When the discharge stops, the man counts seven clean days and immerses. On the eighth day he brings a sacrifice. When a man sees two appearances of discharge on one day or two successive days, then he is a *Zab*, as described above, counts seven clean days, etc., but he is not liable for a sacrifice unless he sees three appearances on one day or one on three successive days.

Parts A-C, M. Zab. 1:1, now take up the ambiguous problem of one who has not fully met the conditions specified above. One who sees only a single appearance of flux clearly enters a different ritual status from a completely clean person. The House of Shammai compare him to a woman who sees blood on the eleventh day of her clean cycle. If she sees it one day, she observes one day in cleanness and is regarded as clean, but if she sees it three consecutive days, she is regarded as a *Zab*. Likewise, one who sees one appearance of flux has to wait; if he sees a second, he is a *Zab* and renders *unclean through lying and sitting* retroactively from the time that he first saw the flux. The Hillelites say he is like one who has suffered a seminal emission. He does not render *unclean through lying and sitting*, but if he sees a second flux, he renders unclean henceforward.

The Houses' opinions are as balanced as possible. That is, each House compares the man's condition to a different circumstance of ritual impurity. They could not have ruled *unclean/clean*; the only way their opinions could have registered with precision is the language before us: KŠWMRT YWM etc. vs. KB'L KRY.

In part B, the ambiguity is an interrupted flux. The man saw one flux, none on the second day, and on the third, two fluxes, or one as abundant as two. The Shammaites regard him as a *Zab*. The Hillelites say he is not completely a *Zab*, therefore is exempt from the offering.

Eliezer b. Judah then corrects the superscription, preserving the same opinions. Eliezer insists that the ambiguity concerns pretty much the same situation, but the specified fluxes occur in different order. The Hillelite ruling would have been *not complete Zab*, vs. the Shammaites' *complete Zab*. But this required a gloss, explaining in what respects the man like a *Zab*, and in what respects he was not. The gloss has survived, and the primary ruling has been dropped.

Parts D, E, F, G, M. Zab. 1:2, pertain to an issue of semen on the third clean day after the fluxes have ended. This is not a flux. The issue is, What happens to the antecedent days? The House of Shammai rule that the seminal issue has cancelled out the two clean days, and the man must start counting the seven clean days anew. The Hillelites say he loses that day, but the antecedent clean days still count. The Houses' lemmas are somewhat developed:

Shammai: It voids the two days *before it*.
Hillel: It voids only its day.

The simplest comprehensible language would have been *two days* vs. *its day* with a gloss of *before it* to clarify *both* the Shammaite and the Hillelite position.

Ishmael and ʿAqiba then (E) debate a more ambiguous situation: If the man saw the semen on the second day. Ishmael seems to follow the Shammaite line. But ʿAqiba then cites the Houses' opinions; no distinction is made between the second and the third day. The sayings of Ishmael and ʿAqiba are definitive evidence that the Houses' dispute took shape before ca. 100.

The Houses then (G) agree about the fourth day, with the Shammaites' coming over to the Hillelite position. The whole is glossed: this pertains to semen, not to flux. In a case of flux, obviously, any appearance cancels out the intervening clean days.

II.ii.121.A. If a man has suffered one issue of flux—

The House of Shammai say, "He is like the woman that awaits day against day."

And the House of Hillel say, "He is like one that has suffered a pollution."

B. And these and these agree that he immerses and eats his *Pesaḥ* at the evening.

The House of Hillel said to the House of Shammai, "Do you not agree that he immerses and eats his *Pesaḥ* at the evening?"

The House of Shammai said to them, "Do you not agree that if he sees [a flux] tomorrow, he is unclean? Lo, he is like a woman that awaits day against day, that if she should see tomorrow, she is unclean [*retroactively*]."

(Tos. Zab. 1:1)

C. If a man caused a shaking of the first observed appearance [of flux]—

The House of Shammai say, "He is suspended (TLWY)."

The House of Hillel say, "He is clean (ṬHWR)."

As to couches and seats he occupied [between the first and second discharge]—

The House of Shammai say, "It [what he sat or lay on] is suspended."

The House of Hillel say, "It is clean."

[Tos. Zab. 1:2 (b. Nid. 72b)]

D. If he saw two appearances, he who caused a shaking of both of them is unclean, according to the words of the House of Shammai.

The House of Hillel say, "He who caused a shaking of the first is clean, and of the second, is unclean."

As to the *lyings and sittings* between the first and the second, the House of Shammai declare [them] unclean, and the House of Hillel declare clean.

E. "If he saw one as abundant as two, he who shifts the whole is unclean," the words of the House of Shammai.

And the House of Hillel say, "The only one who is unclean is he who shifts the last drop only."

(Tos. Zab. 1:3)

F. R. ʿAqiba said, "The House of Shammai and the House of Hillel did not disagree concerning him who sees two, or one as large as two, and on the second [day] it was interrupted, and on the third day he saw one, that this one is not a complete *Zab*.

"Concerning what did they differ?

"Concerning the one who saw on the first day, and on the second it was interrupted, and on the third he saw two.

"The House of Shammai say, 'He is a complete *Zab*.'

"And the House of Hillel say, 'He renders unclean through his *lying and sitting*, and requires immersion in living waters, but is free of the sacrifice.' "

(Tos. Zab. 1:4)

G. When R. ʿAqiba was arranging (ŚDR; alt.: ḤBR) laws for the disciples, he said, "Whoever has heard a reason from his fellow, let him come and say so."

R. Simeon said before him in the name of R. Eleazar b. R. Judah of Bartuta, "The House of Shammai and the House of Hillel did not differ concerning him who saw one on the first day, and on the second it was interrupted, and on the third he saw two, that such a one is not a complete *Zab*.

"Concerning what did they differ?

"Concerning him who saw two, or one that was as abundant as two, and on the second day it was interrupted, and on the third he saw one."

He said, "Not every one that jumps forward is to be praised, but only him who gives the reason [for his words]."

(Tos. Zab. 1:5)

H. R. Simeon said before him, "Thus did the House of Hillel say to the House of Shammai:

" 'What is it to me that he saw one at first and one at the end?'

"They said to them, 'When he saw one at first and two at the end, the [intervening] clean day annulled the appearance [at first], and he has in his hand two appearances [of flux] [But] when he saw two at first and one at the end, since he was required to count seven [clean days], the first appearance cancelled the clean day, and he has in his hand three appearances [of flux].' "

R. ʿAqiba reverted to teach (LHYWT ŠWNH) according to the words of R. Simeon.

I. R. Eleazar b. R. Yannai said in the name of R. Eleazar Ḥisma before Rabbi [Judah the Patriarch], "The House of Shammai and the House of Hillel did not differ about him who saw one [flux] on the first day and one on the second, and on the third it was interrupted, and on the fourth he saw one; and concerning [ʿL for ʿD] one who saw one on the first and on the second it was interrupted, and on the third and fourth he saw two—that such as this is not a complete *Zab*.

"What did they dispute?

"Concerning one who saw two or one as abundant as two, and on the second day it was interrupted, and on the third [and on the fourth] he saw one."

(Tos. Zab. 1:7)

J. One disciple of the disciples of R. Ishmael said before R. ʿAqiba in the name of R. Ishmael, "The House of Shammai and the House of Hillel did not dispute concerning one who saw a seminal emission on the second day, that it makes void the day before it, and concerning him who saw it on the fourth day, that it voids only its day.

"Concerning what did they differ?

"Concerning him who saw [it] on the third day."

(Tos. Zab. 1:1-8, ed. Zuckermandel, pp. 676-7, lines 19-40, 1-8)

Comment: Part A corresponds to M. Zab. 1:1. Part B is new, and the dialogue is built on the supposed agreement. Neither House persuades the other. Here the purpose of the dialogue is to explicate the reasoning of each House.

Part C is found in b. Nid. 72b.

Part F indicates that the Mishnah before us follows ʿAqiba.

Part G-H-I supplies important evidence on how Tannaim envisioned the formation of Houses-materials. They were shaped by the later masters, who had traditions on laws and on Houses' opinions, and, through their own reasoning, figured out what opinions are to be assigned to which legal problems. Clearly, it was conventional to argue the Houses' positions in terms of "they said," working out the logic of each side and setting the whole into debate-form. This shows two things. First, the debate-form is as old as the conventional syzygies. Second, it could be, and was, used for the development of materials long after the Houses had passed from the scene.

Part J corresponds to M. Zab. 1:2.

Note Epstein, *Mevo'ot*, pp. 73, 79, 148, 211.

II.i.121.A. He who gathers together (MKNŚ) many Dough-offerings with the intention of separating them again, but they stuck together—

The House of Shammai say, "They serve as a connective (ḤBWR BṬBWL YWM) [to convey uncleanness from the one to the other if they are touched by one that had] immersed [himself the selfsame] day."

And the House of Hillel say, "They do not serve as a connective ('YNW ḤBWR)."

B. [If] pieces of dough [that were Heave-offering] were stuck together, or [if] loaves [of Heave-offering] were stuck together, or if he bakes a cake [of Heave-offering] on top of another cake before they had formed a crust in the oven, or [if there was] a blown-up skim of froth on water, or the first scum to rise in boiling bean-grits, or scum of new wine (R. Judah says, "Also that of rice")—

The House of Shammai say, "These serve as a connective [to convey uncleanness if they are touched by one that had] immersed [himself the selfsame] day."

And the House of Hillel say, "They do not serve as a connective."

But they agree [that they serve as a connective] if they are touched by any other [grades of] uncleanness, be they slight or grave.

[M. Ṭevul Yom 1:1, trans. Danby, pp. 773-4
(y. Ḥal. 3:5, ed. Gilead, p. 21a = y. Ḥal. 4:1)]

Comment: A man who has become unclean on account of an uncleanness concerning which Scripture says, *He shall be unclean until evening* (Lev. 11:32, 22:6-7), is in a lower state of uncleanness, for he has immersed himself, but only at sunset is he completely clean. The degree of uncleanness is "second grade uncleanness." He does not make common food (*Ḥullin*) unclean, but he does render *Terumah* invalid, that is, he conveys to it third-grade uncleanness, so the Heave-offering is unusable and must be burned. He therefore cannot touch sanctities, which are one degree still more susceptible than Heave-offering and may not go into the Temple beyond the gentiles' court. Such a man is called a *ṭevul-yom*.

The Houses' sayings in both parts are perfectly balanced:

connective [for ṭevul-yom]/not connective.

As often, the Hillelite lemma depends for its protasis on the Shammaite one. The superscriptions are highly articulated and extensive. In part A, the point is that *Ḥallah* is like *Terumah*. The Hillelites hold that, since the man *intends* to separate the loaves, the piece touched by the man is unfit, but the rest is clean. The second part contains disagreement on the same principle. The agreement at the end specifies that the Hillelites accept the Shammaite view in the other grades of uncleanness; the Hillelites make a lenient judgment only in the case of a *ṭevul-yom*.

II.ii.122. If a layer of jelly was formed over the flesh of hallowed flesh, and so too oil floating on wine—

R. Ishmael b. R. Yoḥanan b. Beroqah says, "The House of Shammai say, 'It is a connective for a *ṭevul-yom*.'

"And the House of Hillel say, 'It is not a connective.' "

[Tos. Ṭevul Yom 2:3, ed. Zuckermandel, p. 685, lines 9-11 (y. Suk. 2:8, y. Ter. 5:2)]

Comment: The corresponding Mishnah, M. Ṭevul Yom 2:5, follows the Hillelite view, and for the second case Yoḥanan b. Nuri adheres to the Shammaite opinion, but does not refer to the Houses.

II.i.122.A. All the Holy Scriptures render the hands unclean.

The Song of Songs and Qohelet render the hands unclean.

R. Judah says, "The Song of Songs renders the hands unclean, but about Qohelet there is dissension."

R. Yosi says, "Qohelet does not render the hands unclean, and about the Song of Songs there is dissension."

B. R. Simeon says, "Qohelet is one of the things about which the House of Shammai adopted the more lenient, and the House of Hillel, the more stringent, ruling."

[M. Yad. 3:5, trans. Danby, pp. 781-2 (b. Meg. 7a)]

Comment: See M. ʿEd. 5:3. The Shammaites say it does not render the hands unclean. The debate is Ushan. Simeon does not quote the (theoretical) pericope, merely refers to it. M. ʿEd. constructs the whole in standard form. Note Epstein, *Mevo'ot*, pp. 125, 424, 436.

II.i.123.A. Olives and grapes that have turned hard (PRYṢY ZYTYM etc.)—

The House of Shammai declare susceptible to uncleanness, but the House of Hillel declare them insusceptible.

Black cummin (HQṢḤ)—

The House of Shammai declare insusceptible to uncleanness, and the House of Hillel declare susceptible.

So, too, [do they differ] concerning [whether it is liable to] Tithes.

B. When do fish become susceptible to uncleanness?

The House of Shammai say, "After they are caught."

The House of Hillel say, "After they are dead."

R. ʿAqiba says, "If they could live [if they were put back into the water, they are not susceptible to uncleanness]."

C. When do honeycombs become susceptible to uncleanness by virtue of being a liquid?

The House of Shammai say, "After [he] smokes out [the bees]."

And the House of Hillel say, "After he breaks [the honeycombs]."

[M. ʿUqṣ. 3:6, 8, 11, trans. Danby, pp. 788-9
(b. Ḥul. 75a, b. B.M. 105a)]

Comment: Part A, M. ʿUqṣ. 3:6, is in standard form: The Houses are in the right order and their opinions are standard: *unclean/clean*. The Shammaites hold the specified items can receive uncleanness as foods; the Hillelites do not regard them as food.

Part B, M. ʿUqṣ. 3:8, is another sort of standard dispute: When does an item become susceptible to uncleanness (or, elsewhere, cleanness)? The Houses' lemmas are perfectly balanced: MŠYṢWDW/MŠYMWTW. ʿAqiba's comes afterward, and does not balance. The Shammaite position is that since fish do not require slaughtering, as soon as they are caught, even while alive, they are capable of receiving uncleanness. ʿAqiba is essentially in line with the Hillelite view, as usual.

Part C, M. ʿUqṣ. 3:11, follows the same form. The Houses' opinions are consistent. The Shammaites hold that when the honey may be reached, even though it has *not* been reached, it has entered the status of a liquid which one wants to make use of. The Hillelites say that only when the honey-combs are flowing is honey an available liquid. The balance is perfect: MŠYḤRḤR vs. MŠYRŠQ.

See Epstein, *Mevo'ot*, p. 78, *re* ʿAqiba; *Mishnah*, p. 268.

VII. Collections of Houses-Disputes in Mishnah-Tosefta

In addition to the individual pericopae, sometimes loosely strung together, which contain Houses-materials, we have observed two sorts of coherent, composites: collections and compilations. The *collections* are as follows:

1. M. Ber. 8:1-8: *Meal*
   1. Day/Wine
   2. Hands/Cup
   3. Napkin—Table/Cushion
   4. Sweep/Wash
   5. Food/Spices
   6. Created Light/Creates Lights
   7. Forgot Grace—Go Back/Do Not Go Back
   8. Wine/Food

   Blessing: Nos. 1, 2, 5, 6, [8]
   Uncleanness: Nos. 2, 3, 4
   Miscellany: No. 7.

2. M. Shab. 1:4-8: *Sabbath*
   Form: *They do not. . . except in order. . . while it is still day + permit*
   1. Soak ink, dyes, and vetches
   2. Place bundles of flax in the oven
   3. Spread nets for beasts, birds, and fish
   4. Sell to gentile, carry with him, and raise up on him [a burden]
   5. Give hides to tanner, clothes to laundryman

   Sabbath-rest for inanimate objects: Nos. 1, 2, 3 (nets). Gentile: Nos. 4-5.

3. M. Yev. 13:1: *Right of Refusal*
   Form: Explanatory matter in first Shammaite lemma:
   1. Shammai: Only betrothed *exercise right of refusal*
      Hillel: Both betrothed and married
   2. Shammai: Husband, *and not* brother-in-law
      Hillel: Husband *and* brother-in-law
   3. Shammai: In his presence
      Hillel: In his presence *and not* in his presence
   4. Shammai: Before the court
      Hillel: Before the court *and not* before the court.

   Projected continuation:
   5. Shammai: Adolescent, not child
      Hillel: Adolescent *and* child
   6. Shammai: Three times [Or: One time] only
      Hillel: [Even] four or five.

4. M. Ned. 3:4: *Vows to Tax-collectors*
   1. *They vow with all*
      House of Shammai: Except oath
      House of Hillel: Even oath.

2. House of Shammai: He may not open for him with a vow
   House of Hillel: He may even open for him
3. House of Shammai: Concerning that which he makes him vow
   House of Hillel: Even not ,, ,, ,,

The most striking *compilation* is M. Beṣ., in the following forms:

M. Beṣ 1:1-3, 5-9:

I. Rule of law
   House of Shammai: Verb +/— negative
   House of Hillel: Verb +/— negative
   1. M. Beṣ. 1:1—egg born on festival
   2. M. Beṣ. 1:2—dirt not prepared preceding day
   3. M. Beṣ. 1:8—picking out pulse (Variation: Choose + eat vs. choose *after his usual fashion*)
   4. M. Beṣ. 2:4—[As reconstructed]—lay on hands, bring whole-offerings

II. House of Shammai: Distinction
   House of Hillel: No distinction
   1. M. Beṣ. 1:1b—olive's bulk S'WR, date's bulk ḤMṢ
   2. M. Beṣ. 1:9 —send portions (Variation: Hillelite position is spelled out in detail)

III. House of Shammai: Negative plus full statement of case
   House of Hillel: Permit
   1. M. Beṣ. 1:3—moving ladder+designating pigeons before festival
   2. M. Beṣ. 1:5—take off cupboard doors
      —lift pestle
      —hide to treading place
      —carry child, Scroll, *Lulav*
   3. M. Beṣ. 1:6—take gifts to priest

IV. Full statement of positions of both Houses
   1. M. Beṣ. 1:7—pounding spices and salt
   2. M. Beṣ. 2:5—make fire on festival for other than cooking

V. Brief statement of positions of both Houses
   1. M. Beṣ. 2:1—two/one
   2. M. Beṣ. 2:2—immerse

M. ‘Ed. contains Houses-collections exhibiting still further forms. M. ‘Ed. was supposedly compiled on the day on which Gamaliel II was deposed at Yavneh. Epstein (*Mevo'ot leSifrut HaTanna'im*, p. 422) demonstrates that the tradition is unlikely: "Some of the traditions derive from a much earlier time than Gamaliel's deposition." The tractate, he says, organizes the undecided disputes from Shammai and

Hillel up to Yavnean times. But the tractate as we have it is not in its first recension, nor is it the single recension of a given Tanna, but an assembly of Mishnahs of various Tannaim, particularly Meir, Judah, and Yosi. Our present interest is to see the principles of organization of Houses-materials, and, as always, to discern which materials may derive from pre-Yavnean times.

II.i.124.A. The House of Shammai say, "A quarter-*qab* of bones (ʿṢMWT MN HʿṢMYM) of [any] bones, whether from two [corpses] or from three, [suffices to convey uncleanness by overshadowing]."

And the House of Hillel say, "[It must be] a quarter-*qab* of bones from a [single] corpse (GWYH), and from bones which are the greater part either in bulk or in number."

Shammai says, "Even [a quarter-*qab*] from one bone." [= M. Oh. 2:1]

B. Heave-offering vetches—

The House of Shammai say, "They soak and rub in cleanness, but they give as food in uncleanness."

And the House of Hillel say, "They soak in cleanness, but they rub or give as food in uncleanness."

Shammai says, "They are to be eaten dry (ṢRYD)."

R. ʿAqiba says, "Whatsoever concerns them may be done in uncleanness." [= M. M.S. 2:4]

C. If a man would change a *sela's* worth of Second Tithe money [outside of Jerusalem]—

The House of Shammai say, "[He may change] coins for the whole *sela* (BKL HŚLʿ MʿWT)."

And the House of Hillel say, "A *sheqel's* worth of silver and a *sheqel's* worth in copper coin (BŠQL KŚP WBŠQL MʿWT)."

R. Meir says, "They may not change silver and produce [together] into [other] silver."

But the sages permit it. [= M. M.S. 2:8].

D. If a man would change a *sela* of Second Tithe money in Jerusalem—

The House of Shammai say, "He must change the whole *sela* into copper coin (BKL HŚLʿMʿWT)."

And the House of Hillel say, "[He may take one] *sheqel's* worth of silver and one *sheqel's* worth in copper coin (BŠQL KŚP WBŠQL MʿWT)."

They that made argument before the sages say, "Three *denars'* worth of silver and one of copper."

R. 'Aqiba says, "Three *denars'* worth of silver and from the fourth [*denar*] a quarter in copper coin."

R. Ṭarfon says, "Four *aspers* in silver."

Shammai says, "Let him deposit it in a shop and [gradually] consume its value." [= M. M.S. 2:9]

E. If a bride's stool lost its seat-boards—

The House of Shammai declare it susceptible to uncleanness.

And the House of Hillel declare it not susceptible.

Shammai says, "Even the frame of a stool [remains] susceptible to uncleanness."

If a stool is fixed to a baking-trough—

The House of Shammai declare it susceptible to uncleanness.

And the House of Hillel declare it not susceptible.

Shammai says, "Even one that was made [to be used] inside it [is susceptible]." [= M. Kel. 22:4]

F. These are things concerning which the House of Hillel changed their opinion to teach according to the words of the House of Shammai:

If a woman returned from beyond the sea and said, "My husband is dead," she may marry again. [And if she said], "My husband died [childless]," she may contract Levirate marriage.

And the House of Hillel say, "We have heard no such tradition save of a woman that returned from the harvest."

The House of Shammai said to them, "It is all one whether she returned from the harvest or from the olive-picking or from beyond the sea; they spoke of the harvest only as of a thing that happened in fact."

The House of Hillel changed their opinion and taught according to the opinion of the House of Shammai. [= M. Yev. 15:1-2]

G. The House of Shammai say, "She may marry again and take her *Ketuvah*."

And the House of Hillel say, "She may marry again, but she may not take her *Ketuvah*."

The House of Shammai answered, "Since you have declared permissible the graver matter of forbidden intercourse, should you not also declare permissible the less important matter of property?"

The House of Hillel said to them, "We find that brothers may not enter into an inheritance on her testimony."

The House of Shammai answered, "Do we not learn from her

Ketuvah-scroll that he thus prescribes for her, 'If you be married to another, you shall take what is prescribed for you?' "

The House of Hillel changed their opinion to teach according to the opinion of the House of Shammai. [= M. Yev. 15:3]

H. "If a man was half-slave and half free, he should labor one day for his master and one day for himself," the words of the House of Hillel.

The House of Shammai say, "You have ordered it [well] for his master, but for him you have not ordered it [well]. He cannot marry a bondwoman, nor can he marry a free woman. Shall he remain fruitless? And was not the world created only for fruition and increase, as it is written, *He created it not a waste; he formed it to be inhabited* [Is. 45:18]? But for the order of the world they compel his master and he sets him free, and the bondman writes him a bond of indebtedness for half his value."

The House of Hillel changed their opinion to teach according to the opinion of the House of Shammai. [= M. Giṭ. 4:5]

I. "An earthenware vessel can protect aught [that is within it from contracting uncleanness from a corpse that is under the same roof]"—according to the words of the House of Hillel.

And the House of Shammai say, "It can protect only foodstuffs, and liquids, and other earthenware vessels." [= M. Oh. 5:3]

J. The House of Hillel said, "Why?"

The House of Shammai said, "Because with an *'am ha'areṣ* it is susceptible to uncleanness, and a vessel that is susceptible to uncleanness cannot interpose [to protect from uncleanness.]"

The House of Hillel answered, "But have you not pronounced the foodstuffs and liquids therein clean?"

The House of Shammai said to them, "When we pronounced the foodstuffs and liquids therein clean, we pronounced them clean for himself; but when *you* declare the vessel clean, you declare it so for yourself as well as for him."

The House of Hillel changed their opinion to teach according to the opinion of the House of Shammai. [= Tos. Ah. 5:11-12]

(M. 'Ed. 1:7-14, trans. Danby, pp. 423-4)

Comment: Part A, M. 'Ed. 1:7, recurs without the Houses-dispute in M. Oh. 2:1, which gives the Hillelite opinion anonymously (above, pp. 277-280). The lemmas are not closely matched:

Shammai:	Quarter [*qab*] of bones of [any] bones, *whether from two or three*
Hillel:	Quarter [*qab*] of bones from the corpse, *whether from most of the bulk or from most of the number.*

The italicized words match approximately, but do *not* relate to one another:

BYN MŠNYM BYN MŠLŠH
MRB HBNYN ʾW MRB HMNYN

Binyan does not match *shenayim*, *minyan* does not match *sheloshah*. Clearly the superscription, *quarter of bones*, is supplied to each lemma. This leaves:

ʿṢMWT MN HʿṢMYM
ʿṢMWT MN HGWYH

So the original dispute consisted of ʿṢMYM and GWYH, that is, a matter of word-choice. Presumably the law referred to was what is here represented, and at the outset the Houses' disagreed only on the language in which the law was phrased. The later masters assumed that a dispute on law, not merely on the language of the tradition, was at issue, so they developed the whole, beginning with quarter [*qab*] of bones, RBʿ ʿṢMWT, and the BYN—BYN glosses. Shammai's lemma poses no problem. It conforms to the earlier, primitive form, ʿṢM ʾḤD, in other words, ʿṢM. The pericope has been substantially developed over the primary Houses-lemmas, and if, as is alleged, the whole was worked out in Yavneh, the original language must have been spelled out and assigned to the Houses sufficiently before that time so that the problem of interpreting precisely what the Houses had been talking about could have been confused with the mere difference in word-choice.

Part J, M. ʿEd. 1:14, has an approximate parallel in Tos. Ah. 5:11-12, with Joshua in place of the House of Hillel, above, p. 280.

We must now ask, By what principle, theme, or common form have the foregoing pericopae been strung together? Parts F, G, H, and I clearly form one sub-unit, brought together by the common superscription and subscriptions that the Hillelites reverted to the Shammaite position. The individual pericopae all contain the same statement and presumably were completed before being brought together. A single editorial hand surely would have imposed unities of form and deleted obvious redundancies. Whoever was responsible for the present form of M. ʿEd. 1:12-14 actually did little more than collect what already was in final form. Parts C and D are a pair and occur together in their original place, M. M.S. 2:8-9. Parts A and B are related by the theme of uncleanness, but the specific problems have nothing to do with one another. Part E is another uncleanness problem, unrelated to that of part A. We therefore see two coherent sub-units, parts C-D and F-G-H-I-J. Parts A-B, furthermore, present a single form:

House of Shammai
House of Hillel
+
Shammai

Part B further glosses with ʿAqiba. The reason for bringing together these parts is therefore the common *order* of authorities. In that case, parts C-D may have been added because Shammai appears (part D), and this would further explain the inclusion of part E.

M. ʿEd. 1:1-14 therefore consists of two collections, separate but juxtaposed. The first collection is characterized by the order of opinions: the Houses, then Shammai, most strikingly in M. ʿEd. 1:7, and M. ʿEd. 1:11, parts A and E. *If* the collection of M. ʿEd. was in some form such as we now have it by early Yavnean times, then the inclusion of Meir in Part C is a later gloss; and the addition of ʿAqiba, with and without Ṭarfon, in parts B and D, would represent a somewhat earlier, intermediate, stage of development. (Note also Epstein, *Mevo'ot*, p. 429).

The second collection is easier to discern, consisting, as I said, of M. ʿEd. 1:12-14, parts F-J, united by the common subscriptions about Hillelite reversion. Parts I-J certainly are problematical, for Joshua elsewhere stands in place of the Hillelites, and it may be that those pericopae are considerably later than the earliest Houses-materials. In its present form, in any case, the whole cannot come before Meir.

The first collection is thus the *Houses + Shammai*, the second, the *Reversion of the Hillelites.*

II.i.125.A. In these things the House of Shammai adopted the more lenient, and the House of Hillel the more stringent ruling:

B. An egg was laid on a Festival-day—

The House of Shammai say, "It may be eaten."

And the House of Hillel say, "It may not be eaten."

The House of Shammai say, "An olive's bulk of leaven and a date's bulk of what is leavened."

And the House of Hillel say, "An olive's bulk of either." [= M. Beṣ. 1:1; M. Beṣ. 3:8]

C. If a beast was born on a Festival-day, all agree that it is permitted; but if a chicken was hatched from an egg, all agree that it is forbidden.

D. If a man slaughtered a wild animal or a bird on a Festival-day—

The House of Shammai say, "He may dig with a mattock and cover up [the blood]."

And the House of Hillel say, "He should not slaughter unless he had earth set in readiness [to cover up the blood]."

But they agree that if he had slaughtered, he may dig with a mattock and cover up [the blood]; [moreover they agreed] that ashes of a stove may be regarded as set in readiness. [= M. Beṣ. 1:2]

E. The House of Shammai say, "[If produce is proclaimed] 'ownerless' for [the benefit of] the poor, [it is accounted] ownerless [and tithe-free]."

And the House of Hillel say, "[It can only be accounted] ownerless [and tithe-free] if [it is proclaimed] ownerless [equally] for [the benefit of the] rich as in the year of Release."

The sheaves in a field were each of one *qab's* weight but one was of four *qabs;* if this was forgotten—

The House of Shammai say, "It may not be deemed a Forgotten Sheaf."

And the House of Hillel say, "It may be deemed a Forgotten Sheaf." [= M. Pe'ah 6:1, 5]

F. If a sheaf lies near to a wall or to a stack or to the oxen or to the implements, and is forgotten—

The House of Shammai say, "It may not be deemed a Forgotten Sheaf."

And the House of Hillel say, "It may be deemed a Forgotten Sheaf." [= M. Pe'ah 6:2]

G. Fourth year fruit—

The House of Shammai say, "The rules of the [Added] Fifth and of Removal do not apply."

And the House of Hillel say, "The rules of the Fifth and of Removal do apply."

The House of Shammai say, "The laws of Grape-gleanings and of the Defective Cluster apply, and the poor redeem the grapes for themselves."

And the House of Hillel say, "The whole yield goes to the wine-press." [= M. Pe'ah 7:6, M. M.S. 5:3]

H. A jar of pickled olives—

The House of Shammai say, "One need not broach."

And the House of Hillel say, "One needs to broach."

But they agree that if it had been broached and the lees block up the breach, it is not susceptible to uncleanness. [= M. Maksh. 1:1; b. Yev. 15b, Tos. Yev. 1:11-13]

I. If a man anointed himself with clean oil and then became unclean, and he went down and immersed himself—

The House of Shammai say, "Even though he still drips [with oil], it is clean."

And the House of Hillel say, "[It is unclean so long as there remains] enough to anoint a small member."

J. And if it was unclean oil at the outset—

The House of Shammai say, "[It remains unclean, even after he has immersed himself, so long as there remains] enough to anoint a small member."

And the House of Hillel say, "[So long as it remains] a moist liquid (MŠQH ṬWPḤ)."

R. Judah says in the name of the House of Hillel, "So long as it is moist enough to moisten aught else." [= y. Ber. 8:3]

K. "A woman is betrothed by [the gift of] a *denar* or a *denar's* worth," according to the words of the House of Shammai.

And the House of Hillel say, "By a *peruṭah* or a *peruṭah's* worth."

And how much is a *peruṭah*? The eighth part of an Italian *issar*. [= M. Qid. 1:1]

L. The House of Shammai say, "A man may dismiss his wife with an old bill of divorce."

And the House of Hillel forbid.

What is an old bill of divorce? If he continued alone with her after he had written it for her [it becomes an old bill of divorce].

M. If a man divorced his wife and she then lodged with him in an inn—

The House of Shammai say, "She does not need another bill of divorce from him."

And the House of Hillel say, "She needs another bill of divorce from him."

This applies when she was divorced after wedlock; but if she had been divorced from him after betrothal [only], she does not need another bill of divorce from him, since he is not yet shameless before her. [= M. Qid. 1:1; M. Giṭ. 8:4, 8:9]

N. The House of Shammai permit Levirate marriage between the co-wives and the surviving brothers.

And the House of Hillel forbid it.

If they performed *ḥaliṣah*—

The House of Shammai declare them ineligible to marry a priest.

And the House of Hillel declare them eligible.

If they had been taken in Levirate marriage—

The House of Shammai declare them eligible.

And the House of Hillel ineligible.

Notwithstanding that these declare ineligible and the others declare eligible, yet the House of Shammai did not refrain from marrying women from the House of Hillel, nor the House of Hillel from marrying women from the House of Shammai.

And all the disputes about what is clean and unclean, wherein these declare clean and the others declare unclean, neither refrained from making clean things with the other. [= M. Yev. 1:4]

O. If there were three brothers, two married to two sisters, and one unmarried, and one of the married brothers died, and the unmarried brother bespoke the widow, and then his second brother died—

The House of Shammai say, "His [bespoken] wife abides with him, and the other is free as being his wife's sister."

And the House of Hillel say, "He must put away his [bespoken] wife both by bill of divorce and by *ḥaliṣah*, and his brother's wife by *ḥaliṣah*."

This is a case whereof they have said, "Woe to him because of [the loss of] his wife, and woe to him because of [the loss of] his brother's wife!" [= M. Yev. 3:5]

P. If a man vowed to have no intercourse with his wife—

The House of Shammai say, "[She may consent] for two weeks."

And the House of Hillel say, "For one week [only]." [= M. Ket. 5:6]

Q. If a woman miscarried on the night of the eighty-first day—

The House of Shammai declare [her] exempt from an offering.

And the House of Hillel declare [her] liable. [= M. Ker. 1:6]

R. A linen garment, as to fringes (ŚDYN BṢYṢYT)—

The House of Shammai declare exempt.

And the House of Hillel declare liable. [= Mid. Tan. to Deut. 22:12]

S. A basket of fruit intended for the Sabbath—

The House of Shammai declare exempt [from Tithes].

And the House of Hillel declare liable. [= M. Ma. 4:2]

T. If a man vowed to be a Nazirite for a longer spell (NZYRWT MRBH) and fulfilled his Nazirite-vow and afterward came to the Land [of Israel]—

The House of Shammai say, "He [need continue] a Nazirite [only for] thirty days [more]."

And the House of Hillel say, "He is a Nazir as from the beginning."

If two pairs of witnesses testified of a man, the one testified that he had vowed two Nazirite-vows, and the other that he had vowed five—

The House of Shammai say, "The testimony is at variance, and the Nazirite-vow is not here."

And the House of Hillel say, "The two are included within the five, so that he must be a Nazirite for two [spells]." [= M. Naz. 3:6-7]

U. If a man was put there below the split—

The House of Shammai say, "He does not give passage to the uncleanness."

And the House of Hillel say, "A man is hollow, and [his] upper side gives passage to the uncleanness." [= M. Oh. 11:3]

(M. ʿEd. 4:1-12, trans. Danby, pp. 429-30)

II.i.126.A. R. Judah says, "Six opinions of the House of Shammai's lenient, and the House of Hillel's more stringent, rulings":

B. The blood of the carcass—

The House of Shammai declare it clean.

And the House of Hillel declare it unclean. [= b. Ker. 21a, b. Shab. 77a, b. Men. 104a]

C. "An egg from a [bird's] carcass is permitted if it is in like condition to them that are sold in the market, otherwise it is forbidden," according to the words of the House of Shammai.

And the House of Hillel forbid it [in any condition]. But they agree that an egg from a bird that is *ṭerefah* is forbidden, since it was fashioned in what was forbidden. [= y. Beṣ. 1:1]

D. The blood of a gentile woman and the blood of the purifying of a woman that is a leper—

The House of Shammai declare unclean.

And the House of Hillel say, "It is like to her spittle or her urine." [= M. Nid. 4:3]

E. According to the House of Shammai, they may eat Seventh Year produce by favor [of the owner] or without favor.

And the House of Hillel say, "They may only eat it by favor [of the owner]." [= M. Shev. 4:2]

F. A water skin—

The House of Shammai say, "[A water-skin can contract *midraś*-uncleanness] when it is tied up with a durable knot (ṢRWRH WʿMDT)."

And the House of Hillel say, "Even when it is not tied up (ʾP ʿL PY ŠʾYNH ṢRWRH)." [= M. Kel. 26:4]

G. R. Yosi says, "Six opinions of the House of Shammai's more lenient, and the House of Hillel's more stringent, rulings":

H. According to the House of Shammai, a fowl may be served up on the table together with cheese, but it may not be eaten with it.

And the House of Hillel say, "It may neither be served up with it nor eaten with it." [= M. Ḥul. 8:1]

I. According to the House of Shammai, Heave-offering may be

set apart from olives instead of from oil or from grapes instead of from wine.

And the House of Hillel say, "They do not give Heave-offering." [= M. Ter. 1:4 has it reversed.]

J. If a man sowed seed within a space of four cubits [from the vines] of a vineyard—

The House of Shammai say, "He renders forfeit one row."

And the House of Hillel say, "He renders forfeit two rows." [= M. Kil. 4:5]

K. Flour-paste—

The House of Shammai declare exempt [from Dough-offering].

And the House of Hillel declare it liable. [= M. Ḥal. 1:6]

L. According to the House of Shammai, they immerse themselves in a rain-stream.

And the House of Hillel say, "They do not immerse." [= M. Miq. 5:6]

M. A man who became a proselyte on the day before Passover—

The House of Shammai say, "He immerses himself and consumes his Passover-offering in the evening."

And the House of Hillel say, "He that separates himself from his uncircumcision is like one that separates himself from the grave." [= M. Pes. 8:8]

N. R. Simeon [Ishmael] says, "Three opinions of the House of Shammai's more lenient, and the House of Hillel's more stringent, rulings":

O. According to the House of Shammai [the Book of] Qohelet does not render the hands unclean.

And the House of Hillel say, "It renders the hands unclean." [= M. Yad. 3:5; b. Meg. 7a]

P. Sin-offering water which has fulfilled its purpose—

The House of Shammai declare it clean.

And the House of Hillel declare it unclean.

Q. Black cummin—

The House of Shammai declare insusceptible to uncleanness.

And the House of Hillel declare it susceptible.

So, too, [do they differ] concerning [whether it is liable to] Tithes. [= M. ʿUqṣ. 3:6].

R. R. Eliezer [or, Eleazar] says, "Two opinions of the House of Shammai's more lenient, and the House of Hillel's more stringent rulings":

S. The blood of a woman that has not yet immersed herself after childbirth—

The House of Shammai say, "It is like spittle or her urine."

And the House of Hillel say, "It conveys uncleanness whether wet or dried up."

But they [Shammaites] agree that if a woman gave birth while she had a flux, it renders unclean whether [the blood was] wet or dried up. [= M. Nid. 4:3; Tos. Nid. 5:5-6]

T. If two of four brothers married two sisters, and the two that married the two sisters died, the sisters must perform *ḥaliṣah* and may not contract Levirate marriage; and if the brothers had already married them, they must put them away.

R. Eliezer [or, Eleazar] says in the name of the House of Shammai, "They may continue the marriage."

And the House of Hillel say, "They must put them away." [= M. Yev. 3:1; Tos. Yev. 5:1, Tos. ʿEd. 2:9]

(M. ʿEd. 5:1-5)

Comment: M. ʿEd. 4:1-12 and 5:1-5 are organized around the leniencies of the Shammaites and the strict rulings of the Hillelites, in the presumption that everything else is easily assigned, according to the content, to one or the other House. The first such list, M. ʿEd. 4:1-22, is anonymous. It has a superscription, then consists of a string of pericopae, all of which occur elsewhere. The second set of lists is attributed to masters:

Usha	Judah b. Ilai	six
	Yosi b. Ḥalafta	six
Yavneh	Simeon [Ishmael]	three
	Eliezer (or, Eleazar)	two

That is, the longer, then the shorter lists. The first three are Ushans, the last is presumably Eliezer b. Hyrcanus, who should therefore be set off by himself; variants give Ishmael for Simeon, thus the pair would be from Yavneh.

II.i.125, part A, M. ʿEd. 4:1, is the superscription for the whole. Parts H-I-J, M. ʿEd. 4:6, have no equivalent in the Mishnah.

Part H is in standard form; the difference between the Houses is in the negative, which here is given to the Shammaites, yielding for them the lenient position. The issue is whether the brine has made the olives susceptible to receive uncleanness. The Shammaites hold this particular moisture is not regarded as liquid within that definition. The Hillelites go over to the Shammaite opinion for the agreement. Since the man has shown he does not intend to make use of the brine, it is not in the category of a "liquid."

Part I is elliptical in form:

He who anoints pure oil and is unclean, descended and immersed	
House of Shammai:	Even though he drips, it is clean.
House of Hillel:	As much as for anointing a small limb [= *unclean*].

These opinions do not relate to one another. One has to supply the Hillelites with *unclean* to make sense of their lemma, that is, if so much oil remains on him, the oil is unclean, but less than that is clean. The difficulty even now is not easily resolved, for the referent of *clean/unclean* could be the man, not the oil.

Part J continues the problem:

If it was unclean oil to begin with	
House of Shammai:	As much as for anointing a small limb
House of Hillel:	Moist liquid (MŠQH ṬWPḤ)

Now the Shammaites have the Hillelite lemma. A common progression as a case becomes more extreme is for the former lenient side to take up the opposition's stringent position at the next stage. Now the Hillelites say if there remains this quantity of oil, the oil is unclean; some commentaries hold the oil is clean. No one now refers to the man himself, and presumably those who do so in the first case, part I, are in error. The Hillelites say that if there is enough oil to moisten the hand, the oil is unclean; and some explain (Albeck, *Seder Neziqin*, p. 300) that if the oil is sufficient to wet the hand, it is clean, but more than *that* sufficiency is unclean.

Parts K-L-M, M. ʿEd. 4:7, form a little collection of marriage-rulings.

Apart from the superscription of part A, we may thus discern the following subdivisions, centered on common themes:

1. Parts B, C, D, Festival law
2. Parts E, F, G, Agricultural law
3. Parts H, I, J, Cleanness (Liquids)
4. Parts K, L, M, N, O, P, Marital law (Betrothal; Cessation of marriage: Bill of Divorce, then, *Ḥaliṣah*/Levirate Marriages; then, Imposed Divorce because of Vow)
5. Part Q, Miscarriage (Sacrifice)
   Part R, Fringes on linen garments
   Part S, Tithing
6. Part T, Nazirites
7. Part U, Cleanness (Tents)

The first four groups of pericopae and no. 6 form substantial collections. No. 5 seems to be the only composite without a common theme; one might regard Part Q as an extension of the marital law, but nothing unites parts R and S. Logically, part U should have been in juxtaposition with parts H, I, J, though it can as well stand by itself; the theme in common with *liquids* is general—cleanness.

I see no principle to explain the order of the legal themes. What come first are substantial collections, then follow the miscellaneous ones. Perhaps, therefore, considerations of quantity were important, as in M. ʿEd. 5:1-5.

*II.i.*126: *Part B* has no counterpart in the Mishnah. In M. ʿEd. 8:1, Joshua b. Bathyra testifies to the ruling of the Shammaites, but the Houses do not appear.

Part C likewise is a singleton. The Shammaites rule that if the egg has a hard shell, it is permitted, otherwise, prohibited. The Hillelites prohibit it under all circumstances. The form of part B is standard: Superscription, Houses, ṬM'/ṬHR.

Part C has the standard superscription, but the Houses' sayings are not balanced. The Shammaite one poses the problem. A more primitive form would have put the conditional clause into the superscription (as it indeed is now), but instead of *and if not, prohibited*, it would have had, *the House of Shammai permit*, balanced by *the House of Hillel prohibit*. The *if—not* clause is of no value, since both Houses agree on that point; at best it could have produced an element of the agreement at the end.

Part F has no counterpart in Houses-materials. M. Kel. 26:4 has Yosi taking the Shammaite position. But the approximate parallel is to Tos. Kel. B. M. 11:3, above, p. 263:

The water-skin	*Tos.*	*Mishnah*
House of Shammai say, Is filled and stands	ML'H W'WMDT	ṢRWRH W'WMDT
House of Hillel say, Is filled and bound	ML'H WṢRWRH	'P 'L PY Š'YNH ṢRWRH

The parallel is not close, but the superscription is identical. See Epstein, *Mishnah*, pp. 128-9.

Yosi's list, *parts G-M*, follows a somewhat different form. He starts with the Shammaite opinion, to which he appends *according to the words of the House of Shammai*. Then the brief Hillelite lemma follows, just as in the corresponding Mishnah.

Part N is either Simeon or Ishmael. Albeck gives Ishmael; hence the last two authorities would come from Yavnean times. But Epstein, *Mishnah*, p. 1193, shows it must be Simeon. The items all pertain to the *Purities*.

Part P, M. ʿEd. 5:3, has no counterpart in the Mishnah. M. Par. 12:4 reads, "For they have said, 'The water of the sin-offering that has served its purpose does not convey uncleanness' "—that is, the Shammaite position here, but there it is not explicitly attributed to Shammaites.

Parts R, S, and T are Eliezer's list, the briefest of all.

Part T, M. ʿEd. 5:5: The Mishnah is cited without reference to the superscription, assigning the citation to Eliezer to begin with.

Epstein, *Mevo'ot*, pp. 434-5, assigns all of M. ʿEd. Ch. 4 to Meir. As to Ch. 5, the attributions are clear, and all are *contrary* to Meir (p. 437). See his *Mishnah*, pp. 86-7, 125, 128 (*re* 5:1), 399, 964, 1193.

II.ii.123. And the House of Hillel say, "We have heard only concerning the one who comes from the harvest."

The House of Shammai said to them, "Are not all the days of the year [a time of] harvest? When the harvest of barley is done, the harvest of wheat comes, when the harvest of wheat is done, the grape-harvest comes, when the grape-harvest is done, the olive-harvest comes, so all the days of the year are harvest-time."

The House of Hillel said to them, "We find that the brothers do not inherit on the strength of her testimony."

The House of Shammai said to them, "From the Writ of her *Ketuvah*, let us learn, for it is written in it, 'When you be agreeable and marry another, take what is written in your *Ketuvah* and go forth.' "

The House of Hillel reverted to teach according to the words of the House of Shammai.

(Tos. ʿEd. 1:6, ed. Zuckermandel, p. 455, lines 19-24)

Comment: See M. Yev. 15:3, above, p. 200.

II.ii.124.A. Twenty-four things of the lenient rulings of the House of Shammai and the stringent rulings of the House of Hillel:

B. The House of Shammai say, "A man does not cause his son by vow to become a Nazir."

And the House of Hillel say, "A man causes his son by vow to become a Nazir." [= Tos. Naz. 3:17]

C. An egg that was born on the festival. [= M. Beṣ. 1:1]

D. If a man anointed himself with clean oil and was made unclean, he went down and immersed—

The House of Shammai say, "Even though it [the oil] drips and falls, he [it] is clean."

And the House of Hillel say, "[So long as there remains] enough to anoint a small member, he is unclean; if there is less than that, he is clean." [= M. ʿEd. 4:6, above, II. i. 124. I]

[E. Here follows the story of R. Eleazar b. R. Ṣadoq and Yoḥanan b. HaḤoranit, cited above, Tos. Suk. 2:3, p. 155.]

[F. The law always follows according to the words of the House of Hillel, and he who wishes to be stringent with himself to behave according to the House of Shammai and according to the House of Hillel, etc. As above, Tos. Suk. 2:3, p. 156.]

(Tos. ʿEd. 2:2-3)

G. The House of Hillel [sic] say, "A man does not free his wife with an old *Geṭ*, so that her *Geṭ* should not be older than her son." [= M. Giṭ. 8:4]

H. R. Simeon b. Eleazar said, "They did not dispute concerning one who divorces his wife, and she spends the night with him in an inn, that she does not require from him a second *Geṭ*.

"Concerning what did they dispute?

"Concerning if he had intercourse with her." [= Tos. Giṭ. 8:8]

I. He who vows his wife from [having with him] sexual relations, (for) the House of Shammai say, "Two weeks, like the birth-period of a female."

And the House of Hillel say, "One week, like the birth-period of a male and like the days of her period.

"More than this, he should send her out and pay the *Ketuvah*." [= M. Ket. 5:6]

J. The basket of food set aside for the Sabbath—(and) the House of Shammai declare free of liability, and the House of Hillel declare liable.

R. Judah says, "Hillel himself would prohibit." [= M. Ma. 4:2]

K. [There follows the set of pericopae in which R. Judah reports, "Hillel himself would prohibit." (See I, pp. 284-285.)]

L. R. Ishmael b. R. Yoḥanan b. Beroqah, "The House of Shammai and the House of Hillel did not dispute concerning him who had two groups of witnesses, that he is a Nazir according to the smaller [number of days specified by] them.

"Concerning what did they dispute?

"Concerning him who had two witnesses testifying concerning him, for

"The House of Shammai say, 'Their testimony is divided, and no Naziriteship is here.'

"And the House of Hillel say, 'There are in the category of five two, so he should be a Nazir for two.' " [= M. Naz. 3:7, Tos. Nez. 3:1]

(Tos. ʿEd. 2:4)

M. R. Judah says five things of the lenient rulings of the House of Shammai and the stringent rulings of the House of Hillel:

"The blood of carcasses—the House of Shammai declare unclean [sic], and the House of Hillel declare clean." [= M. ʿEd. 5:1, II.i.125.B, with the opinions reversed, for obvious reasons.]

N. R. Yosi b. R. Judah said, "Even when the House of Hillel declared unclean, they did not declare unclean except blood which is as much as a quarter [*log*], so that if it should congeal, there should be in it as much as an olive's bulk.

"They agree concerning the egg of a *terefah*-bird that it is prohibited, since it grew up in a prohibition.

"Concerning what did they disagree?

"Concerning the egg of a carcass, for the House of Hillel prohibit.

"And the House of Shammai say, 'If such as this are sold in the market, it is permitted, and if not it is prohibited.' " [= M. 'Ed. 5:1, II.i.125.C]

(Tos. 'E d. 2:5)

O. R. Eliezer b. Jacob says one thing of the lenient rulings of the House of Shammai and the stringent rulings of the House of Hillel:

The House of Shammai say, "Two sprinklings render fit in a sin-offering and one sprinkling in all [other] sacrifices."

And the sages [*sic*] say, "It is all the same for a sin-offering and for all the rest of the sacrifices—one sprinkling renders fit *and* makes *piggul*." [= M. Zev. 4:1, Tos. Zev. 4:9]

(Tos. 'Ed. 2:6)

P. R. Simeon says three things of the lenient rulings of the House of Shammai and the stringent rulings of the House of Hillel:

"Qohelet does not render the hands unclean," the words of the House of Shammai.

And the House of Hillel say, "It renders the hands unclean." [= M. Yad. 3:5]

Q. Sin-offering water which has served its purpose—the House of Shammai declare clean, and the House of Hillel declare unclean. [= M. 'Ed. 5:3, M. Par. 12:4]

R. A woman in hard labor, how much must she have relief (TŠPH) so that [if she sees a flux] she should be a *Zab*? R. Eliezer says, "From time to time" [= twenty-four hours], and the law follows his words.

R. Simeon b. Judah says in the name of R. Simeon, "The House of Shammai say, 'Three days.'

"And the House of Hillel say, 'From time to time' [= twenty-four hours].' " [= M. Nid. 4:4 without the Houses; and Tos. Nid. 5:7]

(Tos. 'Ed. 2:7)

S. R. Eliezer says two things of the lenient rulings of the House of Shammai and the stringent rulings of the House of Hillel:

"The blood of one who is in childbirth who *has not given birth* [*sic*] renders unclean when moist but does not render unclean when dry," the words of the House of Shammai.

And the House of Hillel say, "It renders unclean both moist and dry."

[Compare M. ʿEd. 5:4, M. Nid. 4:3. The text here is obviously defective, and the italicized words should be *who has not immersed.*]

(Tos. ʿEd. 2:8)

T. If of four brothers, two marry two sisters, and the two who have married the sisters die, lo, these perform *ḥaliṣah* and do not enter Levirate marriage, and if they [the remaining brothers] went ahead and married them, they must put them away.

R. Eleazar [*sic*] says, "The House of Shammai say, 'They may continue the marriage,' and the House of Hillel say, 'They must put them away.' "

R. Simeon says, "They may continue the marriage."

Abba Saul says, "The House of Hillel had a voice (QWL) (Alt.: *the lenient position*, as above) in this matter." [= M. Yev. 3:1, Tos. Yev. 5:1]

(Tos. ʿEd. 2:2-9, ed. Zuckermandel, pp. 457, lines 9-32, 458, lines 1-21)

Comment: This composite of pericopae opens with a superscription, promising twenty-four things, but promptly ignores it. The superscription is followed by the following items:

1. Nazir
2. Egg
3. Clean oil
4. Old *Geṭ*
5. Vow against sex
6. Basket
7. Nazir-testimony
8. Blood of carcass
9. Sprinklings
10. Qohelet
11. Sin-offering water
12. Woman in hard labor
13. Blood of childbirth
14. Four brothers.

It seems to me that at best the superscription might read *fourteen*. But more likely, the superscription is correct, a stock-phrase borrowed from elsewhere, and, like much that follows, has simply been deposited here as part of a disorganized collection of materials. As indicated, nearly everything has already been seen elsewhere, generally in M. ʿEd., sometimes in other Toseftan passages. But we cannot suppose that the "editor" has systematically assembled pertinent Tosefta materials. The composite seems to me random and aimless.

See Lieberman, *Tosefet Rishonim* II, pp. 183-4; Epstein, *Mevo'ot*, p. 435.)

VIII. Tables

		I	II.i	II.ii
I.	*House of Shammai Alone*	*Tannaitic Midrashim*	*Mishnah*	*Tosefta*
1.	Between two evenings	Mekhilta deR. Simeon b. Yoḥai, p. 12, lines 4-5		
2.	Blessing of savory does not exempt food cooked in pot		M. Ber. 6:5	
3.	Almoners collect food and distribute it to those who tithe		M. Demai 3:1	
4.	Weasel		M. Kil. 8:5	
5.	Trough of Jehu broken by Shammaites		M. Miq. 4:5	
6.	Kneading trough filled with pots		(M. Miq. 6:5 = Judah)	Tos. Miq. 5:2
7.	Stream of porridge conveys uncleanness		M. Maksh. 5:9	

II. *House of Hillel Alone*	*Tannaitic Midrashim*
Little children liable to make appearance (see Sifré Deut. 143)	Mekhilta deR. Simeon b. Yoḥai, p. 218, lines 28-9

		I	II.i	II.ii
III.	*House of Hillel and House of Shammai*	*Tannaitic Midrashim*	*Mishnah*	*Tosefta*
1.	Liable for intention to steal	Mekhilta deR. Ishmael Nez. 15:49-55		
2.	Abortion on eight-first day	Sifra Tazriʿa 3:1	(M. Ker. 1:6 reverses)	
3.	Strands of *ṣiṣit*	Sifré Deut. 234 (Sifré Num. 115 reverses)		

House of Hillel and House of Shammai	I *Tannaitic Midrashim*	II.i *Mishnah*	II.ii *Tosefta*
4. Clean table			(M. Shab. 21:3 Tos. Shab. 16:7 reverses)
5. Where do they shake *Lulav*		M. Suk. 4:9	
6. Gather grapes in grave-area		M. Oh. 18:1	
7. Maturity at 20/18		M. Nid. 5:9	
8. Woman after childbirth cannot touch purities		M. Nid. 10:6	

IV. *House of Shammai and House of Hillel*	I *Tannaitic Midrashim*	II.i *Mishnah*	II.ii *Tosefta*
1. Inspect *tefillin*	Mekhilta deR. Ishmael Pisḥa 17:210-216		
2. Bailiff pays according to hour of removal	Sifra Vayiqra 13:13		Tos. B.M. 3:12
3. Burn unclean holy things in Temple court (compare M. M.S. 3:9)	Sifra Ṣav 8:6	M. Sheq. 8:6-5	
4. Baby born circumcized	Sifra Tazri'a 1:5		Tos. Shab. 15:9
5. Abortion on eighty-first day	(Sifra Tazri'a 3:1 reverses)	M. Ker. 1:6 M. 'Ed. 4:10	Tos. Ker. 1:9
6. Unclean bloods	Sifra Tazri'a 3:6 Sifra Meṣora' 4:3	M. Nid. 2:6	
7. Grape-gleanings and defective cluster	Sifra Qedoshim 3:7	M. 'Ed. 4:5b M. M.S. 5:3 M. Pe'ah 7:6	
8. No festive pilgrim offering on holiday/Sabbath	Sifra Emor 15:5		
9. Fruit of field which has been prepared	Sifra Behar 1:5	M. Shev. 4:26 M. 'Ed. 5:1	
10. Strands of *ṣiṣit*	Sifré Num. 115 (Sifré Deut. 234 reverses) Midrash Tannaim to Deut. 22:12		

		I	II.i	II.ii
	House of Shammai and House of Hillel	*Tannaitic Midrashim*	*Mishnah*	*Tosefta*
11.	Reciting Shema'	Sifré Deut. 34 (Midrash Tannaim to Deut. 6:8)	M. Ber. 1:3	Tos. Ber. 1:4
12.	Leaven	Sifré Deut. 131	M. Beṣ. 1:1	Tos. Y.Ṭ. 1:4
13.	Who is child? (See Mekh. deR. Simeon, p. 218)	Sifré Deut. 143	M. Ḥag. 1:1	
14.	Fleece	Sifré Deut. 166	M. Ḥul. 11:2	
15.	Grounds for divorce	Sifré Deut. 269	M. Giṭ. 9:10	
16.	*Ṣiṣit* on linen cloak	Midrash Tannaim to Deut. 22:12	M. 'Ed. 4:10	
17.	Day/wine		M. Ber. 8:1 M. Pes. 10:2	Tos. Pisḥa 10:2-3 Tos. Ber. 5:35-30
18.	Wash hands/mix cup		M. Ber. 8:2	
19.	Napkin on table/cushion		M. Ber. 8:3	
20.	Sweep/wash		M. Ber. 8:4	
21.	Spices/food		M. Ber. 8:5a	
22.	Created light/creates lights		M. Ber. 8:5b	
23.	Forget grace		M. Ber. 8:7	
24.	One blesses for all			Tos. Ber. 5:30
25.	Wine/food		M. Ber. 8:8	
26.	New Year-Sabbath—how many blessings, etc.			Tos. Ber. 3:13 Tos. R.H. 2:17
27.	*Pe'ah* from plots sown with grain		M. Pe'ah 3:1	
28.	Ownerless		M. Pe'ah 6:1 M. 'Ed. 4:3	
29.	Sheaf left near wall		M. Pe'ah 6:2 M. 'Ed. 4:4	Tos. Pe'ah 3:2
30.	Sheaf to city		M. Pe'ah 6:3	Tos. Pe'ah 3:2
31.	Forgotten sheaf—three/four		M. Pe'ah 6:5	
32.	Grapes of Fourth-year vineyard		M. M.S. 5:3 M. Pe'ah 7:6 M. 'Ed. 4:5	
33.	*Demai* and sweet oil		M. Demai 1:3	Tos. Demai 1:26-7
34.	Sell olives only to *ḥaver*		M. Demai 6:6	Tos. Ma. 3:13
35.	Space between plots with different crops		M. Kil. 2:6	
36.	Vineyard patch		M. Kil. 4:1	
37.	How many vines constitute etc.		M. Kil. 4:5 M. 'Ed. 5:2	

	House of Shammai and House of Hillel	I *Tannaitic Midrashim*	II.i *Mishnah*	II.ii *Tosefta*
38.	Trellised vine		M. Kil. 6:1	
39.	Weasel		M. Kil 8:5	
40.	Caper-bush in vineyard			Tos. Kil. 3:17
41.	Shoot over stone			Tos. Kil. 4:11
42.	Ploughing tree planted field before Seventh Year		M. Shev. 1:1	
43.	Produce of prepared field in Seventh Year		M. Shev. 4:2 M. 'Ed. 5:1	
44.	Thinning out olive trees in Seventh Year		M. Shev. 4:4	
45.	Cutting down trees in Seventh Year		M. Shev. 4:10	
46.	Digging up produce in Seventh Year		M. Shev. 5:4	
47.	Selling ploughing heifer to non-observant in Seventh Year		M. Shev. 5:8	
48.	Selling produce in Seventh Year		M. Shev. 8:3	
49.	Watering plants in Seventh Year			Tos. Shev. 1:5
50.	Tithing pods (*hyssop*)			Tos. Shev. 2:6 Tos. Ma. 1:5
51.	Selling field to non-observant in Seventh Year			Tos. Shev. 4:5
52.	'Aqiba followed both Houses in tithing			Tos. Shev. 4:21
53.	Sell produce for produce, not coins in Seventh Year			Tos. Shev. 6:19
54.	If Heave-offering is given from olives instead of the oil		M. Ter. 1:4 M. 'Ed. 5:2	(Tos. Ter. 2:5; Tos. Ter. 3:14)
55.	Proper measure of Heave-offering		M. Ter. 4:3	
56.	Unclean Heave-offering neutralized in clean		M. Ter. 5:4	Tos. Ter. 6:4
57.	Heave-offering from variant kinds of same species			Tos. Ter. 2:5
58.	Make vat unclean			Tos. Ter. 3:12
59.	Crushed olives, olive oil or olives			Tos. Ter. 3:14
60.	Heave-offering from grapes that end up raisins			Tos. Ter. 3:16
61.	Tithing Sabbath-fruit		M. Ma. 4:2 M. 'Ed. 4:10	Tos. 'Ed. 2:4
62.	One who sifts by hand liable for tithes			Tos. Ma. 3:10

		I	II.i	II.ii
	House of Shammai and House of Hillel	*Tannaitic Midrashim*	*Mishnah*	*Tosefta*
63.	Heave-offering of fenugreek		M. M.S. 2:3	Tos. M.S. 2:1
64.	Heave-offering of vetches		M. M.S. 2:4 M. 'Ed. 1:8	Tos. M.S. 2:1
65.	Change *selas* for *denars*		M. M.S. 2:7	
66.	Change *sela* of Second Tithe money outside Jerusalem		M. M.S. 2:8 M. 'Ed. 1:9	
67.	Change *sela* of Second Tithe money in Jerusalem		M. M.S. 2:9 M. 'Ed. 1:10	
68.	Not yet fully harvested produce passes through Jerusalem		M. M.S. 3:6	Tos. M.S. 2:11
69.	Olive-presses in Jerusalem wall		M. M.S. 3:7	Tos. M.S. 2:12 Tos. 'Arak. 5:15
70.	Second Tithe produce unclean in Jerusalem		M. M.S. 3:9 M. Sheq. 8:6	Tos. M.S. 2:16 Tos. Sheq. 3:16
71.	Open jars to give Heave-offering		M. M.S. 3:13	Tos. M.S. 2:18
72.	*Issar* of Second Tithe money		M. M.S. 4:8	
73.	Removal of cooked food		M. M.S. 5:6	
74.	Removal of Second Tithe produce in this time		M. M.S. 5:7	Tos. M.S. 3:13
75.	Separate tithe of *Demai*			Tos. M.S. 3:15
76.	*Ḥallah* from flour paste and dumplings		M. Ḥal. 1:6 M. 'Ed. 5:2	
77.	Unclean mixture renders unclean in less than an olive's bulk		M. 'Orlah 2:4-5	
78.	Finishing work before Sabbath	Mekh. deR. Simeon b. Yoḥai, p. 149	M. Shab. 1:4-9	
79.	Using stove on Sabbath		M. Shab. 3:1	Tos. Shab. 2:13 Tos. Pisḥa 7:2
80.	Cleaning table on Sabbath		M. Shab. 21:3	Tos. Shab. 16:7 (reverses Houses)
81.	Pharisaic *Zab* not eat with outsider-*Zab*			Tos. Shab. 1:14
82.	Uncleanness conveyed by ox-goad			Tos. Shab. 1:18
83.	He who forgets vessels under water-pipe on eve of Sabbath			Tos. Shab. 1:19
84.	Carrying on Sabbath			Tos. Shab. 14:1
85.	Kill louse on Sabbath			Tos. Shab. 16:21
86.	Distribute charity on Sabbath			Tos. Shab. 16:22

	House of Shammai and House of Hillel	I *Tannaitic Midrashim*	II.i *Mishnah*	II.ii *Tosefta*
87.	To render alleyway valid		M. ʿEruv. 1:2	
88.	When give right of access		M. ʿEruv. 6:4a	
89.	ʿ*Eruv* for five groups in same room		M. ʿEruv. 6:6	
90.	Partition for cistern		M. ʿEruv. 8:6	
91.	Search wine vault		M. Pes. 1:1	
92.	Work in Galilee on night before 14th of Nisan		M. Pes. 4:5	
93.	Proselyte on day before Passover		M. Pes. 8:8 M. ʿEd. 5:2	Tos. Pisḥa 7:14
94.	*Hallel* on Passover		M. Pes. 10:6	
95.	Burn unclean and clean meat			Tos. Pisḥa 1:6
96.	Excess funds for *sheqel* sin-offering		M. Sheq. 2:3	
97.	Old *Sukkah*		M. Suk. 1:1	
98.	*Sukkah* with timber-roof		M. Suk. 1:7	
99.	*Sukkah* too small to hold table		M. Suk. 2:7	
100.	*Etrog* of *Demai*-produce		M. Suk. 3:5	
101.	Egg laid on festival		M. Beṣ. 1:1 M. ʿEd. 4:1	Tos. ʿEd. 2:2
102.	Dirt to cover blood of slaughtered animal		M. Beṣ. 1:2 M. ʿEd. 4:2	
103.	Move ladder on festival		M. Beṣ. 1:3	Tos. Y.Ṭ. 1:8
104.	Prepare pigeons before festival		M. Beṣ. 1:3	Tos. Y.Ṭ. 1:8, 1:10
105.	Take off cupboard doors, etc.		M. Beṣ. 1:5	Tos. Y.Ṭ. 1:10
106.	Take gifts to priest on festival		M. Beṣ. 1:6	Tos. Y.Ṭ. 1:12-14
107.	Pound spices and salt on festival		M. Beṣ. 1:7	Tos. Y.Ṭ. 1:11 Tos. Y.Ṭ. 1:15
108.	Picking pulse on festival		M. Beṣ. 1:8	Tos. Y.Ṭ. 1:21
109.	Send prepared portions as festival gift		M. Beṣ. 1:9	
110.	One or two *tavshilin*		M. Beṣ. 2:1	Tos. Y.Ṭ. 2:4
111.	Immersion for Sabbath-festival		M. Beṣ. 2:2	
112.	Lay hands on festival sacrifice		M. Beṣ. 2:4 M. Ḥag. 2:2 M. Ḥag. 2:3	Tos. Ḥag. 2:10
113.	Make fire on festival		M. Beṣ. 2:5	
114.	Cover hot food on festival for Sabbath		M. Beṣ. 2:6	
115.	Put together candlestick on festival		M. Beṣ. 2:6	
116.	Bake large loaves on festival		M. Beṣ. 2:6	

		I	II.i	II.ii
	House of Shammai and House of Hillel	*Tannaitic Midrashim*	*Mishnah*	*Tosefta*
117.	Collect scattered things in enclosure and gathered things in field, etc.			Tos. Y.Ṭ. 3:10
118.	New Year of trees		M. R.H. 1:1	
119.	Cost of *re'iyyah* and *ḥagigah* sacrifices		M. Ḥag. 1:2	Tos. Ḥag. 1:4
120.	Source of funds for festal sacrifices		M. Ḥag. 1:3	Tos. Ḥag. 1:4
121.	Pentecost on Friday—when to slaughter festal sacrifices		M. Ḥag. 2:4	
122.	Overturning couch of mourner before festival			Tos. M.Q. 2:9
123.	Levirate marriage of co-wives		M. Yev. 1:4 M. 'Ed. 4:8	Tos. Yev. 1:7-13
124.	Marriage followed by Levirate obligation		M. Yev. 3:1 M. 'Ed. 5:5	Tos. Yev. 5:1 Tos. 'Ed. 2:9
125.	Effect of *ma'amar* in case of Levirate marriage		M. Yev. 3:5 M. 'Ed. 4:9	
126.	Estate of woman awaiting Levirate marriage, etc.		M. Yev. 4:3 M. Ket. 8:6 M. B.B. 8:8-9	Tos. B.B. 10:13
127.	Abstain from sex after two children		M. Yev. 6:6	Tos. Yev. 6:6
128.	Refusal-collection		M. Yev. 13:1	Tos. Yev. 13:1
129.	Woman testifies in death of husband		M. Yev. 15:2 M. 'Ed. 1:12	
130.	Disposition of woman who testifies *re* death of husband		M. Yev. 15:3 M. 'Ed. 1:12	Tos. 'Ed. 1:6
131.	Vow against intercourse		M. Ket. 5:6 M. 'Ed. 4:10	Tos. 'Ed. 2:4
132.	Estate of woman awaiting marriage		M. Ket. 8:1	
133.	Vow in mistaken assumption		M. Ned. 3:2	
134.	Vow to murderers-collection		M. Ned. 3:4	
135.	Father and husband annul girl's vows			Tos. Ned. 6:4
136.	Substitute language for Nazir		M. Naz. 2:1-2	Tos. Nez. 1:1
137.	Nazir from abroad		M. Naz. 3:6 M. 'Ed. 4:11	
138.	Division of testimony *re* Nazir		M. Naz. 3:7 M. 'Ed. 4:11	Tos. Nez. 3:1 Tos. 'Ed. 2:14
139.	Thing dedicated in error		M. Naz. 5:1, 2, 3	
140.	Nazirite vow in error		M. Naz. 5:5	Tos. Nez. 3:19

	House of Shammai and House of Hillel	I *Tannaitic Midrashim*	II.i *Mishnah*	II.ii *Tosefta*
	House of Shammai and House of Hillel	*Tannaitic Midrashim*	*Mishnah*	*Tosefta*
141.	Vow without specifying term			Tos. Nez. 2:10
142.	Impose vow of Nazir			Tos. Nez. 3:17 Tos. 'Ed. 2:2
143.	Sage rules vow binding			Tos. Nez. 3:19
144.	Husband dies before water-ordeal		M. Soṭ. 4:2	Tos. Soṭ. 4:7
145.	Woman commits adultery with minor son			Tos. Soṭ. 4:7
146.	Half-slave, half-free		M. Giṭ. 4:5 M. 'Ed. 1:13	
147.	Old *Geṭ*		M. Giṭ. 8:4 M. 'Ed. 4:7	Tos. Giṭ. 8:3 Tos. 'Ed. 2:4
148.	Impaired *Geṭ*		M. Giṭ. 8:8	Tos. Giṭ. 8:8
149.	Spent night together after divorce—is new *Geṭ* needed?		M. Giṭ. 8:9	Tos. Giṭ. 8:8
150.	How much money for betrothal?		M. Qid. 1:1 M. 'Ed. 4:7	
151.	Agent becomes witness			Tos. Qid. 4:1
152.	Return stolen beam or its cost			Tos. B.Q. 9:5
153.	Intermediate people go to Gehenna and come back			Tos. Sanh. 13:3
154.	Sin-offering requires two sprinklings		M. Zev. 4:1	Tos. Zev. 4:9 Tos. 'Ed. 2:6
155.	Slaughter with hand-sickle		M. Ḥul. 1:2	Tos. Ḥul. 1:6
156.	Chicken and cheese on table		M. Ḥul. 8:1 M. 'Ed. 5:2	Tos. Ḥul. 8:23
157.	Number Israelite for firstling		M. Bekh. 5:2	Tos. Bekh. 3:15-16
158.	Sanctifies property and divorces wife			Tos. 'Arak. 4:5
159.	Added fifth to additional payment			Tos. 'Arak. 4:22
160.	Siphon in tent		M. Kel. 9:2	
161.	Articles made from nails		M. Kel. 11:3	
162.	When does tube (etc.) become insusceptible (ḤBL/ḤBR)		M. Kel. 14:2	Tos. Kel. B.M 4:5 (tube) Tos. Kel. B.M. 11:7 (matting)
163.	Measure chest		M. Kel. 18:1	Tos. Kel. B.M. 8:1
164.	Trough for mixing mortar		M. Kel. 20:2 (M. 'Ed. 5:1)	Tos. Kel. B.M. 11:3
165.	When does sheet become insusceptible		M. Kel. 20:6	

	House of Shammai and House of Hillel	I *Tannaitic Midrashim*	II.i *Mishnah*	II.ii *Tosefta*
166.	Stool fixed to baking trough		M. Kel. 22:4	Tos. Kel. B.B. 1:12
167.	Wrappers for garments and purple wool		M. Kel. 26:6	Tos. Kel. B.B. 4:9
168.	Scroll-wrappers		M. Kel. 28:4	
169.	Shaft of trowel		M. Kel. 29:9	Tos. Kel. B.B. 7:4
170.	Vessels of alum-crystal		(M. Kel. 2:1)	Tos. Kel. B.Q. 2:1
171.	Peat in cool oven		(M. Kel. 9:5)	Tos. Kel. B.Q. 6:18
172.	Shovel without blade			Tos. Kel. B.M. 3:8
173.	Mustard-strainer		(M. Kel. 14:8)	Tos. Kel. B.M. 4:16
174.	Girdle			Tos. Kel. B.B. 5: 7-8
175.	Backbone and skull		M. Oh. 2:3	
176.	Baking oven in house with arched outlet—overshadows corpse		M. Oh. 5:1-4	Tos. Ah. 5:11-12
177.	Cooking pot protects from uncleanness		M. Oh. 5:2-3	
178.	Protecting entrances of room with corpse		M. Oh. 7:3	Tos. Ah. 8:7
179.	Split in roof		M. Oh. 11:1	Tos. Ah. 12:1
180.	Man gives passage to uncleanness		M. Oh. 11:3-6 M. ʿEd. 4:12	
181.	Candle-stick protected by basket		M. Oh. 13:1	
182.	Do holes join place for rod		M. Oh. 13:4	Tos. Ah. 14:4
183.	Man in forecourt of tomb-vault		M. Oh. 15:8	
184.	Gather grapes in grave-area		M. Oh. 18:1	Tos. Ah. 17:9
185.	Examine grave-area for Nazir		M. Oh. 18:4	Tos. Ah. 17:13
186.	What do they examine		M. Oh. 18:8	Tos. Ah. 16:6
187.	Quarter-*qab* of bones, etc.		(M. Oh. 2:1) M. ʿEd. 1:7	Tos. Ah. 3:4
188.	Bottle plugging grave			Tos. Ah. 15:9
189.	When do olives receive uncleanness		M. Ṭoh. 9:1	Tos. Ṭoh. 10:2
190.	Olives left to be salted		M. Ṭoh. 9:5	
191.	Bringing part of olives to press		M. Ṭoh. 9:7	
192.	Putting grapes into press		M. Ṭoh. 10:4	

		I	II.i	II.ii
	House of Shammai and House of Hillel	*Tannaitic Midrashim*	*Mishnah*	*Tosefta*
193.	Leaving vessels with *'am-ha'areṣ*			Tos. Ṭoh. 8:10
194.	Cleaning pool		M. Miq. 1:5	Tos. Miq. 1:7, 10
195.	Vessels under waterspout		M. Miq. 4:1	
196.	Immerse vessels in rain-stream		M. Miq. 5:6 M. 'Ed. 5:2	
197.	Immerse hot water in cold, etc.		M. Miq. 10:6	
198.	Two test-rags for every act		M. Nid. 2:4	
199.	Colors of unclean blood		M. Nid. 2:6	
200.	Blood of gentile woman, etc.		M. Nid. 4:3 M. 'Ed. 5:1, 4	Tos. Nid. 5:5-7 Tos. Nid. 2:7-8
201.	Marriage of girl before puberty		M. Nid. 10:1	Tos. Nid. 9:7-9
202.	Women die as menstruants		M. Nid. 10:4	
203.	Woman after childbirth must immerse		M. Nid. 10:7	
204.	Suffered flux on eleventh day		M. Nid. 10:8	Tos. Nid. 9:19
205.	Nursing mother remarries 18/24 mos.			Tos. Nid. 2:2
206.	Shakes tree—what of water?		M. Maksh. 1:2-4	Tos. Maksh. 1:1-4
207.	Water leaks into jar of fruit		M. Maksh. 4:4	
208.	Water leaks into trough		M. Maksh. 4:5	Tos. Maksh. 2:6
209.	Ambiguous *Zab*-state		M. Zab. 1:1-2	Tos. Zab. 1:1-8
210.	Connective for *ṭevul-yom*		M. Ṭ.Y. 1:1	
211.	Jelly as connective for *ṭevul-yom*		(M. Ṭ.Y. 2:5)	Tos. Ṭ.Y. 2:3
212.	Ecclesiastes renders hands unclean		M. Yad. 3:5 M. 'Ed. 5:3	Tos. 'Ed. 2:7
213.	Hard olives and grapes susceptible to uncleanness		M. 'Uqṣ. 3:6 M. 'Ed. 5:3	
214.	When do fish become susceptible to uncleanness		M. 'Uqṣ. 3:8	
215.	When do honeycombs become susceptible to uncleanness		M. 'Uqṣ. 3:11	
216.	Broach pickled jars		M. 'Ed. 4:6	
217.	Oil on body after immersion		M. 'Ed. 4:6	Tos. 'Ed. 2:2
218.	Sin-offering water that has served its purpose		M. 'Ed. 5:3 (M. Par. 12:4)	Tos. 'Ed. 2:7
219.	Blood of carcasses		M. 'Ed. 5:1	Tos. 'Ed. 2:5

South Florida Studies in the History of Judaism

240001	Lectures on Judaism in the Academy and in the Humanities	Neusner
240002	Lectures on Judaism in the History of Religion	Neusner
240003	Self-Fulfilling Prophecy: Exile and Return in the History of Judaism	Neusner
240004	The Canonical History of Ideas: The Place of the So-called Tannaite Midrashim, Mekhilta Attributed to R. Ishmael, Sifra, Sifré to Numbers, and Sifré to Deuteronomy	Neusner
240005	Ancient Judaism: Debates and Disputes, Second Series	Neusner
240006	The Hasmoneans and Their Supporters: From Mattathias to the Death of John Hyrcanus I	Sievers
240007	Approaches to Ancient Judaism: New Series, Volume One	Neusner
240008	Judaism in the Matrix of Christianity	Neusner
240009	Tradition as Selectivity: Scripture, Mishnah, Tosefta, and Midrash in the Talmud of Babylonia	Neusner
240010	The Tosefta: Translated from the Hebrew: Sixth Division Tohorot	Neusner
240011	In the Margins of the Midrash: Sifre Ha'azinu Texts, Commentaries and Reflections	Basser
240012	Language as Taxonomy: The Rules for Using Hebrew and Aramaic in the Babylonia Talmud	Neusner
240013	The Rules of Composition of the Talmud of Babylonia: The Cogency of the Bavli's Composite	Neusner
240014	Understanding the Rabbinic Mind: Essays on the Hermeneutic of Max Kadushin	Ochs
240015	Essays in Jewish Historiography	Rapoport-Albert
240016	The Golden Calf and the Origins of the Jewish Controversy	Bori/Ward
240017	Approaches to Ancient Judaism: New Series, Volume Two	Neusner
240018	The Bavli That Might Have Been: The Tosefta's Theory of Mishnah Commentary Compared With the Bavli's	Neusner
240019	The Formation of Judaism: In Retrospect and Prospect	Neusner
240020	Judaism in Society: The Evidence of the Yerushalmi, Toward the Natural History of a Religion	Neusner
240021	The Enchantments of Judaism: Rites of Transformation from Birth Through Death	Neusner
240022	Åbo Addresses	Neusner
240023	The City of God in Judaism and Other Comparative and Methodological Studies	Neusner
240024	The Bavli's One Voice: Types and Forms of Analytical Discourse and their Fixed Order of Appearance	Neusner
240025	The Dura-Europos Synagogue: A Re-evaluation (1932-1992)	Gutmann
240026	Precedent and Judicial Discretion: The Case of Joseph ibn Lev	Morell
240027	Max Weinreich *Geschichte der jiddischen Sprachforschung*	Frakes
240028	Israel: Its Life and Culture, Volume I	Pedersen
240029	Israel: Its Life and Culture, Volume II	Pedersen
240030	The Bavli's One Statement: The Metapropositional Program of Babylonian Talmud Tractate Zebahim Chapters One and Five	Neusner

240031	The Oral Torah: The Sacred Books of Judaism: An Introduction: Second Printing	Neusner
240032	The Twentieth Century Construction of "Judaism:" Essays on the Religion of Torah in the History of Religion	Neusner
240033	How the Talmud Shaped Rabbinic Discourse	Neusner
240034	The Discourse of the Bavli: Language, Literature, and Symbolism: Five Recent Findings	Neusner
240035	The Law Behind the Laws: The Bavli's Essential Discourse	Neusner
240036	Sources and Traditions: Types of Compositions in the Talmud of Babylonia	Neusner
240037	How to Study the Bavli: The Languages, Literatures, and Lessons of the Talmud of Babylonia	Neusner
240038	The Bavli's Primary Discourse: Mishnah Commentary: Its Rhetorical Paradigms and their Theological Implications	Neusner
240039	Midrash Aleph Beth	Sawyer
240040	Jewish Thought in the 20th Century: An Introduction in the Talmud of Babylonia Tractate Moed Qatan	Schweid
240041	Diaspora Jews and Judaism: Essays in Honor of, and in Dialogue with, A. Thomas Kraabel	Overman/MacLennan
240042	The Bavli: An Introduction	Neusner
240043	The Bavli's Massive Miscellanies: The Problem of Agglutinative Discourse in the Talmud of Babylonia	Neusner
240044	The Foundations of the Theology of Judaism: An Anthology Part II: Torah	Neusner
240045	Form-Analytical Comparison in Rabbinic Judaism: Structure and Form in *The Fathers* and *The Fathers According to Rabbi Nathan*	Neusner
240046	Essays on Hebrew	Weinberg
240047	The Tosefta: An Introduction	Neusner
240048	The Foundations of the Theology of Judaism: An Anthology Part III: Israel	Neusner
240049	The Study of Ancient Judaism, Volume I: Mishnah, Midrash, Siddur	Neusner
240050	The Study of Ancient Judaism, Volume II: The Palestinian and Babylonian Talmuds	Neusner
240051	Take Judaism, for Example: Studies toward the Comparison of Religions	Neusner
240052	From Eden to Golgotha: Essays in Biblical Theology	Moberly
240053	The Principal Parts of the Bavli's Discourse: A Preliminary Taxonomy: Mishnah Commentary, Sources, Traditions and Agglutinative Miscellanies	Neusner
240054	Barabbas and Esther and Other Studies in the Judaic Illumination of Earliest Christianity	Aus
240055	Targum Studies, Volume I: Textual and Contextual Studies in the Pentateuchal Targums	Flesher
240056	Approaches to Ancient Judaism: New Series, Volume Three, Historical and Literary Studies	Neusner
240057	The Motherhood of God and Other Studies	Gruber
240058	The Analytic Movement: Hayyim Soloveitchik and his Circle	Solomon
240059	Recovering the Role of Women: Power and Authority in Rabbinic Jewish Society	Haas

240060	The Relation between Herodotus' *History* and Primary History	Mandell/Freedman
240061	The First Seven Days: A Philosophical Commentary on the Creation of Genesis	Samuelson
240062	The Bavli's Intellectual Character: The Generative Problematic: In Bavli Baba Qamma Chapter One And Bavli Shabbat Chapter One	Neusner
240063	The Incarnation of God: The Character of Divinity in Formative Judaism: Second Printing	Neusner
240064	Moses Kimhi: Commentary on the Book of Job	Basser/Walfish
240066	Death and Birth of Judaism: Second Printing	Neusner
240067	Decoding the Talmud's Exegetical Program	Neusner
240068	Sources of the Transformation of Judaism	Neusner
240069	The Torah in the Talmud: A Taxonomy of the Uses of Scripture in the Talmud, Volume I	Neusner
240070	The Torah in the Talmud: A Taxonomy of the Uses of Scripture in the Talmud, Volume II	Neusner
240071	The Bavli's Unique Voice: A Systematic Comparison of the Talmud of Babylonia and the Talmud of the Land of Israel, Volume One	Neusner
240072	The Bavli's Unique Voice: A Systematic Comparison of the Talmud of Babylonia and the Talmud of the Land of Israel, Volume Two	Neusner
240073	The Bavli's Unique Voice: A Systematic Comparison of the Talmud of Babylonia and the Talmud of the Land of Israel, Volume Three	Neusner
240074	Bits of Honey: Essays for Samson H. Levey	Chyet/Ellenson
240075	The Mystical Study of Ruth: *Midrash HaNe'elam* of the Zohar to the Book of Ruth	Englander
240076	The Bavli's Unique Voice: A Systematic Comparison of the Talmud of Babylonia and the Talmud of the Land of Israel, Volume Four	Neusner
240077	The Bavli's Unique Voice: A Systematic Comparison of the Talmud of Babylonia and the Talmud of the Land of Israel, Volume Five	Neusner
240078	The Bavli's Unique Voice: A Systematic Comparison of the Talmud of Babylonia and the Talmud of the Land of Israel, Volume Six	Neusner
240079	The Bavli's Unique Voice: A Systematic Comparison of the Talmud of Babylonia and the Talmud of the Land of Israel, Volume Seven	Neusner
240080	Are There Really Tannaitic Parallels to the Gospels?	Neusner
240081	Approaches to Ancient Judaism: New Series, Volume Four, Religious and Theological Studies	Neusner
240082	Approaches to Ancient Judaism: New Series, Volume Five, Historical, Literary, and Religious Studies	Basser/Fishbane
240083	Ancient Judaism: Debates and Disputes, Third Series	Neusner
240084	Judaic Law from Jesus to the Mishnah	Neusner
240085	Writing with Scripture: Second Printing	Neusner/Green
240086	Foundations of Judaism: Second Printing	Neusner

240087	Judaism and Zoroastrianism at the Dusk of Late Antiquity	Neusner
240088	Judaism States Its Theology	Neusner
240089	The Judaism behind the Texts I.A	Neusner
240090	The Judaism behind the Texts I.B	Neusner
240091	Stranger at Home	Neusner
240092	Pseudo-Rabad: Commentary to Sifre Deuteronomy	Basser
240093	FromText to Historical Context in Rabbinic Judaism	Neusner
240094	Formative Judaism	Neusner
240095	Purity in Rabbinic Judaism	Neusner
240096	Was Jesus of Nazareth the Messiah?	McMichael
240097	The Judaism behind the Texts I.C	Neusner
240098	The Judaism behind the Texts II	Neusner
240099	The Judaism behind the Texts III	Neusner
240100	The Judaism behind the Texts IV	Neusner
240101	The Judaism behind the Texts V	Neusner
240102	The Judaism the Rabbis Take for Granted	Neusner
240103	From Text to Historical Context in Rabbinic Judaism V. II	Neusner
240104	From Text to Historical Context in Rabbinic Judaism V. III	Neusner
240105	Samuel, Saul, and Jesus: Three Early Palestinian Jewish Christian Gospel Haggadoth	Aus
240106	What is Midrash? And a Midrash Reader	Neusner
240107	Rabbinic Judaism: Disputes and Debates	Neusner
240108	Why There Never Was a "Talmud of Caesarea"	Neusner
240109	Judaism after the Death of "The Death of God"	Neusner
240110	Approaches to Ancient Judaism	Neusner
240112	The Judaic Law of Baptism	Neusner
240113	The Documentary Foundation of Rabbinic Culture	Neusner
240114	Understanding Seeking Faith, Volume Four	Neusner
240115	Paul and Judaism: An Anthropological Approach	Laato
240116	Approaches to Ancient Judaism, New Series, Volume Eight	Neusner
240119	Theme and Context in Biblical Lists	Scolnic
240120	Where the Talmud Comes From	Neusner
240121	The Initial Phases of the Talmud, Volume Three: Social Ethics	Neusner
240122	Are the Talmuds Interchangeable? Christine Hayes's Blunder	Neusner
240123	The Initial Phases of the Talmud, Volume One: Exegesis of Scripture	Neusner
240124	The Initial Phases of the Talmud, Volume Two: Exemplary Virtue	Neusner
240125	The Initial Phases of the Talmud, Volume Four: Theology	Neusner
240126	From Agnon to Oz	Bargad
240127	Talmudic Dialectics, Volume I: Tractate Berakhot and the Divisions of Appointed Times and Women	Neusner
240128	Talmudic Dialectics, Volume II: The Divisions of Damages and Holy Things and Tractate Niddah	Neusner
240129	The Talmud: Introduction and Reader	Neusner
240130	*Gesher Vakesher:* Bridges and Bonds The Life of Leon Kronish	Green
240131	Beyond Catastrophe	Neusner

240132	Ancient Judaism, Fourth Series	Neusner
240133	Formative Judaism, New Series: Current Issues and Arguments Volume One	Neusner
240134	Sects and Scrolls	Davies
240135	Religion and Law	Neusner
240136	Approaches to Ancient Judaism, New Series, Volume Nine	Neusner
240137	Uppsala Addresses	Neusner
240138	Jews and Christians in the Life and Thought of Hugh of St. Victor	Moore
240140	Jews, Pagans, and Christians in the Golan Heights	Gregg/Urman
240141	Rosenzweig on Profane/Secular History	Vogel
240142	Approaches to Ancient Judaism, New Series, Volume Ten	Neusner
240143	Archaeology and the Galilee	Edwards/McCullough
240144	Rationality and Structure	Neusner
240145	Formative Judaism, New Series: Current Issues and Arguments Volume Two	Neusner
240146	Ancient Judaism, Religious and Theological Perspectives First Series	Neusner
240147	The Good Creator	Gelander
240148	The Mind of Classical Judaism, Volume IV, The Philosophy and Political Economy of Formative Judaism: The Mishnah's System of the Social Order	Neusner
240149	The Mind of Classical Judaism, Volume I, Modes of Thought:: Making Connections and Drawing Conclusions	Neusner
240150	The Mind of Classical Judaism, Volume II, From Philosophy to Religion	Neusner
241051	The Mind of Classical Judaism, Volume III, What is "Israel"? Social Thought in the Formative Age	Neusner
240152	The Tosefta, Translated from the Hebrew: Fifth Division, Qodoshim, The Order of Holy Things	Neusner
240153	The Theology of Rabbinic Judaism: A Prolegomenon	Neusner
240154	Approaches to Ancient Judaism, New Series, Volume Eleven	Neusner
240155	Pesiqta Rabbati: A Synoptic Edition of Pesiqta Rabbati Based upon all Extant Manuscripts and the Editio Princeps, V. I	Ulmer
240156	The Place of the Tosefta in the Halakhah of Formative Judaism: What Alberdina Houtman Didn't Notice	Neusner
240157	"Caught in the Act," Walking on the Sea, and The Release of Barabbas Revisited	Aus
240158	Approaches to Ancient Judaism, New Series, Volume Twelve	Neusner
240159	The Halakhah of the Oral Torah, A Religious Commentary, Introduction and Volume I, Part One, Between Israel and God	Neusner
240160	Claudian Policymaking and the Early Imperial Repression of Judaism at Rome	Slingerland
240161	Rashi's Commentary on Psalms 1–89 with English Translation, Introducion and Notes	Gruber
240162	Peace, In Deed	Garber/Libowitz
240163	Mediators of the Divine	Berchman
240164	Approaches to Ancient Judaism, New Series, Volume Thirteen	Neusner
240165	Targum Studies, Volume Two: Targum and Peshitta	Flesher
240166	The Text and I: Writings of Samson H. Levey	Chyet

240167	The Documentary Form-History of Rabbinic Literature, I. The Documentary Forms of Mishnah	Neusner
240168	Louis Finkelstein and the Conservative Movement	Greenbaum
240169	Invitation to the Talmud: A Teaching Book	Neusner
240170	Invitation to Midrash: The Workings of Rabbinic Bible Interpretation, A Teaching Book	Neusner
240171	The Documentary Form-History of Rabbinic Literature, II. The Aggadic Sector:Tractate Abot, Abot deRabbi Natan, Sifra, Sifré to Numbers and Sifré to Deuteronomy	Neusner
240172	The Documentary Form-History of Rabbinic Literature, III. The Aggadic Sector: Mekhilta Attributed to R. Ishmael and Genesis Rabbah	Neusner
240173	The Documentary Form-History of Rabbinic Literature, IV. The Aggadic Sector: Leviticus Rabbah and Pesiqta deRab Kahana	Neusner
240174	The Documentary Form-History of Rabbinic Literature, V. The Aggadic Sector: Song of Songs Rabbah, Ruth Rabbah, Lamentations Rabbati, and Esther Rabbah I	Neusner
240175	The Documentary Form-History of Rabbinic Literature, VI. The Halakhic Sector: The Talmud of the Land of Israel A. Tractates Berakhot and Shabbat through Taanit	Neusner
240176	The Documentary Form-History of Rabbinic Literature, VI. The Halakhic Sector: The Talmud of the Land of Israel B. Tractates Megillah through Qiddushin	Neusner
240177	The Documentary Form-History of Rabbinic Literature, VI. The Halakhic Sector: The Talmud of the Land of Israel C. Tractates Sotah through Horayot and Niddah	Neusner
240178	The Documentary Form-History of Rabbinic Literature, VII. The Halakhic Sector: The Talmud of the Land of Israel A. Tractates Berakhot and Shabbat through Pesahim	Neusner
240179	The Documentary Form-History of Rabbinic Literature, VII. The Halakhic Sector: The Talmud of Babylonia B. Tractates Yoma through Ketubot	Neusner
240180	The Documentary Form-History of Rabbinic Literature, VII. The Halakhic Sector: The Talmud of Babylonia C. Tractates Nedarim through Baba Mesia	Neusner
240181	The Documentary Form-History of Rabbinic Literature, VII. The Halakhic Sector: The Talmud of Babylonia D. Tractates Baba Batra through Horayot	Neusner
240182	The Documentary Form-History of Rabbinic Literature, VII. The Halakhic Sector: The Talmud of Babylonia E. Tractates Zebahim through Bekhorot	Neusner
240183	The Documentary Form-History of Rabbinic Literature, VII. The Halakhic Sector: The Talmud of Babylonia F. Tractates Arakhin through Niddah and Conclusions	Neusner
240184	Messages to Moscow: And Other Current Lectures on Learning and Community in Judaism	Neusner
240185	The Economics of the Mishnah	Neusner
240186	Approaches to Ancient Judaism, New Series, Volume Fourteen	Neusner
240187	Jewish Law from Moses to the Mishnah	Neusner
240188	The Language and the Law of God	Calabi

240189 Pseudo-Rabad: Commentary to Sifre Numbers — Basser
240190 How Adin Steinsalz Misrepresents the Talmud — Neusner
240191 How the Rabbis Liberated Women — Neusner
240192 From Scripture to 70 — Neusner
240193 The Levites: Their Emergence as a Second-Class Priesthood — Nurmela
240194 Sifra — Ginsberg
240195 Approaches to Ancient Judaism, New Series, Volume Fifteen — Neusner
240196 What, Exactly, Did the Rabbinic Sages Mean by the "Oral Torah"? — Neusner
240197 The Book of Job with a Commentary for Our Times — Sacks
240198 Symbol and Theology in Early Judaism — Neusner
240199 The Ecological Message of the Torah: Knowledge, Concepts and Laws Which Made Survival in a Land of "Milk and Honey" Possible — Hütteman
240200 Pesiqta Rabbati: A Synoptic Edition of Pesiqta Rabbati Based upon All Extant Manuscripts and the Editio Princeps, Volume II — Ulmer
240201 Concepts of Class in Ancient Israel — Sneed
240202 The Rabbinic Traditions about the Pharisees before 70, Part I, The Masters — Neusner
240203 The Rabbinic Traditions about the Pharisees before 70, Part II, The Houses — Neusner
240204 The Rabbinic Traditions about the Pharisees before 70, Part III, Conclusions — Neusner

South Florida Academic Commentary Series

243001 The Talmud of Babylonia, An Academic Commentary, Volume XI, Bavli Tractate Moed Qatan — Neusner
243002 The Talmud of Babylonia, An Academic Commentary, Volume XXXIV, Bavli Tractate Keritot — Neusner
243003 The Talmud of Babylonia, An Academic Commentary, Volume XVII, Bavli Tractate Sotah — Neusner
243004 The Talmud of Babylonia, An Academic Commentary, Volume XXIV, Bavli Tractate Makkot — Neusner
243005 The Talmud of Babylonia, An Academic Commentary, Volume XXXII, Bavli Tractate Arakhin — Neusner
243006 The Talmud of Babylonia, An Academic Commentary, Volume VI, Bavli Tractate Sukkah — Neusner
243007 The Talmud of Babylonia, An Academic Commentary, Volume XII, Bavli Tractate Hagigah — Neusner
243008 The Talmud of Babylonia, An Academic Commentary, Volume XXVI, Bavli Tractate Horayot — Neusner
243009 The Talmud of Babylonia, An Academic Commentary, Volume XXVII, Bavli Tractate Shebuot — Neusner
243010 The Talmud of Babylonia, An Academic Commentary, Volume XXXIII, Bavli Tractate Temurah — Neusner
243011 The Talmud of Babylonia, An Academic Commentary, Volume XXXV, Bavli Tractates Meilah and Tamid — Neusner

243012	The Talmud of Babylonia, An Academic Commentary, Volume VIII, Bavli Tractate Rosh Hashanah	Neusner
243013	The Talmud of Babylonia, An Academic Commentary, Volume V, Bavli Tractate Yoma	Neusner
243014	The Talmud of Babylonia, An Academic Commentary, Volume XXXVI, Bavli Tractate Niddah	Neusner
243015	The Talmud of Babylonia, An Academic Commentary, Volume XX, Bavli Tractate Baba Qamma	Neusner
243016	The Talmud of Babylonia, An Academic Commentary, Volume XXXI, Bavli Tractate Bekhorot	Neusner
243017	The Talmud of Babylonia, An Academic Commentary, Volume XXX, Bavli Tractate Hullin	Neusner
243018	The Talmud of Babylonia, An Academic Commentary, Volume VII, Bavli Tractate Besah	Neusner
243019	The Talmud of Babylonia, An Academic Commentary, Volume X, Bavli Tractate Megillah	Neusner
243020	The Talmud of Babylonia, An Academic Commentary, Volume XXVIII, Bavli Tractate Zebahim A. Chapters I through VII	Neusner
243021	The Talmud of Babylonia, An Academic Commentary, Volume XXI, Bavli Tractate Baba Mesia, A. Chapters I through VI	Neusner
243022	The Talmud of Babylonia, An Academic Commentary, Volume XXII, Bavli Tractate Baba Batra, A. Chapters I through VI	Neusner
243023	The Talmud of Babylonia, An Academic Commentary, Volume XXIX, Bavli Tractate Menahot, A. Chapters I through VI	Neusner
243024	The Talmud of Babylonia, An Academic Commentary, Volume I, Bavli Tractate Berakhot	Neusner
243025	The Talmud of Babylonia, An Academic Commentary, Volume XXV, Bavli Tractate Abodah Zarah	Neusner
243026	The Talmud of Babylonia, An Academic Commentary, Volume XXIII, Bavli Tractate Sanhedrin, A. Chapters I through VII	Neusner
243027	The Talmud of Babylonia, A Complete Outline, Part IV, The Division of Holy Things; A: From Tractate Zabahim through Tractate Hullin	Neusner
243028	The Talmud of Babylonia, An Academic Commentary, Volume XIV, Bavli Tractate Ketubot, A. Chapters I through VI	Neusner
243029	The Talmud of Babylonia, An Academic Commentary, Volume IV, Bavli Tractate Pesahim, A. Chapters I through VII	Neusner
243030	The Talmud of Babylonia, An Academic Commentary, Volume III, Bavli Tractate Erubin, A. ChaptersI through V	Neusner
243031	The Talmud of Babylonia, A Complete Outline, Part III, The Division of Damages; A: From Tractate Baba Qamma through Tractate Baba Batra	Neusner

243032	The Talmud of Babylonia, An Academic Commentary, Volume II, Bavli Tractate Shabbat, Volume A, Chapters One through Twelve	Neusner
243033	The Talmud of Babylonia, An Academic Commentary, Volume II, Bavli Tractate Shabbat, Volume B, Chapters Thirteen through Twenty-four	Neusner
243034	The Talmud of Babylonia, An Academic Commentary, Volume XV, Bavli Tractate Nedarim	Neusner
243035	The Talmud of Babylonia, An Academic Commentary, Volume XVIII, Bavli Tractate Gittin	Neusner
243036	The Talmud of Babylonia, An Academic Commentary, Volume XIX, Bavli Tractate Qiddushin	Neusner
243037	The Talmud of Babylonia, A Complete Outline, Part IV, The Division of Holy Things; B: From Tractate Berakot through Tractate Niddah	Neusner
243038	The Talmud of Babylonia, A Complete Outline, Part III, The Division of Damages; B: From Tractate Sanhedrin through Tractate Shebuot	Neusner
243039	The Talmud of Babylonia, A Complete Outline, Part I, Tractate Berakhot and the Division of Appointed Times A: From Tractate Berakhot through Tractate Pesahim	Neusner
243040	The Talmud of Babylonia, A Complete Outline, Part I, Tractate Berakhot and the Division of Appointed Times B: From Tractate Yoma through Tractate Hagigah	Neusner
243041	The Talmud of Babylonia, A Complete Outline, Part II, The Division of Women; A: From Tractate Yebamot through Tractate Ketubot	Neusner
243042	The Talmud of Babylonia, A Complete Outline, Part II, The Division of Women; B: From Tractate Nedarim through Tractate Qiddushin	Neusner
243043	The Talmud of Babylonia, An Academic Commentary, Volume XIII, Bavli Tractate Yebamot, A. Chapters One through Eight	Neusner
243044	The Talmud of Babylonia, An Academic Commentary, XIII, Bavli Tractate Yebamot, B. Chapters Nine through Seventeen	Neusner
243045	The Talmud of the Land of Israel, A Complete Outline of the Second, Third and Fourth Divisions, Part II, The Division of Women, A. Yebamot to Nedarim	Neusner
243046	The Talmud of the Land of Israel, A Complete Outline of the Second, Third and Fourth Divisions, Part II, The Division of Women, B. Nazir to Sotah	Neusner
243047	The Talmud of the Land of Israel, A Complete Outline of the Second, Third and Fourth Divisions, Part I, The Division of Appointed Times, C. Pesahim and Sukkah	Neusner
243048	The Talmud of the Land of Israel, A Complete Outline of the Second, Third and Fourth Divisions, Part I, The Division of Appointed Times, A. Berakhot, Shabbat	Neusner
243049	The Talmud of the Land of Israel, A Complete Outline of the Second, Third and Fourth Divisions, Part I, The Division of Appointed Times, B. Erubin, Yoma and Besah	Neusner

243050	The Talmud of the Land of Israel, A Complete Outline of the Second, Third and Fourth Divisions, Part I, The Division of Appointed Times, D. Taanit, Megillah, Rosh Hashannah, Hagigah and Moed Qatan	Neusner
243051	The Talmud of the Land of Israel, A Complete Outline of the Second, Third and Fourth Divisions, Part III, The Division of Damages, A. Baba Qamma, Baba Mesia, Baba Batra, Horayot and Niddah	Neusner
243052	The Talmud of the Land of Israel, A Complete Outline of the Second, Third and Fourth Divisions, Part III, The Division of Damages, B. Sanhedrin, Makkot, Shebuot and Abldah Zarah	Neusner
243053	The Two Talmuds Compared, II. The Division of Women in the Talmud of the Land of Israel and the Talmud of Babylonia, Volume A, Tractates Yebamot and Ketubot	Neusner
243054	The Two Talmuds Compared, II. The Division of Women in the Talmud of the Land of Israel and the Talmud of Babylonia, Volume B, Tractates Nedarim, Nazir and Sotah	Neusner
243055	The Two Talmuds Compared, II. The Division of Women in the Talmud of the Land of Israel and the Talmud of Babylonia, Volume C, Tractates Qiddushin and Gittin	Neusner
243056	The Two Talmuds Compared, III. The Division of Damages in the Talmud of the Land of Israel and the Talmud of Babylonia, Volume A, Tractates Baba Qamma and Baba Mesia	Neusner
243057	The Two Talmuds Compared, III. The Division of Damages in the Talmud of the Land of Israel and the Talmud of Babylonia, Volume B, Tractates Baba Batra and Niddah	Neusner
243058	The Two Talmuds Compared, III. The Division of Damages in the Talmud of the Land of Israel and the Talmud of Babylonia, Volume C, Tractates Sanhedrin and Makkot	Neusner
243059	The Two Talmuds Compared, I. Tractate Berakhot and the Division of Appointed Times in the Talmud of the Land of Israel and the Talmud of Babylonia, Volume B, Tractate Shabbat	Neusner
243060	The Two Talmuds Compared, I. Tractate Berakhot and the Division of Appointed Times in the Talmud of the Land of Israel and the Talmud of Babylonia, Volume A, Tractate Berakhot	Neusner
243061	The Two Talmuds Compared, III. The Division of Damages in the Talmud of the Land of Israel and the Talmud of Babylonia, Volume D, Tractates Shebuot, Abodah Zarah and Horayot	Neusner
243062	The Two Talmuds Compared, I. Tractate Berakhot and the Division of Appointed Times in the Talmud of the Land of Israel and the Talmud of Babylonia, Volume C, Tractate Erubin	Neusner
243063	The Two Talmuds Compared, I. Tractate Berakhot and the Division of Appointed Times in the Talmud of the Land of Israel and the Talmud of Babylonia, Volume D, Tractates Yoma and Sukkah	Neusner
243064	The Two Talmuds Compared, I. Tractate Berakhot and the Division of Appointed Times in the Talmud of the Land of Israel and the Talmud of Babylonia, Volume E, Tractate Pesahim	Neusner
243065	The Two Talmuds Compared, I. Tractate Berakhot and the Division of Appointed Times in the Talmud of the Land of Israel	

	and the Talmud of Babylonia, Volume F, Tractates Besah, Taanit and Megillah	Neusner
243066	The Two Talmuds Compared, I. Tractate Berakhot and the Division of Appointed Times in the Talmud of the Land of Israel and the Talmud of Babylonia, Volume G, Tractates Rosh Hashanah and Moed Qatan	Neusner
243067	The Talmud of Babylonia, An Academic Commentary, Volume XXII, Bavli Tractate Baba Batra, B. Chapters VII through XI	Neusner
243068	The Talmud of Babylonia, An Academic Commentary, Volume XXIII, Bavli Tractate Sanhedrin, B. Chapters VIII through XII	Neusner
243069	The Talmud of Babylonia, An Academic Commentary, Volume XIV, Bavli Tractate Ketubot, B. ChaptersVII through XIV	Neusner
243070	The Talmud of Babylonia, An Academic Commentary, Volume IV, Bavli Tractate Pesahim, B. Chapters VIII through XI	Neusner
243071	The Talmud of Babylonia, An Academic Commentary, Volume XXIX, Bavli Tractate Menahot, B. Chapters VII through XIV	Neusner
243072	The Talmud of Babylonia, An Academic Commentary, Volume XXVIII, Bavli Tractate Zebahim B. Chapters VIII through XV	Neusner
243073	The Talmud of Babylonia, An Academic Commentary, Volume XXI, Bavli Tractate Baba Mesia, B. Chapters VIII through XI	Neusner
243074	The Talmud of Babylonia, An Academic Commentary, Volume III, Bavli Tractate Erubin, A. ChaptersVI through XI	Neusner
243075	The Components of the Rabbinic Documents: From the Whole to the Parts, I. Sifra, Part One	Neusner
243076	The Components of the Rabbinic Documents: From the Whole to the Parts, I. Sifra, Part Two	Neusner
243077	The Components of the Rabbinic Documents: From the Whole to the Parts, I. Sifra, Part Three	Neusner
243078	The Components of the Rabbinic Documents: From the Whole to the Parts, I. Sifra, Part Four	Neusner
243079	The Components of the Rabbinic Documents: From the Whole to the Parts, II. Esther Rabbah I	Neusner
243080	The Components of the Rabbinic Documents: From the Whole to the Parts, III. Ruth Rabbah	Neusner
243081	The Components of the Rabbinic Documents: From the Whole to the Parts, IV. Lamemtations Rabbah	Neusner
243082	The Components of the Rabbinic Documents: From the Whole to the Parts, V. Song of Songs Rabbah, Part One	Neusner
243083	The Components of the Rabbinic Documents: From the Whole to the Parts, V. Song of Songs Rabbah, Part Two	Neusner
243084	The Components of the Rabbinic Documents: From the Whole to the Parts, VI. The Fathers According to Rabbi Nathan	Neusner
243085	The Components of the Rabbinic Documents: From the Whole to the Parts, VII. Sifré to Deuteronomy, Part One	Neusner

243086	The Components of the Rabbinic Documents: From the Whole to the Parts, VII. Sifré to Deuteronomy, Part Two	Neusner
243087	The Components of the Rabbinic Documents: From the Whole to the Parts, VII. Sifré to Deuteronomy, Part Three	Neusner
243088	The Components of the Rabbinic Documents: From the Whole to the Parts, VIII. Mekhilta Attributed to Rabbi Ishmael, Part One	Neusner
243089	The Components of the Rabbinic Documents: From the Whole to the Parts, VIII. Mekhilta Attributed to Rabbi Ishmael, Part Two	Neusner
243090	The Components of the Rabbinic Documents: From the Whole to the Parts, VIII. Mekhilta Attributed to Rabbi Ishmael, Part Three	Neusner
243092	The Components of the Rabbinic Documents: From the Whole to the Parts, IX. Genesis Rabbah, Part One, Introduction and Chapters One through Twenty-two	Neusner
243093	The Components of the Rabbinic Documents: From the Whole to the Parts, IX. Genesis Rabbah, Part Two, Chapters Twenty-three through Fifty	Neusner
243094	The Components of the Rabbinic Documents: From the Whole to the Parts, IX. Genesis Rabbah, Part Three, Chapters Fifty-one through Seventy-five	Neusner
243095	The Components of the Rabbinic Documents: From the Whole to the Parts, X. Leviticus Rabbah, Part One , Introduction and Parashiyyot One through Seventeen	Neusner
243096	The Components of the Rabbinic Documents: From the Whole to the Parts, X. Leviticus Rabbah, Part Two, Parashiyyot Eighteen through Thirty-seven	Neusner
243097	The Components of the Rabbinic Documents: From the Whole to the Parts, X. Leviticus Rabbah, Part Three, Topical and Methodical Outline	Neusner
243098	The Components of the Rabbinic Documents: From the Whole to the Parts, XI. Pesiqta deRab Kahana, Part One, Introduction and Pisqaot One through Eleven	Neusner
243099	The Components of the Rabbinic Documents: From the Whole to the Parts, XI. Pesiqta deRab Kahana, Part Two, Pisqaot Twelve through Twenty-eight	Neusner
243100	The Components of the Rabbinic Documents: From the Whole to the Parts, XI. Pesiqta deRab Kahana, Part Three, A Topical and Methodical Outline	Neusner
243101	The Components of the Rabbinic Documents: From the Whole to the Parts, IX. Genesis Rabbah, Part Four, Chapters Seventy-six through One Hundred	Neusner
243102	The Components of the Rabbinic Documents: From the Whole to the Parts, IX. Genesis Rabbah, Part Five, A Methodical and Topical Outline; Bereshit through Vaere, Chapters One through Fifty-seven	Neusner
243103	The Components of the Rabbinic Documents: From the Whole to the Parts, IX. Genesis Rabbah, Part Six, A Methodical and Topical Outline; Hayye Sarah through Miqqes, Chapters Fifty-eight through One Hundred	Neusner
243104	The Components of the Rabbinic Documents: From the Whole to the Parts, XII., Sifré to Numbers, Part One, Introduction and Pisqaot One through Seventy-one	Neusner

243105 The Components of the Rabbinic Documents: From the Whole to the Parts, XII., Sifré to Numbers, Part Two, Pisqaot Seventy-two through One Hundred Twenty-two — Neusner

243106 The Components of the Rabbinic Documents: From the Whole to the Parts, XII., Sifré to Numbers, Part Three, Pisqaot One Hundred Twenty-three through One Hundred Sixty-one — Neusner

243107 The Components of the Rabbinic Documents: From the Whole to the Parts, XII., Sifré to Numbers, Part Four, A Topical and Methodical Outline — Neusner

243108 The Talmud of the Land of Israel: An Academic Commentary of the Second, Third, and Fourth Divisions, I. Yerushalmi Tractate Berakhot (Based on the Translation by Tzvee Zahavy) — Neusner

243109 The Talmud of the Land of Israel: An Academic Commentary of the Second, Third, and Fourth Divisions, II. Yerushalmi Tractate Shabbat. A. Chapters One through Ten — Neusner

243110 The Talmud of the Land of Israel: An Academic Commentary of the Second, Third, and Fourth Divisions, II. Yerushalmi Tractate Shabbat. B. Chapters Eleven through Twenty-Four and The Structure of Yerushalmi Shabbat — Neusner

243111 The Talmud of the Land of Israel: An Academic Commentary of the Second, Third, and Fourth Divisions, III. Yerushalmi Tractate Erubin — Neusner

243112 The Talmud of the Land of Israel: An Academic Commentary of the Second, Third, and Fourth Divisions, IV. Yerushalmi Tractate Yoma — Neusner

243113 The Talmud of the Land of Israel: An Academic Commentary of the Second, Third, and Fourth Divisions, V. Yerushalmi Tractate Pesahim A. Chapters One through Six, Based on the English Translation of Baruch M. Bokser with Lawrence Schiffman — Neusner

243114 The Talmud of the Land of Israel: An Academic Commentary of the Second, Third, and Fourth Divisions, V. Yerushalmi Tractate Pesahim B. Chapters Seven through Ten and The Structure of Yerushalmi Pesahim, Based on the English Translation of Baruch M. Bokser with Lawrence Schiffman — Neusner

243115 The Talmud of the Land of Israel: An Academic Commentary of the Second, Third, and Fourth Divisions, VI. Yerushalmi Tractate Sukkah — Neusner

243116 The Talmud of the Land of Israel: An Academic Commentary of the Second, Third, and Fourth Divisions, VII. Yerushalmi Tractate Besah — Neusner

243117 The Talmud of the Land of Israel: An Academic Commentary of the Second, Third, and Fourth Divisions, VIII. Yerushalmi Tractate Taanit — Neusner

243118 The Talmud of the Land of Israel: An Academic Commentary of the Second, Third, and Fourth Divisions, IX. Yerushalmi Tractate Megillah — Neusner

243119 The Talmud of the Land of Israel: An Academic Commentary of the Second, Third, and Fourth Divisions, X. Yerushalmi Tractate Rosh Hashanah — Neusner

243120	The Talmud of the Land of Israel: An Academic Commentary of the Second, Third, and Fourth Divisions, XI. Yerushalmi Tractate Hagigah	Neusner
243121	The Talmud of the Land of Israel: An Academic Commentary of the Second, Third, and Fourth Divisions, XII. Yerushalmi Tractate Moed Qatan	Neusner
243122	The Talmud of the Land of Israel: An Academic Commentary of the Second, Third, and Fourth Divisions, XIII. Yerushalmi Tractate Yebamot, A. Chapters One through Ten	Neusner
243123	The Talmud of the Land of Israel: An Academic Commentary of the Second, Third, and Fourth Divisions, XIII. Yerushalmi Tractate Yebamot, B. Chapters Eleven through Seventeen	Neusner
243124	The Talmud of the Land of Israel: An Academic Commentary of the Second, Third, and Fourth Divisions, XIV. Yerushalmi Tractate Ketubot	Neusner
243125	The Talmud of the Land of Israel: An Academic Commentary of the Second, Third, and Fourth Divisions, XV. Yerushalmi Tractate Nedarim	Neusner
243126	The Talmud of the Land of Israel: An Academic Commentary of the Second, Third, and Fourth Divisions, XVI. Yerushalmi Tractate Nazir	Neusner
243127	The Talmud of the Land of Israel: An Academic Commentary of the Second, Third, and Fourth Divisions, XVII. Yerushalmi Tractate Gittin	Neusner
243128	The Talmud of the Land of Israel: An Academic Commentary of the Second, Third, and Fourth Divisions, XVIII. Yerushalmi Tractate Qiddushin	Neusner
243129	The Talmud of the Land of Israel: An Academic Commentary of the Second, Third, and Fourth Divisions, XIX. Yerushalmi Tractate Sotah	Neusner
243130	The Talmud of the Land of Israel: An Academic Commentary of the Second, Third, and Fourth Divisions, XX. Yerushalmi Tractate Baba Qamma	Neusner
243131	The Talmud of the Land of Israel: An Academic Commentary of the Second, Third, and Fourth Divisions, XXI. Yerushalmi Tractate Baba Mesia	Neusner
243132	The Talmud of the Land of Israel: An Academic Commentary of the Second, Third, and Fourth Divisions, XXII. Yerushalmi Tractate Baba Batra	Neusner
243133	The Talmud of the Land of Israel: An Academic Commentary of the Second, Third, and Fourth Divisions, XXIII. Yerushalmi Tractate Sanhedrin	Neusner
243134	The Talmud of the Land of Israel: An Academic Commentary of the Second, Third, and Fourth Divisions, XIV. Yerushalmi Tractate Makkot	Neusner

South Florida-Rochester-Saint Louis Studies on Religion and the Social Order

245001	Faith and Context, Volume 1	Ong
245002	Faith and Context, Volume 2	Ong
245003	Judaism and Civil Religion	Breslauer
245004	The Sociology of Andrew M. Greeley	Greeley
245005	Faith and Context, Volume 3	Ong
245006	The Christ of Michelangelo	Dixon
245007	From Hermeneutics to Ethical Consensus Among Cultures	Bori
245008	Mordecai Kaplan's Thought in a Postmodern Age	Breslauer
245009	No Longer Aliens, No Longer Strangers	Eckardt
245010	Between Tradition and Culture	Ellenson
245011	Religion and the Social Order	Neusner
245012	Christianity and the Stranger	Nichols
245013	The Polish Challenge	Czosnyka
245014	Islam and the Question of Minorities	Sonn
245015	Religion and the Political Order	Neusner
245016	The Ecology of Religion	Neusner
245017	The Shaping of an American Islamic Discourse	Waugh/Denny
245018	The Muslim Brotherhood and the Kings of Jordan, 1945–1993	Boulby
245019	Muslims on the Americanization Path	Esposito/Haddad
245020	Protean Prejudice: Anti-semitism in England's Age of Reason	Glassman
245021	The Study of Religion: In Retrospect and Prospect	Green
245024	Jacques Ellul on Religion, Technology and Politics: Conversations with Patrick Troude-Chastenet	France
245025	Religious Belief and Economic Behavior	Neusner

South Florida International Studies in Formative Christianity and Judaism

242501	The Earliest Christian Mission to 'All Nations'	La Grand
242502	Judaic Approaches to the Gospels	Chilton
242503	The "Essence of Christianity"	Forni Rosa
242504	The Wicked Tenants and Gethsemane	Aus
242505	A Star Is Rising	Laato
242506	Romans 9–11: A Reader-Response Analysis	Lodge
242507	The Good News of Peter's Denial	Borrell
242508	ΛΟΓΟΙ ΙΗΣΟΥ, Studies in Q	Vassiliadis
242509	Romans 8:18–30: "Suffering Does Not Thwart the Future Glory"	Gieniusz